THE RACE CARD

THE RACE CARD

CAMPAIGN STRATEGY, IMPLICIT MESSAGES,

AND THE NORM OF EQUALITY

Tali Mendelberg

PRINCETON UNIVERSITY PRESS   PRINCETON AND OXFORD

Copyright © 2001 by Princeton University Press
Published by Princeton University Press, 41 William Street,
Princeton, New Jersey 08540
In the United Kingdom: Princeton University Press,
3 Market Place, Woodstock, Oxfordshire OX20 1SY
All Rights Reserved.

ISBN 0-691-07070-9
ISBN 0-691-07071-7 (pbk)

This book has been composed in Berkeley Book

Printed on acid-free paper. ∞

www.pup.princeton.edu

Printed in the United States of America

1 3 5 7 9 10 8 6 4 2

1 3 5 7 9 10 8 6 4 2 (pbk.)

Contents

Illustrations

Tables

Preface

THIS BOOK is about implicit communication. It is a study of change and continuity in electoral communication about inequality, particularly racial inequality in the United States. I have attempted to understand why race is often absent from the surface of American electoral campaigns but very much present underneath. When I began this project, I believed that the explanation lay with the racial divide in the party system and the political psychology of white voters. But eventually I realized that just as important was an understanding of norms. Much of the book is devoted to understanding how elites communicate with voters when electoral imperatives dictate a message that is unacceptable according to the norm.

The book became my attempt to understand why elites sometimes guard their message, conveying meaning in an ambiguous or indirect way, and why they sometimes say exactly what they mean. But my focus remained on citizens. The primary question of this book is, "What makes white voters respond when leaders denigrate or subordinate African Americans?" Elites have a great capacity to move the public; but in a democracy, the citizens have the last say. In the final analysis, it is their response that must be understood.

For this reason, the book focuses on white citizens. To be sure, subordinate groups, when allowed basic rights and the ability to organize, can do a great deal to shape the course of equality. There is much that we need to know about African-American voters and racial communication. But ultimately, although I show that they can be influenced by the actions of members of the subordinate group, the members of the dominant racial group are those who decide how egalitarian a polity will be. African Americans' response requires a full-fledged treatment of its own, one that I cannot provide here.

While the book concentrates on race in the United States, it draws implications for other social cleavages and other countries. I have tried to understand why members of dominant groups sometimes rely on their stereotypes, fears, and resentments in reaching decisions that affect subordinate groups, and other times do not. My explanation tries to connect elites' strategic messages with voters' responses by attending to norms, electoral coalitions, and individual consciousness—consciousness, that is, of the meaning of the message and of the voter's own response.

My argument rests on multiple methods. The first part of the book relies on historians' detailed case studies of racial politics in the nineteenth and twentieth centuries and on my own analysis of political communication. Racial appeals arise from a party system shaped by issues of race, and are spurred by significant change in racial arrangements. As long as the party system is based

on race, racial appeals will remain common, even when norms become egalitarian. However, racial appeals do respond to normative change: they become
more implicit. In this part of the book I also explain the mechanisms that make
implicit appeals more effective today.

The evidence in the second part of the book comes from surveys and especially from experiments I designed to test my argument that implicit appeals
are more effective today at mobilizing racial resentment. My conclusions here
are based primarily on the responses of citizens who participated in one of two
experiments I conducted. The experiments allow me to conclude with greater
confidence about the causal impact of implicit messages and to contrast implicitly racial appeals against explicitly racial appeals, counter-stereotypical appeals, and conservative appeals that have no racial meaning of any kind. I
supplement these studies with a content analysis of news coverage of the 1988
presidential campaign, matched with voters' responses over the course of the
campaign. I show how an implicit appeal is constructed and conveyed by candidates and the media, and how it loses its implicitness—and its effectiveness—when it is challenged and rendered explicit.

Taken as a whole, this book is based on a rich and varied set of data. Voters'
opinions were measured through both closed-ended and open-ended survey
formats, some recorded during phone conversations and others in person.
Some responses followed subjects' exposure to television news stories, some
of which were real and some of which I manufactured. The settings ranged
from campus buildings to respondents' homes. Some samples were national,
while others were local. The elite and media discourse I analyze is quite varied
as well, ranging over time, office, and region. I also ventured beyond the American context and examined secondary accounts of European politics. The variety of methods and settings thus enables me to construct an argument of broad
scope, with greater confidence in the validity of the evidence.

The data collection and analysis, however, ultimately serve the purpose of
commenting on the big questions that led me to this project. I conclude that
while racism continues, it has changed in a significant way. Racial appeals,
because they must be subtle to work, are now susceptible to exposure in a way
that the overt appeals of the past were not. The implicit message today is
far more vulnerable to the dissemination of information than was the explicit
message of the past. The same norm that today leads candidates to convey a
racial message implicitly also rewards the counterstrategy of antiracist messages. Public protest by black elites, if echoed by influential white elites, works
precisely because it brings race to mind rather than allowing it to remain hidden. An antiracist message is not only likely to mobilize African Americans;
less intuitively, it leads resentful whites to downplay their own resentment in
making political choices.

My results also allow me to conclude more generally about equality, change,
and communication. I have told a story of the tension between new norms and

lingering conflict. This story can travel to any situation in which egalitarian change fails to eliminate conflict over inequality. We can expect implicit appeals whenever egalitarian change produces a norm against derogating a newly accepted group, yet leaves a legacy of inequality. The key variables are the norm—egalitarian or not—and institutionalized conflict over equality—present or not. The key relationship is an interaction between egalitarian norms and institutionalized conflict. Sometimes the conflict over equality bypasses institutions, failing to ground itself in electoral coalitions. In such cases, we should not expect implicit appeals. By the same token, sometimes the clash of interests becomes institutionalized but norms are not egalitarian. In these cases, too, implicit appeals are likely to be scarce. Implicit communication arises when the norm and the conflict are equally institutionalized, equally strong, and must battle it out.

ACKNOWLEDGMENTS

This book bears my name only, but I did not produce it alone. My thanks go, first and foremost, to Uri and Hava Mendelberg. Over the years I spent working on this book, my parents set aside their own work, traveled long distances every few weeks, and pitched in to do whatever needed doing. They helped to care for my children, cooked, cleaned, shopped, ran errands, offered to get up at night with the babies, and in general allowed me the breathing room to get the book done. They provided the concrete and emotional support I needed. They also put their social science training to use reading drafts and discussing the book's problems with me. I would never have thought to study social change and justice if they had not raised me to think, to learn, and to care about those things. I could not have finished this book without their help. I thank them for their love and extraordinary support.

I also wish to thank Avi, my partner in life, who keeps me happy and sane, and Leora and Daniella, my amazing children, who enrich my life in countless ways. I am immeasurably grateful to each of them for sustaining me during the bad times and celebrating the good ones with me. My thanks also go to my brother, Gabriel, who, as I began the book, was mystified by the enterprise but by the end had himself become a writer with whom I could share the trials and satisfactions of writing.

I owe many intellectual debts. The first and most important is to Donald Kinder, and also to Stephen Rosenstone, Michael Dawson, and Patricia Gurin, who guided me through the dissertation that was the early version of this book. I am grateful in particular to Don, who taught me most of the correct things I know (the incorrect things are mostly other people's fault). I am privileged to have been able to learn from a master craftsman.

My early research also evolved through interaction with an excellent bunch of fellow graduate students in the Race and Politics Program at the University of Michigan's Institute for Social Research. I feel especially fortunate to have known Lynn Sanders and Thomas Nelson, two people whose kindness and very sharp minds supported and stimulated my graduate work there.

A big thanks goes to Martin Gilens, James Glaser, and especially to my best friends Jeff Spinner-Halev and Gary Shiffman, for providing, at crucial times, large doses of moral support with their insightful comments. Hanes Walton and Kent Jennings also encouraged me during the dissertation phase.

Many people at Princeton generously commented on portions of the book, often beyond the call of duty. Most of all I owe Larry Bartels, who first offered me a job, and then listened to my attempts to wrestle with the book, read several drafts, and advised me on what to do. Jennifer Hochschild and Amy Gutmann read a draft of much of the manuscript and provided helpful comments. Jeff Lewis saved me from making a significant ($p \le .05$) mistake in my analysis of the 1988 NES. Sheri Berman was a terrific soundboard for my attempt to apply the argument to European politics. Keith Whittington deserves a prize for his high ratio of incisive (many) to trivial or ill-advised (none) comments on the historical chapters. Eric Oliver provided extremely helpful comments on Chapter 1, just when I needed them most. I also thank for their helpful feedback Doug Arnold, Oliver Avens, Adam Berinsky, Dan Carpenter, John Darley, Mark Fey, Fred I. Greenstein, Stanley Kelley, Jr., Andrew Koppelman, Jonathan Krasno, Michele Lamont, Dale Miller, Elijah Millgram, Gordon Moskowitz, Deborah Prentice, Anna Seleny, and Karen Stenner.

The Annenberg School for Communication at the University of Pennsylvania provided a warm and stimulating home for a year and a generous fellowship stipend. There I had the chance to discuss my work in depth with Elihu Katz, Kathleen Hall Jamieson, Larry Gross, Joseph Cappella, and my fellow Annenberg Fellows Ravina Aggarwal, Ron Jacobs, Hannah Kliger, Yitzhak Roeh, and Jeff Strange. With their help I gained an appreciation for the complexities of communication and a more urgent curiosity about its role in politics.

I had several valuable opportunities to present parts of this book. In particular I wish to thank for their thoughtful reactions Jack Citrin, Leonie Huddy, Stanley Feldman, Kathleen McGraw, Robert Luskin, James Kuklinski, Sam Winslow, and participants in the political psychology seminar at Columbia University, the Rutgers University political science seminar, the University of Nebraska political science seminar, and the Hebrew University's Departments of Communication and Political Science. I am fortunate to have made several lasting friendships in the process. I am also extremely grateful to Lawrence Bobo, who published the first piece of this project, and to Chuck Myers at Princeton University Press for his enthusiasm for this book.

I received help on the technical side from many capable and dedicated people. A big thanks goes to my friend Lisa D'Ambrosio for astute comments and a good partnership in statistical detective work. I benefited from the able and dedicated research assistance of Deborah Schildkraut, Paul Gerber, Chris Mackie-Lewis, and Deborah Cohen. Many talented undergraduates assisted me at Michigan and Princeton, including Jamil French, Trineca Johnson, Sue Rhee, Emma Soichet, Roberta Stennet, and Sally El-Sadek. Diane Price and the staff of the Department of Politics at Princeton graciously pitched in to meet my many research needs.

The Institute for Social Research and the Department of Communication at the University of Michigan, the Woodrow Wilson School's Survey Research Center at Princeton University, the Department of Politics at Princeton, and the Princeton Theological Seminary provided space and equipment for the experiments. At each institution I was fortunate to find production experts who donated their time to guide me through the filming and editing of the video materials. I also could not have completed the research without the Vanderbilt Television News Archive, the National Election Studies, and the Lexis-Nexis news database.

The National Science Foundation generously supported me for three years through its graduate fellowship. The Graduate School and the Department of Political Science at the University of Michigan did their indispensable part in this too. Princeton University unstintingly provided repeated research funds, without which one of the experiments would not have been conducted. The Annenberg School at the University of Pennsylvania generously supported my work for a year. The Barone Center at Harvard's Kennedy School granted me a Goldsmith Award for a portion of this work—along with a check that came at a crucial moment.

Part One

THE ORIGIN OF IMPLICIT RACIAL APPEALS

CHAPTER 1

A Theory of Racial Appeals

AMERICANS REMEMBER the presidential election of 1988 as the Willie Horton election. A young black man convicted of murder and sentenced to life in a Massachusetts prison, Horton escaped while on furlough and assaulted a white couple in their home, raping the woman. George Bush made Horton a household name by repeatedly mentioning Horton's story and pinning the blame on his Democratic opponent, Massachusetts governor Michael Dukakis. Several years after the election, when voters were asked what they remembered about the 1988 campaign, they provided three names: Dukakis, Bush, and Horton.[1]

The Willie Horton message was obviously about race. Or was it? During nineteen of the twenty-two weeks of the campaign, no one in America seemed to think so. Bush and his aides spoke only about criminal justice, and they never mentioned Horton's race. Dukakis and his running mate, Lloyd Bentsen, said nothing about the racial element of the message. No other Democrat even hinted at the possibility that the message was racial. Journalists, too, seemed blind to the racial element of the story; not one of the hundreds of editorials, articles, or television news stories about Horton noted the racial aspect of the Horton appeal. Horton's race was repeatedly shown in menacing photos, but it was never spoken. Horton may as well have been French and his victims Swedish for all the notice his race drew.

Not so after October 21. On that day Jesse Jackson, the eminent civil rights activist who had been runner-up for the Democratic presidential nomination, accused the Bush campaign of using Horton with racial intent. The Horton story was an appeal to white voters' racial fears, Jackson charged; it was a political play on injurious stereotypes whites had developed about black men's proclivity to rape white women. From the moment Jackson made his charge, race pervaded media coverage of the Horton story and of the campaign. Bush and his campaign officials vehemently denied the charge of racism; Jackson and Bentsen (though not Dukakis) repeated it; and journalists and commentators considered whether the charge was true, most concluding that it was not.

Although he had finished the primary season far behind Dukakis in the polls, Bush's prospects shot up in June with his first mention of the Horton story. In October, when the Horton message reached its greatest intensity, Bush pulled ahead decisively. Soon after race entered the discussion, however,

---

[1] Based on the focus group transcript in Jamieson (1992, 15–16).

Bush's ratings began a steep slide. In the end, of course, Dukakis lost the election. The debate about race came too late to completely undo the effect of the Horton message. It was not until Bush's veto of the 1990 civil rights bill that Jackson's charge was adopted by journalists as the conventional interpretation of the Horton appeal. That the Willie Horton campaign was about race was obvious only three years after it transpired.

In the aftermath of the campaign, scholars and commentators concluded that Bush won through negative attacks that distorted the truth and mangled the issue of crime, attacks that Dukakis was too inept to counter. But for all that the Horton story has been vilified as the epitome of dirty campaigning, we still have not grasped the most significant aspect of the campaign: it communicated about race implicitly. In fact, *the racial message was communicated most effectively when no one noticed its racial meaning.* When people finally noticed, the racial message lost much of its power. Despite all that has been written about the 1988 election, it has gone unremarked that Bush's fortunes suffered just when race went from subtext to text.

The most important and underplayed lesson of the Horton message is that, in a racially divided society that aspires to equality, the injection of race into campaigns poses a great danger to democratic politics—so long as the injection of race takes place under cover. When a society has repudiated racism, yet racial conflict persists, candidates can win by playing the race card only through implicit racial appeals. The implicit nature of these appeals allows them to prime racial stereotypes, fears, and resentments while appearing not to do so. When an implicit appeal is rendered explicit—when other elites bring the racial meaning of the appeal to voters' attention—it appears to violate the norm of racial equality. It then loses its ability to prime white voters' racial predispositions. As a consequence, voters not only become more disaffected with the candidate, but also prevent their negative racial predispositions from influencing their opinion on issues of race. Political communication that derogates African Americans does little harm if it is widely, immediately, and strongly denounced. In an age of equality, what damages racial equality is the failure to notice the racial meaning of political communication, not the racial meaning itself.

The Horton story is not an isolated case. With more or less racial intent, many party officials, candidates, and campaign officials have conveyed implicitly racial appeals, and some have reaped the electoral benefits. The presidential campaigns of Barry Goldwater in 1964 and Richard Nixon in 1968 relied on implicitly racial appeals, the former driven by Goldwater's southern backers and the latter by Nixon's own ambition. Ronald Reagan came to political prominence nationally in part through his use of the welfare queen anecdote, perhaps not told with racial intent but likely with racial result. The 2000 presidential election featured the third presidential candidacy of Pat Buchanan, who in his infamous 1992 Republican National Convention speech attacked the behavior of inner-city residents, who are disproportionately black. In the 1996 primaries, Buchanan proved to be Bob Dole's main challenger, winning in New Hampshire and several other early states. He ardently defended South Carolina's practice of flying the Confederate flag above the state capitol as a symbol of southern heritage, and advocated building a wall at the border to restrict Mexican immigration, which he linked to welfare dependency and crime. Buchanan, however, has been the least successful of these presidential candidates, in part because he has been the least subtle. His use of the term "José" to refer to Mexican immigrants, his aides' well-publicized ties to anti-Semitic, paramilitary, and racist groups, and similar aspects of his campaigns led 54 percent of a national sample of Americans in 1996 to consider him too extreme.

The issues of welfare and crime have a long history of entanglement with race and a continuing salience in American politics. When officials disparage welfare recipients or focus attention on the perpetrators of violent crime, they often convey a racial message—not always intentionally, not always consciously, nor even inevitably. Still, they or their campaign aides sometimes consciously convey implicit racial meaning, and, regardless of the campaigners' intent and awareness, implicit racial meaning is often communicated by the media and received by voters.

Because candidates need not be fully intent on conveying a racial message, implicit racial messages are conveyed not only by conservative but by more moderate candidates, too. In 1994, when 42 percent of Americans named crime as the nation's worst problem, moderate Republican gubernatorial candidates in California (Pete Wilson), Illinois (Jim Edgar), and Texas (George W. Bush) ran ads showing blurry black-and-white images of (fictional) gun-toting rapists. Jim Edgar also ran an anti-welfare ad featuring African Americans. Getting tough on welfare dependency is a strategy that George W. Bush pursued during his 1998 gubernatorial reelection campaign in Texas.

Candidates for Senate, Congress, and lesser offices rely on implicit racial messages, too. David Duke, who ran as a Republican for the Senate and then for governor in Louisiana (followed by a run for president), is perhaps the best known and least successful in this category, having been unable to fully shed the baggage of his Ku Klux Klan past. James Glaser, in his recent study of competitive congressional elections in the South, found that in fact implicit racial messages are central to the Republican strategy and that, indeed, "some racial appeals seem to arise in nearly every election" (1996, 73).

Implicit racial appeals can be found in campaigns at all levels, and although they may be more evident in the South, they are not confined to that region. In northern states with a substantial racial minority, electoral campaigns often include implicit racial messages with oblique, subtle references to race. For example, in his 1999 reelection campaign, New York mayor Rudolph Giuliani put out a press release entitled, "Ruth Messinger Throws a Party for a Murderer," charging that his Democratic opponent had hosted a party for an inmate convicted of killing a guard during the racially charged Attica prison riots in 1971. Republican governors who have risen to prominence in recent years, such as Tom Ridge in Pennsylvania, Jeb Bush in Florida, and George Pataki in New York, all ran election campaigns that featured ads attacking their opponents for being lax on violent crime. These messages, by design or by circumstance, whether on their own or as conveyed by the news media, tended implicitly to refer to violent black criminals. Other prominent Republican governors were elected in part by highlighting their tough anti-welfare stance, a message that the media often conveys with visual references to African Americans. As the Republican party evaluated the reasons for its humiliating showing in the 1998 congressional elections, Republican governors argued that the party should move away from religious issues and focus in part, as the governors said they had done successfully in 1998 and before, on crime and welfare.

Thus some of our most salient political issues are entangled with race, and so are many of the campaign messages that discuss these issues. When public figures discuss matters of welfare or crime, they often—though not always—do so in a way that conveys derogatory references to African Americans. Often—though not always—these references are conveyed implicitly. To understand the relevance of race to the party system and to the conduct of electoral campaigns, implicitly racial communication must be understood.[2] We must understand what makes a message implicit rather than explicit or nonracial. We must also understand the causes of implicit messages and their consequences. To understand when, how, and why implicit meaning exists in campaigns, and when, how, and why it does not, we must understand party strategy, norms, and voters' political psychology.

The power of implicitly racial appeals today is due to the coexistence of two contradictory elements in American politics: powerful egalitarian norms about race, and a party system based on the cleavage of race. Politicians convey racial

[2] Several caveats should be kept in mind about this book. First, I assume that white politicians are running in majority-white areas. Racial appeals made in majority-black areas will likely be detected and denounced, causing the candidate to lose the election. Candidates inclined to make such appeals are likely not to run. Second, this book sets aside implicit pro-black appeals. Democrats who wish to mobilize black voters without alienating whites have incentives to make pro-black statements but mask them in some way. The way such a strategy tends to find expression, however, is not with implicit references to race but via a "surgical" approach, using black radio and black churches (Glaser 1996; McCormick and Jones 1983; Persons 1983; Perry 1991). This strategy is important and worth investigating, but it is beyond the scope of this book. Third, subtle appeals to race are also important in biracial contests featuring white and nonwhite candidates, as Reeves (1997) has shown, but this book focuses on white-white contests as a "harder," less obvious case. In biracial contests, as Reeves argues, "we can assume that race is always a factor" (1997, 30), but in white-white contests, race is a variable rather than a constant. Finally, my book does not directly examine anti-Latino appeals because they are still in their infancy. However, Chapter 9 moves my argument well beyond the American black-white dynamic.

messages implicitly when two contradictory conditions hold: (1) they wish to avoid violating the norm of racial equality, and (2) they face incentives to mobilize racially resentful white voters. White voters respond to implicitly racial messages when two contradictory conditions hold: (1) they wish to adhere to the norm of racial equality, and (2) they resent blacks' claims for public resources and hold negative racial stereotypes regarding work, violence, and sexuality. Today, these conditions hold for most Republican politicians and for many—arguably most—white voters. The contradiction among these conditions can be resolved most effectively through implicit racial communication. Politicians appeal to race implicitly because in order to win they need to mobilize whites' racial resentment while adhering to the norm of racial equality established during the 1960s. In other words, they face incentives to mobilize race in the age of equality. White voters respond to implicitly racial messages because they do not recognize these messages as racial and do not believe that their favorable response is motivated by racism. In fact, the racial reference in an implicit message, while subtle, is recognizable and works most powerfully through white voters' racial stereotypes, fears, and resentments.

To understand implicitly racial appeals, we need to understand the role of consciousness in public opinion—voters' consciousness of the racial meaning of a message and of their racial response to it. And we need to understand why elites might try to communicate indirectly rather than directly. Are the sender and receiver aware of the full meaning of an implicit message? Does the receiver know which of her own predispositions is activated by the message? These are general questions that matter for our understanding of public opinion, elections, and political communication. The case of racial politics, however, sharpens these questions like no other. Race is perhaps the central social cleavage of American political life. Yet American society has committed itself to making race irrelevant. The tension between the existence of racial conflict and the inability to express it produces indirect forms of communication, and makes consciousness a central variable in the political psychology of white citizens.

To understand why implicit appeals exist, why they work, and why they cease to work when they are explicit, we must understand the influence of racial stereotypes, fears, and resentments; party coalitions based on race; and the ability of a message to prime racial predispositions in white voters' minds. But while indispensable, these causes are insufficient. They cannot explain why a candidate would choose to convey a message under cover of some other issue. And they cannot explain why the candidate's supporters would respond more positively to an implicit message. Norms and consciousness are the necessary and missing factors. White Americans recognize that it is no longer acceptable to seem like a racist, not for elites or for citizens (Schuman et al. 1997; van Dijk 1991). Most people want to avoid not only the public perception that they are racist, but also thinking of themselves as racist. The norm of racial equality explains why racially conservative candidates seek to avoid the perception that their message is racial, and why their opposition's most effective strategy is to uncover the racial meaning of the message. Voters' awareness that the message violates the norm, and their awareness that their response to the message violates the norm, varies. This variation explains why the same voters respond to the message when it is hidden but repudiate it when it is obvious.

The history of racial norms reveals that as the racial norm changed during the twentieth century from inegalitarian to egalitarian, racial communication was transformed. The century began with highly explicit political communication about race, but as the century progressed, the explicit turned implicit. When the norm is inegalitarian, racial messages must be explicit to be effective. Otherwise, they fail to convey the commitment of the speaker to racial inequality. An inegalitarian norm causes white voters to expect candidates to establish racist credentials. Conversely, when the norm is egalitarian, explicit messages backfire, and only implicit messages, which appear to adhere to the norm, can succeed. When an egalitarian norm prevails, an inverse relationship exists between the explicitness of the message and its effectiveness in mobilizing voters, and a direct relationship exists between the implicitness of the message and its effectiveness. The reason is that voters can respond to the racial meaning of a message without being aware that the message has a racial meaning or that they are responding to that meaning. Without understanding the relationship between elections, norms, communication, and consciousness, and the dynamics of that relationship, it is difficult to evaluate just what has changed and what remains the same in the politics of race. To understand these dynamics is to understand the ongoing mobilization of race in the age of equality.

IMPLICIT VERSUS EXPLICIT COMMUNICATION

What exactly is the difference between implicit and explicit messages? First, consider what makes an appeal explicitly racial. By my definition, a racial appeal is explicit if it uses racial nouns or adjectives to endorse white prerogatives, to express anti-black sentiment, to represent racial stereotypes, or to portray a threat from African Americans. An explicit message uses such words as "blacks," "race," or "racial" to express anti-black sentiment or to make racially stereotypical or derogatory statements.

Explicitly racial appeals have nearly disappeared, but contemporary examples can still be found. Jesse Helms, for example, charged in 1984 that his Democratic opponent in the North Carolina senatorial contest was colluding with Jesse Jackson to register "hundreds of thousands of blacks" who would vote as a bloc against him (Luebke 1990, 131). Northern examples exist, too. The 1983 mayoral election in Chicago marked the first time that a black politician, Democrat Harold Washington, was elected to that office. This was, not coincidentally, the first time that Chicago's black citizens mobilized in a concerted effort to gain greater representation for themselves. White backlash to Washington's primary victory in the overwhelmingly Democratic city and to the historic mobilization of black voters was loud and far from subtle. "No matter what anyone tells you, this election has come down to *race*," stated an anti-Washington campaign flier distributed in police stations (Pinderhughes 1987).[3]

Implicit racial appeals convey the same message as explicit racial appeals, but they replace the racial nouns and adjectives with more oblique references to race. They present an ostensibly race-free conservative position on an issue while incidentally alluding to racial stereotypes or to a perceived threat from African Americans. Implicit racial appeals discuss a nonracial matter and avoid a direct reference to black inferiority or to white group interest. They forego professions of racial antipathy and do not endorse segregation or white prerogatives. They convey a message that may violate the norm of racial equality by submerging it in nonracial content. In an implicit racial appeal, the racial message appears to be so coincidental and peripheral that many of its recipients are not aware that it is there.

Implicit racial appeals can be generated with words alone. But finding words that have a clear racial association yet seem to be nonracial is a difficult undertaking. Visual images are a more effective way to communicate implicitly. Images play an important and distinctive role in the way people perceive their world. Communication research has long argued that television is a unique (and highly influential) medium because it is primarily visual (Jamieson 1992). Indeed, visual images have proven to be powerful cues for evoking racial stereotypes (Hurwitz and Peffley 1997). Stereotypical or threatening images can communicate derogatory racial meaning in a more subtle way than an equivalent verbal statement.

Consider, for example, the stereotypical images of black men broadcast by local television news programs to millions of viewers in metropolitan areas across the country (Entman 1992; Gilliam et al. 1995). These images constitute a "crime script" that portrays violent crime "with a black face," implicitly suggesting that black men pose a physical threat to whites. Imagine if a television journalist were actually to announce, "Today violent black men once again victimized innocent whites." The journalist who says this would be fired, or at least publicly rebuked in the strongest terms. White viewers are likely to perceive the words, much more than they did the images, as racist, and reject the

---

[3] Many observers also considered Republican candidate Bernard Epton's campaign slogan— "Epton . . . Before it's too late"—an explicitly racial appeal; however, according to my definition it was not, because it contains no verbal reference to race.

messenger and the message. Racial images on their own can communicate their derogatory message much more effectively than images joined with words. Perhaps the most important example of implicit campaign appeals is the Willie Horton message as it existed for much of the 1988 campaign. The Horton message was a conservative message about crime and criminal justice that made no verbal mention of race, but included visual cues to racial resentments, fears, and stereotypes.

What makes implicit appeals distinctively effective is also their Achilles' heel. To counter an implicit appeal one can render it explicit. Today, this can be done by using racial words to describe the content or intent of the message. There are two ways to do so. One way, which the news media can pursue, is to communicate an implicit campaign message with an overlay of racial words. Rather than convey a message with a racially derogatory image but without racial words, the news media can convey the story with racial words, thus making clear that race is the subject of the message. Doing so will make voters aware of the racial nature of the message. The other way to render the message explicit is to point out that it steps outside the bounds of the norm of racial equality and thus of acceptability.[4] Doing so not only makes white voters aware of the racial nature of the message, but reminds them of their commitment to the norm of racial equality and invites them to apply it to the campaign.

RACIAL VERSUS NONRACIAL COMMUNICATION

While racially tinged issues lend themselves to implicit racial appeals, they are not only about race. Racially tinged issues also represent nonracial dilemmas. States' rights in the 1950s and 1960s, criminal justice in the late 1960s, 1980s, and 1990s, and welfare dependency from the late 1960s onward are cases in point. These issues involve matters of race, but they also raise nonracial questions. What is the optimal division of power between the federal government and the states? How should we balance the rights of crime victims and the rights of the accused? What are the most effective means to end welfare dependency? It must be possible to make a conservative appeal on these issues that is not racial. Not every defense of states' rights is designed to keep blacks down; not every appeal to end welfare is a derogation of African Americans; not every exhortation to crack down on criminals is a call for racist action.

Criminal justice and welfare dependency can undoubtedly be discussed as part of a nonracial strategy of appealing to conservative considerations—con-

---

[4] This is not a perfect classification scheme. For example, highly stereotypical visual references would be classified as implicit rather than explicit because they are visual. Still, this classification scheme provides clear decision rules and allows me to proceed with analyses that yield intuitive yet new results.

cern about crime, or anger over undeserving welfare recipients. A candidate may genuinely aim to address nonracial concerns rather than appeal to racial predispositions or mobilize white voters. And when candidates are elected, their anti-welfare or anti-crime policies are not necessarily motivated by race. Nevertheless, some candidates or their campaign aides intend to refer to race when they run campaigns. Those who brought the implicit strategy to national prominence, including southern politicians and Richard Nixon and his aides, seem to have been quite conscious of the fact that the voters they targeted for mobilization were white and had racial concerns. Many Republican officials from the 1960s on knew that the racial make-up of their winning coalition was no accident. Similarly, as the evidence in Chapter 5 shows, the Willie Horton appeal in 1988 was in fact designed largely, though not exclusively, as a racial strategy; other implicitly racial campaigns, such as those discussed in Chapter 3, also show a consistent pattern of racial intent. Still, intent is a cause, not a characteristic, of racial appeals. We cannot rely on intent alone to distinguish between implicit and nonracial appeals.

How, then, can we distinguish purely conservative appeals from implicitly racial ones? First we must define an implicitly racial appeal as one that contains a recognizable—if subtle—racial reference, most easily through visual references. People can debate at length the question of whether a verbal reference has racial associations. But a visual image is much less ambiguous. Of course, the racial significance of a black image can be ambiguous, and it is this ambiguous significance that allows the image to be used with deniability. But once the visual image is noted in a conscious way, and linked to a violation of the norm of racial equality, its negative racial reference becomes much less ambiguous. An appeal on welfare or crime that avoids images of African-American welfare recipients or criminals, if it is communicated this way by the media, distances itself from implicit racial appeals.

However, the clearest way for a candidate to separate an implicit racial appeal from a purely conservative appeal is to refer to whites in place of blacks, even if indirectly. A truly nonracial appeal is a counter-stereotypical appeal. This definition is validated by the finding that an anti-welfare message accompanied by images of white welfare recipients does not activate racial predispositions, while an identical message accompanied by images of black welfare recipients does. An unflattering image of blacks makes the message racial. An image of whites transforms the same message into a counter-stereotypical communication. This simple distinction makes a significant difference to white voters' racial response. A conservative message does not activate racial predispositions if it is accompanied by counter-stereotypical images of whites. Thus, the strict definition of a nonracial appeal on an issue entangled with race is that it replaces derogatory or threatening images of African Americans with similar images of whites.

With a clear definition in hand of implicit, explicit, and counter-stereotypical messages, I must now distinguish between voters' racial and nonracial responses. Just as it is possible for candidates to intend purely conservative appeals, it is possible for voters to endorse appeals out of nonracial considerations. A white citizen may vote for a candidate or oppose a policy out of many different considerations, only some of which are racial. Just because an implicit appeal strengthens opposition to affirmative action, for example, does not necessarily mean that the appeal worked because it was racial. Meaning is in the ear of the listener, as Just, Neuman, Crigler and their colleagues have shown (Just et al. 1996; Kern and Just 1995; Neuman et al. 1992). The question is how to tell whether the listener hears "race" as part of the message.

The optimal measure of the racial impact of a message is racial priming: an increase in the effect of racial stereotypes, fears, and resentments, leading to increased opposition to racial policies (such as government aid to blacks) and to greater support for the candidate who conveys the message. Each study I conducted was designed to contrast the strength of racial priming obtained with an implicit appeal against that obtained with other types of appeals. But racial priming does not settle the question of nonracial impact. A message might also result in racial priming but in simultaneous, and more powerful, nonracial priming. The key to knowing whether a message has a racial impact or not is to contrast the increased effect of racial predispositions against the increased effect of nonracial considerations. A message about crime that shows a black criminal will, I expect, evoke racial predispositions more strongly than it evokes nonracial worries about crime. A message about the need to reduce welfare payments that features black welfare recipients should, by the same token, prime racial predispositions more powerfully than it does a conservative orientation toward politics.

I have now considered three aspects of racial messages: whether they are constructed with racial intent or awareness; whether they are racial; and whether they work through voters' racial predispositions. The key to classifying a racial appeal is not through the first or the last, but through the middle: a racial appeal is defined by its content, not by its cause or by its effect. Having clarified my definitional scheme, I turn to the matter of cause and effect.

NORMS MATTER, NOT JUST PARTY COALITIONS

More than any other cleavage, race now serves as the line dividing the two major parties. This can be seen in Table 1.1, which displays the difference that each salient social cleavage makes to the Democratic vote for president. During the past decades, the electoral fortunes of the two major parties have been strongly tied to the cleavage of race. Moreover, the social cleavage of race divides the parties far more than does any other social cleavage. The distinctive

TABLE 1.1

Relationship of Social Characteristics to Presidential Voting, 1944–1996

	Election Year													
	1944	1948	1952	1956	1960	1964	1968	1972	1976	1980	1984	1988	1992	1996
Racial voting[a]	27	12	40	25	23	36	56	57	48	56	54	51	41	47
Regional voting[b]														
Among whites	—	—	12	17	6	-11	-4	-13	1	1	-9	-5	-10	-8
Among entire electorate (NES surveys)	—	—	9	15	4	-5	6	-3	7	3	3	2	0	0
Among entire electorate (official election results)	23	14	8	8	3	-13	-3	-11	5	2	-5	-7	-6	-7
Union voting[c]														
Among whites	20	37	18	15	21	23	13	11	18	15	20	16	12	23
Among entire electorate	20	37	20	17	19	22	13	10	17	16	19	15	11	23
Class voting[d]														
Among whites	19	44	20	8	12	19	10	2	17	9	8	5	4	6
Among entire electorate	20	44	22	11	13	20	15	4	21	15	12	8	8	9
Religious voting[e]														
Among whites	25	21	18	10	48	21	30	13	15	10	16	18	20	14
Among entire electorate	24	19	15	10	46	16	21	8	11	3	9	11	10	7

Source: Abramson, Aldrich, and Rhode (1996, 103).

Note: All calculations are based on major-party voters.

[a] Percentage of blacks who voted Democratic minus percentage of whites who voted Democratic.

[b] Percentage of southerners who voted Democratic minus percentage of voters outside the South who voted Democratic.

[c] Percentage of members of union households who voted Democratic minus percentage of members of households with no union members who voted Democratic.

[d] Percentage of working class that voted Democratic minus percentage of middle class that voted Democratic.

[e] Percentage of Catholics who voted Democratic minus percentage of Protestants who voted Democratic.

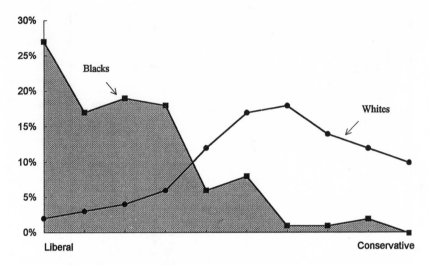

Figure 1.1. Opinion on race policy, separately for blacks and whites. Opinion on race policy is an unweighted average of answers to six questions about what should be done to ameliorate racial inequality, including questions about guaranteeing equal opportunity, providing federal aid to African Americans, and practicing affirmative action. The figure displays answers to these questions, arranged from the most liberal—favoring more action in these areas—to the most conservative—favoring less action in these areas. The circles represent the percentages of whites; the squares represent the percentages of African Americans. Reprinted with permission from University of Chicago Press. (Kinder and Sanders 1996, 27)

power of race does not surprise when we consider Figure 1.1, which displays the distribution of whites' and African Americans' opinions about racial inequality. Actually, Figure 1.1 shows not one but two distributions—one black and the other white, one favoring active government intervention in matters of race and the other opposed. The distributions overlap, suggesting that there is some common ground between blacks and whites, but are still clearly separate. Race is not only an important divide in electoral politics; it is, in the words of Kinder and Sanders, "a divide without peer" (1996, 27).

Thus, the landmark breaks with legal discrimination did not remove race from electoral politics. In fact, these changes only enhanced the importance of race in elections. On the matter of government intervention in racial inequality, the Republican party moved to the right, the Democratic party to the left. As Carmines and Stimson (1989) and Huckfeldt and Kohfeld (1989), among others, have shown, white voters formerly loyal to the Democratic party began to defect to the Republican party, especially in presidential contests, in large measure because of race. African-American voters decisively deserted the party of Abraham Lincoln and the Emancipation Proclamation for the party of Lyndon Johnson and the Civil Rights Act. The result is a party system firmly rooted in the cleavage of race. Commenting on the partisan alignment in the contemporary South, Earl Black noted:

> Because they drew almost all of their votes from whites and won much higher shares of the white vote than the black vote, the victorious white Republicans both symbolized and perpetuated the *rule of white majorities*. Whether or not they resorted to overt racial appeals—and few did in 1994 (at least not of the sort traditionally recognized as craven attempts to win white support)—the white Republicans' thoroughgoing conservatism was ideally designed to attract substantial white majorities in districts where most voters were whites. . . . White Democrats [however] . . . could not possibly succeed without doing well—in different ways— among both whites and blacks. . . . White Democratic victories rested upon the *rule of biracial coalitions*. (Black 1998, 602–604; emphasis in the original)

To a large extent, Black's story about southern elections fits some elections in other regions, too, and it fits national elections. Figure 1.2 shows the percentages of black and white major-party voters who voted Democratic in each presidential election from 1944 to 1996. The Democrats won over 50 percent of the white vote in three of the six elections held between 1944 and 1964, but in only two of the eight elections since 1964. The Democrats won an absolute majority of the total white vote in two of the six elections between 1944 and 1964, but never since then (Abramson et al. 1998, 101–102). In election after election, a majority of white voters has shied away from choosing a Democrat for president. For their part, the Republicans have received almost no black votes since symbolically turning their back on civil rights in 1964 by nominating for president one of the few senators to vote against the historic Civil Rights Act. And while 1964 is a watershed for the racial party system, Figure 1.2 shows that race is no less a divide in the 1990s. In fact, the racial gap was larger in the 1990s than in 1964.

Each party thus faces a distinct combination of racial pitfalls and incentives. Democrats win when the white vote is split among Republican and third-party candidates, when they avoid alienating moderate whites, and when they mobilize blacks. The Democratic party thus must walk a fine line between alienating blacks, its most loyal constituency, and losing further support from racially conservative whites. Republicans, on the other hand, win with effective appeals to whites; the party's challenge is to mobilize racial conservatives without alienating moderate whites (Axelrod 1972, 1986; Carmines and Huckfeldt, 1992; Carmines and Stimson 1989; Edsall and Edsall 1991; Huckfeldt and Kohfeld 1989; Kinder and Sanders 1996).

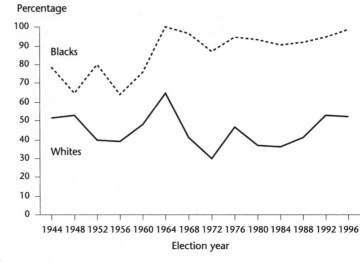

Figure 1.2. Percentage of major-party voters who voted Democratic for president, by race, 1944–1996. Reprinted with permission from Congressional Quarterly Inc. (Abramson, Aldrich, and Rhode 1996, 102)

But to fully understand the Republican dilemma, and the range of strategic choices open to Democrats, it is not enough to know how parties cobble together groups with clashing preferences. True, the need to appeal simultaneously to racially conservative and moderate whites can explain why Republicans try to appeal to racial conservatives without alienating racial moderates. But the need to balance electoral demands by itself cannot explain why Republicans embed their racial message in messages about other issues and deny that they are discussing race. The balancing act cannot explain why even racial conservatives might be more effectively mobilized by implicit appeals.

A coalition-based analysis also falls short of a full explanation of the Democratic strategy. The logic of electoral coalitions predicts that Democrats would remain silent on race, as they in fact often do. But that is not the beginning and end of the Democratic strategy. The Democrats' most effective counterstrategy—which, as I show, they do pursue, albeit occasionally—is to point out how racial the Republican message really is. But why would Democrats benefit from highlighting race in the Republican message? If Democrats always lose when race is on the agenda, as the pure coalitional model predicts—because their core constituency demands a racially liberal position that is anathema to the moderate voters the Democrats need—then it is never in the Democrats' interest to raise the issue of race. The pure coalitional model cannot explain why Democrats might benefit by bringing race to the surface. Yet highlighting the racial element of the opposition's implicit appeals is the Democrats' most effective strategy short of abandoning their racial liberalism, adopting the Republican position on race, and foregoing their attempt to represent the interests of blacks.

The missing link in the pure coalitional model is the norm of racial equality. The social prohibition against making racist statements in public acts as a constraint against playing the race card in a recognizable fashion. Violating this norm is costly for Republicans. In fact, as I will show, it is costly even with their core constituency of racially resentful whites. The norm of racial equality is the only factor that drives Republicans to engage in implicit rather than explicit messages. If Republicans fail to conform to this norm, they risk losing supporters from their own base. The norm of racial equality also renders the strategic choice for Democrats into a decision of whether to be silent in the face of an implicit strategy or to make the implicit message explicit. Campaign messages are of course shaped by electoral strategy, by a calculation of what the core constituency demands, and to what swing voters will object. But decisions about campaign messages also respond to norms of public discourse.

What is a norm? I use the term to describe an informal standard of social behavior accepted by most members of the culture and that guides and constrains behavior. Cialdini and Trost (1998) point out that although laws and material punishments or rewards can reinforce a norm, a norm by definition exercises a social force independent of laws and material costs and benefits. According to DeRidder and his colleagues, perhaps the most distinctive aspect of a norm is its "obligatory character" (1992, 22). But the obligation is of a specific kind. People follow a norm not because they fear the arm of the law or physical punishment but because they wish to avoid social censure or the pangs of conscience. Put more positively, people follow a norm because they seek social approval or a virtuous conception of self.

A new political norm often arises from the concerted actions of a social movement seeking to ameliorate the powerlessness of a group. To gain substantial numbers of adherents, however, a new political norm must be communicated actively and deliberately by influential leaders. The cooperation of influential leaders is necessary especially if the new norm competes with an opposite established norm. The most effective way to combat an old norm and establish a new one is to pass landmark legislation, to issue momentous judicial rulings, and to engage in other highly salient signals of commitment to the new norm. Discrediting the adherents of the old norm is also an effective way to undermine the old norm, but must be supplemented by actions that actively establish the new norm. Once the new norm has passed this initial stage, it may be communicated more passively. Candidates imitate the successful strategies of other candidates who adhere to the new norm. Politicians strive to anticipate and avoid the censure of influential elites who have signaled a commitment to the norm. Voters learn about the new norm from cultural elites and socialization agents in a gradual process of cultural and social diffusion, with successive generations internalizing the norm in an increasingly more effective way. The norm then becomes *descriptive*—providing information about what a typical member of the culture does, about how everyone acts; and, more importantly, *injunctive*—providing information about what actions a typical member of the culture approves or disapproves, about what everyone condones. At its most powerful, the norm is internalized and becomes *personal*—specifying how one's ideal self would act.[5]

The norm of racial equality in the United States was established in just such a fashion. Beginning in the 1930s and 1940s, and even more so in the 1950s and 1960s, segregation, disenfranchisement, lynching, and a host of other racist practices came under increasing cultural attack. Cultural leaders increasingly communicated the notion that racial inequality was an immoral principle. The norm of racial equality gained momentum through landmark legislation and court rulings that signaled that racial equality should now be the injunctive norm. The norm of racial equality was also furthered by the civil rights movement, through its moral rhetoric and through actions that prodded and enabled landmark legislation and discredited the white southern adherents of the old inegalitarian norm. The practices of racial inequality, and the ideology of white supremacy that justified them, were challenged, deliberately and directly.

Thus, over the course of the twentieth century, and particularly during the 1960s, influential elites became increasingly committed to basic racial equality, in particular to equal opportunity. African-American political organizations mobilized against white supremacy with growing effectiveness. The central political institutions of the United States gradually aligned themselves in opposition to this ideology and to the legal segregation it defended.[6] The idea of biological inferiority was discredited. The racist rhetoric of the era of segregation was gradually retired. Citizens' endorsement of basic racial equality became nearly universal. In the age of equality, neither citizens nor politicians want to be perceived or to perceive themselves as racist. The norm of racial equality has become descriptive and injunctive, endorsed by nearly every American.

[5] This terminology is usefully laid out by Cialdini and Trost (1998).

[6] The landmark legislation and court rulings had a far greater normative than material impact. The actual number of people who were formally found to be violators of the law and who suffered adverse material consequences as a result is small (Hochschild 1999; Rosenberg 1991). These laws mattered a great deal, but perhaps as cultural norms more than material punishments.

For most white Americans, it is a personal norm as well. Whites do not simply pay lip service to equality and continue to derogate blacks in private. Almost all whites genuinely disavow the sentiments that have come to be most closely associated with the ideology of white supremacy—the immutable inferiority of blacks, the desirability of segregation, and the just nature of discrimination in favor of whites. In this sense, nearly every white person today has a genuine commitment to basic racial equality in the public sphere.

This dramatic and hugely significant change in norms, however, coexists with a racial divide embedded in the party system. The change in norms did not eliminate racial conflict. Neither did it mitigate the racial base of the party system. Because the civil rights era came and went without fully resolving the problems of racial inequality, individuals and institutions are forced to continue to reach decisions about racial matters, matters that count among the most difficult of our national problems. Racial segregation and inequality have lessened to some extent. But in some ways they are now even more entrenched than they were before the civil rights era (Farley and Allen 1987; Hochschild 1984; Massey and Denton 1993; Wilson 1987, 1996). The problems of race still simmer, periodically getting a turn on the political front burner. Government did not withdraw from the arena of racial problems after the landmark laws and rulings of the 1960s guaranteed African Americans the right to use public accommodations, to have equal employment opportunities, and to cast the ballot. Since the 1960s, a variety of policies designed to cure the ills of racial inequality, including affirmative action in government contracts, in employment, and in higher education, and equal financing and desegregation of public schools and public housing, have been debated, and often resisted by a majority of white voters. So have policies related to racial inequality, including liberal measures in the areas of criminal justice and assistance to the poor. Republicans have incentives to appeal to white voters' racial resentments and fears over these matters, and to the stereotypes that many whites still have about race, crime, and poverty. Democrats in turn must hang on to at least some of the resentful white members of their biracial coalitions but keep up black support. Conflict over race has become institutionalized in the party system.

The norm of racial equality thus restricts but does not eliminate candidates' racial appeals. The norm makes white citizens' response to those appeals contingent on awareness, but does not eliminate it. Egalitarian norms, a racial party system, and white voters' racial stereotypes and resentments jointly explain why race is virtually absent from the surface of campaigns but very much present underneath. Racially conservative candidates avoid the words "black" and "white" and respond to accusations of racism as if they were accusations of immorality of the worst kind. But the electoral incentives and costs they face lead them to try to convey conservative racial meaning in an implicit way.

THE POLITICAL PSYCHOLOGY OF IMPLICIT MESSAGES

The tension between egalitarian norms and negative racial predispositions also explains why many white voters respond quite differently to a racial message depending on its implicitness. The norm of racial equality has not eliminated all racial stereotypes, fears, and resentments, but it does regulate when and how much whites rely on these racial predispositions in making political choices. Whites rely on racial predispositions in reaching decisions about politics when they can do so in a way that is indirect and deniable, not just to others but to themselves as well. The norm of racial equality is not only a public norm that shapes what people do when in the company of others; as we will see in Chapter 8, even a confidential decision is shaped by the norm. Thus, in the case of race, white citizens' opinion is motivated to a significant degree by negative stereotypes and resentment of blacks, but also by egalitarian considerations, including internalized moral views about the need for equal opportunity. The tension between equality and racism allows messages to influence the political response. Some messages allow the egalitarian norm to win, while others allow racial predispositions free reign.[7]

The key to the outcome is awareness of racial priming. Racial predispositions can be activated without the awareness of those who hold them. The likelihood of racial priming without awareness is greater with exposure to implicit than to explicit appeals. An implicit appeal is less likely to be perceived as having violated the norm of racial equality. It is likely to be perceived not as a statement that derogates blacks or suggests a threat from blacks, but rather as a message that includes race only incidentally and neutrally. The same message made explicitly is likely to be perceived as having crossed the line of public acceptability, and it will be rejected. In rejecting the appeal, citizens are likely to become more vigilant about their own racial response. As a result, they reject their racial predispositions as grounds for reaching decisions. I will discuss the various psychological mechanisms at greater length in Chapters 4 and 8. For now, the important point is that implicit appeals work through racial priming—activating negative racial predispositions—and that this happens when self-censorship mechanisms, triggered by a violation of the norm of racial equality, fail to work. Implicit appeals are more effective than explicit messages because they bypass the self-censorship mechanisms of whites.

Political campaigns do not much change people's racial resentments, stereotypes, and fears, as will become evident in later chapters. A longstanding tenet in the literature on voting is that campaigns mobilize rather than convert (Berelson et al. 1954). Campaigns thus rarely alter racial predispositions, but they

---

[7] My definition of implicit appeals is related to but separable from the concept of implicit racism developed by psychologists. See Chapter 4.

do activate or deactivate racial predispositions in the mind, leading citizens to give greater or lesser weight to them. Several recent studies of racial attitudes have demonstrated that the connection between long-standing racial predispositions and political choices grows or shrinks with political circumstances (Kinder and Sanders 1996; Sears 1998). Huckfeldt and Kohfeld (1989) underscore the point in their discussion of Chicago's highly racialized 1983 mayoral election: "Were there significantly fewer racists in Chicago during the 1979 mayoral election than during the 1983 mayoral election? Probably not, but conditions in 1983 provoked levels of racial animosity that were unimagined four years earlier."

What these studies have not considered is that today, campaigns often activate racial predispositions without voters' awareness. In fact, campaigns are most successful when they rely on messages that contain racial cues but are not perceived by most voters as racial.

WHAT WE KNOW—AND DON'T KNOW—OF IMPLICIT APPEALS

It seems, then, that knowledge of implicit appeals is important to our understanding of race, elections, and political communication. However, we know very little about how racial messages operate, in electoral campaigns and in political discourse more generally. What determines when a candidate will use an implicit or explicit racial appeal, and how is each appeal neutralized? How do American political institutions, particularly the media and parties, assist or neutralize implicit racial appeals? Do white voters read the message as a covert yet clear signal of the candidate's racial ideology—or do they view the message as a principled, nonracial conservative stand? These questions must be answered if we are to understand how racial meaning is communicated in American politics. But studies of communication, voters, and campaigns have not yet turned their full attention to these questions. To understand what is to be done in the study of implicit communication, we must first understand what we have not yet done.

The notion that campaigns attempt to appeal to racial predispositions without appearing to do so is not novel, of course. The term "code word"—which means a deniable verbal reference to race—is now fairly common among journalists. Kathleen Hall Jamieson's analysis of the 1988 presidential campaign suggests that the Bush campaign's manipulation and distortion of fact, journalists' amplification of that distortion, and white voters' inclination to allow their racial fears to shape their interpretation of the facts all combined to create a racist response. But how do we know whether the response was racial? And was 1988 a fluke, or part of a pattern? What explains the decision to use a racial appeal? To obtain the answers, we need a systematic effort to discover what makes a message racially coded and how it works. We need to understand the historical circumstances that gave rise to implicit messages, and to investigate effective counterstrategies. Finally, we need to compare communication about race with communication about other social cleavages.

Although most political observers and some scholars now take the existence of implicit racial appeals for granted, they nevertheless tend to neglect their significance. The conventional view seems to be that they are used, at some times and places, but as just a minor variant either of explicitly racial appeals or of purely conservative appeals. This has led scholars to underestimate just how common and powerful racial communication is.

For example, in the 1970s edition of his classic *Dynamics of the Party System*, James Sundquist argued that the issue of race might have become a source of partisan realignment, but had not because it was abandoned by the Republican party. He believed this largely because he believed that local Republican organizations, in the South as well as the North, were unwilling to engage in blatant appeals to racism, and it would take such a blunt tool to make a dent in conservative Democrats' party affiliation.

In the 1983 edition of the same book Sundquist moderated his conclusion only slightly. Even the local Republican organizations in the Deep South, he claimed, were divided on whether to try to recruit George Wallace voters. They knew it could be done: "The Democrats could be labeled the 'black man's party' and the GOP established as the defenders of southern racial traditions" (1983, 364). But many Republicans "had no stomach for such an overt appeal to racism. . . . No one arose to take Wallace's place as leader of a southern protest movement based on race, and the region entered . . . a period marked by the rapid and pronounced abatement of the powerful racial issue that had dominated southern politics through most of history." Instead of making appeals to race, Republicans chose to mend fences through such symbolic overtures as appointing token African Americans to their staffs. Sundquist did not consider the possibility that Republicans might come to rely on the "interlinked" issues of race and crime (and race and welfare) to make less overt racial appeals. He believed that the Democrats had moved to the right in tandem with white opinion and thus forestalled Republican gains from subtle racial appeals.

As a consequence, Sundquist underestimated the extent to which party coalitions were becoming fundamentally shaped by issues of race. And he overestimated the continuing resistance of racial conservatives to identification with the Republican party (e.g., Giles and Hertz 1994). Sundquist knew, while he was writing during the 1970s and 1980s, that racial conservatives split their tickets with a vengeance. But he assumed that this was as far as the Republicans could get. He made a mistake in part because he neglected the frequency with which Republicans relied on implicit racial appeals, and the influence such appeals had on white voters. He briefly noted Nixon's implicitly racial tactics, but dismissed their effect: "Nixon . . . used the 'code words' and created the 'symbolism' that appealed to segregationists. But that did not mean they had realigned as Republicans" (1983, 370). Sundquist believed that Nixon's was an isolated case, and that his appeals had only limited influence over voters.

Studies of elections outside the South have also passed over the significance of implicit racial appeals. In their comprehensive study of mayoral elections, Metz and Tate (1995) made clear their intention to study implicit appeals. They defined racialized elections as those in which

> one or both of the two major candidates make explicit appeals to members of their own racial group; when the major candidates limit their campaign appearances to members of their racial group, and when the candidates raise issues that are *explicitly or implicitly* racial. . . . The types of issues that candidates raise can be overtly racial, such as the city's affirmative action policy, or *covertly racial*, as sometimes is the case in a candidate's exclusive focus on the city's crime (read: Black) problem. (263, 267; emphasis added)

However, Metz and Tate did not measure implicit appeals. They conclude that white candidates' racial appeals have declined since 1969.[8] Their measure of racialized campaigns, however, misses the important distinction between explicit and implicit rhetoric. Had they measured implicit and explicit appeals separately, they likely would have found an increase in the first and a decrease in the second. Ignoring implicit appeals leads to an underestimate of the importance of racial appeals today. It also results in a murky view of how racial appeals change over time, what leads candidates to use them, and how voters respond to them.

Plaintiffs in voting rights cases and scholars who testify on their behalf have also tended to neglect implicit appeals in pressing their case. The greatest opportunity for testifying about implicit appeals presented itself before the 1990s, while the courts still relied on a "totality of circumstances" test to decide whether a violation of the Voting Rights Act had occurred (but see Grofman and Handley 1998a). Even then, however, because subtle appeals to race were difficult to prove, they were little discussed in the courts, despite the explicit inclusion of "overt or subtle appeals" in the list of seven factors used to establish a violation of Section 2 (Grofman 1992, 200–201; Thernstrom 1987, 194–195). The single exception seems to be the sociologist Paul Luebke, who has documented instances of implicitly racial campaign appeals in North Carolina (1990; Grofman 1992, 208). While testifying as an expert witness in *Gingles v. Edmisten*, he defined a racial appeal this way: "One candidate calls attention to the race of his opponent or his opponent's supporters, or if media covering a campaign disproportionately call attention to the race of one candidate or of

---

[8] The highest-scoring elections are the 1983 Chicago mayoralty, characterized by quite explicitly racial appeals (Kleppner 1985), and the 1979 Birmingham contest in which candidate Frank Parsons stated, "Whites need to vote to prevent a Black mayor." No implicitly racial campaigns make their way to the top of the scale.

that candidate's supporters" (Grofman 1992, 206–207). But how are judges to decide that a candidate called attention to race if he never used any explicitly racial references? Is the common use of the phrase "bloc vote," for example, meant as a racial reference, and does it evoke associations with the "black vote"? "Because overt racial appeals may be absent," wrote Grofman, "testimony about more subtle and covert forms of racial appeal such as the use of code words and of themes associated with white supremacy and antiblack sentiment may be required if this element of the totality of circumstances test is to be proved" (1992, 208). Yet how can such testimony convince if "a racial campaign appeal, like pornography, is in the category of 'I know it when I see it' " (1992, 206)? We need a more systematic definition of implicit appeals, and a theory of how they work, in order to proceed with Grofman's exhortation.[9]

Scholars of parties and elections have not been alone in their neglect of implicitly racial appeals. How an implicit racial message might be received by the audience is a question that has been passed over by the field of public opinion. Studies of public opinion long underscored the view that citizens do not think coherently or do not think much at all (Converse 1964). More recently, scholars have explored the possibility that citizens think several thoughts at once, generate opinions without forethought, make use of values and feelings, and think in shortcuts (Feldman and Zaller 1992; Marcus et al. 1995; Popkin 1991; Sniderman, Brody, and Tetlock 1991; Zaller 1992). We now know that people's minds are sometimes empty, sometimes unmade and disorderly, often ill-informed, and often ambivalent or uncertain, and we attend to the implications of this. We also understand that the media does not have "minimal effects," that it can shape opinion in part by priming one consideration over another (Iyengar and Kinder 1987). All this is important to know. But it does not explain—or even ask—how implicit communication works. It does not tell us whether implicit communication matters, or how it might matter. It does not speak to the possibility that voters respond to some messages with full consciousness and to others without. It does not explain why the overt content of some messages (for example, crime) may affect opinions on an entirely different issue domain (for example, affirmative action).

Political communication is the most likely field to have engaged in an intensive study of implicit campaign appeals, but for the most part it has joined the other fields in neglecting the subject. Studies of political communication have moved toward a constructionist model of communication in which politi-

---

[9] Jamieson (1992) and Himelstein 1983 are the only studies I know that focus on implicitly racial appeals. Kousser (1991), Luebke (1990), Pettigrew and Alston (1988), and Reeves (1997) engage this phenomenon in a more limited way. To my knowledge, Black's (1976) analysis of southern governors and Metz and Tate's (1995) chapter on racial strategy are the only systematic treatments of changes in white candidates' racial rhetoric over time, but they do not focus on implicit appeals. Holly (1989) provides an interesting though brief and general exploration of politicians' implicit communication.

cians, journalists, and citizens actively construct messages and interpret meaning (Crigler 1996; van Dijk 1988). But the constructionist view has rarely led scholars to attend to the distinction between overt and covert meaning. With few exceptions (Jamieson 1992 and van Dijk 1991 important among them), political communication scholars, when they analyze multiple layers of meaning, skim over the possibility that the subtext of a message does much of its work. The few exceptions do not provide evidence about the impact of implicit messages. Thus we do not know how voters process implicit messages versus other kinds of messages. We do not yet understand implicit political communication.

OVERVIEW OF THE CHAPTERS

Part I of this book explains how and why many white politicians make racial appeals, and when these become implicit. Part II shows how the racial meaning of implicitly racial appeals is conveyed by the news media, and how it is received by white audiences, influencing voters without their full awareness. Part III asks what is distinctive about race in relation to gender, sexual orientation, ethnicity, and immigration, and offers remedies to the damage that implicit communication inflicts on equality.

Using historical analysis, Chapters 2 and 3 establish the importance of two causes of implicit racial campaign appeals: the norm of racial equality and a party alignment based on race. Racial appeals—implicit and explicit—are only used when the party system is structured by the issue of race. They are most prominent following a large shock to the status quo, such as the emancipation of slaves in the nineteenth century or the Supreme Court's *Brown v. Board of Education* decision in the twentieth. Explicit racial appeals were common in the national elections of Reconstruction and in the southern elections of the disenfranchisement period, as Chapter 2 shows. However, for a brief time, while Radical Republicans were in power, the norm changed, and explicit appeals waned somewhat in favor of slightly more implicit appeals. Implicit appeals, then as now, allowed politicians to appeal to white voters' racial predispositions without triggering condemnation from egalitarian-minded elites.

Norms about race changed slowly but radically after 1930, and politicians increasingly tried to legitimize their racist discourse as a result, as Chapter 3 shows. Southern politicians made increasingly implicit references to white supremacy, black inferiority, or black threat, and decreased their reliance on explicit references to race. In the 1960s the Republican party forged a national strategy that relied on implicit appeals to build, eventually, winning Republican coalitions in presidential elections and, with time, in southern congressional and gubernatorial elections. As in the nineteenth century, a race-based party system is producing racial appeals, but now the norm of racial equality is so strong that these appeals must be made implicitly.

Part II explains the success of implicit racial messages in the contemporary period. In Chapter 4 I lay out a psychological theory of implicit appeals. Implicit appeals prime white citizens' racial resentment while circumventing their mechanisms of self-censorship. The enormous shift in public norms of racial discourse, documented in Chapter 3, created a near-universal tendency to self-censor. Some people censor themselves because they aspire to be egalitarian, others because they wish to conform to the social pressure of norms of discourse. Implicit appeals are more effective than explicit appeals because they avoid the conscious perception that they derogate African Americans and thus circumvent self-censorship.

Chapter 5 examines in detail how the tactic of implicit racial appeals is implemented by elites and how it is conveyed by the news media. It also examines how that tactic is challenged and how the challenge is in turn conveyed by the media. My conclusions are based on a comprehensive content analysis of television and newspaper coverage of the story of Willie Horton, beginning with the 1988 presidential campaign and ending ten years later.

Chapters 6 through 8 test the implications of the theory for white voters. Chapter 6 analyzes the real-time vote choices of a national sample exposed first to an implicit and then to an explicit phase of a presidential campaign. Chapter 7 reports on an experiment designed to test the distinct effects of otherwise identical implicit and explicit racial messages and to contrast these with a counter-stereotypical message that shows white welfare recipients. I conducted this study in the homes of a random sample of Michigan voters, lending the results a rare degree of external validity. Here the issue is welfare rather than crime. Chapter 8 investigates the impact of norms and of the perception of the message by adding an additional manipulation in which New Jersey voters were provided with false feedback that placed them either within or outside the norm.

Throughout these chapters I will ask two questions: how strongly do racial messages prime racial predispositions? And by contrast, how strongly do they prime nonracial predispositions? My findings show that implicitly racial messages are much more effective at priming racial than nonracial predispositions; that they influence opinion on racial much more than on nonracial policies; and that they do all this much more effectively than either explicit messages or nonracial messages. Racial resentment exercises the strongest impact when politicians and the media convey implicit racial messages. The effective way to counter implicit messages is to expose their underlying racial meaning. Chapter 8 finds that voters' feelings about the norm, and their perceptions of racial messages, can each inhibit the impact of racial appeals.

Part III generalizes the framework and concludes with implications for racial equality, egalitarian change, and democratic politics. Communication between elites and citizens is far more complex than scholars generally recognize, with the subtext at times more powerful than the text. Voters' political psychology is also more complex than commonly assumed, with consciousness at times playing a central role. Before the benefits of a liberal exchange of information can be realized, communication must shift from the implicit to the explicit level. As long as it remains implicit, voters cannot process information with full awareness of the message or reach decisions based on consciously selected predispositions. As long as implicit communication persists, efforts to improve the status of African Americans will be resisted by a white majority that believes it is living up to the promise of racial equality. And implicit racial communication will persist—until the party system realigns on an issue other than race. The argument I develop about racial communication explains why African Americans' position in American politics is distinctive relative to the position of other subordinate groups. The electoral politics of race is different from that of gender and sexual orientation because of the uneasy coexistence of a norm of equality with political conflict. But the same logic that illuminates the politics of race applies to other situations in which egalitarian norms are strong, yet conflict persists over the status of a subordinate group.[10] Chapter 9 suggests how the logic applies to anti-ethnic and anti-immigrant politics in Europe.

This book is my attempt to advance a comprehensive theory of implicit messages, to tell a full story about this form of political communication: its causes, its institutional and psychological mechanisms, and its political consequences. Implicit appeals are driven by cultural, political, and psychological forces. They require an analysis that recognizes all three forces, one that is anchored by norms, electoral strategies, and voters' psychology.

As the next chapter will show, in the nineteenth century, a party system based on the issue of race emerged in the United States, generating explicit appeals to race. But the party system was not the only cause of the rise of explicit racial appeals. The norm of racial inequality was the other factor.

---

[10] In this book I use the terms "dominant" and "subordinate" to refer to the general difference in power, privilege, influence, resources, and status between white Americans and African Americans, men and women, heterosexuals and gays, and citizens and noncitizens. Of course, no pejorative meaning is intended in my use of "subordinate."

CHAPTER 2

The Norm of Racial Inequality, Electoral Strategy, and Explicit Appeals

> At first glance, it seems not unjust that the term
> "strategy" should be derived from "cunning" and
> that, for all the real and apparent changes that war
> has undergone since the days of ancient Greece,
> this term still indicates its essential nature.
> —Clausewitz, *On War*

WHY DO SOME elections include racial appeals while others do not? Why are some racial appeals implicit and others explicit? To reach a fuller understanding of how and why implicit appeals exist today and why explicit appeals have disappeared, we need to find out why explicit appeals existed in the past and why implicit appeals were absent.

Racial appeals appeared prominently on the American political scene with the rise of the national party system of the 1860s, and intensified with the shock of emancipation. The parties positioned themselves on the issue of political rights for African Americans, with Democrats to the right, Republicans to the left.

Simply occupying the right or the left, however, did not by itself dictate a rhetorical strategy. The Democrats could have, for example, appealed exclusively to the idea of states' rights, an idea they did in fact make salient in their campaigns. But they chose to appeal not only to states' rights but also to derogatory views about blacks. Their position against extending citizenship rights to African Americans was communicated with explicitly racial messages that derogated African Americans in a direct and overt way. Similarly, the Republicans could have appealed to notions of equality or humanitarianism in communicating their position on African American rights, as did some abolitionists. But for the most part, they appealed to neither. Instead, they chose to make explicitly racial appeals of their own, along with appeals to anti-southern, sectionalist sentiment. Why did each party pursue the rhetorical strategy that it did? Understanding the alignment of the parties on the issue of blacks' status is necessary—but not sufficient—to explain the parties' rhetorical strategies.

The factor of norms is the missing piece of the puzzle. During the nineteenth century, the norm dictated conformity to the basic precepts of white superiority and black inferiority. This norm of racial inequality led Democrats, intent on denying African Americans their citizenship rights, to craft a strategy that featured explicit attacks on the character of blacks. The norm in turn drove Republicans to justify their advocacy of rights for African Americans with a strategy that included an explicit affirmation of white supremacy. Thus, during national electoral campaigns, Republicans' defense of racial equality was puny, and their racist appeals to whites loud and clear. Just as today it is political suicide for politicians to appear to violate the norm of racial equality, then it was suicide to appear to violate the norm of racial inequality. During both centuries, the party system aligned on the issue of race and created incentives to engage in racial appeals. But in the nineteenth century the norm of inequality rendered those appeals explicit; in the twentieth century, the norm of equality rendered those appeals implicit.

Thus, a party's rhetorical strategy depends not only on its position on the issues, but also on the dictates of norms. Norms, however, are not fixed. They respond to social and political conditions. In the twentieth century, the norm would change markedly. But even during the nineteenth century, the norm was susceptible to change. The passage of the Fourteenth and Fifteenth Amendments during Reconstruction, and Republicans' commitment to enforcing them, created a new norm of limited political equality. The new norm was weak and as short-lived as Reconstruction. It co-existed with, rather than replaced, the older norm of racial inequality. But for a brief time, while the new norm had some force, Democrats were reluctant to engage in explicitly racial appeals.

The end of Reconstruction brought an end both to the norm of limited political equality for blacks and to a national party system based on the issue of race. Democrats and Republicans no longer took different positions on the question of blacks' status, and the question itself was set aside. Racial appeals subsided as the party system that had given rise to them dissolved. They reappeared in the South at the turn of the century, as the party system in that region briefly structured itself along the issue of race, with Populists aligning themselves with black voters against Democrats. The Populists too could not fly in the face of the norm of racial inequality without compensating in some way. They made both racially egalitarian and racially derogatory appeals to white voters. Democrats crushed the Populist revolt in part with an intense barrage of explicitly racial appeals, disenfranchising blacks in the process. The party system in the South ceased to revolve around race, and racial appeals accordingly faded from campaigns.

The content of racial appeals during the nineteenth century was remarkably constant across campaigns. It drew on deeply rooted stereotypes, fears, and resentments, and the enduring notion of racial inferiority. African Americans were portrayed as having a proclivity toward three evils: sexual immorality, criminality and the desire to subjugate whites, and economic dependency and laziness. Many campaigns that included racial appeals had all three of these dimensions. One or another dimension sometimes overshadowed the others, but each tended to recur over time.

The notion that blacks were fundamentally different from whites when it came to sex, violence, and work lent itself to the argument that blacks' character made them fit to occupy an inferior position in society. If blacks were inadequate, went the argument, then they deserved to get only low occupations, receive meager pay, and inhabit only warm climates (therefore, they should be shipped to Africa or at least prohibited from residing in many Midwestern states). Notions of black difference justified blacks' lower economic position, physical removal, and political disempowerment. Throughout the nineteenth century and well into the twentieth, whites almost universally believed that blacks should not fully mix with whites. Even those who wanted to improve blacks' position—Republicans during Reconstruction, Populists during the 1890s—often reassured whites that the fundamentals of white superiority would not change.

WHITE AMERICANS' RACIAL PREDISPOSITIONS

During the century leading up to the founding of the American nation, racial slavery became a fundamental institution in every North American colony. Because it was intertwined with race, and because it pervaded the social fabric of every colony, slavery created across the nation a set of deeply rooted, elaborate, and widespread notions about racial inferiority (Kolchin 1993). These were more than individual prejudices. By the nineteenth century, they constituted an entrenched national norm.

Negative racial predispositions were quite strong on both sides of the divide over slavery.[1] The point of contention between pro-slavery and anti-slavery forces was not whether slaves were inadequate people, but rather the causes—and thus the implications—of their inadequacy. Radical abolitionists believed that blacks' condition was treatable, and some, particularly late in the struggle against slavery and during Reconstruction, announced their belief in full equality (McPherson 1992). But most abolitionists described slaves as "brutish, ignorant, idle, crafty, treacherous, bloody, thievish, mistrustful, and superstitious," and led purposefully segregated lives (Franklin 1989, 134–135, 137–139; Fredrickson 1971; Jordan 1974, 116). Most opponents of slavery, North and

---

[1] Negative racial predispositions, from the beginning, were not tantamount to a simple hatred of blacks. Many who accepted the inevitability of slavery or defended restrictions on free blacks had negative views of what they perceived as the current unfortunate characteristics of blacks, but did not dislike blacks as a general matter (Jackman 1994). Those who wished not to eliminate but to reform slavery, for example, argued that slaves needed and deserved Christianity because they were meek, helpless, and servile. Also, even public figures castigated for the extremity of their anti-black rhetoric sometimes denied that they were against blacks at all, arguing that they were simply pro-white (Degler 1982, 74).

South, were motivated by the perception that slavery harmed whites (Degler 1982, 27). "It is not for the good of Negroes but for that of the whites that measures are taken to abolish slavery in the United States," wrote Tocqueville (1988, 1:360). As the debate over slavery reached its peak in the late 1850s and early 1860s, there was near universal concession of the current inferiority of slaves. Most Republicans and Democrats shared in common the view that blacks lacked the character dimensions necessary to have an equal place in the political, economic, and social life of the society.

The theme of sexuality existed early, continuously, and prominently in whites' actions regarding race (Davis 1988, 462–463). Prohibitions against interracial sexual relations were codified quite early in the North American colonies (Giddings 1984; Ruchames 1969, 71). The theme of African men's lust for white women was especially pronounced in the worldviews of the North American colonists (Jordan 1974, 79–80). The early colonial laws prescribing castration only for the rape of white women by black men further demonstrate the particular significance attached by white men to this crime.[2]

Often the myth that black men had designs on white women had overtones of illicit power and violent threat. Sexual retribution by black men became a salient worry during times when whites' control over blacks seemed more tenuous or when blacks made political gains (Williamson 1984). Reports of planned revolts were often accompanied by rumors that slaves planned to kill white men and rape white women, rumors that some historians have suggested were often outright fabrications, perhaps representing anxieties stemming from white men's own sexual exploitation of black women (Jordan 1974, 80; Takaki 1990, 49–55).

The theme of sexuality was also tied to reproduction. The rise of social Darwinism after the 1830s brought a great deal of anxiety about the reproductive consequences of the sexual mixing of the races. In the white imagination of the time, racial amalgamation and the "degeneration" of the white race through interracial sexual relations would inexorably follow egalitarian measures (Fredrickson 1971, 49).

As the nineteenth century began, criminality and laziness joined sexuality as racial themes. The worry about violence committed by African Americans and about their work ethic sharpened as the free black population grew in the early decades of the nineteenth century. The perception of them as thieves and

---

[2] Castration had no precedent in English law and was considered, even in the colonies, to be an inhumane punishment. Yet laws in several colonies were firm in reserving it as the only suitable punishment for the most horrible of crimes. For example, Virginia's castration law (reserved for crimes by blacks), which was repealed on humanitarian grounds in 1769, remained available for punishment in cases of rape of white women (Jordan 1974, 82). The view that nothing was sufficiently cruel to compensate for the cruelty imposed on white women by black rape was alive and well nearly a century and a half before it was articulated as a defense of lynching. It remained alive and well through much of the first half of the twentieth century, as can be seen from the rate at which black men were sentenced to death for the crime of rape.

as fomenters of slave revolts became widespread. Their supposed propensity to engage in criminal behavior was deemed to go hand in hand with a propensity to avoid honest work. Each was taken to originate in inherent laziness (Ruchames 1969, 421).

Northerners as well as southerners worried about the threat of black crime and violence. The worry grew to the extent that nearly every northern state restricted the right of free blacks to vote to one degree or another, and many restricted the right of blacks to immigrate (Litwak 1961; Meier and Rudwick 1994, 92–93; Malone 1999, 2). The worry about perceived black deficiencies seems to have intensified when the increasing number of blacks began to affect the outcome of some state and national elections.

In a pattern that would recur for the next two centuries, the threat that racial inequality would lessen sparked the first alignment of state parties on an issue of race, leading to the first known use of racial campaign appeals at the state level. In New York, after blacks had provided Federalists with a narrow margin of victory in the election of 1800, the opposition party countermobilized against the perceived threat of black political equality. Jeffersonians campaigned with the slogan "Federalists with Blacks Unite," and subsequently tried to disenfranchise blacks with speeches such as this: "The minds of blacks are not competent to vote. They are too degraded to estimate the value, or exercise with fidelity and discretion this important right. . . . Look to your jails and penitentiaries. By whom are they filled? By the very race, whom it is now proposed to clothe with the power of deciding upon your political rights" (Malone 1999, 28–30).

Even those who defended the right of African Americans to vote adhered to the norm of racial inequality by describing free blacks with terms such as "degraded," "vicious," and having "loose manners" and "depravity of conduct" (Fredrickson 1971, 4, 5; Jordan 1974, 220).[3] In 1798 New Jersey abolitionists declared their belief that free blacks were "given to Idleness, Frolicking, Drunkenness, and in some few cases to Dishonesty"; nine years later, New Jersey became the second state outside the southern and border states to disenfranchise blacks. As other northern states followed suit, local racial appeals appeared.[4]

---

[3] Among the most ardent defenders of blacks' right to vote was Peter Jay, who argued during New York's disenfranchisement convention that blacks were not inherently inferior but that slavery had made blacks in general "inferior to whites in knowledge and industry": "Unaccustomed to provide for themselves, and habituated to regard labor as an evil, it is no wonder that when set free, they should be improvident and idle, and that their children should be brought up without education, and without prudence and forethought" (Malone 1999, 31).

[4] During Pennsylvania's constitutional convention of 1838, in which blacks were disenfranchised, delegates argued that if blacks were allowed to keep voting, "every negro in the State, worthy and worthless, degraded and debased, as nine tenths of them are, will rush to the polls in senseless and unmeaning triumph" (Litwack 1961, 75). Attempts to send African Americans to

The worry about black crime and violence also shaped southern politics. The southern fear of a "race war" was so intense that several historians consider it the main force behind the secessionist movements of the 1820s to the 1860s, including the final break with the Union (Channing 1970, 289; Franklin 1989, 96; Freehling 1992 [1966], 51). The prominent citizens of Charleston exhorted the South Carolina legislature to constant vigilance: "We should always act as if we had an enemy in the very bosom of the State, prepared to rise upon and surprise the whites, whenever an opportunity be afforded" (Wade 1967, 226–227).

Thus, on the eve of the Civil War, negative racial predispositions were extremely common. Their basic themes of sex, violence, and work resonated with nearly all whites. They were found among whites of the South and the North, defenders of slavery and abolitionists. They had given rise to codes, laws, practices, and political movements that were designed, in one way or another, to protect white privilege. The norm of racial inequality was firmly in place. But racial predispositions had yet to be mobilized in electoral politics in a concerted way. Racial campaign appeals, and a party system based on the issue of race, were still in their infancy.[5] For racial appeals to surface in a prominent way, and for voters' racial predispositions to be mobilized in elections, the issue of race had to make its way to the party system. The parties would have to take different stands on the issue.

THE PARTY SYSTEM OF THE 1860s GIVES BIRTH TO EXPLICIT RACIAL APPEALS

By the presidential election of 1860, controversy over slavery had worked itself into the national party system (Sundquist 1983). As late as 1858, the views of Democrats and Republicans on slavery were more in accord than not (Burns 1985; Zarefsky 1990). But already during the election of 1856, and especially during the Civil War, the parties moved far apart on the issue of blacks' status. As the sectional conflict between North and South grew heated and Republican numbers swelled, Democrats began to emphasize the racial aspects of the Republican platform. The stage was set for defenders of slavery and, after the war, defenders of racial hierarchy, to "whip up public hostility against Republicans and Negroes" (Wood 1968, 10). These racial appeals relied on the familiar

---

Africa, or resettle them some place outside the nation's borders, became quite popular in the North. Nine northern state legislatures voted in 1824 to urge the federal government to finance the gradual emancipation of slaves and their subsequent expatriation to Africa (Degler 1982, 23; Fredrickson 1971, 6–12).

[5] The Lincoln-Douglas senatorial contest of 1858 was a prominent precursor. The rash of state restrictions on blacks during the early decades of the nineteenth century were also accompanied by state-level racial appeals, though the extent of these appeals is not yet known (Malone 1999).

themes of sex, violence, and work. In general, the derogatory "Black Republican" label of the late 1850s well captured the Democratic strategy of the coming decade, and symbolized the problem that the Republican counterstrategy strove to avoid. Republicans, especially once the Civil War began, primarily relied on two rhetorical moves in rebuttal: the threat of southern domination, and, to a lesser extent, racist appeals of their own.

The alignment of the parties on the issue of race set the stage for racial appeals, but the issue was to become much more salient with emancipation. Emancipation acted as a shock, galvanizing the Democrats and sending the Republicans scrambling for an effective response. Emancipation gave rise to the first prominent use of racial appeals in a political disagreement of national scope. Before the war there was sufficient anxiety about race for politicians to use, but ultimately there seemed to northern opponents of emancipation little chance that emancipation would ever be directly espoused by the federal government. Once emancipation loomed as a reality, the opposition became determined to resist with all the means available. Now the prospect of free blacks migrating Northward and Westward in large numbers seemed to northern whites imminently near (Klinker and Smith 1999, 61; Wood 1968, 17–18). The themes present in whites' fears, stereotypes, and resentments came to figure prominently in explicitly racial electoral appeals.

The Democrats' explicit focus on race and the Republicans' response in kind make sense when we consider how strong the norm of racial inequality was then. Racial appeals were safe since there were no social constraints against espousing racial inequality—quite the opposite. Even once empowered to vote, African Americans did not seem to expect Republicans to repudiate the idea of racial inequality. In fact, many African-American leaders seemed to significantly limit their expectations for equality (Foner 1988). Consequently, racial messages were highly explicit on both sides, although the tactic was prominent for Democrats and peripheral for Republicans. Democrats used explicit appeals to attack, Republicans to defend. The partisan press was a central means of communicating these messages. Journalists began for the first time to draw negative images of blacks (Wood 1968, 12, 34). Politicians also conveyed racial appeals in stump speeches and in official pronouncements. Party organizations did their part through pamphlets and broadsides.

Democratic Racial Rhetoric: The Fear of Racial Equality

The Democrats relied primarily on the charge that Republicans desired complete equality between the races. Lincoln faced this charge in his senatorial campaign in 1858 and afterward (Wood 1968, 19; Zarefsky 1990). The Democratic National Executive Committee distributed a campaign pamphlet in 1860 that suggested, with explicitly racial language, that Lincoln wanted to repeal "all laws which erect a barrier between you and the black man." Republicans, claimed the pamphlet, believe that the black man "is your equal, entitled to vote, hold office, sit at the same table with you, and marry your daughter." The New York Weekly Day Book claimed Lincoln would "elevate the negro at whatever cost to the Saxon" while the Detroit Free Press sarcastically urged the president to relocate to Haiti or Liberia, where he would find a more "congenial atmosphere" (Wood 1968, 19–20). The charge that Republicans desired complete and disastrous racial equality was widespread and may have had significant political results in New Jersey and New York as well as the Midwest, particularly in states with a large southern-born population, such as Indiana, Illinois, and Ohio (McPherson 1988, 561–562).

The theme of sexuality was also present, primarily in the fear of racial amalgamation. It was featured in the opposition to the mobilization of black Union troops in the North. The New York World covered the departure of the 20th Regiment of Colored Volunteers from New York by lamenting the sight of white women giving support "to a regiment of hypothetical Othellos." The Chicago Times reported that at the send-off for the First Illinois Colored Regiment, "white women were there in attendance to bid farewell to black husbands, around whose necks they clung long and fondly. Black women, too, and men almost white, were locked in each other's arms" (Wood 1968, 42–43).

Another anti-emancipation argument that found widespread use relied on the familiar stereotype of black laziness. Aiding freed slaves, the argument went, would be onerous and unfair to white working people. "Are the white working men of this country willing to bind this heavy yoke around their necks, and entail it upon their children?" asked a Democratic newspaper editor (Wood 1968, 24). In what was to be a recurring argument, John Van Evrie, perhaps the most widely cited racist writer of the 1860s, warned that freed blacks would refuse to work, thus increasing the tax burden and draining local social services (Foner 1988).

Democratic appeals were also characterized by the theme of black violence and crime. The Democratic press repeatedly printed stories of black violence, using highly charged terms such as "outrage" even though most of the incidents were minor (and in at least some cases, clearly fabricated). Stories of supposed atrocities committed by blacks in other lands abounded in Democratic newspapers and found their way to speeches and pamphlets, accompanied by warnings about a similar fate following the emancipation of slaves. Van Evrie described, in what was one of the most popular racist pamphlets of the 1860s, how rioting blacks "marched with spiked infants on their spears," "sawed asunder" white men, and raped white women "on the dead bodies of their husbands" (Wood 1968, 28).[6]

---

[6] The newspapers that carried these stories and accusations were not only the extremist racist newspapers of the day, but even those considered mainstream.

As the prospect of greater black equality neared, the power and explicitness of campaign appeals that derogated blacks increased. Just after Lincoln announced his preliminary Emancipation Proclamation in September 1862, the Democrats' slogan in Ohio, "The Constitution as it is, the Union as it was," was amended with the additional "and the Niggers where they are." A series of publications and speeches there seemed to prime resentment over competition for jobs (Klinker and Smith 1999, 61; Wood 1968, 22). The Democratic gains from that election allowed the legislature to amend the state Constitution to prohibit the entry of blacks to the state. Elsewhere, too, Democratic newspapers, including the *New York World*, the leading Democratic newspaper in the North, and the *Philadelphia Age*, launched a barrage of appeals, charging that the newly freed blacks would present an economic threat to the white working class.[7]

The concern with sex, violence, and work was thus increasingly exploited and mobilized by Democratic politicians in the early 1860s, as emancipation became a growing worry and the parties increasingly diverged on the issue of black emancipation. This mobilization, in accord with the norm of racial inequality, was nothing if not explicitly racial.

Republican Racial Rhetoric: Free White Soil for Free White Men

As the Republican party was increasingly moving to the left on the issue of citizenship rights for blacks, many Republicans nevertheless did their best to dissociate from the public perception that they were allies of blacks (Nieman 1991, 42–43). Republicans of the late 1850s and early 1860s developed an increasingly radical program of political equality for blacks. They advocated basic citizenship rights in the North and the gradual, "natural" extinction of slavery in the South (Gerring 1998, 108–111). But a large number of Republicans saw full equality as unthinkable and abhorrent; they hated slavery in part because it required the presence of many blacks; and they planned to permanently separate whites from blacks should emancipation come about. When it came to running a national campaign, the Republicans faced a difficult dilemma. They responded by developing a strategy that included attempts to show that Republicans were no more sympathetic to full equality with blacks than anyone else.[8]

---

[7] "A vote for [Horatio] Seymour is a vote to protect our white laborers against the association and competition of southern negroes" (Wood 1968, 20). Klinker also describes explicitly racial appeals in Illinois (1999, 61).

[8] That is not to say that Republicans did not favor more racial equality than Democrats did. Gerring's analysis of party platforms reveals that in the elections of 1860 and 1864 the Republican platform underscored civil rights for blacks while the Democratic platform underscored opposition to civil rights (1998, 110). However, Republicans distinguished between basic citizenship

The core Republican idea was "free soil" for "free men." One version of it was consonant with radical abolitionism, and was motivated by the desire to liberate black slaves, grant them human dignity, and ensure their humane treatment. But for most Republicans, it represented, in part, racial homogeneity—the desire to preserve the United States as a "white man's country" (Foner 1990, 12–13). While campaigning on behalf of the Republican ticket of 1860, William H. Seward, the leading Republican of the 1850s, noted: "The great fact is now fully realized that the African race here is a foreign and feeble element, like the Indians incapable of assimilation . . . and it is a pitiful exotic unnecessarily transplanted into our fields, and which it is unprofitable to cultivate at the cost of the desolation of the native vineyard" (Fredrickson 1971, 141).[9] For many Republicans, slavery was immoral because it required the presence of blacks. More specifically, white Republicans believed that enslaved blacks were denying the land and its fruits to slaveless whites. Slave labor, colored black, posed an undesirable competition to free labor, colored white (Foner 1970).

Regardless of their motivation, Republicans advocated colonization (the removal of blacks) in a deliberate way, to counter the charge of pro-black advocacy and demonstrate their conformity to the norm of racial inequality. Such prominent Republicans as Horace Greeley and Abraham Lincoln favored colonization (Fredrickson 1971, 138–164). The influential senator Lyman Trumbull of Illinois supported the plan to expatriate blacks to Latin America with repeated professions of his—and, more generally, Republicans'—belief in white superiority. The Republicans were "the white man's party," and they would "settle the territories with free white men"; blacks, he said, "should not be among us" (Fredrickson 1971, 148–149).[10]

In addition to adopting the language of white rule and racial separation, Republicans also turned the Democratic charges of racial egalitarianism

---

rights that, they came to believe, ought to be universal, and social equality, which they believed was a privilege, not a right (Condit and Lucaites 1993; Zarefsky 1990). They advocated rudimentary legal safeguards to such rights as testifying in court, owning property, and immigrating between states (Nieman 1991, 43–44). They were aware that even this program, which did not advocate social equality, was not popular with many white voters. In 1860, Lincoln carried New York, for example, but voters there also defeated that year's black suffrage proposal (Malone 1999, 32). Malone writes that "politicians were willing to support the enfranchisement of blacks if they saw gain in doing so and were able to obviate the effects of race-mongering politicians" (1999, 45). Often during the nineteenth century, however, these politicians were not able to neutralize the race baiting of the opposition with egalitarian rhetoric, and had to resort to other means.

[9] In the 1850s Seward proclaimed in a Senate speech: "The white man needs this continent to labor upon. His head is strong, and his necessities are fixed. He must and will have it" (Fredrickson 1971, 141).

[10] Republicans also made use of the free labor ideology to mobilize support for the war. The war's project, according to Republicans, was to export the superior northern civilization, with its overflowing bounty, spirituality, and glory, and thus ensure its continuity. The less benevolent

around, and accused their opponents of practicing amalgamation. During the Lincoln-Douglas debates, on September 18, 1858, Lincoln delivered a speech on racial equality in Charleston, Illinois. Here he attempted to rebut the charge that he favored that ultimate measure of racial equality, racial amalgamation. Not only did he not favor racial amalgamation, Lincoln said, but his opponent was apparently worried about his own "base" impulse to engage in sexual relations with black women:

> I will say then that I am not, nor ever have been in favor of bringing about in any way the social and political equality of the white and black races, that I am not nor ever have been in favor of making voters or jurors of negroes, nor of qualifying them to hold office, nor to intermarry with white people; and I will say in addition to this that there is a physical difference between the white and black races which I believe will forever forbid the two races living together on terms of social and political equality. . . . It seems to me quite possible for us to get along without making either slaves or wives of negroes.
>
>   . . . I have never had the least apprehension that I or my friends would marry negroes if there was no law to keep them from it, but as Judge Douglas and his friends seem to be in great apprehension that they might, if there were no law to keep them from it, I give him the most solemn pledge that I will to the very last stand by the law of this state, which forbids the marrying of white people with negroes. . . . I do not understand there is any place where an alteration of the social and political relations of the negro and the white man can be made except in the state legislature—not in the Congress of the United States—and as I do not really apprehend the approach of any such thing myself, and as Judge Douglas seems to be in constant horror that some such danger is rapidly approaching, I propose as the best means to prevent it that the Judge be kept at home and placed in the state legislature to fight the measure. (Holzer 1993, 189–190)

Many Republicans in the early 1860s relied on Lincoln's strategy, and accused the Democrats and slaveowners of being the real "Nigger worshippers" (Wood 1968, 31).[11] Not only were they not racial egalitarians, Republicans insisted, but it was the Democrats who blurred the lines of race. Thus, while the parties increasingly diverged on the matter of rights for blacks, the Republican rhetorical strategy was, by design, quite similar to the Democrats'. The issue of race pulled the parties apart, giving rise to frequent racial appeals, but the norm of inequality pushed their campaign appeals close together, making each side's appeals explicitly racial.

---

version had clear racial overtones; it reserved a privileged place in this civilization to whites. The more benevolent streak of free labor ideology extended the idea of opportunity to blacks.

   [11] Publications such as Horace Greeley's, and pamphlets making use of sarcastic humor, also argued that the Democratic strategy was simply too extreme and based on irrational racial hate (Wood 1968, 17).

THE RECONSTRUCTION CAMPAIGNS: EXPLICIT APPEALS
VERSUS ANTI-SOUTHERN SECTIONALISM

As the Republican effort to grant African Americans citizenship accelerated at war's end, the parties refined the racial rhetorical strategies they had developed during the early 1860s. Democrats continued to play on the racial themes of sex, violence, and work, and on the threat to white supremacy. Republicans, whose platform emphasized civil rights for blacks, nevertheless continued to forge their own racist rhetoric and tried to avoid the language of racial equality. But Republicans succeeded most of all by mobilizing anti-southern sentiment. The party system became even more firmly structured along the issue of race— what to do about the millions of newly emancipated blacks. But it was also firmly structured along the issue of sectionalism—what to do about the millions of newly defeated southern whites. The Democrats tried to make use of the former, the Republicans of the latter. Democrats gained when the issue of race trumped the issue of sectionalism; Republicans gained when the reverse was true. Each side was still unencumbered by anything resembling a norm of racial equality. Racial speech was very explicitly racial.

The 1864 Presidential Election

Just as Lincoln's preliminary Emancipation Proclamation had sparked racial appeals in the 1862 election, so the official proclamation, issued in 1863, sparked racial appeals in the election of 1864, with George McClellan running against Lincoln on a promise to undo emancipation (McPherson 1988, 769–72). The 1864 presidential election marked the first widespread national use of racial appeals for political gain. The election was, more than anything, a referendum on the war, but the issue of emancipation was prominent in the discourse of the campaign (Wood 1968, 53). Strongly worded general denunciations of African Americans and their white supporters were frequent and loud. Speakers at the 1864 Democratic National Convention derogated "flat-nosed, woolly-headed, long-heeled, cursed of God and damned of man descendants of Africa," and the "negro-worshippers of old Abe Lincoln" (Wood 1968, 71). In his address, S. S. Nicholas, one of the party's leading theoreticians, mixed the paternalistic racist position, which emphasized the harm to blacks of removing them from their rightful lower place, with the more antagonistic themes common in the Democratic newspapers (Wood 1968, 29–30).[12] These delegates were not the extremist Democrats who opposed the northern war

---

[12] By highlighting the Republican temerity on racial equality, and playing up their own supposed concern for the best interests of blacks, Democrats played on the theme of hypocritical leadership, and attempted to remove the Republicans from the higher moral ground.

effort and who gathered in a convention of their own; they were mainstream Democrats.

The issue of black troops was a convenient way to indirectly criticize the war while warning against the growing fluidity of racial arrangements under Republican rule. In an inversion of today's explicit appeals, taking issue with the Civil War in an overt way was politically risky; doing it implicitly, under cover of the much more acceptable rhetoric of racial inferiority, served the Democrats well. During the campaign, the Democratic National Committee distributed several publications that accused Republicans of racial favoritism toward blacks and warned of the dangers of blacks bearing arms.[13] In 1864, forty-three Democratic members of Congress signed and published a petition that denounced the arming of black men as a Republican attempt to equalize "the right of suffrage and also of social position" (Wood 1968, 42).[14] Several Democratic newspapers carried numerous and exaggerated stories of violence by black soldiers, including a story printed during the 1864 campaign of the rape of a white woman by three black soldiers, told with great detail (Wood 1968, 50). Stereotyped notions of black criminality and laziness were brought into play as well. Black troops, Democrats charged, would refuse to work and to support themselves after the coddling they were supposedly receiving from the government, and would turn to a life of crime.[15]

No racial element was played upon more strongly than the fear of miscegenation. The term itself was introduced in a sham pamphlet designed in late 1863 by the editors of the *New York World* to discredit Republicans. "Miscegenation" immediately came to mean "illicit interracial sexual relations" (Wood 1968, 54). The sham pamphlet laid out a quite radical defense of interracial sexual unions, and was sent anonymously to prominent Republicans with an invitation to respond in support of its contents. The plan, which failed, was to print these affirmations in the Democratic papers (Wood 1968, 56).

Several newspapers nevertheless took up the charge that the Republicans favored interracial sexual liaisons. The Democratic National Committee featured the issue in a pamphlet suggestively titled "Miscegenation: Indorsed [*sic*] by the Republican Party." The pamphlet cited a Republican speaker who reportedly said that after the war the "brave Othellos of the South would come

---

[13] In one publication the committee accused Senator Henry Wilson of saying that black soldiers were "equal to the white in everything, and superior to him in endurance" (Wood 1968, 45).

[14] "White soldiers were being murdered as a result of exposure to unnecessary risks, while Abraham Lincoln petted Negroes" (Wood 1968, 46). Two weeks before the election of 1864, in a speech printed and widely circulated by the Democratic National Committee, a Democratic campaign speaker denounced government favoritism to blacks (Wood 1968, 48).

[15] The *Philadelphia Age*, for example, complained that black troops included "only the worst Negroes—criminals, ruffians, vagabonds, idlers, and former slaves—who would not adapt willingly to a life of self-support" and who, after the war, would constitute "a huge black mass, [with] fearful energy [for] mischief, hovering directly over us" (Wood 1968, 51).

North and claim their fair Desdemonas" (Wood 1968, 65). The Democrats who signed the "Congressional Address" declared that the "corruption of race [is] a violation of natural law" (Wood 1968, 66; Fredrickson 1971, 174).

The first injection of race prejudice into national politics ended, for the most part, with the large-scale demise of the Democrats in the wake of the Republican electoral victory of 1864. The lopsided election results suggest that the miscegenation controversy had little impact (Wood 1968, 60–61). One reason racial appeals failed in 1864 is that Republicans were unanimous and loud in repudiating the pro-miscegenation position attributed to them. Perhaps most importantly, the war and the economy were dominant issues. By early fall of 1864 the North had won decisive victories, reinvigorating the electoral prospects of the Republicans (McPherson 1992). Republicans combined their explicitly racial appeals with appeals to patriotism that highlighted their success in the war. Most white voters in turn seemed to say that as much as they worried about the shifting status of blacks, they hated the rebellious South even more. Andrew Johnson well captured the Republican rhetorical strategy and the sentiment of many northern whites: "Damn the Negroes, I am fighting those traitorous aristocrats, their masters" (Foner 1990, 20; Gerring 1998, 110).

The Fourteenth Amendment and the Election of 1866

In the war's aftermath, as the parties grew increasingly polarized on the issue of what to do about the newly freed blacks, and as Republican legislation continued to make that issue salient, racial appeals spread to more elections and grew in intensity. "More than anything else," writes Foner, "the election [of 1866] became a referendum on the Fourteenth Amendment" (1990, 119). Racist rhetoric was especially prominent in the 1866 gubernatorial contests of Ohio and Pennsylvania, where the Democratic candidates made repeated use of the miscegenation issue, circulating some of the most racist pictorial depictions of black men ever to appear in American politics (see Fig. 2.1) (Wood 1968, 78–79). These efforts were in vain, however. Most of the Ohio Democratic slate went down to defeat, and the Pennsylvania Democrats met with failure as well (Foner 1990, 118–119; Wood 1968, 79).

The Republican victory once again rested not on white voters' endorsement of rights for blacks, but rather on their desire to use political rights for blacks as a means of quelling what they perceived as continuing southern rebellion (Rable 1984, 59; Riddleberger 1979). Southern whites' efforts to resubjugate blacks and their rejection of Union rule added up to a portrait of an incorrigibly traitorous region that many believed must be forcibly resubdued.[16] This por-

---

[16] As Benjamin S. Hedrick of North Carolina put it, "If the northern people are forced by the South to follow Thad Stevens or the Copperheads, I believe they will prefer the former" (Foner

Figure 2.1. African Americans were represented as lazy, with exaggerated physical features, taking advantage of government handouts at the expense of hardworking whites. Used in the congressional and gubernatorial campaign of 1866 in Pennsylvania. (Courtesy of the Library of Congress)

trait is evident in the language of the Fourteenth Amendment. Of the amendment's four substantive sections, three deal with former Confederates; only one deals with equality before the law. Republicans did point to blacks' dedicated military service to justify political rights for African-American men. But even this seemed to draw force from the contrast with the rebellious and traitorous white South. Congressman Josiah Grinnel put it simply: "I will never prefer a white traitor to a loyalist black" (Fredrickson 1971, 184). In the election of 1866, northerners wanted, above all, to get tough with the South, and the Republican rhetorical strategy highlighted this theme at the expense of the Democrats' explicitly racial appeals.

1990, 119). By framing the election as a vote against "murder, arson, robbery, torture, cruelty, oppression, systematic swindling and lynch law," Greeley and the Republicans succeeded in winning votes (Rable 1984, 59).

State Suffrage Referenda and the Election of 1867

The Republican proposal to grant suffrage to blacks represented an unprecedented opportunity for Democrats to mobilize whites' racial resentments and
fears.[17] Voting rights for blacks met with widespread resistance from northern
as well as southern whites. Out of the eleven state referenda on the issue held
in the North between 1865 and 1869, eight were rejected (Kousser 1992).
Both state legislatures and voters turned down suffrage proposals in 1865 and
1867 in Connecticut, Wisconsin, Kansas, Ohio, and Minnesota, despite the
popularity and numerical advantage of Republicans and the support of Republican leaders. Similar scenarios played out in Maryland, New Jersey, and Michigan, among others (Wood 1968). Democrats mobilized negative racial predispositions quite effectively in these elections, some of which also featured
contests for state offices. Prominent Democrats made suffrage a focus of their
campaign speeches. The Democratic gubernatorial candidate in Ohio, Allan G.
Thurman, promised he would "save the state from the thralldom of niggerism"
(Foner 1990, 135). The Democratic party of New York proposed to nominate
Dan Rice of Pennsylvania for president because of his role in defeating black
suffrage in Ohio (Wood 1968, 86). "Any Democrat who did not manage to
hint that the negro is a degenerate gorilla would be considered lacking in enthusiasm," wrote the French journalist (and later prime minister) Georges
Clemenceau (Wood 1968, 86). Galvanized by the shock of black political
equality in their own states, northern Democrats spared no effort to communicate explicit racial appeals. Black voting was a real threat to the norm of racial
inequality, and Democrats accurately calculated that if they said so loudly and
explicitly, they would win.

Thus a prominent argument against black suffrage was that it would inexorably lead to the ultimate threat to racial inequality, racial intermarriage.[18] The
notion that suffrage would set off a domino effect toward racial equality found
repeated expression, often in quite stereotypical form. The concern with interracial sex was not made into a campaign theme by a concerted effort, unlike
in 1864. But it did receive play.

The radical Republicans' attempt to provide minimal government assistance
to the newly freed slaves provided another source of explicitly racial appeals
for Democratic campaigners. This one centered on the theme of work and

[17] At the end of the Civil War, eighteen of twenty-five Union states did not allow blacks to vote.
By the ratification of the Fifteenth Amendment in 1870, thirteen of twenty-six non-Confederate
states still prohibited the black vote (Wood 1968, 85–86).

[18] The goal of such complete racial equality was so farfetched at the time that the majority of
black leaders did not make it part of their agenda (Condit and Lucaites 1993; Woodward 1966,
193, 195, 219). A mixed-race Republican convention held in North Carolina in 1867 declared
that "no sensible person of any complexion desires or expects social equality" (Wood 1968, 154).

unearned advantage. Blacks aided by the Freedmen's Bureau were said to be on the road to a ruined work ethic. Besides, many whites complained, whites had never been privileged to receive similar aid. Upon vetoing the 1866 Freedmen's Bureau bill, Andrew Johnson called the bill an "immense patronage" unwarranted by the Constitution and unaffordable by the government. Congress, Johnson complained, had never provided economic relief, established schools, or purchased land for "our own people." These special privileges were not only unfair to whites; they threatened the "character" and "prospects" of blacks (Foner 1990, 112–113).[19]

Republican politicians, although increasingly damaged in the eyes of white voters by the taint of black rights, for the most part attempted to remain silent on the issue of race. Several state Republican platforms in the North did advocate voting rights for northern blacks, as did Rutherford B. Hayes in his gubernatorial campaign in Ohio. But for the most part, Republican campaigners did not stake out a clear racially egalitarian stance. Those who did were at times chided by their own side for "a sacrifice of political strength on the altar of consistency" (Foner 1988, 314).[20]

Republicans suffered significant electoral losses as the Democrats' racial strategy finally seemed to succeed. Democrats made sweeping gains in many states, and reduced the size of the 1866 Republican majorities by three-quarters (Foner 1990, 136). In Ohio, despite a slim Republican advantage in voter turnout, both houses went Democratic, the governor's office nearly did as well, and the suffrage amendment failed by a large margin (Wood 1968, 86). Democrats made inroads even in Republican stronghold states (Wood 1968, 109). The state suffrage amendments that won did so by narrow margins, even where, as in Iowa, Republicans outnumbered Democrats by two to one (Wood 1968, 86).

When Republicans again seized on the issue of sectionalism after 1867, they were able to trump the Democratic racial appeals, and black suffrage gained ground. Republicans were able to make headway with sectionalism when former Confederates were reinstated in the South, priming the sectionalist resentment of northern voters and providing a powerful impetus for black suffrage (Foner 1990, 103, 109, 111; Franklin and Moss 1988, 206; Fredrickson 1971, 183–184). "As for negro suffrage," wrote journalist Charles Dana, "the mass of the Union men in the Northwest do not care a great deal. What scares them is the idea that the rebels are all to be let back . . . and made a power in the government again, just as though there had been no rebellion" (Foner 1990, 103). A crucial distinction that allowed Republicans to marshal northern sec-

---

[19] Voting rights for blacks also drew forth simple affirmations of the need for white supremacy. The legislative controversy over suffrage for the District of Columbia resembled many of the state contests in this regard (Wood 1968, 94).

[20] In California, where the worry was primarily about Chinese-American suffrage, the gubernatorial candidate, George C. Gorham, employed humanitarian rhetoric, arguing that "the same God created both Europeans and Asiatics."

tionalist resentments for their cause was between universal suffrage imposed on the South and its absence elsewhere (Riddleberger 1979, 30). The 1868 Republican platform made clear this distinction (Wood 1968, 87). As before, Republicans won elections and advanced black rights by coupling anti-south-ern appeals with messages that demonstrated their adherence to the norm of racial inequality.[21]

The Presidential Election of 1868

The interplay of the norm and party strategy, reflected in explicitly racial ap-peals, was brought to a head in the 1868 election. Republicans, adroit at milk-ing the sentiments of vengeance against a recalcitrant South, went up against a Democratic party convinced it would win by pointing out that the increasing connection between racial equality and the Republican party constituted a vio-lation of a bedrock norm. Democratic candidate Horatio Seymour campaigned mostly on economic issues, but he did not shy away from making appeals to race. His running mate, Francis P. Blair, Jr., campaigned almost entirely on the race issue (McPherson 1992, 423; Wood 1968, 126).

There was nothing subtle or indirect about the Democratic racial appeals. Spurred by their successes in the elections of 1867, Democrats campaigned explicitly on an anti-black, pro-white platform. A Democratic campaign badge featured pictures of Seymour and Blair with the words: "Our Motto: This is a White Man's Country; Let White Men Rule" (Foner 1988; see Fig. 2.2). "Is there no pride in your blue eyes, light hair, white faces, and intelligent brains? If there be, let it be aroused to save your white brothers from the impending struggle," declared former Ohio congressman Samuel S. Cox while touring Maine, Pennsylvania, and New York (Wood 1968, 1). The Democratic National Convention of 1868 featured accusations that the Republicans had subjected

---

[21] The Republican party, with its radical wing in ascendance, went on to enact the Fifteenth Amendment despite widespread popular opposition. Radical Republicans were likely motivated in this regard by moral concerns (McPherson 1992). But a great many Republicans held their noses at granting blacks what they saw as undeserved political equality. The influential Republican congressman James Garfield wrote to a colleague: "[I have] a strong feeling of repugnance when I think of the negro being made our political equal and I would be glad if they could be colonized, sent to heaven, or got rid of in any decent way" (Fredrickson 1971, 185). Most Republicans' motivation was partisan, anti-southern, or some combination of the two. Republicans anticipated and in fact derived a direct electoral gain in the South by enfranchising blacks (Gillette 1965; Kousser 1992, 152). Many Republicans also believed that only suffrage would finally settle the troublesome "Negro question" in the South (Foner 1990, 449). Not to be neglected is the fact that the amendment, ratified only by Republican state legislatures obedient to the party and by south-ern states required to ratify it to rejoin the Union, passed where state suffrage referenda, voted on by white citizens, had failed (Smith 1997, 314). In some states Republicans lost control of the legislature (Wood 1968, 102).

Figure 2.2. An explicitly racial appeal by the Democratic presidential candidate in 1868. (Courtesy of the New York Public Library, Schomburg Center for Research in Black Culture)

the South "to military despotism and negro supremacy" (Wood 1968, 117). The catchphrase "negro supremacy" was written into the Democratic platform (Franklin 1971; Wood 1968, 124). The theme of the "uncontrolled power" that "barbarous Africans" would hold with universal suffrage was repeated throughout the campaign (Wood 1968, 117, 124). Several state Democratic conventions featured warnings of impending black violence against whites, even an all-out race war (in fact, race riots were primarily attacks against blacks). Seymour, who had earlier rejected a racial strategy, now condemned the Republicans' "negro military policy" as a "cause of all the country's financial troubles," and predicted that universal suffrage would cause the "government of the South to go into the hands of the negroes" (Wood 1968, 125).

The themes of crime and sexuality were salient in the Democrats' explicit appeals. Exaggerated stories of black crime appeared prominently on a near-daily basis during the campaign, primarily in the major Democratic newspapers. A favorite genre was the story of rapes of white women and girls by black men. These were widely circulated by newspapers and often involved such gruesome embellishments as a pregnant woman dying with her unborn child.

During the spring and summer of 1868 Democratic newspapers in New York, Indianapolis, and Columbus ran stories accusing prominent national and local Republicans of practicing miscegenation (Wood 1968, 145–150). Like the campaign speeches, the stories were explicitly racial; fear of blacks and the need to maintain white power was a dominant, primary theme, not a subtext.

The Democratic racial appeals seem to have backfired somewhat later in the campaign, as Blair's racist rhetoric turned increasingly extreme. Blair took Republicans to task for turning the South over to "a semi-barbarous race of blacks who are worshippers of fetishes and polygamists" and who longed to "subject the white women to their unbridled lust" (Foner 1990, 145). He offered social Darwinistic pronouncements on the inability of mixed-race offspring to reproduce and their retarding effect on the evolution of superior civilization. His speaking tour provoked Republican replies such as the following, published in the *New York Tribune* in October 1868:

> Blair, Blair, Black sheep
> Have you any wool?
> Yes, my master, seven bags full—
> Nigger scalps from Georgia,
> Ku-Klux got them all,
> So many less nigger votes
> Against us in the Fall. (Wood 1968, 128)

The *Tribune's* taunt was in part aimed at Blair's exaggerated racism, but more than that, it suggested that Blair was the servant of that ultimate bogeyman, the southern rebel. Anti-southern patriotism remained the Republicans' trump card. Seymour's public sympathy with draft rioters during the war made an easy target (Foner 1990, 145). Republicans such as William Garrison waved the "bloody shirt" and successfully stirred up anger at the supposedly southern-sponsored assassination of Lincoln in 1865 and at the anti-Union defiance that the pre-Reconstruction Black Codes of the South were made to symbolize, independent of race (McPherson 1992, 423; Wood 1968, 165). They spoke of the plight of blacks, but often to emphasize the evils of the South and of the Democratic party. Blacks were placed in the role of victims so that Republicans could place Democrats in the role of tyrants. Republicans also countered Democratic racial appeals by casting them as pro-southern.

Republicans also made sure to say nothing that would portray themselves as the black man's friend. Some Republicans used racial rhetoric against Democrats, revisiting Lincoln's bout with Douglas in what was becoming a familiar Republican strategy: attributing Democratic anti-miscegenation proposals to the supposed Democratic inability to practice self-restraint. David Locke satirized Democrats by suggesting that they expected "their" white women to be easily tempted into interracial unions (Wood 1968, 151).

Republicans in the South were an exception to this, appealing to black voters with assurances of free schools (usually, separate from whites) and the guarantee of political rights such as voting, holding office, and securing legal justice, and many followed through on their promises (Degler 1982, 235–238, 252). But in speaking to whites, white Republicans in the South were prone to emphasize instead that the new political rights for blacks would not threaten whites' status. And they tended to discourage blacks—sometimes with public threats—from running for powerful and visible offices so as not to provoke white backlash, which white Republicans feared would damage their own political fortunes (Degler 1982, 242–243, 246; Holt 1979, 102–107).

In addition, Republicans in the North took great care not to appear to violate the norm of inequality by limiting their program of black rights to the South, which, in the view of many northern white voters, deserved it as punishment. The Republican platform of 1868 reflected this strategy clearly; federally mandated black suffrage was desirable in the South, but undesirable in the North in deference to the principle of states' rights (Foner 1990).[22]

In the end, the Democrats' racial strategy was not effective enough to win. However, it may well be that had the Democrats not adopted their racial strategy, they would have fared worse. Republican Ulysses S. Grant won the election, but with a minority of the white popular vote (Franklin 1971; Foner 1990). And the Democrats' racial strategy was profitable at the state level, where Democrats made inroads (Smith 1997, 314).

The Republican party that dominated Congress during Reconstruction had firmly supported a position that, by any but contemporary standards, was radically egalitarian. The policies of the Radical Republicans were in fact a clear violation of the norm of racial inequality. To limit the electoral damage from this violation, the party's campaigns tried to reassure white voters that its fundamental view of blacks was actually just as anti-egalitarian as the Democrats'. Even when dominated by egalitarian radicals, the Republican party could not run on a platform of racial equality; instead, it most often ran on a platform of getting tough with the traitorous, Democratic South. The Democratic party had no reservations about engaging in explicitly racial appeals. When Democrats lost, it was not because their racial strategy did not resonate. Republicans won elections, and the passage of universal suffrage, in part through explicitly racial campaign appeals meant to demonstrate their adherence to the norm of racial inequality, and by finding a more powerful issue with which to trump the Democrats' racial strategy.

---

[22] The contest was framed as one between a war hero intent on the motto "Let Us Have Peace," who promised to restrain the run-away radicals of his party and keep southern rebels in check (Foner 1990, 146; Mantell 1973), and an unexciting governor of New York with questionable patriotic credentials, trailing an unappealing vice presidential candidate (Franklin 1971; Wood 1968, 129).

PRECURSORS TO IMPLICITLY RACIAL RHETORIC

Democrats Back Away from Explicit Rhetoric

While Republicans continued to try to limit the perception that they violated the racial norm, that very norm was changing with each significant implementation of the party's program. The ratification of the Fourteenth and Fifteenth Amendments undermined the norm of racial inequality. In turn, the changing norm caused a shift in the nature of racial rhetoric. The passage of these amendments changed the rules of the game for the party of the racial right. The Democrats understood that they might suffer adverse consequences if they did not signal, in some symbolic way, an acceptance of the new rules. The explicit opposition to racial equality continued into the 1870s, with its spokesmen arguing that "the races could not live together as equals" (Condit and Lucaites 1993, 117), and that blacks were "absolutely unfit for these public positions" (Woodward 1966, 76). But now this was supplemented with more indirect rhetoric and with symbolic gestures toward racial equality reminiscent of the implicit rhetoric of today. Those who had opposed the new laws made concessions to the basic aim of Reconstruction, assuring northerners that the principle of equality before the law, newly enshrined in the Constitution, would be respected.

The representatives of this approach in the Deep South, such as South Carolina's Wade Hampton, even engaged in limited appeals to black voters and provided patronage to black leaders (Meier and Rudwick 1994, 188–189; Walton 1992).[23] These appeals were genuinely meant to win votes from blacks, whose turnout for gubernatorial contests in some southern states hovered around 60 percent even into the 1880s (Grossman 1992; Kousser 1992, 141; but see Degler 1982). During the 1880s and early 1890s, Deep South Democrats succeeded in winning some black votes, particularly after Republicans had ceased to protect black rights, though it is unclear how much of this success was due to intimidation and fraud (Meier and Rudwick 1994, 195, 199). Wade Hampton, for example, promised black voters that he would not purge them from the rolls—so long as they voted for him (Meier and Rudwick 1994, 189). For two decades after the Fifteenth Amendment was enacted, Democrats in northern and midwestern areas with a large black constituency were careful to refrain from racist rhetoric. In some of these states civil rights laws were passed, and in Ohio Democrats even eliminated all formal racial distinctions, although most Democratic governors between 1877 and 1910 were in fact

---

[23] Hampton distributed campaign propaganda entitled, "*Free Men! Free Ballots!! Free Schools!!! The Pledges of Gen. Wade Hampton . . . to the Colored People of South Carolina, 1865–1876*" (Woodward 1966, 55). "Not one single right enjoyed by the colored people shall be taken from them," he pledged (Fredrickson 1971, 198).

former Republicans (Foner 1988, 510; Grossman 1992). Some southern Democrats during radical Reconstruction held barbecues and picnics for black voters and spoke before mixed-race audiences; in Louisiana, the Democratic party platform even declared in 1870 that "the interests of both white and black men are identical. . . . Whatever rights and privileges either enjoy under the constitution are sacred, and it is the duty of every citizen to see that they are maintained" (Degler 1982, 240).

But soon it became apparent that black voters were not interested in barbecues and false promises. With a few exceptions, Reconstruction-era Democrats in the Deep South and in much of the outer South did not expect to get—and in fact did not get—more than a handful of (actual) black votes (Meier and Rudwick 1994, 188). Their support was nearly all white. Their continuing rhetorical overtures to blacks during radical Reconstruction may have been designed to woo black voters even in the face of frequent rejection, but more likely were meant to reassure powerful Republicans leaders (among them recently empowered black officials). It is clear that southern whites very much wanted to get the North and the Republicans to leave the South alone (Foner 1988, 417; Williamson 1990, 406–417). In South Carolina, Democrats went to great lengths to publicly show off and exaggerate the number of those few blacks who did support them (Williamson 1990, 410).[24] The show was likely meant for Republican influentials who were forging a norm of political equality for blacks. And it worked to some extent. As the Fifteenth Amendment became a fact on the ground, for example, northern observers in such bastions of white supremacy as South Carolina thought they witnessed a genuine change of heart among whites there (Degler 1982, 237).

The urgency to appease the Republican norm shift was enhanced by several laws enacted by Congress within the first year of the ratification of the Fifteenth Amendment (Kousser 1992, 139). Included among these laws were three vigorous "force" bills. These may not have been well enforced in all parts of the South, but in states such as South Carolina these laws allowed blacks to exercise their right to vote so effectively that they gained control over the state legislature, the congressional delegation, and many appointed and local offices (Williamson 1990, 360; but see Holt 1979). Along with their direct impact on black voting, these laws also had a less direct effect. They signalled that Republicans in Congress were prepared to take seriously the protection of voting rights. The Republican-controlled Congress seemed to use these force bills and other laws as a signal of its desire for signs from white southerners that they had accepted the will of Congress on the matter of black rights. The congressional bill readmitting Virginia to the Union in 1870, for example, was expressly intended to bring "the southern states to a sense of their real depen-

---

[24] In the late 1870s and 1880s, South Carolina Democrats did succeed in attracting more than a few black votes, but this followed upon the destruction of the Republican party (Holt 1979).

dence upon Congress" (Foner 1988, 453). Influential Republicans promulgated laws in an effort to change the norm of racial inequality.

As the norm began to change, so did the explicit nature of racial rhetoric. As part of the effort to appease Republican elites, white southerners emphasized less the negative qualities of blacks and the imperatives of white supremacy, and began to talk more of the virtues of laissez-faire government. In several states, Democratic leaders convened Taxpayers' Conventions whose platforms criticized Reconstruction legislatures, populated by significant numbers of black legislators, for having raised taxes and expenditures (Foner 1990, 181; Holt 1979). The tax protests targeted the growing size of state budgets, as well as their spending priorities, which, for the first time in southern history, included school systems and social services (Foner 1990, 156, 161, 181–182; Franklin and Moss 1988, 218; Holt 1979; Williamson 1990). In theory, the tax protests were motivated not by resentment of government assistance to blacks but by anger at the increasing tax burden imposed by state governments. However, the racial composition of these governments, the intent of the state governments to assist blacks (and poor whites), and the need to hide the still-intense concern with racial equality all combined to imbue the laissez-faire arguments with racial meaning. Implicit racial rhetoric ascended as explicit discourse declined.

The other rhetorical element that replaced explicitly racial discourse was silence. Already in 1870, with the victory of the Fifteenth Amendment, most Democratic state platforms made no mention of racial issues (Wood 1968, 157). Those members of Congress who had been staunch racists drew quiet on the issue. In mid-1871, the unadulterated racist Clement Vallandigham of Ohio argued for a break with past Democratic party strategy on the grounds that the Fifteenth Amendment had come to pass, and "secession, slavery, and inequality before the law were dead" (Wood 1968, 158). Democrats did not entirely break with their racial strategy when the norm changed. But by contrast with the preceding decade, the first few years of the 1870s were relatively quiet.

The efforts of southern white conservatives to placate the North were accompanied by not-so-subtle words and actions. Explicit racial rhetoric was less often used, particularly during elections, but it was not gone. The Taxpayers' Conventions at times grumbled about growing black political power (Foner 1990, 182). Violence and fraud accompanied some of the most pro-black rhetoric produced by conservative gubernatorial candidates in the South (Foner 1990, 240–241; Holt 1979; Williamson 1990). Blacks and their white allies were sometimes murdered en masse in the course of electoral campaigns (Degler 1982; Foner 1990, 184–188; Kousser 1992). The more their actions betrayed their resistance, however, the more important it was for the Redeemers to reassure those national elites who still cared that they meant to conform to the new norm of minimal political equality.

The Presidential Election of 1872

The Republican efforts to shift the norm were short-lived. When they died away, so did the party system based on the issue of race, and so did racial appeals. After 1872, race increasingly dissolved into individualist rhetoric, and then faded from national elections. The presidential election of 1872, pitting the Liberal Republican candidate Horace Greeley—a Republican backed by Democrats—against the Republican incumbent Ulysses S. Grant, marked the entry of anti-black individualism into electoral discourse. But rather than define partisan differences, the election underscored the emerging partisan similarities. The very existence of the Liberal Republicans reflected the increasing internal division among Republicans on how to deal with the race question (Foner 1988). The division was less apparent in Congress, as the Republicans during the early 1870s continued to propose and pass protective legislation with a good deal of party unity (Kousser 1992). But after 1872, anti-black individualism increasingly took hold in the Republican party, the party gradually abandoned its pro-equality position on matters of race, and the norm of racial inequality underwent a slow but sure resurgence.

The Republican shift was driven by disunity and frustration with the continuing difficulties of Reconstruction (Foner 1990, 214). The basic rights guaranteed by the Reconstruction amendments were, many Republicans believed, as much as blacks deserved. Greeley had been a staunch abolitionist before the war. But during his presidential campaign, he at first ignored African Americans altogether, and then, in an April 1872 issue of the newspaper he edited, he charged that they lacked initiative (Riddleberger 1960, 95–96). He invented what may be the meanest slogan ever applied to blacks: "Root, Hog, or Die!" (Foner 1990, 214). Blacks, believed Greeley, had obtained all they deserved of fundamental rights. Now, like hogs, they should root in the dirt to meet their basic needs, and if not, they deserved to die.

Greeley's anti-black rhetoric was echoed by other Liberal Republicans, who took up the cause of free enterprise and a society unfettered by the clumsy, inevitably corrupt hand of government and connected it quite explicitly to the need to abandon blacks. Blacks, the Liberals said, had gotten their freedom; it was now up to them to determine how they fared in the struggle for survival: "The negro is now a voter and a citizen," stated an Illinois newspaper; "let him hereafter take his chances in the battle of life" (Foner 1988, 449). Many whites, including northerners sympathetic to the former slaves, believed that African Americans would, by nature, land at the bottom, at least for the foreseeable future (Fredrickson 1971; Powell 1980, 78). These whites acknowledged that blacks were not always allowed to exercise their political rights. But government's role did not extend to vigorous protection of black civil rights, and law could not legislate away society's ills. Blacks should do for themselves what the state could not or should not.

Accompanying these declarations of the virtue of self-help were blame-the-victim statements, many with an explicitly racial character. Reconstruction, Liberals said, was a "failed experiment" in which former Confederates—now leaders of "intelligence and culture" rather than traitorous villains—had been misguidedly replaced by a "degraded" race that could only make a mockery of citizenship. The unprecedented legislation to improve the social and economic condition of blacks and poor whites, churned out by biracial southern legislatures, was for the Liberals evidence that universal (male) suffrage was not such a great idea after all (Foner 1990, 212–213).

For the most part, those engaging in explicitly anti-black rhetoric were not the Democrats who had come to prominence with the aid of racist rhetoric. These politicians, such as Samuel Cox, now uttered not a word about race (Wood 1968, 162). It was the right wing of the Republican party that had turned against its other half. The Democrats were still constrained by the limited norm against making explicit racial appeals. Former members of the Republican party, however, who had a long pedigree of abolitionism, could make these appeals without adverse consequences.

The remaining Republicans reacted to this turn of events by moving to the right alongside their former colleagues. Several weeks after Greeley's nomination, Republicans in Congress legislated Confederate office-holding back to life, contravening the Fourteenth Amendment in the process (Foner 1990, 215). At the same time, they resorted to their well-oiled strategy of waving the bloody shirt, denouncing "Ku Klux outrages and midnight murders and marauding" but linking southern outrages to black misbehavior (Foner 1990, 216). They promised to eliminate corruption in the South, with corruption now associated with black rule. They even echoed the Liberal view of Reconstruction as a "failed experiment." In the South, particularly in areas where the Republican rank-and-file was majority black, Republican appeals were much more careful to endorse blacks' political rights (Degler 1982). But elsewhere, the party went in the other direction.

In the end, Greeley was soundly defeated by Grant, with a margin twice that of Grant's 1868 victory, and nearly twice that of Lincoln's over McClellan in 1864. In fact, Grant's 55 percent of the vote was larger than any percentage of the presidential vote between 1836 and 1892. This seems to have been more a function of partisan confusion at the mass level than of the failure once again of racial politics to yield electoral victory at the presidential level; 1872 was, after all, the election that introduced the derogatory terms "Republic-rat" and "Dem-ican" (Foner 1990, 216; Wood 1968, 164).

But while the Liberal Republicans and their Democratic allies had lost the battle, they won the war. Radical Reconstruction from that point on began to lose its place on the national agenda and as an organizational force within the Republican party. Republican electoral campaigns, and the party's legislative fiats for racial equality, had been powered on anti-southern rhetoric; as "bloody

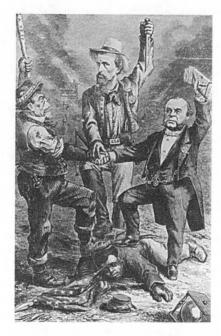

Figure 2.3. Thomas Nast's cartoon, "This is a White Man's Government." As did similar Republican appeals, this one appeals for racial equality indirectly by showing the need to restrain flagrant abuses of power by the traitorous South. According to Foner, this image shows "the former slave as innocent victim of Irish Immigrants, Confederate veterans, and Wall Street financiers (ostensibly, the three pillars of the Democratic party)." (Foner 1988, following p. 386; originally published in *Harper's Weekly* September 5, 1868)

shirt" sentiments declined in the North, so did the Republican sectionalist strategy, and with it, the party's will and ability to protect the rights of blacks (Wood 1968, 165). Then, too, white Republicans increasingly held the view that they could retain power without those costly and controversial measures required to protect southern black votes (Smith 1997; Woodward 1991).[25] Increasingly they gravitated toward the Liberal and Democratic agenda for race, which was, essentially, to keep federal hands off it (Degler 1982, 264). Thomas Nast, whose drawings in the mid-1860s had portrayed blacks as valiant Union soldiers or downtrodden victims of southern barbarism, in the mid-1870s turned out derogatory images of black legislators making a mockery of their office (Figs. 2.3 and 2.4). Newspapers with Republican sympathies began

[25] Woodward's work on the Compromise of 1877, *Reunion and Reaction*, argues that already during 1876 the northern Republican party was deciding to try to convert the Republican party in the South to a white base (1991, 8).

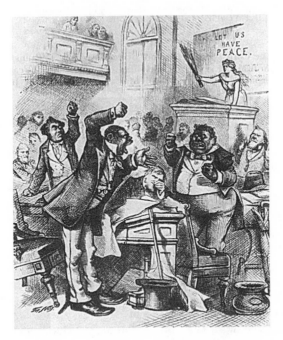

Figure 2.4. "Colored Rule in a Reconstructed (?) State." According to Foner, this cartoon shows "black legislators as travesties of democratic government." Republican Thomas Nast's drawings of African Americans changed from 1868, when they portrayed blacks as victims of a secessionist, traitorous Democratic party, to 1874, when they portrayed blacks as incompetent to govern. (*Harper's Weekly* March 14, 1874)

adopting the same white supremacist rhetoric purveyed by Democrats over three presidential elections (Foner 1990, 223).[26]

Greeley's defeat in 1872 was accompanied by eventual victory for northern Democrats, beginning just two years later in 1874 with Democratic control of the House of Representatives and five northern governorships (Holt 1979, 197). The presidential election of 1876 still included the familiar Republican bloody shirt rhetoric, even though the Republican platform condemned appeals to sectionalism (Woodward 1991, 23; Foner 1988, 567). But Republicans in the North said little about Reconstruction, including the rights of African

---

[26] The Republican administration refused to intervene in the face of an armed and thoroughly unconstitutional insurrection by Democrats in Mississippi in 1875, but just two years later, in 1877, it sent federal troops to confront laborers on strike. Grant himself noted when he became an elder statesman that the Democrats and many Republicans refused "to protect the lives of negroes"; "now, however, there is no hesitation about exhausting the whole power of the government to suppress a strike on the slightest intimation that danger threatens" (Foner 1990, 247).

Americans, except to try to reassure white voters that Republican corruption would cease. They all but wrote off the votes of southern blacks (Foner 1988, 569). Except for white supremacists in South Carolina, Democrats spoke about corruption and the economic depression, consciously choosing to bury the race issue in the hope that this would in turn bury the sectional issue that had so worked against them (Foner 1988, 568; Gerring 1998, 239; Grossman 1992). "By abandoning explicit appeals to the race issue and absorbing a highly visible group of Liberal Republicans," writes Foner, "they partially dissolved their old association with racism and disloyalty, while in no way altering their intention of undoing federal protection for blacks' rights" (1988, 510–511).

Each party had decided that abandoning the issue of race best served its electoral purpose. Republicans abandoned the issue from a lack of will and a sense of futility; Democrats abandoned it because their position on the issue had acquired a strong association with their position in favor of southern whites. Republicans wanted to move to issues on which they could find a common purpose and which had greater urgency for them; Democrats wanted to regain the legitimacy lost when they had been tarred as the allies of the traitorous South. For Republicans it was a way to move on ideologically, for Democrats a way to move on politically. The parties moved away from race and sectionalism, and toward class and economic issues (Rosenstone et al. 1984, 64–65; Woodward 1991, 36). Accordingly, all racial appeals, explicit or otherwise, faded from electoral campaigns.

THE NORM OF RACIAL INEQUALITY RETURNS FULL-FORCE

As it became increasingly clear after 1876 that compromise between North and South on the status of blacks was the new order, the norm of racial inequality was reestablished. It had never gone away, but it had been somewhat weakened by Reconstruction. After 1876, support for racial equality came to be seen increasingly as a violation of the resurgent norm of racial inequality. Simultaneously, the parties ceased to divide on matters of race. Campaigns no longer featured racial appeals; in fact, with the exception of 1884, 1892, and 1904, Democratic platforms were entirely silent on the matter of race in every presidential election between 1880 and 1936 (Gerring 1998, 239). But in a reflection of the resurgent norm of inequality, when public figures spoke on matters of race, their rhetoric took a more explicit turn relative to the early 1870s. Southern whites still had to go through some rhetorical motions of conforming to the Fourteenth and Fifteenth Amendments, which explains such famous slogans as "equal accommodation for each race, but separate." But the language of group conflict and racial threat was used freely, sometimes intermixed with the white supremacy of noblesse oblige (Condit and Lucaites 1993, 130, 133–134). The weaker the national expectation that white southerners protect the rights of blacks, the bolder they grew in defying it, first in actions, then in words.

The notion that black political power was undesirable was expressed with clear racial labels. In 1885, Henry Grady, an editor of the *Atlanta Constitution* who was widely considered an exemplar of the modernizing New South and was a major figure in Georgia politics, justified the "domination of the white race in the South" as a legitimate assertion "of the right of character, intelligence, and property to rule." "This continent belongs to those who conquered the wilderness, who have taught to the world how a people can govern themselves, and who want no foreign element, white or black, to control their destiny, or to debase their civilization," declared Senator Wade Hampton in 1890. "She [the white South] is not to be ruled by the blacks," wrote Walter Hill, "nor by white men at home or from abroad who owe their election exclusively to the blacks." "The white race," declared Senator Thomas J. Heflin, "is the superior race, the king race, the climax and crowning glory of the four races of black, yellow, red and white. The South's doctrine of white supremacy is right and it is fast becoming the doctrine of the American Republic" (Condit and Lucaites 1993, 311 n. 58).

The North's growing inegalitarian norm contributed to the white South's freedom to say what was on its mind. In turn, southern spokesmen reinforced the North's derogatory views of blacks. From the 1880s to the 1930s, virulent white supremacist views replaced white northern optimism about the possibility of "elevating" blacks to citizenship (Woodward 1971; Williamson 1984, 118). Ideas about the moral decline of the black race were commonplace, popularized in novels, essays, and newspaper stories (Meier and Rudwick 1994, 211). Whites worried that the elimination of slavery meant that blacks had returned to their "natural" inclination to be "lazy, thriftless, intemperate, insolent, dishonest, and without the most rudimentary elements of morality" (Fredrickson 1971, 260). Even supporters of black rights became disillusioned with blacks' political performance (Holt 1979, 196). Reconstruction came to be seen as the era of corrupt black rule. "Corruption in high circles did not disqualify whites for self-government, but somehow it did seem to disqualify the Negroes, who had been notably less corrupt," write Meier and Rudwick (1994, 192). Statistical evidence of the criminality of the black race was widely used in the beginning of the twentieth century to establish African Americans' supposed propensity to engage in illegal acts, particularly the rape of white women (Condit and Lucaites 1993, 155). The emerging field of criminology attempted to show that blacks had a greater tendency to commit crimes, particularly those of "passion" (Woodward 1966, 94). Medical practitioners and biological researchers measured every human organ they could examine for evidence of blacks' exaggerated sexual capacity or puny intellectual ones (Gould 1981). Scholarly books with such titles as *The American Negro as a Dependent, Defective, and Delinquent* were published during the first two decades of the twentieth century. A spate of best-selling racist novels, further popularized by the now-infamous, then-beloved film *The Birth of a Nation*, contributed to the ascendancy of the stereotype of black men as rapacious beasts (Fredrickson 1971, 281). The titles for the silent film came from Woodrow Wilson's *A History of the American People*, which condemned Reconstruction as the rule of "ignorant negroes"; Wilson widely publicized his White House screening of the film and praised it as "History written with lightning" (Franklin 1993 [1976], 69; Klinker and Smith 1999, 110).

These elements of American culture constituted perhaps the strongest norm of racial inequality ever present throughout the United States (Fredrickson 1971). Between the 1880s and 1920s, all sectors of white American society, from the cultural and political elite to the least educated and the most powerless voters, expressed derogatory racial stereotypes that justified blacks' subordination.

This norm was a bonanza for political efforts to further deny blacks their rights. Southern members of Congress repeatedly referred to the image of the black beast in their speeches. The black man was "a fiend, a wild beast, seeking whom he may devour," South Carolina senator Benjamin Tillman liked to say (Fredrickson 1971, 276, 281–282). The theme of African American sexual aggression was present in arguments against appointing blacks to government posts and in favor of formally segregating them once hired (Ayers 1992, 299). In particular, the worry was that white women working for the government would come into contact with black men. Between 1890 and 1920, the number of lynchings exceeded the number of other state-sponsored executions, and the proportion of lynchings targeting blacks increased (Condit and Lucaites 1993, 156, 158; Feldman 1995, 201; Williamson 1984, 117, 184; Woodward 1971, 351). The theme of criminality found further expression in the argument, used during the antebellum years and reintroduced at this time, that blacks should not receive much education because, as they were destined for eternal serfdom, it created immoral and unrealistic expectations in them and made them into "thieves and vagrants in companies, battalions and armies" (Condit and Lucaites 1993, 156; Harlan 1958; Meier and Rudwick 1994, 202). The norm of racial inequality was sufficiently powerful that for much of the period 1880–1920, efforts to subjugate blacks sparked almost no significant opposition from national white elites.

Thus, the norm of racial inequality again reigned, in the North and South. At the same time, the national Republican party no longer concerned itself with the status of African Americans. The party system had ceased to revolve around matters of race. With no institution willing to represent the rights of African Americans, the issue of race died. The national party system revolved around other concerns. National campaigns no longer featured racial appeals.

For a brief time, however, the South took a different course. During the 1890s, the party system there, pitting Democrats against Populists, aligned itself along the issue of race, and explicit racial appeals rose to prominence.[27]

THE SOUTHERN PARTY SYSTEM AND EXPLICIT APPEALS

The Southern Populists

The southern Populists, who came into existence in response to economic crisis, realized that to amass sufficient power against the Democrats on the issue that drove them to politics—the well-being of farmers and laborers—they would have to obtain the votes of large numbers of blacks. The party quickly decided to align itself on the issue of race and developed a racial rhetorical strategy. Many Populists, though not all, campaigned explicitly in favor of black rights, addressing audiences of mixed races with such statements as the following:

> You are made to hate each other because upon that hatred is rested the keystone of the arch of financial despotism which enslaves you both. You are deceived and blinded that you may not see how this race antagonism perpetuates a monetary system which beggars you both. . . . The colored tenant . . . is in the same boat with the white tenant, the colored laborer with the white laborer. . . . The accident of color can make no difference in the interests of farmers, croppers, and laborers. . . . [We will] wipe out the color line and put every man on his citizenship irrespective of color. (Woodward 1966, 63)

The Populists' rhetorical commitment was sometimes underscored by meaningful action. They appointed blacks to influential party positions, included black speakers at campaign events, (more rarely) listed black and white candidates together on the party's ballots, and wrote platforms that included planks against lynching and the convict lease system (Meier and Rudwick 1994, 198–199). Tom Watson, perhaps the most well known Populist to speak for black rights, clearly condemned the Democratic racial strategy: "The bugaboo of negro domination," he said, was "the most hypocritical that unscrupulous leadership could invent" (Goodwyn 1978; Woodward 1966, 63–64, 89–90; see also Degler 1982, 340).

The Populists' egalitarian words and actions were driven by the racial party alignment in the South. They believed that the only way to challenge the domi-

---

[27] The earlier Readjuster movement in Virginia had a similarly egalitarian platform of political rights, and also was crushed with a concerted campaign of racial appeals, fraud, and violence. A Democratic flier during the campaign of 1880 exhorted voters, "White Men of Virginia! Remember

nant Democrats was to ally with black voters. But their strategy was extremely risky considering just how far they departed from the racial norm of their day. It is difficult to overstate the radical nature of these racially egalitarian appeals. Nearly everyone else was executing a full-scale retreat from racial equality— black leaders from political life, white egalitarians from the rights they had worked to write into the Constitution, national Republicans from attempts to incorporate black voters. But the Populists were uttering the words and follow-ing through with the deeds that enabled blacks, for a brief time, to exercise some of their political rights.[28] It was a marriage based on mutual interest and political necessity, not on an ideological commitment to black rights (Degler 1982; Meier and Rudwick 1994, 200). The Populists only challenged the norm because they had no other means. And they only challenged the norm as much as was absolutely necessary.

To compensate for their radical appeals to blacks, the white Populists en-gaged in the same kind of rearguard racist rhetoric that Republicans had used when they were the party of racial equality. It was the Democrats who favored the mixing of the races, the Democrats who gave out patronage to blacks, and the Democrats who harmed the interests of whites, charged the Populists. A popular defense against the charge of pro-blackness was to point out that Democrat Grover Cleveland had invited Frederick Douglass and his white wife to the White House (Degler 1982, 349). A Populist newspaper in Birmingham, Alabama, declared: "We are farther from advocating or practicing social equal-ity than any ballot box stuffer [Democrat] alive. Our objection does not relax at the going down of the sun. We have got no children at the Tuskegee normal school or kindred there" (Degler 1982, 349). Democrats accused Populists of opening the door to black domination, and Populists keenly felt the need to deny the charge. " 'Dominate' what? 'Dominate' how? 'Dominate' who?" asked Tom Watson of his audience. "It takes Intellect to dominate: haven't we got it? It takes Majorities to dominate: haven't we got them? It takes Wealth to dominate: Haven't we got it?" (in Degler 1982, 349). "The heart of the Populist argument in behalf of political participation by blacks," concludes Degler, "was that it would not threaten white supremacy" (1982, 351). The Populists' rhetorical strategy was designed to resolve the contradiction between a plat-form that advanced black rights and the need to adhere to the norm of racial inequality.

---

the fight in your State will settle the political question of either white or colored supremacy. Which shall it be?" (Degler 1982, 292).

[28] "It was quite common in the 'eighties and 'nineties," wrote Woodward, "to find in the *Nation*, *Harper's Weekly*, the *North American Review*, or the *Atlantic Monthly* northern liberals and former abolitionists mouthing the shibboleths of white supremacy regarding the Negro's innate inferi-ority, shiftlessness, and hopeless unfitness for full participation in the white man's civilization" (1966, 70).

The Anti-Populist Response

The Populists' anti-black rhetoric was benign compared to the explicitly racial appeals of their opponents. As they had during the early years of Reconstruction, some Democrats at first tried limited appeals to black voters in an attempt to beat the Populists at their own game (Degler 1982, 343). But this effort consisted primarily of the familiar round of picnics and barbecues, with some false promises added for good measure. The Populists, Democrats soon realized, could only be crushed, not preempted. And crush them they did, with all the means at their disposal: violence, fraud, and electoral campaigns that repeatedly derogated blacks in no uncertain terms. It did not take long for many Populists to cede the field or, in some cases, to decisively abandon their coalition with blacks.

The backlash against the Populist mobilization of blacks was so strong that throughout the South, it turned into a large-scale electoral mobilization to disenfranchise blacks with formal measures.[29] The growing concern with black criminality made for a useful justification for the disenfranchisement of blacks. V. O. Key, in his book *Southern Politics in State and Nation*, argued that some of these state constitutional amendments were designed with stereotypical assumptions in mind. The long residency period was assumed to affect blacks disproportionately because of "their supposedly peripatetic habits." Requiring that voters certify their payment of poll taxes was thought to weigh more heavily on black voters because of "the absence among Negroes of a predilection for the preservation of records." The understanding clause was seen as a way out for illiterate whites but not for illiterate blacks, since "it was not expected that sophistication on constitutional matters would be general among Negroes." The crime conviction measure, which disallowed voting when a person was convicted of a crime, appears to have had stereotypical origins too (Key 1949, 537–538).[30]

Many of the Populists who stayed in politics abandoned their egalitarian stance and joined Democrats in the effort to mobilize white views of black criminality in the service of disenfranchisement (Degler 1982; Goodwyn 1978). The disenfranchisement campaign, argued Woodward, was largely accomplished with "an intensive propaganda of white supremacy, Negrophobia, and race chauvinism. Such a campaign preceded and accompanied disfranchisement in each state." This was necessary to circumvent opposition by lower

---

[29] Aside from Mississippi, which had done so in 1890, all former Confederate states enacted some form of vote restriction at this time and many more segregation laws were passed than before (Key 1949, 537–539; Meier and Rudwick 1994, 201–204; Woodward 1966, 83).

[30] The stereotype of black criminality shaped state and federal Supreme Court decisions on voting rights (Condit and Lucaites 1993, 162).

class whites, who feared their own disenfranchisement.[31] To that end, proponents of black disenfranchisement appealed to the necessity of healing political rivalries among whites by excluding blacks (Key 1949, 540–541; Woodward 1966, 85).[32]

Criminality was not the only theme of these explicit appeals. Some appeals referred to black political domination. An 1892 Democratic broadside in North Carolina showed a black man, with exaggerated facial features and an evil grin, lying in a comfortable bed and holding a sign, which read "BALLOT: HARRISON AND THE FORCE BILL; REPUBLICAN PARTY IN NORTH CAROLINA; NOT DEAD BUT SLEEPING" (Ayers 1992, 39).[33] In 1894, while Benjamin Tillman campaigned in South Carolina for a constitutional disenfranchisement convention, he told dissenters who threatened to mobilize black voters: "If these people want to warm this black snake into life . . . we are ready to meet them and give them the worst drubbing they have ever had in their lives" (Key 1949, 548).

Often, blacks' exercise of power was deliberately linked with the notion that blacks had a propensity for crime, and resulted not only in electoral victories and disenfranchisement but in violence against blacks. In Georgia and elsewhere in the Deep South, the press featured stories of black crime, particularly rape, and general "instances of arrogance, impertinence, surly manners, or lack of prompt and proper servility in conduct" (Woodward 1966, 85–86). "Virtually every issue of every southern newspaper contained an account of black wrongdoing," Ayers found in his thorough research of the era; rape was a favorite theme (1992, 153). The *Atlanta Journal*, which Hoke Smith edited while he ran for governor on a disenfranchisement platform, was especially prone to such stories, printing them daily during the 1906 campaign (Woodward 1966, 85–86).[34] The massive rioting in Atlanta by whites against blacks,

---

[31] The professed aim of disenfranchisement proponents at the constitutional conventions was disenfranchisement not of Populists, but of blacks. "The annals of conventions and legislatures," Key found, "abound with candid declarations of the intent to accomplish an end forbidden by the Constitution of the United States—denial of suffrage on account of color. Few open expressions of intent to disfranchise the troublesome Populists (along with a goodly number of white Republicans) are to be found" (1949, 544).

[32] Rebecca Latimer Felton of Georgia, the first woman appointed to the U.S. Senate, echoed a common argument when she told a group of her supporters in 1897: "[Rapes of white women] will grow and increase with every election where white men equalized themselves at the polls with an inferior race and controlled their votes by bribery and whiskey. . . . If it takes lynching to protect woman's dearest possession from drunken, ravening human beasts, then I say lynch a thousand a week if it becomes necessary" (Williamson 1984, 128). Fifteen years earlier she had publicly taken the Democrats to task for "their crusade against the colored race" (in Degler 1982, 289).

[33] The caption explained: "The colored man in the picture is not dead, but asleep, and he has a ballot for 'Harrison and the force bill' in his hand. He pretends to be dead, but he will be awake in time to cast that ballot in November."

[34] Smith was pushed toward racial appeals and black disenfranchisement not only by his more conservative opponent, but also by his Populist supporter Tom Watson (Lewis 1993, 335).

and Georgia's disenfranchisement of blacks, noted Du Bois, were direct results of the gubernatorial campaign. Over ten thousand white soldiers, wielding guns, beat and killed blacks and wrecked their homes and businesses (Ayers 1992, 436; Lewis 1993, 333–335). Smith's strategy succeeded in winning him the election and secured the passage in 1908 of disenfranchisement in Georgia with 66.5 percent of the popular vote (Key 1949, 550). Explicitly racial campaign appeals had real and horrific consequences for blacks.

North Carolina's Populist movement, the most successful in the South, was brought to an end during the 1898 election with the use of explicit appeals and with appalling consequences. The North Carolina Populists had fused with black Republicans and made it possible for more blacks to hold office during the mid-1890s then had during Reconstruction (Degler 1982, 345). The election that would legally end black voting featured an armed coup and exaggerated or false stories of black misdeeds, printed daily in the largest newspaper in the state, the *Raleigh News and Observer*, among others (Degler 1982, 362; Meier and Rudwick 1994, 200). Throughout much of the South, electoral campaigns were accompanied by stories of black criminality, sparking violence against blacks, and leading to the passage of disenfranchisement amendments (Ayers 1992; Fredrickson 1988; Woodward 1966, 86).[35]

These intense and explicit appeals to whites' racial stereotypes, fears, and resentments were caused by the rise of a party system structured along the issue of race and by the shock of the Populists' success. The Populists' ability to mobilize blacks and their efforts to safeguard blacks' rights presented a threat to the norm of racial inequality. The party supporting racial hierarchy responded with explicitly racial appeals, and succeeded in intimidating the Populists into abandoning the cause of racial equality. Racial hierarchy, as a result, became safer still.

The disenfranchisement campaigns illustrate not only the by-now familiar interaction of norms, party coalitions, and racial appeals, but also the fact that race is not always the least acceptable grounds for action. When national norms against racist expression are nonexistent, and racism is fully accepted, racism serves as a convenient cover behind which other things may hide. During the Civil War, Democrats who wanted to oppose the war had to find patriotic-sounding reasons for their position. Stereotypical pronouncements about black Union troops served that purpose, as genuinely felt as they were. Similarly, as they crushed the Populists, southern Democrats had to hide their class motivation, and stereotypical rhetoric about miscegenation and criminality served

---

[35] The significance of the racist campaign to put down the Populist revolt and disenfranchise black men goes beyond its immediate results. According to Key, the conservatives and their campaign of black repression created a long-term "distorted" process of one-party rule and transient factions in the South (1949). The racial appeals of the disenfranchisement campaigns thus shaped the internal party structure of the South and permitted the South to exercise veto power both in presidential nominations and in congressional legislation.

that purpose, genuinely felt as it was. Race was not only a means to a true, nonracial end. But it did serve as a means as well as an end. Today, politicians find derogatory racial appeals too risky, and racial problems and solutions often cost too many votes to discuss directly—hence the use of nonracial language to justify actions that may be interpreted as racist. In the South of the turn of the century, the reverse was true.

For a brief time, the Populists had created an alternative, egalitarian racial rhetoric that was to reappear as the racial norm changed during the twentieth century. Eventually their rhetorical strategy would find expression in twentieth century challenges to anti-black appeals.

CONCLUSION

During the nineteenth century and well into the twentieth there existed in the United States a universal norm of racial inequality. When, in the 1860s and 1870s, the party system aligned on the question of what the federal government should do about the status of African Americans, each party's rhetorical strategy was responsive to the racial norm. The norm not only allowed Democrats to craft an effective racial strategy for winning elections. It also constrained the rhetorical strategy of the Republican party. Sex, violence, and work were the chief dimensions of whites' racial predispositions. As the parties competed with each other for power, and tried to highlight their own adherence to the norm and their opponents' violation of it, these dimensions became prominent in electoral appeals. The national parties' split on race was an important cause of the rise of national electoral appeals to race, as was the shock provided by emancipation. White citizens did not vote to uphold racism unless politicians asked them to do so. And politicians in turn had no reason to ask when no threat to racial hierarchy appeared imminent.

Most important in overcoming the impact of racial appeals was the fact that the party system also revolved around the question of what to do about the southern rebellion. During most of the 1860s, when racial appeals were heavily used in national electoral campaigns, anger toward and fear of southern rebellion was more powerful than anger toward and fear of blacks. At least, this was the case in the North, where elections were won.

My claims about racial alignments and racial predispositions will be familiar to readers of historical scholarship on the South. True, the theme of race is surprisingly muted in the large majority of accounts of elections, either taken for granted or dismissed as unimportant. The racial appeals of elites, and the racial considerations of voters, are on the margins in many of these accounts, even as slavery occupies center stage. Still, some historians have paid a good deal of attention to racial discourse (although rarely in the context of elections).

What has been given no attention, even in accounts that do consider racial campaign appeals, is the factor of racial norms.

My account suggests that while party alignments and the shock of major events such as emancipation are necessary to an understanding of racial appeals, they are not sufficient. The missing piece is the factor of norms. When the norm is inegalitarian, the left party cannot defend its egalitarian position on racial grounds without suffering the electoral consequences. During the nineteenth century, the parties of the racial left chose instead to emphasize their conformity to the norm by engaging in (relatively limited) racist appeals. The same norm made it highly profitable for Democrats, as the party of the right, to mobilize voters with appeals that derogated blacks. The notion of states' rights, which the party had championed during the 1850s, had nowhere near the electoral force of explicitly racial appeals in the 1860s. Once they positioned themselves to the right on the issue of race, Democrats had to choose among the rhetorical strategies consonant with that position. The rhetorical strategy of explicitly racial appeals had the higher payoff.

But a norm, however strong, is not immutable. The Reconstruction period suggests that even in highly racist times, if events create a window of opportunity, a limited norm of equality can arise, and shape racial campaign discourse. The window of opportunity was the emancipation of slaves born of the urgencies of the Civil War (see Klinker and Smith 1999 for a developed argument). The norm that emerged with the victory of radical Reconstruction was a norm of limited political equality for blacks. For a brief time during the early 1870s, Democrats, who in the mind of northern voters had become the party of southern treason and of the blatant repression of blacks linked to this treason, grew reluctant to make explicitly racial appeals. Explicitly racial appeals signaled Democratic recalcitrance in the face of the Fourteenth and Fifteenth Amendments, a recalcitrance the party believed it could not afford to show to Republican elites, who were in control of the federal government and many state offices and who had enshrined their program in the Constitution. Republicans, however, because they were the party crafting the new equality, were, with the exception of southern Republicans directly beholden to black voters, under much less pressure to avoid appeals that explicitly derogated blacks. The nascent and weak norm of racial equality still competed with the norm of racial inequality, and so it was limited in its partisanship. The losing party had to show that it conformed to the new norm; the winning party had to show that it conformed to the still-powerful old norm. The Republican party ultimately succumbed to the pressure, and quit its effort to uphold the normative constraint on Democrats.

It is a measure of how poorly the issue of racial equality was settled during the 1860s and 1870s that it dissipated from the party system after a decade. As we shall see in the next chapter, the fact that the issue of race today continues to find its way into electoral appeals, several decades after it reemerged as a national issue, is a mark of the institutionalization of competing racial interests. Paradoxically, that is good news for racial equality; it means that African Americans and their white allies have managed to gain a more permanent foothold in the party system than ever before. That in turn prompts the opposition party to continue to make appeals to its own side.

The presence of racial appeals is not always a good sign, however. We can infer that the more explicit the racial appeal, the stronger the norm of racial inequality. We can also infer that the more frequent and intense the explicit appeals, the stronger the efforts by the party of the racial right to buttress racial inequality. The presence of explicit and intense racial appeals in the South of the 1890s indicated an all-out attempt to crush the Populist coalition with African Americans and their disenfranchisement. Thus, the more explicit and intense the appeal, the more inegalitarian the norm that gives rise to it, and the greater the risk to a program of black advancement.

From the perspective of implicit racial communication, it is striking how little of it existed during the nineteenth century. This too is a measure of the weakness of the attempts to institute political equality. Only for a few years during the early 1870s did racist politicians hesitate to speak their minds in public. During much of the time that race was used for political gain, it was done unabashedly. Blacks were clearly derogated as blacks, whites elevated as whites. The stereotypes of sexual perversity, violence, and laziness were unconcealed and spoken in clearly racial terms. Images that depicted these stereotypes were quite extreme, and words that made reference to them were nothing if not blatant. The threat of black political "domination" was discussed with much wringing of hands, at times even by the same whites who had worked to bring the suffrage to the emancipated slaves.

In the twentieth century, politicians again mobilized negative racial predispositions for electoral gain when the parties once more took different positions on the issue of race. However, a crucial change in style characterizes the racial appeals of today. In the 1930s, the norm of racial equality gradually began to replace the norm of racial inequality. In the second half of the twentieth century, as the new norm vanquished the old, explicit appeals became nearly extinct. But racial appeals did not disappear. Whites endorsed the idea of racial equality and rejected the idea that blacks were biologically inferior. But they were still predisposed to believe that blacks had a tendency to engage in sexual excess and violence and to avoid work. The brief blip of implicit appeals evident during Reconstruction became the new way to appeal to whites' racial predispositions.

CHAPTER 3

The Norm of Racial Equality, Electoral Strategy, and Implicit Appeals

> The weaker the forces that are at the disposal of the
> supreme commander, the more appealing the
> use of cunning becomes. In a state of weakness and
> insignificance, when prudence, judgment, and
> ability no longer suffice, cunning may well appear
> the only hope.
> —Clausewitz, *On War*

WHAT IS DISTINCTIVE about the modern politics of race is not the intersection of race with nonracial issues. Race has been bound up with concerns about sexuality, violence, and work, with notions of deviance and competition, at least since the early nineteenth century. The entanglement of the American ethos of economic self-reliance with racial stereotypes, fears, and resentments is quite old. From the beginning, political appeals that made use of race often made use of something else to go along with race. What is new to the age of equality is that race is much more muted in political discourse than it used to be. Politicians now appeal to race under cover. What created this historical break, in part, was the shift in attitudes about racial equality—more precisely, the repudiation of racism. The ideology of white supremacy was displaced by an ideology of racial equality. The norm of racial inequality began to erode in the 1930s, replaced in the 1960s by the norm of racial equality.

Still, the political need for racial appeals continues. Racial tensions go unresolved, and elites have incentives to make appeals to them. The interests of African Americans are now represented in an institutionalized way. The issues of racial equality are now perennially before all branches of the federal government. White citizens continue to subscribe to negative views of African Americans even as they endorse the ideology of racial equality. Two forces—one compelling elites to endorse the new norm of racial equality, and the other compelling them to appeal to racial stereotypes, fears, and resentment—generate the now-dominant strategy of implicit racial appeals. The older racial strategy relying on explicitly racial appeals has greatly diminished. In its place we now see not the absence of racial appeals, but the presence of implicit ones. Racial appeals did not disappear; they were transformed, often consciously and strategically.

As we saw in the previous chapter, during the nineteenth century the racial norm was inegalitarian and racial appeals were explicit. Silence on race meant the absence of racial appeals. Now, however, while silence on race sometimes means just that, it can mean instead the presence of racial appeals that are subtle. The changes of the mid-twentieth century brought about a renewed impetus to racial appeals, but at the same time made them implicit. As it had during the mid-nineteenth century, the party system of the mid-twentieth century arranged itself along racial lines. As in the nineteenth century, a shock was necessary to instigate racial appeals at the national level. That shock was the successful mobilization of the civil rights movement and black rebellion in the cities, coupled with the dramatic actions of powerful national institutions.

INSTITUTIONS BEGIN TO REJECT THE NORM OF RACIAL INEQUALITY

The key to the story is the emergence of the norm of racial equality, which evolved in several ways simultaneously. Chief among them was the political reawakening of African Americans, which went hand-in-hand with African Americans' attempt to shift the norm of public discourse. By 1930, the Great Migration had begun, 21 percent of African Americans lived in the North, and local African-American mobilization there was underway (McAdam 1982; Tindall 1967). A new generation of African-American elites was flexing its political muscle at the national level as well. The NAACP was born two decades earlier, but in 1930 it finally cut its political teeth in its attempt to defeat Judge John J. Parker's nomination to the Supreme Court (Goings 1990; Tindall 1967, 541). The NAACP argued to members of Congress that Parker should be defeated because he had made racist statements while running as a lily-white Republican candidate for governor of North Carolina in 1920. At that time he said, "Experience has demonstrated that the participation of the Negro in the political life of the South is harmful to him and to the community, and is a fruitful source of that racial prejudice which works to his injury. As a class he has learned this lesson. He no longer desires to participate in politics. The Republican party of North Carolina does not desire him to participate in the politics of the state" (Goings 1990, 23).

The NAACP proved by its lobbying that African Americans did indeed desire to participate in politics. But as important from the perspective of norms, the NAACP's action signaled that racist rhetoric would be challenged thereafter. Certainly it was too soon for any candidate to worry about losing because he had run for office with the aid of explicitly racial appeals. But by targeting the rhetoric of a candidate, the NAACP was attempting to undermine the norm of racial inequality. Civil rights would come to mean not only formal legal equality, but also the absence from politics of recognizably racist speech.

A battle over racist rhetoric was Roy Wilkins's first move as head of the NAACP. In 1934 he organized a protest campaign against Will Rogers, who had used the word "nigger" repeatedly in a broadcast on NBC radio. Wilkins finally got NBC to force Rogers to switch to the (then) more "acceptable" term "darky" (Branch 1988, 51).

Other African-American mobilization efforts also resulted in a change—however small—in the norm of racial inequality. The NAACP's anti-lynching campaign, among the most important of its activities, was meant primarily to spur a federal anti-lynching bill. But it also had the effect of undermining the acceptability of lynching. The NAACP was not able to prevent lynchings, but its activities did a great deal to embarrass local authorities in the South. "Even though the NAACP failed to secure either the convictions of lynchers or the punishment of law officers guilty of complicity," writes the historian William Brundage, "it helped direct the spotlight of national scorn on rural communities where lynching persisted." By 1950 the pressure of changing national norms increased so much that public lynchings nearly disappeared. Secret violence against African Americans, however, continued. Lynching was increasingly conducted underground. Explicit racial appeals were about to undergo a similar transformation (Brundage 1993, 231, 252).

African-American activists eventually found allies within an important national institution with a great deal of normative influence—the mass media. The national press was the first mainstream institution to take sides in what became a national conflict between African Americans and their white allies on one side and a majority of southern whites on the other. From 1930 to 1940 the national press printed stories that, while paternalistic and focused on racial differences, nevertheless emphasized African Americans' accomplishments and positive characteristics. Editorials chastising the "blindness" of white southerners began to appear. During World War II, the press took a more firmly egalitarian stance, emphasizing similarities between the races and stressing the ability of blacks and whites to live and work together. At least as important was the press's condemnation of the ideology of white supremacy. During the 1950s the press stood firmly in support of the Supreme Court's *Brown v. Board of Education* decision, and continued excoriating southern spokesmen (Condit and Lucaites 1993, 161, 172).

Intellectuals, artists, and public figures, many of whom had contributed to the norm of inequality (passively or actively), now began to exercise their normative influence against racism. "Racial discrimination," warned Eleanor Roosevelt, "is the weak spot in our democracy" (in Klinker and Smith 1999, 225). The scientific community in the 1920s and 1930s began to edge away from the hereditarian view of race (Barkan 1992). Social scientists began to make optimistic pronouncements about inequality and said that racial differences would inevitably decline (Myrdal 1962 [1944]). The southern white liberal movement grew more popular, at least for a time (Feldman 1995, 139).

In the wake of these emerging trends, northern members of Congress, some with new African-American constituencies, became increasingly vocal on behalf of fair treatment in the South (Condit and Lucaites 1993). The growing challenge to white supremacy took shape, in part, as a challenge to voting restrictions in the South, especially the white primary (Key 1949, 644). The Supreme Court, too, reversed course during the 1940s and began to produce a stream of egalitarian decisions (McAdam 1982; Sitkoff 1978).

These normative changes were accompanied by a shift in the presidential rhetoric of Franklin Roosevelt and especially Harry Truman (Condit and Lucaites 1993, 11–12; O'Reilly 1995, 154–155). Several earlier presidents had made infrequent but notable rhetorical strides in that direction, although they were also completely indifferent even to egregious violations of African-American rights (Casdorph 1981, 7–10; Condit and Lucaites 1993, 165). Truman, however, became the most outspoken pro–civil rights president of the first six decades of the century.

Thus, the central political institutions of the United States began to converge on the notion that southern segregation and the ideology of white supremacy were illegitimate. No federal branch was yet willing to take strong measures to correct the problem. Still, white supremacists began to feel the weight of national disapproval.

In response, southern white politicians at first returned to various explicit defenses of racial inequality. In the 1940s and 1950s, the new norm of racial equality was only emerging; it was sufficiently weak that racial conservatives decided to attack it. The pressure of conformity still favored the more established norm of racial inequality.

SOUTHERN RHETORICAL RESPONSES IN THE 1940s:
MORE OF THE SAME

At first, white southerners defended racial inequality in the same explicitly racial terms they had used before. One difference was that now, new civil rights organizations served as a focal point. White supremacists attacked the NAACP and its Legal Defense Fund for its electoral mobilization and for prompting the Supreme Court to outlaw the white primary.[1] Other themes were more familiar: equality, they argued, would give rise to black political corruption, interracial mixing, and black domination. Eugene Talmadge, in his 1946 gubernato-

---

[1] The rise of black mobilization and the tentative New Deal gestures toward blacks may have been responsible for the spike in supremacist rhetoric during the primary elections of 1942 in the South. In Louisiana a senatorial candidate told voters stories of "colored organizations . . . sitting around midnight candles." In South Carolina Eugene S. Blease promised to reform Washington, where "white ladies are ordered to call Negro officials Mister" (Tindall 1967, 722).

rial campaign in Georgia, made statements that the opposition party had "received 99 percent of the Negro vote. Such block voting by an uneducated group does not further the cause of good government." Mississippi senator Theodore Bilbo was even more blunt while campaigning at home in 1946: "You and I know what's the best way to keep the nigger from voting. You do it the night before the election. I don't have to tell you any more than that. Red-blooded men know what I mean" (Key 1949, 636, 646, 653; Dittmer 1994, 2).

White supremacists continued to express their explicit and extreme defense of inequality in congressional debates. The significance of including African Americans in the ranks of fighting men was not lost on them, as it had not been lost on Democrats during the Civil War. The color line had to be reemphasized, they felt, after it had been eroded by such measures as extending the GI bill to African Americans and allowing soldiers to vote by absentee ballot (Egerton 1994, 221). One of the most influential of the South's senators, Mississippi's James O. Eastland, charged that African-American troops were not only lazy, irresponsible, and "of very low intelligence"; they also raped white women in Allied-occupied Europe (Egerton 1994, 174). In general, Eastland declared, "The Negro race is an inferior race. I say quite frankly that I am proud of the white race. I am proud that the purest of white blood flows through my veins. I know that the white race is a superior race. It has ruled the world. It has given us civilization. It is responsible for all the progress on earth.' "[2] His colleague in the House, John E. Rankin, railed against "niggers" on the House floor (Egerton 1994, 221).

Thus, racial conservatives' immediate response to the erosion of the norm of racial inequality was to buttress the norm. But when it was time to conduct a national electoral campaign, they realized that they would have to make some rhetorical concessions.

THE 1948 PRESIDENTIAL CAMPAIGN

The Dixiecrat rebellion of 1948 brought the first concerted use of racial appeals in a twentieth-century presidential contest. Tellingly, it was the first presidential election that featured an effort to legitimize the defense of white supremacy.

The cause of racial appeals was, as usual, a shock to racial arrangements. In 1948 this shock was the co-occurrence of three events: blacks' growing political mobilization, the massive mobilization of blacks for the war effort, and the

[2] U.S. Senate, 79th Congress, 2d Session, Hearings Before the Special Committee to Investigate Senatorial Campaign Expenditures, 1946 (Washington, D.C.: Government Printing Office, 1947), 390–92; *Cong. Rec.*, 1945, 6994–96, 7000.

conduct of the Cold War on the grounds of human rights and democracy (Klinker and Smith 1999). As in response to past shocks, the parties repositioned themselves to take electoral advantage of the change in circumstances. In particular, Truman offered unprecedented proposals on behalf of African Americans. Under pressure from the black labor leader A. Philip Randolph and from the NAACP, and outfitted with a concrete electoral plan from his aide Clark Clifford, Truman advocated such radical measures as an anti-lynching law, the elimination of the poll tax, and—the only one he fought for—the desegregation of the armed forces. He was also the first president to speak to the NAACP and to speak in Harlem (Branch 1988, 67; O'Reilly 1995, 160–161; Sitkoff 1971, 600–610).

While Truman sought to take advantage of the egalitarian shock by moving to the left, others sought to do so by moving to the right. Truman's actions represented a decision to place the Democratic party to the left of center on the issue of race. The opposition—coming from within the Democratic party—lurched toward the right and took up racial appeals. Half the Alabama and all the Mississippi delegates walked out of the Democratic national convention in 1948 upon the approval of a civil rights plank (Key 1949, 335; Rosenstone et al. 1984, 108).[3] The Dixiecrats formed their own States' Rights Democratic party and nominated Strom Thurmond for president.

However, there was now a new limit on what opponents of racial equality could say in their drive for office. For the first time in a presidential contest, the party of the racial right faced a normative constraint on its racial appeals. The Dixiecrats made a rhetorical concession to the erosion of the norm of racial inequality by increasing their reliance on implicit appeals. It was states' rights that motivated them, they insisted, not a hatred of blacks. The problem was undue federal intrusion, they said, not the threat to their privileged racial status. Many Dixiecrats made efforts to distance the movement from white supremacy and focus it firmly on states' rights. Thurmond himself was perhaps their most ardent spokesman for this position: "We consider so-called civil rights legislation and many other like questions to be reserved to the States by the Constitution. Anyone who insinuates that there is any other intention in the States' Rights movement than that of protecting and preserving this constitutional guarantee must undoubtedly be attempting to smear our movement" (Heard 1952). The influence of the growing norm of equality is clear—Thurmond and other prominent Dixiecrats were worried that the "racist" label would taint their movement. During much of the fall campaign, Horace Wilkinson, an influential boss of the States' Rights party, spoke to national and

---

[3] The civil rights plank was passed under the leadership of Hubert H. Humphrey, then mayor of Minneapolis, who launched his national career with a staunch civil rights speech at the convention (O'Reilly 1995; Klinker and Smith 1999, 222).

some southern audiences in moderate racial language, rejecting full racial equality but swearing to uphold racial justice (Feldman 1995, 148).

However, in their zeal to fire up the southern audience, some delegates to the Dixiecrat meeting forgot the need to conform to the growing national norm and used explicitly racial language. Thurmond was careful to rely mostly on paternalism when speaking about blacks, claiming that they had done well under white care, but he had his lapses. "All the laws of Washington," Thurmond told the delegates, "and all the bayonets of the Army cannot force the Negroes into our homes, schools, churches and places of recreation" (Feldman 1995, 132). Texas congressman Lloyd Price told the States' Rights convention in Birmingham that New Englanders were to blame for bringing "howling, screaming savages to this country" (Feldman 1995, 132). Former Alabama governor Frank Dixon complained that civil rights would "reduce us to the status of a mongrel, inferior race" (Klinker and Smith 1999, 222). In the same vein, while campaigning in the South, Horace Wilkinson, who authored the Dixiecrat resolutions carefully framed in the language of states' rights, told his audience that accepting a civil rights plank meant having to "submit to nigger rule," an unacceptable outcome given that "it's a white man's world." In a private letter Wilkinson was even more blunt: "Ultimately we are going to have to deport the Negroes" (Feldman 1995, 133).

Ultimately such language helped paint the Dixiecrats as too extreme, as violators of the emerging national norm on race. Even some white southern newspapers took the Dixiecrats to task for their explicitly racial language: their convention "did little more than bellow and cry 'nigger,'" commented the *Montgomery Advertiser* (Feldman 1995, 132, 133, 141). The Dixiecrat campaign was the first presidential contest (possibly excepting 1872) in which explicitly racial appeals were coupled with nonracial appeals to principle. It was also the last presidential contest in which explicit appeals dominated. The norms were in flux in the nation, with neither the old norm of racial inequality nor the emerging norm of racial equality dominating. Political rhetoric aimed at a national audience had to straddle the two.

The erosion of the norm of racial inequality also explains why Truman did not counterbalance his move to the racial left with appeals to racial stereotypes, fears, and resentments, as had his Republican counterparts of the 1860s. As noted in Chapter 2, Republicans then had felt the need to show their conformity to the norm of racial inequality by coupling their racially liberal proposals with racist appeals. The Democrats of the late 1940s apparently felt no need to do so.[4]

---

[4] Too much, however, should not be made of Truman's move to the racial left. He gave only one public speech on civil rights during the campaign—in Harlem (Rosenstone et al. 1984, 109). His policy proposals on race, and the rhetorical strategy he formed to go with them, were not central to his agenda.

Truman's moves and the Dixiecrat rebellion foreshadowed the split between Democrats and Republicans that would emerge in the 1960s. The Dixiecrats' immediate impact, however, was to convince the Democratic party that experimenting with racial equality was too dangerous for its health. During Truman's second term his civil rights agenda effectively died. In his 1952 presidential campaign, Adlai Stevenson continued Truman's rhetorical retreat from racial egalitarianism, and even went a step in the other direction.[5] The party system had hovered on the brink of an alignment based on issues of race, sparking electoral appeals to race. As the Democratic party abandoned its plan to mobilize blacks in presidential elections, the southern dissenters in the party no longer saw a need to countermobilize whites with racial appeals. They would continue to engage in racial appeals while campaigning for their own election in the South, particularly after the 1954 *Brown* decision provided another large shock to racial arrangements. But at the national level, racial appeals were few and the parties remained indistinguishable on race until they realigned in the election of 1964 (Carmines and Stimson 1989).

GROWING EGALITARIANISM IN WHITE PUBLIC OPINION AFTER 1950

While the national parties resettled into complacency on race, national norms were continuing their steady change. In the late 1940s, as national elites abandoned the norm of racial inequality and as black activism grew, the views of white citizens began a profound transformation.

In a 1942 National Opinion Research Center (NORC) survey, over half the white sample considered blacks of inferior intelligence and opposed integrating public transportation, and nearly two-thirds explicitly supported segregated schools (Schuman et al. 1985, 9). In the late 1940s, however, these views began inching toward greater racial egalitarianism (Schuman et al. 1985, 17, Table 3.1). Just four years after its 1942 survey, the NORC found that 57 percent of whites—mostly northerners—now endorsed the notion that blacks were as intelligent as whites, the first recorded white majority of that opinion (Schuman et al. 1985, Table 3.4). By the mid-1950s, southern white majorities had joined their northern counterparts in that assessment (Schuman et al. 1985, 125). By the late 1950s, majorities of white samples endorsed the principle of school integration and opposed segregated transportation, even when their own children or residence were hypothetically involved (as long as blacks

---

[5] Stevenson engaged in limited but clear appeals to states' rights, applauded the Confederate South's "political genius" and the New South's "great progress," and castigated "insensitive observers" who mistakenly attributed racial inequality in the South to race prejudice (Huckfeldt and Kohfeld 1989, 7–8; Stevenson 1953, 26–27, 153).

were a numerical minority).[6] By 1963 most whites, by large margins, said blacks should have the right to attend the same public facilities, go to the same schools, and have as good a chance at a job as whites.

Whereas the early 1940s were characterized by widespread white endorsement of the basic tenets of white supremacy, the late 1950s and (especially) the 1960s were characterized by the repudiation of the norm of racial inequality. This did not mean, however, that whites were increasingly committed to implementing significant racial change. While increasingly large majorities of whites repudiated the ideology of white supremacy, most whites remained steadily opposed to significant government intervention. I will return to this point below and in Chapter 4.

SOUTHERNERS MOVE TOWARD IMPLICITLY RACIAL RHETORIC IN CONGRESS: THE 1950s

As the norm of racial equality continued to spread, southerners' explicit defense of racial inequality dwindled, particularly before a national audience. This rhetorical change is evident in the words uttered in Congress. During the 1950s, explicit defenses of white supremacy by members of Congress gradually declined. They were replaced by assurances that equality in the South had been achieved. "The public image of the fire-eater," write Condit and Lucaites, "was once again replaced by the benign visage of the patriarch promising fair treatment for blacks" (1993, 12). The uncompromising defense of the ideology of white superiority diminished, although the defense of the practice of segregation continued.

One rhetorical tactic was similar to what antebellum defenders of slavery had done—to present a vision of a harmonious, peaceful South where whites genially coexisted with blacks. Congressman Harry D. Cooley, for example, said, "I am not aware of the fact that a single man or woman in my congressional district is being oppressed" (*Cong. Rec.* 1956, 13549–50). At the same time, however, southern politicians' rhetoric included explicitly racial references to "white culture," the group rights of whites (which needed protection) and those of blacks (which were overly protected). A theme forged during Reconstruction—the notion that blacks were gaining special, undeserved, or unfair privileges—was revived. "These racial minorities that are always whining about civil rights have a hundred times as many of their own members on the

---

[6] These overall shifts masked a considerable degree of sectionalism, with overwhelming majorities in the North endorsing racial equality in principle, and large majorities in the South opposing it (Schuman et al. 1985, Tables 3.1 and 3.3, 78). But dramatic movements could be seen among southern whites as well. For example, 1964 witnessed the first time a majority of college-educated southern whites endorsed the principle of school integration (Schuman et al. 1985, 78).

Federal pay roll as they are numerically entitled to," whined Congressman John Rankin, among the South's most influential members of Congress (Condit and Lucaites 1993, 182; Egerton 1994, 221).

Familiar, disparaging comments about black characteristics, particularly criminality and sexuality, continued to surface. Now, however, they lacked virulence, and were accompanied by declarations of pure and virtuous motives. Members of Congress such as Senator John Bell Williams focused on "pronounced differences" between the races and brought attention to African Americans' supposed proclivity for crime, illegitimacy, and venereal disease. But he added, "It has not been my purpose in presenting the foregoing to establish one race as the super race or to present the other as a race of degenerates" (*Cong. Rec.* 1956, 5691–92, 5694).[7] A common rhetorical tactic used by congressional segregationists was to point to the threat of racial violence that would erupt upon the dismantling of segregation (Condit and Lucaites 1993, 183).

These qualifiers were not only meant to show conformity to the emerging norm of equality. They were also designed to maintain the notion that southern whites adequately represented black interests. This view is apparent in Senator Williams's assurance that "our Negroes know that we have their interests at heart" (*Cong. Rec.* 1948, 1296). Southern congressmen probably meant to preempt the possibility that the federal government would step in to guarantee black rights. But their rhetoric also reflects the accurate perception that the norm which previously supported racist public expression had eroded.[8]

By 1964, when Congress debated the bill that would become the landmark Civil Rights Act, southern congressmen had learned to bury their explicitly racial references among implicitly racial words. The debate in the Senate, where southerners had perfected the craft of the filibuster in order to block civil rights, was the longest in congressional history. A content analysis of that debate, based on a random sample of ten speeches by senators from the Deep South (all opposed), eight speeches by senators from the Outer South (all opposed), and eight speeches by senators from outside the South (all in favor), reveals how heavily the opponents of civil rights relied on implicitly racial rhetoric. I have classified the words senators used either as explicit ("blacks,"

---

[7] Senator Price Daniels denied knowing anyone who "has ever defended the doctrine of separate and equal schools because of prejudice or a desire to discriminate . . . or a feeling of superiority" (*Cong. Rec.* 1954, 6743).

[8] Another method of masking racist rhetoric was to attach it to anti-Communist arguments. Anti-Communism was undoubtedly genuinely and strongly felt. But it also served the purpose of justifying southern opposition to racial equality. Some members suggested that civil rights activism was tainted by Communist organizing. In fact, some of the most ardent executors of McCarthyism were also the most vocal white supremacists (Egerton 1994; Myrdal 1962, 508). Congressman Bryson called the Fair Employment Practices Committee "the darling of every radical Negro, Communist, and socialistic organization in the Nation" (Condit and Lucaites 1993, 183).

TABLE 3.1

Senators' Explicit, Implicit, and Nonracial Remarks on the 1964 Civil Rights Act

	Senators' Own Remarks			Quotes from Outside Sources		
	Non-South For	Deep South Against	Outer South Against	Non-South For	Deep South Against	Outer South Against
Number of Speeches	8	10	8	8	10	6[a]
Explicit	9.4%	5.4%	3.8%	12.7%	9.3%	18.3%
Implicit	19.4%	16.9%	15.5%	22.5%	8.7%	8.3%
Nonracial	71.2%	77.7%	80.7%	64.8%	82.0%	73.4%
Total	100%	100%	100%	100%	100%	100%

Note: Entries are the percentages of each senator's sentences, averaged separately for proponents and opponents. (Deep South = SC, GA, MS, AL, LA; Outer South = TX, AR, FL, TN, NC, VA.)

[a] Two speeches were missing remarks from outside sources, so they were excluded.

"whites," "race," "racial," "Negroes," "Martin Luther King," "SCLC," and similar words) or implicit ("sit-ins," "agitators," "protest," "boycott," "march," "demand," "activist," "civil disobedience," "constitutional rights," "minority," "mob," "quota," and similar words). A word belongs in the implicit category if it does not directly refer to African Americans or whites but had a racial association at the time (e.g., "activist" can mean a person active on behalf of any cause, but in the context of the civil rights bill and the highly salient activities of the civil rights movement, its primary association is likely to have been a person active on behalf of civil rights).[9]

Table 3.1 shows the percentages of explicit and implicit sentences spoken by senators from the Deep South, Outer South, and outside the South.[10] The table presents two sets of results, one for remarks initiated by the senator himself, and the other for remarks quoted by the senator from newspapers, letters, or other outside sources. Those representing the Deep South probably faced more pressure than those representing the Outer South to demonstrate that they conformed to national norms. It was the Deep South where opposition to racial progress was greatest, and that was considered to be in grossest violation

---

[9] Intercoder reliability for each category is high, ranging from 100 to 96 percent, calculated by check-coding approximately 12 percent of the sample.

[10] I divided the number of each senator's explicit and implicit sentences by the senator's total number of sentences. The totals are calculated separately for each type of rhetorical form (senator's own remarks versus senator's quotes from other sources). Remarks provided as an answer to a question from the floor were set aside. I sampled 480 nonprocedural lines for each speech. Within each region, senators and speeches were sampled randomly with replacement.

of the growing national norm of racial equality. Thus Deep South senators, while speaking in a national forum, may have felt more keenly the need to prove their rhetorical conformity to the national norm. Accordingly, they may have demonstrated a stronger preference for implicit over explicit expression. Responsiveness to the norm should also be higher in senators' own remarks than in quoted remarks that are clearly marked as belonging to others. We might therefore find more explicit remarks in senators' own words than in the words they introduce from outside sources—but only for those senators who intend to oppose civil rights but remain within the norm.

The results in Table 3.1 for senators' own remarks show that proponents of civil rights relied on explicit rhetoric more than opponents. However, each group used roughly the same degree of implicit expressions. Because of their unequal use of explicit sentences, the ratio of implicit to explicit is roughly two to one for proponents of civil rights, but as high as four to one for opponents. Opponents of civil rights were reluctant to rely on explicitly racial rhetoric, but supporters had no qualms about doing so. In place of explicit expressions, opponents of civil rights relied on implicit ones. They—and only they—carried a liability from explicit rhetoric, and thus they—and only they—tried to couch their position in terms that were meant to appear racially neutral.

Senators' use of quotations from outside sources is also revealing. Supporters of civil rights did not distinguish between their own remarks and quotations. They relied on roughly the same percentage of implicit and explicit expressions in quotations and in their own remarks. In both types of comments, these senators used explicit racial language to portray blacks as deserving of civil rights. But the quotations of the opponents had considerably more explicit rhetoric than did their own remarks. These senators felt they could not directly charge that, if given civil rights, blacks would threaten the well-being of whites, commit crimes, perpetrate sexual offenses, or refuse to work. Instead, the opponents used words printed in newspapers and letters to do so for them. Mississippi senator John Stennis, for example, read from a newspaper that "Negroes might start killing the white people in Mississippi pretty soon," a quotation attributed in the newspaper to an African-American man (*Cong. Rec.*, 1964, 7070). That statement, which appears to be uttered by a black person and vetted by an authoritative newspaper, is likely to seem less of a norm violation than a senator's direct assertion that, if given equal rights, blacks would slaughter whites.

There were regional differences among the opponents that suggest the impact of the norm was not uniform. The Deep South senators' percentage of explicit words nearly doubled when using quotations, while the Outer South senators' percentage more than quadrupled. As their use of explicit sentences rose, the opponents' percentage of implicit words dropped—roughly by half. Thus, the implicit-to-explicit ratio for the Deep South's quotations is only one to one, much lower than the three-to-one ratio these senators used in their own remarks. The difference is sharper still among the Outer South senators, whose ratio actually reverses in the quotations from outside sources to two to one in favor of explicit sentences. In their own remarks, opponents of civil rights tended to bury explicitly racial rhetoric among implicit remarks; but when quoting others' words, the reverse is true, with opponents less prone than proponents to submerging explicit rhetoric in implicit language.[11] Opponents apparently felt free to use racial language when they believed that the normative constraints on doing so were weaker.

Senators opposing the landmark civil rights bill in 1964 spoke in a way that suggests a very strong norm against racism. Supporters of civil rights felt considerably freer to use explicitly racial words because they were arguing for greater racial equality. Opponents of civil rights were reluctant to speak frankly of race, preferring to rely on words that had racial associations but avoided direct references. But when explicitly racial language was clearly marked as someone else's, opponents felt freer to use it. Relying on others' words to introduce normatively extreme rhetoric allows the speaker to utter the controversial words without eliciting as much condemnation. That the nature of opponents' racial rhetoric fluctuated across these rhetorical forms (own versus others' words) suggests that the shift from explicit to implicit language came in response to normative pressure.

Thus, as the norm of racial inequality declined, and the norm of racial equality spread, the rhetoric of white supremacy changed. In national forums, white supremacists ceased to warn of "beastly black rapists" and reverted, at first, to paternalistic arguments about the well-being of African Americans, and then to race-free rhetoric. This shift should not be exaggerated—in 1964 white supremacists still attacked black qualifications for equal status and power. But they began to use the language of equality and to criticize African Americans more indirectly. By 1964, congressional debate reflected southern racists' growing wariness of explicitly racial rhetoric and their reliance on implicitly racial rhetoric. They modulated their rhetoric to the audience; at the national level, rhetoric was taking on a more coded character, while resistance in the South was still strident and explicitly racial.

SOUTHERN WHITE POLITICIANS AT HOME, 1950–1965

When speaking to southern audiences, southern politicians were still using relatively explicit racial language and defending racial inequality more stridently than in national forums. This stridency became more pronounced after the shock to racial arrangements provided by the *Brown* decision. Like nothing else, *Brown* spurred southerners to an all-out rhetorical defense of segregation

---

[11] A similar pattern is obtained for words as a percentage of lines spoken.

(Black 1976). The vast majority of southern politicians endorsed the formal Declaration of Constitutional Principles that laid out the South's resistance, thus closing ranks around segregation. The once-moderate governor of Arkansas, Orval Faubus, was simply reflecting southern consensus when he said during the Little Rock Central High crisis of 1957, "I will never open the public schools as integrated institutions" (Woodward 1966, 161–162, 167).

Protecting segregation, however, now called for rhetoric that would legitimize it in the eyes of those with the power to undermine it. Even in the Deep South, segregationist stands were accompanied by rhetorical moves designed to lend greater authority (Braden 1980). Politicians recognized that simply asserting the principles of white supremacy would no longer work, and they turned to other grounds for justifying segregation. Accordingly, white supremacists repeatedly declared their intention to pursue resistance through legal means. In fact, they repeatedly claimed that the Constitution was on their side and had been violated by the Supreme Court and the presidency. They "insisted they were not anti-Catholic or anti-Semitic and not sympathetic with the Klan." In other words, as had the Dixiecrats, they emphasized that their motivation was nonracial. Certainly, they assured the nation, they were innocent of bigotry (Braden 1980, 338–339).

The rhetoric of the Citizens' Councils, the main legal organization established to resist desegregation during the 1950s, makes a good case in point. Their rhetoric evolved from racial to nonracial exactly at the time they attempted to gain influence outside the South. Neil McMillen's study of the Citizens' Councils found that in the beginning, their official publication "was devoted entirely to the race issue." But increasingly, as the organization sought to expand beyond the South, the publication began to deal with such issues as Communism, centralized government, and the welfare state. The leaders of the movement, McMillen found, did this strategically, in order to attract a larger following outside the South, including such states as California.

The architect of the Citizens' Councils effort on behalf of the California anti-open housing initiative in 1966, William K. Shearer, was particularly adept at implicit rhetoric. He was an "avowed white supremacist," according to McMillen, but "preferred the subtleties of innuendo to head-on assault." Rather than referring to California's whites, he referred to the "majority community." Rather than discussing racial minorities, he targeted the "liberal political power structure." He did refer to "racial minority voting blocs" but in conjunction with "economic" and "ethnic" voting blocs (McMillen 1994, 145, 192, 201). As we shall see, Shearer was not a lone rhetorical innovator; many public figures who supported segregation were engaging in similar rhetorical moves at this time.

The *Brown* decision also profoundly shaped southern elections, but in the opposite rhetorical direction. Earl Black found that during the decade after *Brown,* southern elections were powered by quite explicit racial appeals designed to assure white voters that their leaders would protect them from racial change.[12]

Thus, when racial conservatives targeted audiences outside the South, they turned away from explicit and toward implicit resistance to racial equality. But they were doing the opposite when speaking to their constituents at home, particularly while conducting electoral campaigns.

THE NEW NORM IS CODIFIED AND THE NATIONAL PARTY SYSTEM ALIGNS ON RACE

In the 1960s, the advancing norm of racial equality finally intersected with the national party system's lurch toward an alignment on the matter of race. The result was the rise of implicit racial appeals in national campaigns. As in the past, the parties' alignment on race, and the rise of racial campaign appeals, were sparked by a major shock to racial arrangements. The shock came in the form of a crescendo of civil rights activism and a spate of formal government actions on civil rights.

[12] Based on his examination of southern gubernatorial elections during the period 1950 to 1973, Black generated a three-fold typology of campaign rhetoric: militant segregationist, moderate segregationist, and nonsegregationist. Militant segregationists featured unqualified support for segregation in most of their speeches and appealed to racial prejudice. This was the prevalent—and victorious—campaign mode in 1950, when Dixiecrat sentiment still ran high. *Brown* returned it to popularity and victory from 1954 to 1965 (Black 1976, 14). These candidates often vowed, as did J. Lindsay Almond, to "fight relentlessly to prevent amalgamation of races in Virginia" (Black 1976, 14). They often used the term "bloc vote" to taint their opponents with the charge of black support (Black 1976, 239–240). Moderate segregationists also defended segregation, but in a more qualified and subdued way. They concentrated on nonracial issues and did not appeal to racial prejudice. In fact, they sometimes charged the opponent with race-baiting. Between 1954 and 1966, candidates who ran as moderate segregationists during the first Democratic primary often turned extremists in the runoff. This is easily understandable in light of the purpose of the runoff: to test the white supremacist mettle of the candidates, and to allow whites a veto over candidates deemed insufficiently safe for white dominance (Black 1976, 199, 234; Woodward 1971, 373). Moderate segregationists often prevailed in the early 1950s, before *Brown* (Black 1976, 29–30). Moderates include Terry Sanford of North Carolina and Earl Long of Louisiana. Long supported segregation ("I am one million percent for segregation") but also disclaimed race-baiting: "I am the best friend the colored and the white man has ever had. Putting one man against another is not the Christian thing to do. If I have to do that, then I don't want to be governor" (Black 1976, 73–75). Other successful antiracial tactics were to denounce the opponent for "inciting hate" (Black 1976, 15). Black argues that using extreme supremacist rhetoric before the *Brown* decision was less effective than the more moderate kind, pointing to several extremists who failed to get even 10 percent of the primary vote. But his numbers show that users of the extreme strategy were three times more numerous among Democratic nominees (that is, winners of the first primary) than they were among all major Democratic candidates (Black 1976, 30). Some of the most vociferous racist candidates of the early 1950s were also artless campaigners (Black 1976, 34).

Nothing embodied that activism more than the nonviolent direct action of the civil rights movement, which was launched in earnest in 1954 and reached its peak in 1963–65. In a strategic attempt to show the injustice of racial inequality, the movement increasingly engaged in tactics that highlighted the brutality of the South's white supremacy (Branch 1988; McAdam 1982; Morris 1984). It succeeded in dramatically accelerating the pace of change, prodding national institutions to formalize racial equality with major government actions.

The central institutions of the federal government followed suit. The Supreme Court continued to issue racially egalitarian decisions in education, housing, public accommodations, and voting. Although his rhetoric outpaced his actions, in his major addresses John F. Kennedy strongly endorsed the *Brown* decision and the country's general course toward racial equality.[13] The 1963 civil rights bill Kennedy sent to Congress in the wake of the Birmingham clashes between the civil rights movement and white supremacists was, up to then, the most ambitious civil rights legislation of the century (O'Reilly 1995; Sitkoff 1978; Woodward 1966, 181). Upon assuming the presidency, Lyndon Johnson quickly established himself as the most racially egalitarian president in U.S. history. Under his leadership, Congress passed the landmark 1964 Civil Rights Act. His voting rights address to a special joint session of Congress in the wake of the violence in Selma, Alabama, was, according to the historian C. Vann Woodward, "the most stirring appeal yet made by an American President in behalf of civil rights." In it Johnson introduced a powerful new bill to guarantee voting rights, and concluded with the motto of the civil rights movement: "We shall overcome" (Woodward 1966). In a lopsided vote, Congress passed the 1965 Voting Rights Act, perhaps the most effective civil rights law ever passed (Sitkoff 1993, 180).

The president and Congress probably would not have shocked racial arrangements as they did had not the civil rights movement linked the race issue with southern extremism. That link saved the Republican party in the elections during the Reconstruction period, when it moved itself and the country's laws to the racial left. Now that link facilitated the passage of unprecedented egalitarian legislation. As the civil rights movement accelerated its use of nonviolent action, it succeeded in reviving the negative images of the white South, so potent during Reconstruction, making them the most salient ingredient in the civil rights debates of 1963–65. The frame of southern rebelliousness and "intransigence" again dominated white discourse. Kennedy's historic 1963 civil rights speech highlighted not only the principle of equality of opportunity,

[13] At such public moments as his inaugural and State of the Union addresses, he proclaimed the Brown decision "both legally and morally right," touted the aim of equal opportunity, argued for reducing the significance of racial differences, and welcomed racial diversity (Condit and Lucaites 1993, 197–198; Woodward 1966, 172). Kennedy's sympathetic phone call to Coretta Scott King during Martin Luther King's imprisonment in 1960 was also a highly visible symbolic gesture toward both racial equality and black voters (Egerton 1994).

but also the imperative of curbing southern white violence.[14] Witness also the influential journalist Theodore H. White's description of the Senate debate about the Civil Rights Act of 1964:

> For eighty years, ever since the end of Reconstruction, a coalition of southern senators had dominated the Senate of the United States, letting it act only if the Senate chose to act outside of, and indifferent to, the condition of humiliation of the Negro American in the South. Year after year, by threat or use of their unlimited freedom of debate, they had blackmailed Senate and country not to intrude in the relation between black and white Americans in the states of the old Confederacy. Their numbers, their seniority, the outstanding ability of several of them, and, above all, their skill in filibuster and parliamentary process had made the United States Senate their club, their home, their institution. Here they had reconquered by wile and defended by cunning what Lee had surrendered at Appomattox. Now it was being taken away from them. . . .
>
> We shall examine later the mechanical process and the strategy by which the northern and western senators, under the leadership of Hubert Humphrey and Thomas Kuchel, were to impose the will of the nation on the southern irreconcilables. (White 1965, 171–172; emphasis mine)
>
> Every one of these [civil rights] proposals . . . was anathema maranatha to the Old Guard of southern senators who, generation after generation, had here held unbroken the front their grandfathers had lost on the battlefields of the Civil War. Were it not for the titanic importance of the substance of the bill itself, one could say that their defeat in this last stand was the major historic event of the spring of 1964—for their hour had come. (White 1965, 183)

The movement's tactics were the immediate impetus to both pieces of legislation, but especially to the Voting Rights Act. Lyndon Johnson proposed the landmark law just hours after civil rights marchers had been beaten with bullwhips and rubber hoses wrapped in barbed wire in an orgy of white southern violence that was broadcast live during a primetime television broadcast of the film *Judgment at Nuremberg* (Sitkoff 1993, 179–180; Klinker and Smith 1999, 277). The brutality of white southerners seemed to many whites across the country a clear violation of the growing norm of basic racial equality, an at-

---

[14] Kennedy said:

This nation was founded by men of many nations and backgrounds. It was founded on the principle that all men are created equal, and that the rights of every man are diminished when the rights of one man are threatened. . . . It ought to be possible . . . for every American to enjoy the privileges of being American without regard to his race or color. . . . Every American ought to have the right to be treated as he would wish to be treated, as one would wish his children to be treated. But this is not the case. . . . It is better to settle these matters in the courts than on the streets, and new laws are needed at every level. . . . The old code of equity law under which we live commands for every wrong a remedy, but in too many parts of the country wrongs are inflicted on Negro citizens and there are no remedies at law. Unless the Congress acts, their only remedy is in the street. (White 1965, 181)

tempt, as Johnson said in his address, to "flout the Constitution" (Sitkoff 1993, 180). Civil rights laws seemed to many to be, simultaneously, a fitting punishment for that violation and a way to recognize that, as Johnson said, "the real hero of this struggle is the American Negro," who should be elevated for his "persistent bravery and faith in American democracy" (Sitkoff 1993, 179).

Thus from 1964 on, the Democratic party made the civil rights issue its own. The Republican party, quite conspicuously, went in the other direction, hence the intersection of the norm of racial equality with a party split on race.

A drawing that appeared in an early 1860s issue of *Harper's*, featuring a wounded black Union soldier symbolizing patriotic heroism, escorted into Congress by a woman symbolizing liberty and justice, would have fit well with the discourse of the 1960s. The challenge to racial inequality had reached its second historical peak, and the parties once again chose sides, this time with the Republicans on the right and the Democrats on the left.

The 1964 Presidential Campaign

Lyndon B. Johnson was quick to position himself and the Democratic party as the champion of civil rights. His first State of the Union address promised equal opportunity regardless of race in a variety of spheres (Condit and Lucaites 1993, 198). He would accept "nothing less than the full assimilation of more than twenty million Negroes into American life" (Woodward 1966, 184–185). His Great Society vision included equality for African Americans in an explicit way. By fully incorporating African Americans into their society, Johnson stressed, whites would only increase the glory and bounty of their nation, not detract from their enjoyment of it.[15] His vision of a grand civilization decreased the salience of group antagonism and replaced it with the idea of the common good.

The problem with this message is that it was susceptible to undercutting from the right. For the moment, conditions had not sufficiently ripened for the opposition to take advantage of this weakness. Nevertheless, there were attempts to do so.

One challenge from the right came from within Democratic ranks. George Wallace contested Johnson's reelection in 1964 in three northern Democratic primaries, garnering large majorities of white working-class precincts that previously had been firmly in the liberal camp and winning well over a third of the total primary vote in those states. He did this with almost no financial support and despite well-organized opposition (Rosenstone et al. 1984, 110; Woodward 1966, 184).

---

[15] "The Great Society rests on abundance and liberty for all. It demands an end to poverty and racial injustice—to which we are totally committed in our time, but that is just the beginning" (White 1965, 411–412).

Then there was the challenge from the Republican party. Barry Goldwater had been drafted to become the party's presidential nominee, and he was about as disinterested in racial problems as any politician could be in 1964. But a presidential campaign is not a one-person show. At the behest of his advisers and members of his coalition, the Arizona senator criticized the Civil Rights Act, which he had voted against, not because of its goal (he proclaimed that "it is wise and just for Negro children to attend the same schools as whites"), but because it called for federal intervention in states' affairs (Edsall and Edsall 1991, 40). The norm had changed so much that Goldwater could not be expected, even by white southerners, to criticize racial integration on principle, or to defend segregation. Instead, he could—and, given his libertarian orientation, effortlessly did—adopt the language developed over the last decade and a half by southern representatives. This was the language of states' rights and opposition to federal intervention. Goldwater added his own emphasis on libertarianism, stressing the supreme importance of individual choice:

> It is wrong to compel children to attend schools restricted to members of their own race. . . . It is also wrong to forbid children to attend schools restricted to members of another race. I condemn that sort of segregation because it is *compulsory*.
>
> There is another way that people may separate and distinguish themselves from each other. Far from being compulsory, it is the necessary result of freedom—the freedom of association. Throughout this land of ours, we find people forming churches, clubs and neighborhoods with other families of similar beliefs, similar tastes, and similar ethnic backgrounds. No one would think of insisting that neighborhoods be "integrated" with fixed proportions of Anglo-Americans, German-Americans, Swedish-Americans—or of Catholics, Protestants and Jews.
>
> To me, it is just as wrong to take some children out of the schools they would normally attend and bus them to others. . . . It is wrong . . . because it reintroduces through the back door the very principle of allocation by race that makes compulsory segregation morally wrong and offensive to freedom. (Kessel 1968, 209–210; emphasis in original)

Goldwater was doubtlessly sincere. By relying on the principle of laissez-faire, he was not parroting the coded language of southern white supremacists, but speaking his "conservative conscience."

His southern fellow travelers, however, orchestrated his campaign in such a way that the libertarian message took on explicit racial meaning for the right audience. Goldwater personally tried to avoid racial appeals or references of any kind (Kessel 1968, 209). He may have been motivated by moral considerations as well as the necessity of hanging on to liberal Republicans. For these reasons it was not until October 16 that Goldwater made a major campaign speech on the subject of civil rights, in Chicago, and "he did not even mention civil rights in the South until the closing hours of the campaign" (Kessel 1968, 209). However, Goldwater's southern backers only wanted one anti-integration speech. The October 16 address satisfied that criterion handsomely. Much of the speech was repeated in a television program devoted to civil rights and filmed in Columbia, South Carolina, in the company of Strom Thurmond and other well-known segregationists. It was widely broadcast across the South (Kessel 1968, 216).

Aside from the speech on civil rights, Goldwater's appeal to states' rights had no references to "blacks," "whites," or "race." It was not explicitly racial. But because, in 1964, states' rights were inseparably tied to the issue of race, Goldwater's message is likely to have been most effective as an implicitly racial appeal. Indeed, Goldwater's general conservatism was highly unpopular when perceived as an attack on cherished New Deal programs (Kelley 1983; see also Converse et al. 1965). Principled, across-the-board conservatism gained very few votes in 1964. When translated into racial conservatism, however, Goldwater's message did resonate, at least with racially conservative white voters. With the exception of his home state of Arizona, Goldwater managed to carry only the Deep South states. In 1964, as well as historically, the Deep South was the region most intent on maintaining racial hierarchy. There, "each one of the [New Deal] government programs Goldwater sought to overturn had substantial, if not overwhelming, majority support" (Edsall and Edsall 1991, 40). Thus, it was not Goldwater's general conservatism that appealed to most of his voters so much as the racial meaning of his stand.

The 1964 election, and the civil rights revolution in which it was embedded, pushed the party system to align along racial lines. Carmines and Stimson have documented that perceptions of the parties changed markedly in 1964. Before 1964, most Americans saw no difference between the parties on civil rights, while afterward, most were able to correctly point to the Democratic party as the champion of civil rights and the Republican party as the opposition (1989, 165–166). House Democrats moved to the left of House Republicans, Senate Democrats to the left of Senate Republicans (1989, 63).[16] That year also marked the beginning of the geometric increase in black electoral mobilization by Democrats and blacks' decisive abandonment of the party of Lincoln (Huckfeldt and Kohfeld 1989, 14–15).

All this does not mean that most whites made their presidential choice based on racial considerations—quite the contrary. Johnson's large victory margin resulted from framing the contest in New Deal terms (Kelley 1983, 98). As the Edsalls put it, the affiliation of many whites with the Democratic party was grounded in "such programs as Social Security, unemployment compensation, the G.I. Bill, and federal mortgage assistance" (1991, 12). The Democratic party

---

[16] Petrocik (1981) shows that in the 1950s the party cleavage was based on nonracial economic issues, and voters placed both parties at the moderate center on civil rights. In the 1960s the Democrats were placed on the left and the Republicans at center, and by the 1970s, the Republicans were placed on the right.

had provided middle- and working-class whites with a stream of benefits, to the extent that it had become, by their own reckoning, "their" party.

Johnson demonstrated that he understood the strategic importance of trumping racial antagonism with economic well-being. In a speech he delivered on May 8, 1964, to an Atlanta audience, he stressed the economic benefits provided by Democratic administrations to everyone in the South:

> Franklin D. Roosevelt sent me to the South in nineteen and thirty-six to survey conditions in our southern states. . . . The South was then a forgotten and a forbidding land. Its mills were idle and its banks were shut. Misery was on the faces of its farmers and hunger scarred the faces of its children. . . . Many thought the South had suffered its final defeat. These were the faint of heart and I was not among them. And, thank God, the people of Georgia were not among them. The results are here in the new South. The average income in the South has increased six times since nineteen and thirty, rising much faster than the national average. . . . Nearly every home in Georgia has water and electricity and every child can go to school. (Kessel 1968, 234–235)

This emphasis on the New Deal and on common economic concerns allowed Johnson some breathing room with white voters to pursue his platform of racial equality. Also contributing to that breathing room was his rhetoric against race-baiting. As a southern politician, Johnson was familiar with the southern populist dilemma. As did the populists, Johnson was pursuing a racially egalitarian platform while trying to mobilize racially resentful whites—not as whites but as a working class. He pursued a rhetorical strategy first developed by populists in the 1890s: convince working-class whites that their true interests lay with the party of the "common man" and against racial antagonism. In a New Orleans campaign speech he reminded his audience of the deleterious effect of race-baiting: "All they ever hear at election time is "Negro, Negro, Negro!' The kind of speech they should have been hearing is about the economy and what a great future we could have in the South if we just meet our economic problems" (Kessel 1968, 235).

Johnson did not need to make heavy use of his antiracist counterstrategy because economic and class issues worked for him well enough. The Republicans could not yet claim the mantle of defenders of the common man against the "special interests," which became a reference to racial minorities and other liberal groups. Black rebellion in northern cities had begun in the summer of 1964, as had white northern backlash (Woodward 1966, 183), but it still lacked momentum. Working-class whites were still sufficiently satisfied with the Democratic program not to be drawn away by racial appeals.[17]

---

[17] The Edsalls cite Gallup Poll data that an overwhelming majority of nonsouthern whites still supported the civil rights movement as late as March 1965 (1991, 36). Throughout 1965 Johnson's approval ratings remained quite high, and public support for his Great Society programs,

IMPLICIT APPEALS IN SOUTHERN ELECTIONS AFTER 1965

After 1965, the norm of racial equality became sufficiently powerful to affect not only the words intended for national consumption but the last bastion of explicitly racial appeals: southern elections. Landmark legislation passed by Congress, decisions issued by the Supreme Court, firm rhetoric and actions of two presidents, and whites' public opinion all combined to form a norm both injunctive and descriptive.[18] By 1964 a two-thirds majority of whites sampled in national surveys endorsed the right of blacks to buy a home over the right of whites to keep blacks out of white neighborhoods (Schuman et al. 1985, Table 3.2). Also by that year, only 25 percent endorsed segregation as a principle (Schuman et al. 1985, Table 3.1). By the middle to late 1960s, most whites expressed a willingness to vote for a black for president. Educated whites in the South were also abandoning segregation as a principle (Schuman et al. 1985, 78).

In response, the discourse of campaigns at the national level had changed dramatically, from explicit to implicit; now the norm was sufficiently strong to trickle down and affect southern campaign discourse at home. During the early 1970s most southern states began to elect what Earl Black calls nonsegregationist governors. Nonsegregationists fall into one of the following categories:

1. Whatever his private beliefs, the candidate does not campaign openly as a segregationist. For all practical purposes, he seeks to avoid explicit stands on racial issues; he champions neither segregation nor desegregation.

2. The candidate does not describe himself as a segregationist or as an integrationist, but he expresses qualified support for some black demands. Statements concerning race tend to be indirect and highly abstract (for example, the candidate favors "equality of opportunity"). Black support is welcomed.

3. The candidate explicitly and unambiguously favors various Negro rights. Racial segregation may be explicitly repudiated; black support is welcomed. (Black 1976, 15–16)

This campaign style, which began as "a curiosity" in 1965, became increasingly frequent after the mid-1960s.[19]

---

including the least favored—the antipoverty program—was overwhelming (73 percent approved of his antipoverty efforts) (Edsall and Edsall 1991, 47–48). This began to change with the broadcasts of the massive riots in Watts, which broke out eleven days after the signing of the Voting Rights Act.

[18] Kennedy and Johnson were probably influential through somewhat different means of social influence—one by his martyrdom and the other by his former position as a racial conservative from Texas.

[19] Examples include the campaigns of Jimmy Carter in Georgia, John Connally in Texas, Winthrop Rockefeller in Arkansas, and Linwood Holton in Virginia.

One possible explanation for the southern abandonment of explicitly racial appeals is that, with white southern support for Democrats gradually declining after 1966, Democratic candidates found themselves significantly dependent on African-American voters (Black 1976, 85; Sundquist 1983, 364). The year 1965, during which the landmark Voting Rights Act was enacted, clearly emerges in Black's data as a watershed for candidates' campaign styles. The shift toward a nonsegregationist style may thus be due to the enfranchisement of African Americans by that act, as Black argues. Black registration and voting did in fact increase dramatically after 1965. Registration rates among African Americans in the Deep South nearly doubled between 1964 and 1969, surging from 36 to 65 percent. The fifty-eight counties where federal registrars were employed by the Justice Department to eliminate discrimination elected more than 120 African-American officials by 1968 (Nieman 1991, 180). In addition, SNCC's Voter Education Project enhanced the Voting Right Act's effect (Timpone 1995). Thus, the black empowerment explanation seems valid.

However, black empowerment is at best an incomplete answer. Southern politicians could not have been learning their rhetorical lessons from defeat at the hands of black voters, as candidates who used explicit racial appeals fared no worse at the polls than nonsegregationists. Voters were not consistently punishing candidates' rhetorical failure to adhere to the new norm. The nonsegregationist campaign style did in fact become much more common than the alternatives after 1965, but not because it trumped the other styles on Election Day. From Black's data on elections after 1965, it is apparent that with the sole exception of Governor John J. McKeithen's reelection in Louisiana on a nonsegregationist platform, no nonsegregationist candidate who ran against an extreme segregationist won the Democratic first primary in the South until 1973. Nonsegregationist campaigns seem more successful than the others, but only because nonsegregationists ran mostly against each other.[20] When nonsegregationists advanced to the runoff, they ran into a brick wall, losing at high rates to extreme segregationists (based on data reported in Black 1976, 225–226). Despite repeated evidence that segregationist rhetoric was still a winning strategy, segregationist rhetoric declined from 1965. That is, explicitly racial campaigns were in decline for eight years before the alternative proved itself a victorious strategy. At least in the Deep South, explicit messages did not decline and implicit rhetoric did not rise from the electoral defeat of explicitly racial campaigns.

Neither can the anticipation of winning black votes account for the rise of the nonsegregationist campaign style. It cannot explain why even candidates who had very little hope of attracting black votes even with nonsegregationist

---

[20] Black estimates that "three-fifths of the contested first primaries from 1966 through 1973 matched nonsegregationists against each other, compared to less than a tenth of the primaries before 1966" (1976, 194).

rhetoric would abandon explicitly racial campaigns. Black's data show that Republicans, who won with almost no black votes, and white Democrats who decided to forsake black votes in favor of white backlash votes, also abandoned the explicit racial language that went with militant segregationism.

The norm of racial equality can, however, explain the behavior of candidates across the ideological spectrum, Democrats and Republicans, defeated and victorious. Nineteen sixty-five emerges as a watershed year in the switch to nonsegregationism because in that year the president and Congress aligned themselves firmly behind racial equality, nudging the norm of racial equality past the threshold of influence over the Deep South. With the passage of the Voting Rights Act, influential national elites signaled in a powerful way that the nation expected that racial equality would characterize the conduct of southern elections. Increasing numbers of candidates may have decided not to risk the consequences of violating what they perceived to be a well-entrenched national norm.

The danger of alienating crucial white groups closer to home also seems to have been a key to the southern attentiveness to the new norm. In Governor Albert K. Watson's 1970 reelection campaign in South Carolina, for example, business elites at home as well as national newspapers signaled their displeasure with his explicit appeals (Sundquist 1983, 363).[21] The norm most likely spread in part through learning from similarly situated candidates and from party officials. Southern candidates were not each inventing the rhetorical wheel anew in their search for political viability. They were not simply individuals seeking reelection, but a collective body of leaders making its way through a rapidly changing world of racial alignments and public rhetorical norms. Each new candidate had, by the late 1960s, many examples of others similar to himself who had made dramatic changes in their rhetorical tactics. There was not only the rhetorical example set by Barry Goldwater in his presidential bid in 1964, but also those set by southern congressmen who had been negotiating the waters of rudimentary racial codes since the 1950s under the watchful eye of the national press and of northern members of Congress.

Those who abandoned segregationism and explicit appeals, however, did not abandon all appeals to race. Republicans who engaged in what Black calls a moderate segregationist strategy often made relatively implicit appeals. In 1966 and 1973, Republicans employing moderate segregationist campaigns were able to beat Democrats who adopted a nonsegregationist tactic in the

---

[21] "Dozens . . . of South Carolina conservatives from the established world of business and the suburbs were outraged by the pungently racist Republican campaign," reported the columnists Rowland Evans and Robert Novak in the *Washington Post*. More recently, after the NAACP organized a tourism boycott to prod South Carolina to take down the Confederate flag from its state capitol, some local elites urged the state to comply because "this issue . . . [is] casting South Carolina in a very unfavorable light nationally" (Jim Davenport, "Confederate Flag Rally in S. C.," Associated Press, January 17, 2000).

general election, suggesting that moderate segregationism was still a viable strategy well after 1965.[22] In fact, Black's data (through 1973) suggest that Republicans facing nonsegregationist Democrats were slightly more likely to win when they pursued a moderate segregationist strategy than when they pursued a nonsegregationist strategy (based on Black 1976, 262, Table 40).[23] A subtle reference to race may have worked better than an explicit reference and better than no reference at all.

The example of George Wallace illustrates these elements of the argument. George Wallace was the most effective practitioner of implicit appeals in the South. But he did not turn to this style until after the watershed year of 1965. Wallace's 1966 primary campaign (conducted through his wife, Lurleen) was an exemplar of the implicit style. In contrast to Wallace's two previous gubernatorial campaigns, Black writes, "Strident segregationist oratory disappeared, to be replaced by a set of euphemisms which indicated that the Wallaces would firmly resist further racial changes" ("We will continue to stand up for Alabama") (Black 1976, 56). Ray Jenkins wrote of the Wallaces' 1966 gubernatorial campaign:

> An outsider might be astonished to find that nowadays Wallace never deals with the race issue per se in his campaign oratory. Pugnacious outcries such as "segregation today, segregation forever" in his inaugural speech as Governor have now given way to a more sophisticated approach: "We will awaken the nation to the liberal-Socialistic-Communist design to destroy local government in America." This approach is not too subtle for rural Alabama "red-necks" who understand that he means to preserve segregation, nor is it so crude that it entirely robs him of respectability elsewhere in Alabama and the nation. . . . To the southerner, Wallace's philosophy means keeping the status quo; to a small businessman in Peoria, it might mean an outcry against Washington bureaucracy. (quoted in Black 1976, 186)

Wallace gained legitimacy for himself through ambiguity, by forging a set of rhetorical symbols with meanings both racial and nonracial. He thus managed to conform to the new norm of racial equality but still appeal to racially resentful white voters.

---

[22] This was true, for example, as late as 1973, in Virginia. The contest was close enough (a 0.7 percent victory margin) that it may well have turned on the Republican's use of busing to tar his opponent as a radical on racial matters (Black 1976, 274).

[23] There were a few post-1965 defeats of segregationists in general elections (Black 1976, 262). In 1968 and 1970 Republicans who took up the militant segregationist style lost to Democratic nonsegregationists, as did Republicans with moderate segregationist campaigns in 1970 and 1972. However, this apparent success is not what it seems; these Democrats had pursued a segregationist style in the primaries (Black 1976, 261, 269, 272, 275, 326–334). This suggests that to some extent Democrats proved their white supremacist credentials during the primaries, and could afford silence on race during the general election campaign.

Wallace did not employ this strategy in order to win black votes. Wallace could have been under few delusions that blacks would flock to him in significant numbers two years after he had run on a highly segregationist platform (much later, after he had completely changed his racial politics, Wallace did succeed in gaining black votes). More likely, the Voting Rights Act and Johnson's determined stand with the civil rights movement in the South signaled a shift in norms about what was acceptable for southern candidates to say even while on their own turf.

As with the Fifteenth Amendment nearly a century before, it was not the wrath of African-American voters as much as the determination of the most influential whites in the land, backed by crucial white groups in the state, that worried white supremacists. They wanted to show that they conformed to the new law and the new norm in some way, but in the most minimal, symbolic way possible. They had to do so if they were to gain a constituency beyond the Deep South, as Wallace undoubtedly wanted in the mid-1960s (Carter 1996). Yet they needed to keep mobilizing white voters. The solution to these contradictory needs was to craft implicitly racial appeals.[24]

Black's category of moderate segregationism is not the only one that potentially includes implicit appeals. His data suggest that the nonsegregationist style in practice stood for racial conservatism more than for racial liberalism; it too could subsume implicitly racial appeals. Of the sixteen contested first Democratic primaries held between 1965 and 1973 in which nonsegregationists faced each other, ten were won by the more racially conservative of the two leading nonsegregationist candidates (Black 1976, 196), and two featured candidates indistinguishable from each other on race. Only in four of the sixteen did the more racially liberal candidates win (and of these, only two went on to win the general election). The runoff contests show a similar pattern (Black 1976, 238–239). The nonsegregationist style, it seems, is essentially a strategy of silence on race. The virtue of silence is that it can suggest multiple stances, the more extreme of which can be denied, but cultivated by implicit reference.

White southern opinion on race also casts the nonsegregationist style as one conducive to implicit racial appeals. During the period 1972–84, white southerners had moderately positive feelings toward "blacks"; however, these feelings were flanked on one side by overwhelmingly positive evaluations of "whites," and, on the other side, by overwhelmingly negative evaluations of "black militants" (based on pooled NES samples, reported in Black and Black 1987, 62, 69). More recently, Kuklinski et al. found that southerners continue to have more negative attitudes toward African Americans—but conceal them on standard survey measures (1997). This is fertile territory for a strategy based on implicitly racial appeals.

[24] Most likely, candidates who conformed to the new norm eventually experienced a genuine change of heart on the matter of basic civil rights for blacks, but probably not on other matters of race.

Black hints at this in the closing pages of his book: "The decline of explicitly segregationist rhetoric does not necessarily mean that white politicians have given up race as a campaign issue. . . . Many white candidates have found and will find ways to appeal to anti-black prejudices without describing themselves as segregationists" (Black 1976, 304). Southern politics awaits a systematic analysis that rests on the distinction between explicit and implicit messages. But southern politics, while distinctive, is not the only politics that generates implicitly racial appeals.

RACIAL RESENTMENT OUTSIDE THE SOUTH

By the mid-1960s, white voters outside the South were sincerely abandoning the ideology of white supremacy and endorsing the principle of racial equality. In part this change included the abandonment of some racial stereotypes. Blacks were no longer seen as less intelligent than whites or as inherently less able (Kinder and Sanders 1996).

But this did not mean that whites had let go of all their racial stereotypes, fears, and resentments. As soon as the civil rights agenda called for implementing change outside the South, support among whites plummeted. African-American insurgency in the cities did not help in this regard.[25] During 1964 and 1965, many white Americans considered civil rights to be the nation's most important problem, while few expressed concern about "social disorder" (McAdam 1981). But after four years of massive outbreaks of violence and destruction in cities across the country, civil rights dropped from the nation's radar and was replaced by social disorder (Kinder and Sanders 1996, 101–102). Coverage of urban problems in periodicals tripled in the late 1960s (Baumgartner and Jones 1993, 133). Already by September 1966 a majority of the white public expressed disfavor with Johnson's civil rights agenda (Edsall and Edsall 1991, 59). The mid-term election of that year portended ill for it as well: the liberal majority in the House evaporated as the Republicans gained forty-seven seats (Edsall and Edsall 1991, 59). Conservative Republicans gained congressional seats and gubernatorial offices throughout the South and in California and Illinois, often with coded appeals to whites' racial stereotypes, fears, and resentments (Edsalls 1991, 60).

It was not so much, as Schuman et al. (1997) contend, that equality lost support when implementation became the issue. Rather, as in the Reconstruction debates over the Fourteenth and Fifteenth Amendments, northerners thought implementation of civil rights in the South to be a fine idea, but in the

[25] Martin Luther King, Jr., launched his northern initiative by targeting housing discrimination in Chicago in 1966. The Justice Department soon brought school desegregation suits against northern cities for the first time. Button (1978, 10) estimates 329 "significant outbreaks of violence" in 257 cities between 1964 and 1968.

North a bad one. Shifting implementation to the North cost the Democrats support for two reasons: northern resistance to local implementation, and the loss of an external enemy that could be used to stir up negative feelings toward the South. It was much easier to legislate equality when the purpose was to correct the bad behavior of the South. The South had been portrayed as rigging the rules of the game in Congress (dominating committee chairmanships and abusing the filibuster) and violating the rules of the game in the streets (sicking dogs on innocent children, beating well-dressed middle-class people). It therefore deserved to be set straight. Major fiddling with racial arrangements in the North, however, was considered unjustified.

Of course, the problem of race in the North was significantly different from in the South. Solving it in the North was not a matter of whisking away segregationist laws but of addressing poverty, unemployment, crime, family breakdown, and other entrenched social ills.

But there was also considerable overlap in the civil rights agenda for the North and the South. Working for integrated schools, targeting housing discrimination, reining in the brutality of local white police forces, and examining the hiring and promotion practices of employers were salient efforts of both the southern civil rights movement and of northern activists. Whites outside the South were much more sympathetic to these efforts in the South than in their own towns and cities; the problem of civil rights, they believed, had existed in the South, but never in the North. Once southern discrimination was dealt a death blow by Lyndon Johnson's legislation, whites believed that American racism—which was actually southern racism—had ceased to exist (Kinder and Sanders 1996, 103, 105). Blacks were now free to take advantage of the bountiful opportunities of America—each black person advancing as far as the content of his character allowed. When it came to their own backyards, whites decided that equal opportunity was in fact already a reality—no need to intervene in a problem that did not exist. Blacks obviously were still behind in American society, but now it was a matter of individual effort, not of eliminating discrimination. Further efforts on behalf of blacks would undermine the work ethic rather than do good. Blacks were not vilified as an inferior or threatening race, as they had been before the 1940s, but their efforts to alter the racial status quo outside the South sustained racial resentments with very deep roots in American society.

While racial resentment increased over attempts to rectify a problem that did not seem to exist, stereotypic representations of African Americans thrived in popular culture. Coverage of the riots of the late 1960s included "threatening images of black hoodlums and terrorists" even as the media passed along environmental attributions of the causes of rioting (Condit and Lucaites 1993, 201). Photographs of armed Black Panthers protesting gun control legislation in the California assembly were featured on front pages of newspapers across the country (Edsall and Edsall 1991, 59). The Moynihan report focused on black "degeneracy" (a word applied to African Americans since the earliest debates about slavery) and reprised the old themes of African Americans' illegitimate sexual relations and proclivity to crime even as it proposed solutions to the unemployment of African-American men (Giddings 1984).[26] Local television news featured African Americans in stereotypical roles, particularly as criminals. Moreover, black criminals were more likely than similar white criminals to be covered in a dehumanizing way. Their names were presented less often, they were shown handcuffed more often, and they were less likely to be shown speaking for themselves (Entman 1989). Portrayals of welfare recipients took on racial and negative tones, too (Gilens 1997, 1999).

In the years between the presidential elections of 1964 and 1968, then, the target of northern white condemnation shifted from whites in the South to African Americans in the North. Racial problems were featured prominently in the media but, unlike the coverage of the previous two decades, in a way not favorable to African Americans. White citizens were reluctant to back the aggressive implementation of racially egalitarian measures outside the South.

As much as some racial stereotypes, fears, and resentments intensified, however, they did not prevent the norm of racial equality from intensifying too. White Americans outside the South no longer endorsed the notion that blacks were genetically inferior (Kinder and Sanders 1996, 97). By 1972, only 31 percent of a national sample of whites surveyed by the National Election Study (NES) believed that blacks had less of the good things in life because their race was inferior, a percentage that had dropped steadily from the 1940s and would continue to dwindle over time. Explicit defenses of racial inequality were out.

As a consequence, implicit appeals, based on the language of individualism and local control, were in. By 1968, 81 percent of respondents to a Gallup poll agreed that "law and order has broken down in this country" (Edsall and Edsall 1991, 72). The stage was set for the first racial appeal in American history to win a presidency: Richard Nixon's southern strategy.

THE PRESIDENTIAL ELECTION OF 1968: IMPLICIT RACIAL APPEALS WIN

Between 1965 and 1968 the national parties were firmly aligned on the question of race, but that alignment was constrained by the norm of racial equality. Democrats were committed to a program of racial equality; Republicans sought to take advantage of the fact that racial concerns were now salient among whites nationwide, but to remain within the constraints of the norm. As 1968 approached, it was clear to Richard Nixon that racial appeals should play a

---

[26] Daniel Patrick Moynihan, "The Negro Family: The Case for National Action," written for the U.S. Department of Labor as part of President Johnson's "War on Poverty."

key, though coded, role in his campaign. He figured this out not only from the racially selective success of Goldwater's appeal in the South, but also from the success of Wallace's coded racial appeals in the North. The apparent success of implicitly racial rhetoric in both North and South was a happy development for Nixon, as he was deeply indebted to the South for his nomination. As Garry Wills put it, "If Nixon gave more, more flamboyantly, to the South, that was because the whole convention hinged on the South. Others he could soothe or try to placate; these delegates he had to *serve*."[27]

And serve them he did. First he promised them that he would oppose the federal open-housing bill and busing, and that he would appoint an attorney general "who is going to observe the law" and a chief justice to replace the retiring Earl Warren who would "interpret the law . . . and not make it." He would not try to "satisfy some professional civil rights group," and in any case he believed that "the first civil right of every American is to be free from domestic violence" (Page 1978, 143–44; Rosenstone et al. 1984, 111–112; Wills 1969, 261). Second, during the convention he promised to choose a running mate suitable to southern aspirations, a promise handsomely kept in his pick of Spiro T. Agnew, Maryland's governor. Agnew drew Nixon's attention with an April speech condemning moderate African-American leaders for failing to stand up to militant blacks (Wills 1969, 290–292). Agnew subsequently took up implicitly racial rhetoric much like Wallace's on behalf of the ticket. In general, Nixon also portrayed himself as someone with a particular sympathy for the South and affection for things and people southern.

During the campaign, Nixon offered "freedom of choice" in opposition to school busing (especially, though not only, in the South) (Carter 1996, 32). According to Wills,

> [Nixon's] overarching formula "less government interference" allowed him to use rhetoric congenial to each sector's grievances. Much of this rhetorical adjustment was done, of course, at the local level, by his lieutenants—like Thurmond, Callaway, and Tower in the South. All Nixon had to supply was a setting, in which nuanced states' rights arguments (against, for instance, federal withholding of funds to segregated schools) seemed to be consonant with other demands for local control. (Wills 1969, 71)

What one former Alabama senator said of Wallace now applied to Nixon too: "He can use all the other issues—law and order, running your own schools, protecting property rights—and never mention race. But people will know he's telling them, 'A nigger's trying to get your job, trying to move into your

---

[27] Nixon owed his nomination to Strom Thurmond, who vouched for him with other southerners. Thurmond's power lay in the arithmetic of that year's nomination. The South's electoral endorsement of Goldwater in 1964 gave the South nearly half the necessary delegates to nominate the 1968 presidential candidate (Wills 1969, 261–262, 270; Sundquist 1973, 357).

neighborhood' " (Rosenstone et al. 1984, 111).[28] Following Wallace and Goldwater, Nixon formulated a southern strategy, but he carried it out with more
subtlety: "Nixon's fanciful speech on the 'new alignment'—joining New South
to new blacks—was an artful cover for the work being done on a real coalition;
for one must know 'where the ducks are' (as Goldwater put it), but one must
not *say* where they are. One of Clif White's major errors—the kind Nixon did
not repeat—was to confess his strategy" (Wills 1969, 264).[29]

Nixon's deliberate use of implicitly racial appeals is also made quite clear in
Joe McGinniss's account of the filming of Nixon's final television ads. The last
ad dealt with the New York City teachers' strike: "The heart of the problem is
law and order in our schools. I do not think that we can expect teachers to go
into classrooms where there is not discipline and where they are not backed
up by local school boards. . . . Discipline in the classroom is essential if our
children are to learn" (1969, 23). Immediately after recording this, Nixon told
his aides, "Yep, this hits it right on the nose, the thing about this whole
teacher—it's all about law and order and the damn Negro-Puerto Rican groups
out there" (McGinniss 1969, 23).

Those around Nixon could not have been surprised to hear his racial slur;
after all, Nixon constantly used the word "nigger" in private conversation. He
told John Ehrlichman that the Great Society programs would be wasted on
African Americans because "blacks were genetically inferior to whites" (O'Reilly
1995, 327).[30] Law and order for Nixon boiled down to the "damn Negroes,"
but he could not say this in his ad. Sundquist notes that "law and order was a
separable issue from race, but it was not always a *separated* issue" (1983, 383).[31]
However, Nixon did not wed law and order to race in an explicit way. He
intended to convey racial meaning implicitly. He wanted to appeal to racial
stereotypes, fears, and resentments, yet conform to the norm of racial equality.

The main counterstrategy of the Democrats' standard-bearer, Vice President
Hubert H. Humphrey, was nonracial. He pushed the "wasted vote" argument
to prevent Democrats from defecting to Wallace. He also relied on unions

[28] Nixon's public rhetoric was remarkably free of explicit racial appeals. On law and order, for
example, he said: "When both national political parties say we've got to remove the causes of
rioting, looting and burning, they're saying that these anarchists have a cause. . . . Poverty is not
a cause for anarchy." And he said: "People who riot ought to be bopped in the head," though even
this was "too easy" on some rioters (Rosenstone et al. 1984, 132).

[29] Nixon was aided in his aims not least by Kevin Phillips, the "house expert on ethnic voting
patterns," whose self-professed specialty was "the whole secret of politics—knowing who hates
who." During the 1968 campaign he told Wills, then a reporter, that "white Democrats will desert
their party in droves the minute it becomes a black party" (Wills 1969, 264–265).

[30] But it was not his private racism that caused his use of racial appeals. His prejudice had not
prevented him earlier in his career from being a racial liberal (O'Reilly 1995).

[31] Nixon had a series of other campaign ads, equally telling. Some promised punishment for
black violence, some condemned "hand outs" and offered instead a "hand up," some touted black
capitalism in place of welfare (McGinniss 1969).

to retain working-class Democrats in the Democratic column, a strategy that apparently had some effect (Rosenstone et al. 1984, 112). Humphrey accused Nixon of using the phrase "law and order" "as a code word for repression of blacks in reaction to riots in black ghettoes," but he did not dwell on this (Himelstein 1983). He did not shy away from his support of civil rights guarantees, but neither did he put them front and center (Page 1978).

Nixon's strategy appears to have worked. He won a narrow victory over Humphrey and outmaneuvered Wallace on Wallace's own terms. By moving to the right he was able to reduce Wallace's support in the South, and also hold on to important states such as California, Illinois, Ohio, and New Jersey. Of the cluster of salient racial issues of the day, the issue that appeared to matter most to Wallace supporters was urban unrest (Rosenstone et al. 1984, 112–113). Urban unrest in 1968, of course, was synonymous with black rioting. Nixon's adoption of the mantle of law and order was crucial to his attempt to signal Wallace supporters, North and South, that he was interchangeable with their candidate.[32]

The 1968 election was the first in which a majority of whites voted for a Republican party firmly aligned with the center-right. The Democrats, to their electoral detriment, were firmly established as the party of blacks and the left and increasingly lost their attraction for most whites. From 1968 onward the Democratic party experienced high levels of white defection from its ranks, accompanied by eventual conversion to the Republican party.[33]

This was also the very first election in the long history of racial campaigns that seemed to have netted a presidential victory. The apparent success would help to make the strategy popular in all manner of electoral contests. But campaigns that used it took note of the twist Nixon had put on it—they were careful to play the race card with deniability.

---

[32] Nixon continued to pursue his southern strategy while in office (Edsall and Edsall 1991, 81–84; Rosenstone et al. 1984, 113). But he also followed through on his "black capitalism" rhetoric of the campaign, and, initially, supported emerging affirmative action plans, including set-asides for black business contracts (Edsall and Edsall 1991, 86). School desegregation plans went forward even after he assumed office. There are several explanations for this. It may have been in part a bone to the racially liberal wing of the Republican party (Edsall and Edsall 1991, 86–87, 97). It may have been meant to siphon off working-class whites from the Democratic party. Or Nixon may have wanted to maintain the southern panic about desegregation and to have something to mobilize whites against. Consonant with this is the fact that he asked his staff to do just enough to keep school desegregation and affirmative action going, but to make it seem as if it was not their doing (O'Reilly 1995). Nixon used this tactic well in his 1972 campaign, when he attacked his own affirmative action policy. In any case, opposition to busing came to dominate Nixon's racial agenda.

[33] Republicans also obtained advantage by attracting people who normally tend not to vote (Huckfeldt and Kohfeld 1989, 149).

RACIAL APPEALS IN THE AGE OF EQUALITY:
IMPLICIT OVER EXPLICIT

The implicit racial rhetoric developed in the 1950s and 1960s continued into the following decades. It could be found at all political levels and all regions of the country—in mayoral, statewide, and presidential elections. Some attempts at coded rhetoric were not subtle and thus backfired. Others, notably in the 1988 Republican presidential campaign, effectively avoided the label of racism and succeeded handsomely (see Chapters 5–6).

The shape implicit appeals have taken in some southern elections is demonstrated by Jerry Himelstein's case study. He analyzed a 1979 referendum held in Hattiesburg, Mississippi. The referendum proposed to change the electoral system of city government to increase black representation. Himelstein found little change from earlier, explicit defenses of white supremacy, and much continuity—with one important exception: "Themes that had been prominent in the rhetoric of massive resistance to desegregation [in the 1950s and early 1960s] were invoked without overt reference to race" (Himelstein 1983, 157). In fact, the campaign against reforming Hattiesburg's government was conducted, Himelstein says, with complete racial neutrality on the surface: "None of the public statements by official spokespersons contain even one direct reference to race" (Himelstein 1983, 163).[34]

Even racially conservative candidates in the South now attempt to establish their egalitarian credentials, but they are still prone to racial campaigns. They achieve this dual purpose through implicit appeals.[35] "By the 1980s," wrote Paul Luebke, ". . . racial tolerance had become an obligatory position for any

---

[34] The continuing themes were "an alleged state of harmony that the proposed changes would upset"; "the threat of a court fight and federal government intervention"; and "outside agitation." Race predicted 96 percent of the vote. The testimony of campaign workers corroborates the argument that race underlay the debate; they encountered such statements from white voters as "that's just a nigger issue" (Himelstein 1983, 157, 160, 162, 163, 165).

[35] Contests pitting white against black candidates have also featured implicitly racial appeals. One conservative candidate running in 1976 used newspaper ads in eastern North Carolina featuring a picture of his black opponent and a caption that read: "Unless the people come out and vote on September 14, the election will be decided by a relatively small segment of the population." In 1982, the runoff election for the second congressional district in North Carolina between black candidate Mickey Michaux and former state legislator Tim Valentine featured a pamphlet circulated selectively by Valentine that said, "It's not easy to stop and take time to vote, but *you* must. Our polls indicate that the same well organized block [sic] vote which was so obvious and influential in the First Primary will turn out again on July 27. My opponent will again be bussing his supporters to the polling places in record number." References to a "block vote" were used earlier in the century with explicitly racial adjectives (e.g., "negro block"); "bussing" has a shorter but equally racial history. Michaux only won the white votes he had won in the first primary (Luebke 1990, 118–119; emphasis in the original).

aspiring politician, forcing racial traditionalists to use code words to indicate their stand vis-à-vis blacks" (1990, 109). "For the most part," concluded James Glaser, "southern Republicans have recognized that outright racist appeals are no longer socially acceptable. Republican campaign managers vigorously deny that they are trying to appeal to racist attitudes with their campaign tactics, and candidates take great offense when they or their tactics are labeled by others as racist. . . . Their message on race, they claim, is conservative, not racist" (1996, 69–70).[36]

A sign of the strength of the norm against public racist speech among politicians is the way candidates respond when accused of racism. Examples of such accusations from the last few years consistently show that candidates vehemently deny that they are racist and express great offense at being called racist. When Senator Dianne Feinstein ran for reelection in 1994, her Republican opponent was accused of sanctioning restrictive racial covenants in his real estate dealings, to which he replied: "She is a liar. They are saying that I am a racist—this is McCarthyism and Mrs. Feinstein should be ashamed of herself." New York mayor Rudolph Giuliani, accused by the prominent black clergyman Calvin O. Butts of disliking black people, replied, "Reverend Butts called me a racist and he never apologized. You can't do things like that. It's like calling somebody a Nazi."[37]

Instances of the failure to conform to the norm prove just as instructive. North Carolina senator Jesse Helms remains the anomalous example of a politician who continued to use explicitly racial appeals after the early 1970s. However, even he has, from the beginning of his statewide electoral career, mixed implicit and explicit racial appeals. Of Helms's first senatorial race, Luebke wrote, "Although Helms in the past had defended segregation, his campaign messages [in 1972] used codes like 'forced busing' that could not be easily tagged as racist" (1990, 26). In late 1984, however, while campaigning against Democratic governor James Hunt for reelection, Helms did not hesitate to use explicitly racial references: "The big factor in this election will be whether there will be a balance to the efforts of Jesse Jackson, who came into this state earlier this year to meet with Governor Hunt and then announced that he was going

---

[36] Consider for example the Republican governor of North Carolina in the late 1980s, Jim Martin. Martin was reelected to a second term in 1988 with a campaign that stressed prosperity and normalcy and portrayed him as a modern politician of uncertain partisan affiliation. For this purpose, he used images of white and black schoolchildren together. He even bought radio spots on black radio stations. He may have been genuinely attempting to win votes from African Americans, but it is unlikely that this was his main goal. He lost 90 percent of the black vote. Moreover, he won two-thirds of the white vote. It is most likely that he was adhering to the new norm of making rhetorical gestures toward racial equality. Even buying advertising on black radio stations, which at first glance seems designed only to win African-American votes, also serves the purpose of showing that a candidate is appealing to all voters.

[37] Dave Lesher, "Bradley Faults Huffington on Race Issue," *Los Angeles Times*, October 5, 1994; "One Man's Endorsement Is Another's". . . *New York Times*, October 13, 1998.

to register, I-forget-what-it-was, 200 or 300-thousand *blacks* for the sole purpose of defeating Jesse Helms" (Luebke 1990, 131; emphasis mine). And in his 1990 campaign Helms used a now-infamous, explicitly racial ad in which a pair of white hands crumples a job rejection letter with the blame placed on a "minority."

Clearly Senator Helms has not been reluctant to be racially explicit, even at the cost of widespread censure by national elites. What may have allowed Helms to escape rejection as a norm violator was that he situated anti-black messages within the context of a broad attack on liberalism generally. He avoided blanket stereotypical statements about African Americans as a group in favor of the language of group conflict and moral failing, language in which African Americans only figured incidentally (Luebke 1990, 139–140).[38] Also, Helms may have neglected to make his racial rhetoric as implicit as that of others for the same reason that he has not bothered to moderate anything else that offends his colleagues in the federal government and the national media.

Helms remains an anomaly that underscores how unusual explicit appeals have become. Implicit appeals are far more frequent than explicit ones. A rash of campaigns in 1989 and 1990 featured implicit appeals, perhaps in an attempt to emulate the implicit strategy of the 1988 Bush campaign. But these appeals do not only appear in rashes. Like the party alignment on issues of race, implicitly racial appeals are now a stable feature of the American political landscape, although they certainly do not dominate all other issues. Nor are they present everywhere and at all times. But they are the bread and butter of Republican campaigns in the South, where the party system is perhaps most divided along racial lines. In his book on southern congressional campaigns in the 1980s, Glaser concludes: "Not every Republican campaign is as racial as the ones described above, but some racial appeals seem to arise in nearly every election" (1996, 73).[39]

CONCLUSION

As American political institutions began to abandon the norm of racial inequality and to converge on the undesirability of white supremacy, the defenders of racial inequality at first responded in the same explicitly racial terms they had used in the nineteenth century. But as the norm governing what was acceptable

---

[38] Another anomalous example of a campaign that relied on explicitly racial appeals after 1968 is the Chicago mayoral election of 1983 (Pinderhughes 1987; see also Kleppner 1985).

[39] It may be that local elections are more prone to explicitly racial appeals since they are less scrutinized. Similarly, certain media, such as direct mail and radio, are safer for explicit appeals. The demographic make-up of a district may also affect the implicitness of the appeal, although not in a linear fashion. These and many such hypotheses remain outside the scope of this book, but they hint at the many interesting questions that arise from an implicit communication perspective.

to say progressed increasingly in the direction of equality, they changed their language. By the late 1960s they no longer felt free to make explicit references to race, much less stridently defend white superiority. Nevertheless, they were able to use the normative shift for their purpose. They developed increasingly implicit ways of attacking concrete measures designed to implement racial equality.

The shift to implicit rhetoric was not a southern shift alone. Nor was implicit rhetoric only a strategy for the defense of white supremacy. Barry Goldwater, Richard Nixon, and George Bush learned from southern politicians and made implicit discourse their own, not for the purpose of defending white supremacy but for the purpose of mobilizing white voters and winning elections. Nor was the implicit strategy the sole property of one party. It was developed by Democrats when they were the party of white supremacy, then used by Republicans in a concerted effort to win over racially resentful whites and shift the alignment of electoral coalitions in their favor.

Nixon emerges from these pages as the consummate player of the implicitly racial strategy. He went all out for the white vote, but went all out to deny doing so. In his memoirs, which he hoped would rehabilitate his post-Watergate reputation, Nixon continued to deny that he had pursued a racial strategy, had made appeals to racism, or even had sought southern votes. "The Republican Party must have no room for racism. The Deep South had to be virtually conceded to George Wallace. I could not match him there without compromising on the civil rights issue, which I would not do" (Nixon 1978, 316). Clearly he did make room for racism, went after the Deep South, matched Wallace there, and compromised on the civil rights issue. But he denied it to the end, because he perceived that it would gravely harm his reputation. It is a mark of how far the norm of egalitarian public expression has advanced that Nixon felt this way. He is far from alone.[40]

The Democrats have been in a difficult electoral position since they became the party of African Americans in a society still divided by race. The party of the racial left, whether Republican, Democrat, or Populist, is always vulnerable to racial appeals from the right, as we saw in Chapter 2. But that party nevertheless has strategic options, and some are more effective than others. The Democrats of the age of equality made a mistake in adopting a strategy of silence in

---

[40] By the late 1970s even George Wallace had decided that the path to political survival lay in distancing himself as much as possible from the "racist" label. Beginning in 1977, Wallace focused, more than anything, on sanitizing his racist reputation. In an obituary for Wallace, Howell Raines wrote that Wallace "undertook a campaign of apology and revisionist explanation intended to erase the word 'racist' from his epitaph. He argued that his early devotion to segregation was based on his reading of the Constitution and the Bible and was misinterpreted as a racist hatred of black people. 'I was never saying anything that reflected upon black people, and I'm very sorry it was taken that way' " (Howell Raines, "George Wallace, Symbol of the Fight to Maintain Segregation, Dies at 79," *New York Times*, September 15, 1998).

the face of the Republicans' implicit appeals to race. The Edsalls argue that some of that silence on race was motivated, beginning in the 1960s, by a reluctance to strengthen the conservative framing of racial problems (Edsall and Edsall 1991, 114). This reluctance obviously comes from flawed reasoning since, as the Edsalls point out, the conservative framing was already prominent. However flawed their reasoning, Democrats after 1968 often operated as if silence was the best defense against racial appeals. As Glaser notes, "Republicans raise the issue, Democrats often do not respond in public" (1996, 187), and Democrats "state their position, which is the racially liberal position, but they do so cautiously and softly, and they do not elaborate much" (73). They do this to avoid the danger that whites will think of them as the candidates of African Americans, and because African Americans let them do it. African Americans have low expectations of what white Democrats should say in mainstream forums, and African Americans can be appealed to "surgically," in black churches and on black radio (74, 188). Glaser's description of the South fits the Democrats' strategy in presidential elections as well.

The historical record I have examined in this and the previous chapter suggests that, contrary to most Democrats' calculations, silence in the face of implicit racial appeals is a losing strategy. Silence may not lose with African-American voters as long as the crucial legislative votes are cast for black interests, as Glaser says. But it loses in the contest over white voters. And the Democrats cannot afford to lose white voters. For example, Earl Black has shown that white Democrats who win congressional elections in the South get the majority of their votes from white voters, and cannot win unless they get a substantial minority of the total white vote (Black 1998, Fig. 3). In 1994 no white Democrat was sent to Congress with less than 39 percent of the white vote. White voters determine whether a congressional district elects a white Democrat or a white Republican (Black 1998).

An effective defense against implicitly racial appeals requires an issue that trumps race in the considerations of white voters. In the nineteenth century this issue was primarily sectionalism—northern whites' resentment of southern whites' secession. In the twentieth century this issue was primarily economic prosperity and cherished social welfare programs. Each of these appeals unifies the electorate across lines of race, or at least mutes the cleavage of race.

But the counterstrategy must also include a response on the issue of race. Pointing out that an implicit racial appeal is in fact a racial appeal is a sound counterstrategy. Lyndon Johnson and Bill Clinton were familiar with this approach because, as southern politicians, they had inherited the rhetorical strategy developed by southern populists in the 1890s. Black's findings on southern governors illustrate this counterstrategy. In 1970, South Carolina's John West defeated Republican congressman Albert K. Watson in part by challenging his racial appeal. Watson appealed for "discipline" in desegregated schools, much as had Nixon in 1968, and his television commercials asked, "Are we going to be ruled by the bloc? Look what it did in Watts" (the "bloc" being a long-standing term for African Americans) (Black 1976, 84). West countered not with silence but with an antiracist appeal: "I will not by word or deed or action do anything to inflame or polarize class against class, rich against poor, color against color" (Black 1976, 85). Just as the populists did during their campaigns in the 1890s, these speeches highlighted the opponent's racial appeal in a negative way. Notice also how Paul Johnson did this in 1951, in Mississippi:

> They cannot win on a platform that pits race against race, creed against creed, religion against religion and class against class. For twenty years my opponent has known nothing to run on but prejudice, hate, fear and the Negro question; if I had to base my candidacy on race vs. race, class against class, religion against religion, I would . . . get my old shotgun, stand it on its butt, stick my toe to the trigger, and blow my brains out. I don't want to win by making the Negro the whipping boy when he isn't even an issue in the race. (Black 1976, 41)

Thus, when Arkansas governor Bill Clinton announced in 1991 that he was seeking the presidential nomination, he echoed this populist refrain against race-baiting almost word-for-word:

> For twelve years, Republicans have tried to divide us—race against race—so we get mad at each other and not at them. They want us to look at each other across a racial divide so we don't turn and look to the White House and ask, Why are all of our incomes going down? Why are all of us losing jobs? Why are we losing our future? (Germond and Witcover 1993, 99–100)

No doubt the success of George Bush's Willie Horton tactic in 1988 made Bill Clinton determined to inoculate himself in advance of 1992. It was no coincidence that the person most determined to inoculate himself against a racial appeal was a southern member of the party aligned with blacks and rejected by racially resentful whites. Clinton understood that his party was vulnerable to racial appeals, and he had a long southern tradition of combating racial appeals on which to draw. Of course, we require more definitive evidence on whether challenging race-baiting works, and subsequent chapters attempt to provide it.

What of changing the Republican racial strategy from within the party? Is there hope that Republicans would go after the white vote less enthusiastically, and try to mobilize African Americans more enthusiastically? Republican strategist Lee Atwater and other party leaders did in fact publicize their effort to recruit more African Americans in the late 1980s and 1990s. Republicans have cultivated black conservatives, giving them a great deal of publicity and appointing them to prominent positions (Walton 1992). Republican consultants recognize that even getting 20 percent of the black vote, nationally and in southern congressional districts with a considerable proportion of blacks, would give them a huge advantage (Glaser 1996). And Republicans in the South often make efforts to recruit African-American voters.

However, the nature of these efforts shows that Republicans are self-deluded about African-American voters. As their Democratic counterparts of the nineteenth century did, Republicans sometimes assume that they can get black votes with token gestures or patronage. Consider what one southern candidate told Glaser: "We went into Hobson City, a 100 percent black town, and had a blast. Played basketball. Had a parade in the downtown. A barbecue. I got no votes out of that town. My philosophy and my voting record were out the window. Meant nothing." This politician is gravely mistaken on two counts, which together compose the "barbecue syndrome": that barbecues would attract African Americans, and that the substance of his positions meant nothing to them. It is exactly the racially and economically conservative substance of his record—and the record of southern Republicans in general—that prevented him from winning African-American votes. True, African-American voters are socially conservative, and may have moved toward fiscal moderation in recent years; but they are still strongly committed to racially and economically liberal policies (Dawson 1994; Tate 1993). Republicans cannot win the votes of significant numbers of African Americans with racially and economically conservative programs. All the barbecues in the world won't change that.

The barbecue syndrome is common to politicians of whichever party finds itself on the outs with African Americans. In the nineteenth century, southern Democrats were prone to it, as the previous chapter showed. Since the 1960s, southern Republicans, and Republican presidential candidates, have been prone to it. Until they realize their mistake, Republicans will continue to be ineffectual in recruiting African-American support. And they will continue to rely on and try to mobilize the white vote, which they need by large margins in order to win.

Many Republicans seem well aware of the hopelessness of gaining the support of African-American voters on a racially conservative platform. They too expend some effort to appeal to African-American voters. That effort, however, is purely symbolic, designed not to genuinely compete for African-American voters, but to ensure that the media and the opposition will not criticize the candidate for ignoring African Americans. Consider this statement by Gerald Ford's 1976 media consultant, Malcolm MacDougall: "We had given up on the black vote. . . . We'd bought a few spots on black radio so the media couldn't report that we'd given up. Lionel Hampton singing 'Call Ford Mr. Sunshine.' The only black vote we got out of that was Lionel Hampton's" (MacDougall 1977, 233). And maybe not even his. Gerald Ford's own views remain unknown, but some of his campaign officials clearly had no intention of expending a great deal of effort to win African-American votes. They had written off the black vote. What did concern them, however, was the possibility that they would be classified as racially callous, or even worse, as outright racists.

They wanted to avoid the perception that they had violated the norm of racial equality. It was not the direct power of the black vote that led them to make the racially egalitarian gesture of appearing to recruit African-American voters. Rather, it was the anticipated power of national institutions to cast them as violators of the norm. Because they have made themselves into the party of the racial right, Republicans have been engaged in a preventive rhetorical strategy, one designed to avoid the stigma of being labeled racist. They do so not in order to win the votes of people who are unlikely to vote for them, but to secure the votes of people who are reasonably likely to vote Republican.

The Republican strategy, then, has included limited appeals to African Americans, designed to ward off the accusation of racism rather than to win over significant numbers of people who remain the staunchest opponents of the Republican economic and racial agenda. On the white side, the Republican strategy consists of implicit appeals to white voters' racial predispositions, appeals which, when they are very effective, are perceived as silence on the issue of race. In the South in particular, superficial silence on race is not a sign of racial progress, contrary to what some observers believe.[41] The abandonment of explicit rhetoric only reflects a positive development when it is replaced by true silence, but not when it is replaced by implicit rhetoric. If silence conceals opposition to racial equality, it makes that opposition harder to combat. Some fundamental issues of race are no longer fought over, but the degree and pace of change remains a potent and contested issue, and therefore an area ripe for electoral strategizing. White Republican appeals to race are not overt, but neither are they absent. Messages that seem to appeal to conservatism may be just that, but alternatively, they may be implicit appeals to racial stereotypes, fears, and resentments. Knowing into which of these categories the message fits makes all the difference in predicting its impact on voters.

The scholarly neglect of implicitly racial appeals made it easy to underestimate the growing Republican strength in the South. White southerners have been electing Republicans in the 1990s to a much greater extent than many scholars anticipated. This is not the consequence of racial redistricting and the siphoning off of African-American voters from Democratic majorities. Rather, it is due primarily to the success of Republicans' ideological and programmatic appeals to white voters (Grofman and Handley 1998b; Hill 1995; Lublin 1995; Petrocik and Desposato 1998). Chief among these are implicit appeals to whites' negative racial predispositions.

It is the task of the next section of this book to show just how powerful these appeals can be, and that they are powerful because they evoke a racial response. Do implicitly racial appeals in fact evoke a racial response, as I argue,

---

[41] For example, Leslie Dunbar (Black 1976, 305).

or do they instead evoke a nonracial response? Are they in fact more effective than explicit appeals, or less effective? What is the best way to challenge them? The next chapter lays out the psychology of implicit appeals. The following chapters put to the test the proposition that in the age of equality, implicitly racial appeals are exceptionally effective in racial priming.

Part Two

THE IMPACT OF IMPLICIT RACIAL APPEALS

CHAPTER 4

The Political Psychology of Implicit Communication

> Almost without their being aware of it, he acquired
> great prestige and authority over them.
> —Machiavelli, *The Prince*

HOW DO IMPLICIT racial messages work? In this chapter I develop a theoretical framework for understanding how racial messages influence white voters. After briefly outlining the framework, I discuss each building block in depth.

Three facts give rise to this theoretical framework. First, public commitment to basic racial equality reached immense proportions starting in the late 1960s. Second, notwithstanding this commitment, racial resentment continues to thrive among a significant portion of the white public. Third, in response to the first two factors, implicit appeals to racial stereotypes, fears, and resentments have been, since 1968, an important tool for mobilizing support from white voters. Jointly, these three facts give rise to the questions at the heart of this chapter: How do white citizens respond to racial appeals while upholding their commitment to racial equality? How could implicit appeals work at a racial level but still afford deniability? How are whites likely to respond to explicit appeals?

As we saw in Chapter 3, white supremacist politicians from the 1950s onward integrated the language of equality with arguments designed to preserve racial inequality, arguments that drew on racial stereotypes, fears, and resentments. Politicians felt an imperative to adjust their rhetoric to the growing norm of racial equality. Among the most important of these adjustments was the move to shed explicit articulations of racial stereotypes, fears, and resentments, to find ways to communicate them without mentioning race explicitly. Political elites reinvented racial rhetoric, creating a tradition of political communication that rested on oblique and easily deniable references to racial distinctions.

White citizens have also found ways to reconcile racial stereotypes, fears, and resentments with a growing embrace of racial equality as a national principle. The majority of whites have predispositions that, at their core, highlight the perceived deficiencies of blacks, often in terms of economic dependence, criminality, and sexual immorality. Most whites believe that the appropriate public response to these deficiencies is to foster, or, less benevolently, to impose individual responsibility. It is not racism, many whites believe, that stands in the way of black progress, since racism is primarily a problem of the South, and the old South at that. Once civil rights were written into law, and white southerners forced to treat blacks fairly, most whites believed that blacks should be able to advance as their individual abilities and character allow. If more blacks than whites fall far short of the American dream, many whites believe, this is not due in a significant way to unequal life chances (although many whites recognized that these exist), but to the failure of too many blacks to play by the rules of American society. If proportionately more blacks than whites turn to violent crime, according to many whites, that is not a reason to address the causes that lead to crime, but rather to punish black criminals so that they cease to prey on white people—even if whites have more to fear from other whites than from blacks. Individualistic thinking, applied with particular force to the situation of blacks, is not new. It was prominent in the past, especially during the political debates of Reconstruction. It seems new because until the 1950s, it resided in the shadow of a hereditarian form of thinking that cast blacks as unalterably inferior despite their individual efforts. That thinking has been genuinely repudiated. The norm of racial equality is the consensus that the ideology of white supremacy is morally and empirically bankrupt. The norm repudiates the notion that blacks are inalterably inferior and rejects this idea as a justification for treating blacks less favorably than whites.

As a consequence of these developments, racial appeals can have a significant impact on white voters—if they are implicit. The conflict between negative racial predispositions and the norm of racial equality can generate ambivalence; in turn, ambivalence creates a greater susceptibility to messages. A racial appeal thus has the capacity to affect public opinion about matters related to race. It is most likely to do so by making negative racial predispositions—stereotypes, fears, and resentments—more accessible. Once primed by a message, these predispositions are given greater weight when white Americans make political decisions that carry racial associations, such as whether to support affirmative action or spend public funds to assist blacks. Racial priming can take place without the awareness of the individual, safeguarding the person's commitment to egalitarian conduct. Unconscious racial priming, however, is contingent on the message being ambiguously racial, that is, implicit. In situations that remind white citizens of their commitment to racial equality, racial priming is inhibited or overridden. The norm of racial equality is triggered for whites when the message is explicit, resembling the racist appeals whites learned to repudiate in the 1950s and 1960s. In that case, the message will put white individuals on guard against their own negative racial predispositions, and racial priming will not occur.

This is the theory in brief. It rests on four building blocks, which for ease of exposition I call "A" factors: ambivalence about negative racial predispositions;

accessibility and priming; awareness of one's racial response; and ambiguity of the racial content of the message. I elaborate on the building blocks below.

AMBIVALENCE

Universal Commitment to the Norm of Racial Equality

The norm of racial equality today is an injunctive and descriptive norm, specifying both what everyone should do and describing what nearly everyone in fact does. As we saw in Chapter 3, a substantial erosion occurred between the early 1940s and the late 1950s in the norm of racial inequality. In the 1960s, civil rights organizations, public officials, and the laws of government contributed to the birth of a new, diametrically opposed norm. The decades since then have strengthened the new norm of racial equality.

The new norm is perhaps most clearly discernible in public opinion, direct evidence for which comes from survey data. Whites now express near-unanimous condemnation of white supremacist views, and they endorse racial equality as a matter of moral principle. Whereas the early 1940s were characterized by widespread white endorsement of segregation, the late 1950s were characterized instead by repudiation of many of its institutions and justifications (Greeley and Sheatsley 1971; Taylor et al. 1978). By the early 1980s, 90 percent of whites thought black and white children should attend the same schools, 71 percent disagreed with whites' right to keep blacks out of their neighborhoods, over 80 percent indicated they would support a black candidate for president, and 66 percent opposed laws prohibiting intermarriage. As early as the first years of the 1970s, national surveys and polls showed that the proportion of whites favoring the agenda of the southern civil rights movement was staggeringly high. Equal job opportunities were endorsed by a whopping 97 percent of whites; 88 percent opposed segregated public transportation; 88 percent chose blacks' residential rights over the prerogative of whites to keep blacks out; and 88 percent endorsed the right of blacks to use public accommodations with whites (Schuman et al. 1985, Table 3.1).

Desire for social distance from blacks, another facet of public opinion, shows a similarly dramatic decline from the 1940s. By the early 1980s overwhelmingly large proportions of whites indicated they would not object to sending their children to a school attended by a minority of black children, and said they would welcome a black dinner guest. Already in the 1970s, whites had indicated in large numbers that they would have no objection to a black family living next door (Schuman et al. 1985, Table 3.3).

Surveys that asked whites directly whether blacks are as intelligent as whites found a huge change between the mid-1940s and late 1950s. Whereas in 1944 most whites denied blacks were as intelligent as whites, as early as 1956 an overwhelming proportion of whites indicated this was so (Schuman et al. 1985, Table 3.4), a proportion still in evidence today. For example, over 80 percent of white respondents in the 1990 General Social Survey denied that blacks are less well off because of inborn ability.

Studies using the Katz and Braly adjective checklist, a highly direct method of assessing stereotypes, also show a marked decrease over time in negative stereotyping of blacks. In 1933, college students asked to choose characteristics of blacks and whites from a list of adjectives overwhelmingly rated blacks as superstitious (84 percent) and lazy (75 percent), and to a lesser extent happy-go-lucky (38 percent) and ignorant (38 percent), among other negative traits. Whites were largely described with positive traits, particularly as being industrious and intelligent (Katz and Braly 1933). A 1951 follow-up, however, found a reduction of over half in the proportion of students rating blacks with negative traits, and a large decrease in the proportion choosing positive traits for whites. The third adjective checklist study, conducted in 1982, found almost no endorsement of negative stereotypes of blacks, and a growing negative perception of whites (Gaertner and Dovidio 1986, Table 2). The adjective checklist has clear flaws as a method of assessing private stereotypes. But its obtrusive intention—to find out how overtly stereotypical the respondent's thinking is—is useful for gauging the strength of egalitarian norms.

The norm of racial equality is sufficiently strong, in fact, that direct measures of intolerance reveal that the people at greatest risk of having their civil liberties restricted are those identified as racist. Marcus et al. (1995) found that when citizens are asked to choose from a list of eleven political groups the one they most dislike, 67 percent choose either the Ku Klux Klan or "American racists." None of the other groups are disliked by more than 5 percent of the sample. This sentiment, part of what Marcus et al. call a "standing decision" not to tolerate the group, leads people to restrict the political activity of racists more readily and with greater zeal than that of any other group.

Thus, the most telling indicator of the norm—whether a large majority of the citizenry endorses the principle of equal treatment for blacks and rejects the central tenets of white privilege—shows that the norm is, in fact, thriving, and has been for the past three decades. Most whites know that they should treat blacks equally, and they are inclined to chastise those who do not.[1]

---

[1] The norm of equality is also apparent in the way blacks are portrayed in advertisements. In the entertainment industry, depictions of blacks have become more positive and varied in important respects, so that whites are now exposed to significantly more egalitarian representations of blacks than they were before 1970. Magazine advertising in 1950 seldom included blacks at all, and when it did, it was in service occupations and in subordinate roles. During the 1970s and 1980s, however, blacks were reflected in magazine ads at ratios near their population proportion, in varied occupations, and as people of equal status to whites. Television portrayals became more inclusive of blacks as well during the 1960s, and now blacks are portrayed in television commer-

Negative Racial Predispositions

Although whites' near-universal rejection of white supremacy is incontrovertible, and the principle of integration and basic equality is now deeply rooted, it is equally clear that many whites have negative racial predispositions. Although approximately 80 percent of whites surveyed in the mid-1990s opposed laws against marriage between blacks and whites, the percentage approving of intermarriage was close to 60 percent, and less than 10 percent had actually intermarried (Schuman et al. 1997, Fig. 7.1). Many whites still feel uneasy about intimacy with blacks. Of white respondents to the 1990 General Social Survey (GSS), for example, 65 percent opposed the possibility of a close relative marrying a black person, while another 29 percent were neutral, leaving a mere 6 percent in favor. In contrast, whites surveyed by the 1990 GSS were ten to twenty percentage points less opposed to close contact with Asians than with blacks. Similarly, actual rates of white intermarriage show much more progress with Asians and Latinos than with blacks. Not only are whites uneasy about actual close contact; they are also uneasy about practicing thorough integration. In the 1990s, whites were far more willing to send their children to school with "a few" or with "half" black students than to a "majority" black school (the percentages are 96–98 percent, 79–83 percent, and 41–51 percent, respectively) (Schuman et al. 1997, Table 3.3, NORC item). Nearly half of whites say they prefer to live in a predominantly white neighborhood (Schuman et al. 1997, Table 3.3). Whites are much less likely to choose egalitarian alternatives when asked to imagine living their lives in the company of a significant number of blacks, or in intimacy with them.[2]

---

cials in numbers reflecting their proportion of the population. The content of those representations has changed as well; blacks are no longer seen uniformly in service occupations (servants and entertainers), appearing in a diverse set of jobs. Blacks are shown on television taking and giving orders to the same extent as whites (Dovidio and Gaertner 1986, 6–8). Unfortunately, these measures of progress are not unqualified, as I will discuss shortly.

[2] Although it is not a component of negative racial predispositions, also important is the view, popular with most whites, that further attempts to guarantee civil rights are unnecessary in light of the progress already made—progress many whites take to be not flawless, but satisfactory (Bobo and Kluegel 1993; Sigelman and Welch 1991). Most whites sampled by the 1992 NES, for example, felt that civil rights were being advanced at the right pace, and over a quarter more felt the pace was too fast. This view contrasts sharply with those of most African Americans, who tend to be much more pessimistic about blacks' chances of equal treatment, who believe that more must be done to safeguard equal rights, and who have been much more committed than whites to racial integration (Hochschild 1995; Sigelman and Welch 1991). Consistent with this is that whites have shown considerably less movement on the matter of implementing racial equality, particularly once implementation was no longer confined to the South. The 1992 NES, for example, found a majority of whites denying that the government had a responsibility to ensure school integration. There was remarkably little change in opinion about the amount the government should be spending to aid blacks in the decade between 1973 and 1983 (Schuman et al. 1985, Table 3.2); through-

Then there are measures of racial stereotypes. The most direct measures of racial stereotypes, such as the adjective checklist, are not so much valid indicators of negative racial predispositions as they are of the norm of racial equality. Thus it is not surprising that these direct measures draw an egalitarian portrait of white views (Dovidio and Gaertner 1986). Somewhat more unobtrusive measures of racial stereotypes, which measure negative racial predispositions more accurately, paint a different picture (Crosby et al. 1980; Jackman and Muha 1984; Kuklinski et al. 1998; McConahay et al. 1981; McConahay 1986; Sigall and Page 1971). The 1990 General Social Survey, for example, included a series of items asking for seven-point ratings of various social groups on several trait dimensions. Respondents were asked to indicate to what extent members of each group were poor, lazy, violent, unintelligent, living off welfare, or unpatriotic. Subtracting the ratings of whites from those of blacks yields a measure of stereotypical thinking, telling us to what extent blacks are distinctively perceived to be poor, lazy, violent, dumb, prone to reject self-reliance, or unpatriotic (Bobo and Kluegel 1991; Kinder and Mendelberg 1995; T. Smith 1990). According to this definition, most whites do not think in a racially neutral way. Most whites believe that whites have more positive characteristics than blacks. This is particularly true of the long-standing stereotypes of violence, laziness, and, most of all, lack of economic self-sufficiency (Kinder and Mendelberg 1995; T. Smith 1990).

Still more unobtrusive measures of negative racial predispositions, particularly scales measuring symbolic racism, modern racism, or racial resentment, similarly reveal continuing animosity toward blacks (to be discussed further below). Responses to the four symbolic racism items carried by the 1988 Na-

---

out the 1970s pluralities believed the government was already spending a sufficient amount to improve the condition of blacks and only a few believed the government should be spending more. Large majorities maintained—and still do—that blacks and other minorities should help themselves rather than receive assistance from the government (Schuman et al. 1985, Table 3.2; 1992 NES, setting aside missing data). The 1992 NES, for example, found a majority of whites who thought spending to aid blacks was at a satisfactory level, while another quarter thought less money should be spent (only 18 percent thought spending should be increased, setting aside missing data). The only area in which a clear and consistent majority of whites seems satisfied with strong government intervention is the right of blacks to use hotels and restaurants (Schuman et al. 1985, Table 3.2). This is the only question of the comprehensive set tracked by Schuman et al. that specifies that Congress has already passed the law in question, a step likely to substantially increase support for the measure (Sniderman et al. 1991, 212). Hotels and restaurants are also much less important than are neighborhoods, schools, and workplaces, and whites are less likely to think that ensuring equal access to them will devalue the experiences they offer whites. No doubt, whites' resistance to implementing racial equality is not due to negative racial predispositions alone, as Bobo and Kluegel (1993), Kinder and Sanders (1996), and others have shown. Government spending that does not resemble racial redistribution and fits market mechanisms often gains substantial support from white voters. A large majority of 1990 GSS respondents, for example, endorsed spending more on black schools (69 percent) and on black college students (70 percent).

tional Election Study (NES), for example, show that racially resentful expressions on average are endorsed by 61 percent of whites. On the individual items of racial resentment the percentages range from 41 percent who deny that generations of slavery and discrimination hinder blacks to 74 percent who endorse the view that blacks should overcome prejudice without any special favors.[3]

Thus, most white Americans face a tension between two contradictory orientations. A strong descriptive and injunctive norm reinforces in the large majority of whites the belief that blacks and whites are inherently equal and deserve equal treatment. Yet a great many whites have negative racial predispositions. On the one hand almost all white Americans believe strongly that blacks should be treated equally. But on the other hand most whites also believe that blacks fail because they are deficient on the things whites value—they are less prone to work hard, to abide by the law, and to engage in moral sexual behavior. The tension between these two contradictory views creates ambivalence.[4]

Of course, race is not the only area in which public opinion demonstrates ambivalence. In other areas too, a principle weakens in the face of a conflicting principle or predisposition (Feldman and Zaller 1992; Kuklinski et al. 1991; McClosky 1964; Prothro and Grigg 1960; Stouffer 1955; Sullivan et al. 1978, 1982). The case of race, however, is special (see for example Feldman and Zaller 1992, 275 n. 4). As we saw in Chapters 1 and 3, there are additional grounds to expect whites to be ambivalent about racial matters. The civil rights movement helped create a sea change in racial norms, but at the same time it catalyzed a legal and political transformation that incorporated racial conflict into politics. Once Americans began to negotiate their racial arrangements from within political institutions, racial resentments surfaced, and the psychological battle between equality and resentment was on.

Operationalizing Negative Racial Predispositions

It is essential, before leaving the factor of ambivalence, to operationalize more precisely my definition of negative racial predispositions. My focus in subsequent chapters will be on priming—the waxing and waning of these predispo-

---

[3] Resentful expressions have not lessened measurably since 1988; the minimum and maximum percentages from the 1992 NES are, respectively, 38 percent and 74 percent (setting aside missing cases).

[4] This variant of the ambivalence hypothesis draws on Gaertner and Dovidio (1986). There are other variants of the hypothesis. Whites may be highly ambivalent when they think about racial matters because they adhere to conflicting tenets of the American creed (Kuklinski et al. 1991; Myrdal 1944). They may be ambivalent because they entertain both pro-black and anti-black orientations (Katz and Hass 1988; Katz et al. 1986). Regardless of precisely how and why ambivalence about race exists, several strands of literature agree that it is widespread among whites.

sitions as a determinant in whites' political decisions. As I do not have strong a priori expectations of how different elements of racial predispositions might operate, it makes sense to work from a definition sufficiently broad to capture a broad range of elements. Adopting a broad definition of racial predispositions is not a radical departure from standard treatments, even cognitive ones focused on stereotypes. Even such a simple definition of racial stereotypes as that of Hamilton and Torlier (1986), who conceptualize them as beliefs and expectations about groups, suggests that stereotypes may contain different elements. Many of the predispositions that have received attention from scholars, including attributions, affect, stereotypes, and values, are intimately related in the case of race. For example, the stereotype that blacks are lazy, the attribution of racial inequality to blacks' lack of commitment to hard work, and a preference for individual effort over government intervention in the situation of blacks are all logically related to each other. They are also empirically related to each other. A laziness stereotype and an individualistic attribution of racial inequality, for example, are interrelated dimensions of the same underlying construct (Kinder and Mendelberg 1995).

Taken together, these racial feelings and mental representations form a set of negative racial predispositions: sentiments such as fear, resentment, and anger; stereotypes that detail flawed character traits for blacks (particularly those relating to work, violence, and sexual immorality); and attributions for racial inequality that rest on blacks' dispositional faults.

This definition fits the predisposition known as symbolic racism, modern racism, and, most recently, racial resentment. Kinder and Sears defined it as "a blend of anti-black affect and the kind of traditional American moral values embodied in the Protestant Ethic . . . a moral feeling that blacks violate such traditional American values as individualism and self-reliance, the work ethic, obedience, and discipline" (1981, 416). Racial resentment is among the most powerful determinants of opinion on racial matters, ranging from affirmative action in schools and in hiring, to spending on government programs that aid blacks, to the government's role in eliminating racial discrimination and in desegregating schools (Kinder and Sanders 1996). In fact, Kinder, Sears, and other researchers have found that resentment tends to be the most powerful predictor of these opinions even when one takes into account nonracial predispositions such as unease about equality, a commitment to limited government, and economic individualism (Alvarez and Brehm 1997; Kinder and Mendelberg 2000; Kinder and Sanders 1996; Sears et al. 1997).

Consequently, when measuring racial predispositions in subsequent chapters, I will rely on scales of racial resentment. Because the most recent major work on this topic, Kinder and Sanders's *Divided by Color* (1996), is persuasive in arguing that the underlying construct is best labeled racial resentment, I too shall use that term, even though it is not without its problems. I will alternate between the terms resentment and racial predispositions, using the former primarily when I use the items developed by Kinder and Sanders, and the latter primarily when I refer to the construct in a more general way. More detail is available in the appendix.

The Power of Ambivalence

If the norm of racial equality and negative racial predispositions conflict, and if they generate ambivalence, we need to know what ambivalence might do to citizens' political judgments. Among the most compelling demonstrations of the power of ambivalence is Gaertner and Dovidio's studies of aversive racism (1986). Gaertner and Dovidio hypothesized that many whites have a genuine egalitarian self-image but also a proclivity to treat whites more favorably than blacks. Gaertner and Dovidio predicted that whites would be compelled by their egalitarian self-image to avoid discriminating against blacks. But whites would not always succeed. Whites manage not to discriminate only as long as the discrimination seems like discrimination. When the discrimination seems like something else, it is much more likely to happen.

Gaertner and Dovidio conducted a series of experiments to test their hypothesis that whites will only discriminate against a black individual when the discrimination seems to be nonracial. In a typical aversive racism experiment, a black confederate signals a need for help to a white subject. The investigators vary the normative requirement of providing help from strong to weak. In the strong normative condition the victim details his need for help in such a way that it is highly compelling and difficult to refuse. In the weak normative condition the need for help is less clear and easier to refuse. Thus, in the strong normative condition it is difficult to refuse help to a black person without seeming racist. In the weak condition it is possible to refuse to help a black person without seeming to be biased by race, since there is a nonracial reason to refuse—the help does not seem justified. In each condition, the experimenters contrasted whites' behavior toward a black person with their behavior toward an identical white person. They found that in the strong normative condition, when whites' failure to help a black person is likely to seem discriminatory, whites treat blacks and whites the same. But in the weak normative condition, when there are nonracial reasons to refuse help, blacks are helped less often than whites. Whites respond to the normative signals in the situation because they are committed to equality. But because they have negative racial predispositions, whites express them, as long as this expression does not appear to violate egalitarian norms.

The studies of aversive racism are confined to discrimination against a black individual, but they have implications for politics. The ambivalence between the norm of equality and negative racial predispositions is likely to affect not only the behavior of whites toward black individuals but also their political choices about race. Whites inhibit their negative predispositions only when egalitarian norms are salient to them. When these norms are salient, whites behave fairly toward individual blacks and are likely, by the same logic, to make fair political decisions that affect blacks. Thus, we can expect that the desire to maintain an egalitarian self-concept will predominate when a clear signal is sent about what is racist and what is egalitarian and when there are no nonracial grounds for ill-treating blacks. Under these conditions, we can expect more egalitarian political choices.

The implications for racial communication are straightforward. A racial message will have the greatest racial impact when the response it evokes can be explained by a nonracial reason. Racial predispositions will only be primed by a message when the members of the audience can still perceive themselves as conforming to the norm of equality. Conversely, a racial message will have little impact if the response to it cannot be explained by a nonracial reason.

ACCESSIBILITY AND PRIMING

The coexistence of negative racial predispositions with an egalitarian norm, which creates ambivalence, also creates instability in whites' racial response (Katz and Hass 1988; Katz et al. 1986; Gaertner and Dovidio 1986). When a person makes a decision about a political matter, she can give a great deal of weight or very little weight to each of the relevant predispositions. When predispositions conflict with each other, the weights they receive will fluctuate depending on which predisposition seems more appropriate to the situation (Feldman and Zaller 1992; Zaller 1992). In the aversive racism experiments, whites' ambivalence between the norm of equality and their negative racial predispositions makes them highly sensitive to the normative signals around them. The power of a message is greater when it evokes a predisposition about which a person is ambivalent. Ambivalence thus enhances the power of political communication to determine whether negative racial predispositions or a commitment to the norm of equality most influences whites' opinions about race-targeted policies and their evaluations of candidates.

I capture the instability from racial ambivalence through the notion of racial priming. Priming occurs when a person makes greater use of a given predisposition after exposure to communication that cues it in some way (Iyengar and Kinder 1987; Krosnick and Kinder 1990; Krosnick and Brannon 1993; see reviews by Kinder [1998] and by Graber [1984], [1993]). Iyengar and Kinder, for example, manipulated the extent to which viewers were exposed to television news coverage of a given issue and then asked viewers to evaluate the president. They discovered that more coverage of an issue leads viewers to give greater weight to the issue when evaluating the president (1987). Once a message has grabbed attention and been processed by a predisposition, that predisposition is likely to remain accessible—activated and ready for use. It is likely to dominate over other predispositions should viewers find themselves in a position to form and express a political opinion.

The notion that not all predispositions are consulted equally at decision-making time helps to explain the impact of racial messages. This notion derives from the assumption that people spend mental energy not infinitely, but only in pursuit of some goal (Fiske 1993; Fiske and Taylor 1991; Simon 1985; Zaller 1992). Instead of surveying all the predispositions that may apply, people conveniently rely on whatever comes to mind more readily, or whatever seems more relevant or important at the moment. The lens of group membership is among the most central and influential in American public opinion (e.g., Brady and Sniderman 1985; Bobo 1988; Conover 1984, 1985, 1988; Dawson 1994; Sears 1988). Thus it makes sense that, as empirical studies of racial resentment and racial stereotypes document, for many white citizens racial predispositions are often readily accessible.[5] Nevertheless, even chronically accessible predispositions can vary in use (Lau 1989). Ambivalence makes an accessible predisposition still more accessible—under the right conditions, such as the right type of message. The messages in the environment can increase the accessibility of a predisposition, leading the person to give it greater weight in making decisions about politics (Chong 1996; Fazio and Williams 1986; Lavine et al. 1996). Thus, the influence of racial predispositions can wax and wane depending on the message. A message—of the right kind—increases the weight a person gives to her negative racial predispositions. I will refer to this increased weight as racial priming.

In sum, racial messages work through racial priming. A racial message depends for its power on its ability to activate existing predispositions. But a predisposition does not always have the same weight regardless of the informational environment. The news media and political campaigns shape opinion on policies and candidates linked with matters of race by communicating messages that make negative racial predispositions more available for subsequent decisions about politics. Because of ambivalence, racial priming works well with some messages but not others. The question then becomes, how do white individuals resolve the tension between their negative racial predispositions and egalitarian norms?

---

[5] This could be driven by several processes. Perhaps racial predispositions are constantly, chronically accessible, but are given more weight in some decision-making after exposure to particular messages. Alternatively, perhaps racial predispositions are made even more accessible than normal levels, hence the priming effect. Accessibility is an important theoretical element of the priming phenomenon, but there is evidence that it is not necessary for priming (Nelson 1992). That is, implicit messages may not make racial predispositions more powerful determinants of racial views because they are more accessible in memory, but rather because it increases the weight given to racial predispositions in judgment. Simply remembering one's predispositions will not make one act them out, especially in today's political climate, given massive changes in norms of public expression on race.

AWARENESS

Awareness helps to resolve the conflict between contradictory predispositions. A growing literature in social psychology suggests that individuals give weight to their negative racial predispositions without full awareness. A racial message may thus prime racial predispositions even when a person does not attend to the racial nature of the message. In fact, a racial message probably primes racial predispositions especially when its racial meaning is processed outside of awareness. When a message primes racial predispositions with awareness, the audience's commitment to the norm of equality overrides the greater accessibility of racial resentments, fears, and stereotypes, and the message fails at racial priming.

Automatic activation of prejudice is far from a new idea. American intellectual history supplies repeated references to the notion that race prejudice was beyond the feeble corrective attempts of individuals. William Thomas of the University of Chicago, in a widely read article, argued nearly one hundred years ago that racial prejudice "cannot be reasoned with, because, like the other instincts, it originated before deliberative brain centers were developed, and is not to any great extent under their control. . . . [Race prejudice] is an affair that can neither be reasoned with nor legislated about very effectively" (Fredrickson 1971, 315). Twentieth-century history proved Thomas quite wrong. Law, it turns out, had quite a bit to do with changing racial mores in the 1950s and 1960s, and behavior motivated by race prejudice is quite manipulable when social institutions align themselves against it. Race prejudice is indeed under the control of the individual. But paradoxically, Thomas also may have been partly right. Individuals do not control their racial predispositions in every situation, even when they have repudiated racism.

A great deal of contemporary evidence suggests that negative racial predispositions can be primed without the awareness of the individual. Racial categories are so ingrained in American society that they may work at a primitive, visual level, and, like gender, they can dominate over other social categories (Brewer 1988). This kind of categorization can cause biased judgments even while a person performs the most simple and fundamental mental operations, and these operations tend to be those of which we are least aware (Banaji and Hardin 1996; Uleman et al. 1996). In a literature that has come to be known as "implicit stereotyping," social psychologists have repeatedly established that these social categories and their stereotypes can become more accessible for later decisions without the awareness of the individual (Banaji et al. 1993; Bargh and Pietromonaco 1982; Fazio et al. 1986; Greenwald and Banaji 1995; Higgins et al. 1985; Higgins and King 1981; Macrae et al. 1994; Moskowitz and Roman 1992; Moskowitz 1993; Wyer and Srull 1981).[6] Devine and her colleagues have found that anti-black beliefs, among other out-group stereotypes, can be made accessible without awareness (Devine 1989; Devine et al. 1991; Monteith et al. 1993).[7] In fact, priming may have the greatest impact when it takes place outside awareness and without intent (Moskowitz and Roman 1992; Strack et al. 1993). In one study, people instructed to memorize the priming cue but to ignore its meaning still showed priming effects, suggesting that information can influence social judgment despite the intent to use it for a different end (Uleman and Moskowitz 1994). Some studies have shown that even people who hold egalitarian beliefs, and presumably do not intend to make inegalitarian judgments about individuals, can still be led to make such judgments when primed with racist or sexist stimuli outside their awareness (Banaji and Greenwald 1995; Devine 1989).

As powerful as it is, unconscious priming can be controlled if people are motivated and aware enough to guard against it. We humans are biologically unique in our ability to control our unconscious. When American institutions aligned themselves against overt white supremacy, and advocacy of racial inequality became a social taboo, many whites acquired a strong motivation to control their use of racial predispositions, indeed, to regard the entire enterprise of racial distinction with suspicion. Experimental evidence suggests that people are quite capable of exercising control over their social judgments. People make inferences about other people's personality traits spontaneously and almost instantaneously, as they encode information, but they can nevertheless be taught to control this process if given immediate feedback (Uleman et al. 1996). Jury verdicts are influenced by tainted evidence even when the judge instructs jurors to ignore it, but not when jurors are suspicious about the source of the evidence (Fein et al. 1997). When people decide to counter their own stereotype activation, this motivation significantly reduces racial priming, even when cognitive resources are taxed; when cognitive resources are not taxed, the intent to counter stereotypes can completely reverse the priming effect (Blair and Banaji 1996). Whites who believe that blacks lack a work ethic are more prone than other whites to oppose government assistance to blacks; but if the blacks in question are portrayed in a positive, counter-stereotypical light, the effect of the stereotype is reversed (Peffley et al. 1997).

[6] Higgins et al. (1977) and Wyer and Srull (1980) have found that the effects of priming a mental representation on judgments of a target person continued until a week after the priming took place, and even increased over time. Fazio and Williams (1986) found that attitudes toward the 1984 presidential candidates varied in the extent to which they determined later vote choice depending on how accessible they were, and interpreted this result in light of a theory of automatic activation of attitudes outlined by Fazio (1986).

[7] An early assertion of this view among cognitive works is found in Taylor et al. (1978). For an early example of this work from within a classical conditioning paradigm see Tursky et al. (1976).

Thus, racial priming—whites giving their racial predispositions greater weight in making political decisions—is best predicted by a model that grants discretion and activism to individuals. As Thomas Nelson has suggested, we cannot explain the impact of racial messages with a pure accessibility model, that is, a model of racism in which whatever comes to mind finds automatic expression (Nelson 1992; see Fiske 1989 for a similar argument about the role of intent). Krosnick and Brannon suggest that priming is not so much about persuasion as it is about people making a conscious decision to give some considerations less weight than others (1993). While under some circumstances decisions are produced by an automatic process (e.g., E. Smith 1990), under other circumstances a conflicting orientation is used in a conscious way to override the primed predisposition.

Thus, awareness is likely to be a key factor that connects a racial message with a racial response. A conscious effort works to suppress the activation of stereotypes in social judgments, and it may work in the same way to suppress racial priming in political opinions. That conscious effort originates in a variety of psychological sources. It may be that, as Devine (1989) argues, all whites know the content of racial stereotypes and thus all whites are susceptible to racial priming, but some are more powerfully motivated to control it while others are less so. In that case, prejudiced individuals are distinguished from unprejudiced individuals not in the activation of racial stereotypes, but in their expression. Unprejudiced individuals are guided by internal standards while prejudiced individuals are guided by mere social concerns, and so the former succeed in overriding what the latter allow. Fazio and colleagues have challenged the assertion that all whites hold negative views of blacks that can be primed automatically, but they nevertheless agree that some individuals do fit Devine's model. Fazio and colleagues have stressed the finding that a person's motivation to suppress prejudice is an important variable (see also Plant and Devine 1998). Some situations allow individuals to recognize the relevance of exercising this motivation while other situations do not (Fazio et al. 1995; Fazio and Dunton 1997).

Another mechanism that allows whites to control racial priming is self-monitoring. Terkildsen (1993) found that the tendency to monitor one's self in accordance with the social demands of the situation contravenes the impact of prejudice. She found that people who were both prejudiced and self-monitored overcompensated for their prejudice by supporting a dark-skinned (fictitious) black candidate more than his lighter-skinned or white replicas (they also failed to show a preference for the white candidate over the light-skinned black candidate). On the other hand, people who were prejudiced but lacked the tendency to self-monitor simply expressed their prejudice by opposing the two black candidates more than an identical white candidate (opposition to the darker-skinned black candidate was greatest). Thus, once again we see that when prejudiced people fail to control their response, their prejudice influences their political choices. When they do control their response, however, their prejudice is neutralized as a determinant of their choice.[8]

These studies and others in this vein do not provide definitive evidence about whether or not racial predispositions become more accessible with exposure to racial cues. But they do suggest that people may choose (in conscious and nonconscious ways) whether or not to give weight to negative racial predispositions in making political choices. Most likely, that choice is driven in part by the nature of the message that cues negative racial predispositions.

MESSAGE AMBIGUITY

Why Ambiguity Matters

The final "A" factor in my theoretical framework is the ambiguity of the racial content of the message. People increase their reliance on predispositions when there are holes or gaps in the information around them. A message that can be perceived in more than one way will tend to be perceived in a manner consistent with information already in mind. An ambiguous cue will elicit more stereotypic judgments than an unambiguous cue, especially among people who endorse the stereotypes (Bargh and Pietromonaco 1982; Devine 1989; Higgins and King 1981; Higgins et al. 1985; Higgins et al. 1977; Wyer and Srull 1980). Zarate and Smith (1990), for example, showed that when subjects are shown an African-American man, they tend to perceive him primarily as an African American and secondarily as a man. Categorizing a black man as black in turn leads people to increase their reliance on racial stereotypes when they make judgments. Unfortunately, much of what we know about ambiguity comes from studies that document the impact of unambiguous cues (such as explicitly racial category labels) on judgments of ambiguous targets (a person whose race is unclear). We know much less about the impact of ambiguous cues—such as an implicit racial message.

Nevertheless, we can infer that ambiguous messages do in fact lead voters to increase their reliance on their predispositions. Conover and Feldman

---

[8] A less cognitive, more affective theory, proposed by Gray (1982) and elaborated by Frijda (1988), essentially reiterates this analysis. According to Frijda, emotions are subject to what he calls the "law of care for consequence," which dictates that "every emotional impulse elicits a secondary impulse that tends to modify it in view of its possible consequences" (355). Emotions encounter a control mechanism, itself part of the package of emotional response, ubiquitously known as anxiety, although not restricted to it. The existence of this mechanism explains how even very powerful emotions are prohibited from dictating behavior. The emotional variant of the controlled process theory also accommodates communication and the nature of the informational environment. The extent to which emotional control relaxes is directly and powerfully determined by the demands of the situation. Emotional self-monitoring erodes when others seem to be letting themselves go.

(1989), for example, found that the ambiguous environment of a presidential campaign elicits voters' preexisting information structures. These predispositions include voters' own issue preferences, what voters know about the meaning of ideological labels, and the issue positions implied by candidates' party membership. The extent to which voters rely on their predispositions depends on the nature of the informational environment during the campaign. Voters use predispositions because the information needed to evaluate candidates is either lacking or ambiguous. Candidates' issue positions, for example, are often difficult to decipher, and the more ambiguous these positions the more voters rely on their own views (Shepsle 1972; Page and Brody 1972).

If, in general, voters rely on predispositions to a greater extent when confronted with an ambiguous message, perhaps the same logic applies to race. Ambiguity about the racial nature of a candidate's message may lead voters to increase their reliance on their racial predispositions. This prediction about ambiguity is reinforced by the work of Gaertner and Dovidio (1986) on aversive racism. The aversive racism studies find that where there is ambiguity about the applicability of egalitarian norms of behavior, the likelihood of discrimination increases. Conversely, where there is no ambiguity about the meaning of a behavior, that is, no other plausible grounds for ill-treating blacks, whites will behave in an egalitarian manner toward blacks.

The notion that expression of stereotypes is conditional on legitimation is further supported by results from a different line of research. Darley and Gross (1983) suggest an important qualification to the application of stereotypes to ambiguous information. In their experiment, subjects were asked to judge an individual presented as either lower class or upper class. This by itself was insufficient to elicit class stereotypes. When joined with ambiguous information about the individual's intelligence, however, the low-class label triggered the application of class stereotypes in judgments of the individual. Yzerbyt and his colleagues (1994) interpret Darley and Gross's results to mean that people are generally reluctant to apply stereotypes in social judgment, but are much more willing to do so when given individuating information, since then their judgments seem to them individually based. When a message presents both stereotypical information and individuating information, viewers may be more likely to apply stereotypes in later evaluations than when stereotyped information is presented alone.

Implicit racial messages are ambiguous racial cues; it is unclear whether they are about race or not. The racial cue is there but it is dominated by nonracial content. This ambiguity may be the source of their power. Implicit racial messages may be more effective in evoking racial predispositions than unambiguous—that is, explicit—racial messages. Ambiguously racial messages activate racial predispositions but circumvent conflicting considerations such as a commitment to the norm of equality. Racial predispositions remain ready for use later on when voters form and express opinions about racial matters and when they choose among candidates.

Ambiguity and Visual versus Verbal Information

The distinction between visual and verbal information helps to clarify how appeals can be ambiguously racial. Implicit appeals may be most effective when they are visual. The reason is that visual racial content commands less conscious attention than verbal racial content. The visual content seems coincidental, secondary to the point—if it is submerged in verbal content that does not mention race. At the same time, the visual racial cue can activate racial predispositions quite strongly. Hence, implicit appeals are both deniable and powerfully racial.

Visual images are important to the way people perceive their world. Communication research has long argued that television is a unique medium because it is primarily visual (Jamieson 1992; Just et al. 1996; Peffley et al. 1996): "The visual grammar used by television (i.e., the relationships, inferences, and symbols presented through images and pictures) is not only unavailable to other forms of communication but may actually be more persuasive" (Peffley et al. 1996, 6). Studies of human perception have demonstrated that visual information can elicit emotions to a greater extent than verbal information (Fiske 1989; Fiske and Taylor 1991; Frijda 1988; Ortony et al. 1988). The information we see can dominate the process by which we make decisions (Biocca 1991; Petty and Cacioppo 1981, 1986; Fiske and Taylor 1991; Lynn et al. 1985; Neuman et al. 1992; Nisbett and Ross 1981; Paivio 1991).

Research about politics confirms these more general findings. Sullivan and Masters (1988) found that emotional cues in candidates' facial expressions changed candidate evaluations more than did viewers' party identification, issue agreement, or assessment of leadership ability. Lanzetta et al. (1985) found that exposure to the smiling face of Ronald Reagan increased positive evaluations of him, regardless of prior political disposition. The physical attractiveness of a candidate also influences voters' evaluations (Riggle et al. 1992; Rosenberg et al. 1991). Because most voters tend to be relatively uninvolved in politics and pay little attention to political information, they engage in "peripheral processing" and are persuaded by incidental cues (Krugman 1986; Zillmann 1984).[9] Thus, most viewers are likely to be highly susceptible to the influence of visual information.

---

[9] Petty and Cacioppo (1986) discuss two distinct levels of processing persuasive messages, one central and one peripheral. The central route happens when highly involved viewers engage in a high degree of information elaboration and comparisons with prior knowledge, high attention, and thoughtful consideration of the topic. Their attitude structures about the attitude object are

We can infer from these findings that visual cues are a fertile ground for implicitly racial communication. If visual information can trump verbal information, then a visual racial cue will likely have an effect even if the verbal information provided with it is nonracial. Moreover, if visual cues are processed peripherally, then visual images may work in a less conscious way than verbal information. Visual cues to race may work outside of awareness, without interference from people's commitment to the norm of equality. Accordingly, my studies will make use of the split between visual and verbal information to test for the distinctive power of implicit racial messages.

SUMMARY

Four factors determine whether or not a racial appeal works in the age of equality. The most basic is accessibility and priming. This is the mechanism that, when it fails, allows racial predispositions to remain politically disconnected, and when it succeeds, brings them into politics. The other factors— ambivalence, awareness, and ambiguity—determine whether racial priming succeeds or whether it is mitigated by the norm of racial equality. The success of racial priming depends on the message being ambiguously racial, that is, on it being implicit rather than explicit. Ambivalence creates a greater psychological susceptibility to communication and a sensitivity to the racial nature of the message. Awareness of the racial nature of the message and of one's own response allows the norm of racial equality to override racial priming, while the lack of awareness facilitates racial priming.

The framework provided in this chapter implies that white voters will be influenced by racial messages, giving greater weight to their racial predispositions (operationalized as racial resentment) but only when the message is implicitly racial. The more voters' attention is called to a violation of the norm of racial equality, the more their commitment to that norm will come into play, at the expense of the weight they give to their racial predispositions. In such a fashion racial appeals can be neutralized.

---

stable. Peripheral processing happens through heuristics. It happens to viewers low in involvement, when they rely on secondary features of the message, like affective cues in the speaker's facial expressions that are not intrinsic to the content of the message. These perceivers' attitude structures are relatively volatile.

The distinctive power of visual symbols, especially when presented on television, may in part be due to their greater vividness and distinctiveness relative to auditory information. As cognitive misers, viewers will attend to vivid stimuli more than pallid stimuli (Fiske and Taylor 1991). However, there is a controversy about whether there really is a vividness effect or not, and how conditional it is. Frey and Eagly (1993) found that vividness detracts from the persuasiveness of a message, but only when respondents are not very attentive to the message. When viewers are more attentive to the message, its vividness has no impact on either memory or persuasion.

APPENDIX: CONCEPTUALIZING RACIAL PREDISPOSITIONS

In the most influential early treatment of racial predispositions, Gordon Allport defined prejudice as "an antipathy based on a faulty and inflexible generalization. It may be felt or expressed. It may be directed toward a group as a whole, or toward an individual because he is a member of that group" (1954, 9). Allport's conceptualization of racial prejudice was sufficiently elegant and incisive to shape contemporary treatments of racial attitudes through the present. For one thing, he gave weight to both emotional and cognitive elements of racial prejudice (although he seemed to conceive of cognitive details as justifications of underlying hostility); prejudice by definition consisted of hostility and a distinctively unreasonable reason for it, the "faulty and inflexible" racial stereotype. Allport's conceptualization also had the virtue of situating racial prejudice in the context of real world conditions and the power dynamics of social groups. Prejudice existed as part of a society arranged according to racial hierarchy and dominance. It stood to reason that when those arrangements changed, so should prejudice, and in this sense too Allport's conceptualization proves useful for my present purpose. Studies of racial predispositions since the early 1970s have purposefully tended to place cognition at center stage and neglect affective components (Ashmore and Del Boca 1981; Pettigrew 1981). As Dovidio and Gaertner point out, the astronomic growth in studies of stereotyping in the 1970s, a byproduct of the cognitive revolution in social psychology, was concurrent with the decline in studies of prejudice (Gaertner and Dovidio 1986, 13).

Symbolic Racism and Racial Resentment

A contemporary approach that may be the closest heir to Allport's view is variously termed symbolic racism (Kinder and Sears 1981; Sears 1988), modern racism (McConahay 1986; McConahay et al. 1981), and, most recently, racial resentment (Kinder and Sanders 1996).[10] Its logic is that whites' racial preferences are intimately intertwined with the classic American values of self-reliance and individual effort. Sears, Kinder, and McConahay have taken a measurement tack that is unobtrusive yet includes affect. This measurement strategy is also distinctive in situating resentful expressions in a political and moral context.

The items used to measure resentment reflect the two elements of the concept: hostility toward militant black demands, and resentment of benefits be-

[10] Bobo and colleagues have recently added the related concept of "laissez-faire racism" (Bobo et al. 1997).

stowed on blacks—which are perceived as undeserved—or costs imposed on whites—which are perceived as unfair (Sears 1988, 56).[11] Much of the unobtrusive nature of this approach rests on its situating racial antagonism in the context of politics. This makes expressions of resentment appear to be nonprejudicial because they are political, and because they are not ideological defenses of white supremacy.

There is of course a controversy about the validity of symbolic racism and modern racism. Yet much of the controversy is about whether symbolic racism is a valid measure of racial *prejudice* (e.g., Sniderman and Piazza 1993). There seems to be much less controversy about its adequacy as a measure of racial *stereotypes*. In fact, its items fit rather well with a variety of conceptualizations of stereotypes (Gardner 1994). In a recent article, Vertanen and Huddy find that symbolic racism is empirically related to traditional assessments of stereotypes (1998). Kinder and Mendelberg (1995) as well found that symbolic racism items and more overt stereotype measures scale on the same dimension (see also Kinder and Sanders 1996). Scholars concur on the twin points that large numbers of white Americans believe that blacks tend to shirk their responsibilities and that this belief leads whites to oppose many government policies on matters of race. Sniderman and Piazza (1993), for example, disagree that this stereotype measures prejudice (because they conceive of prejudice as a strong, consistent, and simple hostility to blacks); but they agree that it is a stereotype, and a powerful one (105–109). They found that stereotypes that implicate blacks' failure to work hard were the most powerful of the stereotypes they studied. Whites who believed that "blacks on welfare could get a job" or that "blacks need to try harder" or that "black neighborhoods are run down" were much more opposed to more spending for blacks, to ensuring fair job treatment, and to affirmative action—more opposed than whites who rejected these stereotypes and more opposed than whites who endorsed other kinds of racial stereotypes (Sniderman and Piazza 1993, 92–99).

Measuring Racial Predispositions and Racial Resentment

The racial resentment items (or a subset depending on the chapter) serve as the primary individual-level independent variable in this book. The items are listed below. Responses are in five-point Likert format ranging from strongly agree to strongly disagree, with counterbalancing to prevent acquiescence bias.

Most people—blacks and whites alike—agree that the average white person in America is more likely to have a good income, get a good education, and to have a regular job than the average black person. Here are some reasons that have been

---

[11] McConahay had a third category: the sense that discrimination is no longer a problem.

given as to why the average black American is not as well off as the average white American.

1. Irish, Italian, Jewish, and many other minorities overcame prejudice and worked their way up. Blacks should do the same without any special favors.

2. Over the past few years, blacks have gotten less than they deserve.

3. It's really a matter of some people not trying hard enough; if blacks would only try harder they could be just as well off as whites.

4. Generations of slavery and discrimination have created conditions that make it difficult for blacks to work their way out of the lower class.

These items are affectively charged, they contain an internal attribution for racial inequality, they explicitly refer to blacks, and they directly implicate traditional standards of conduct such as self-reliance. Therefore, they are powerful, they are specifically racial, and they represent the core of whites' complaints about blacks' behavior. Because they are not couched in the language of inherent inferiority, and they do not directly invite a judgment of the characteristics of blacks as a group, they are less obtrusive than traditional measures of racism. An extensive validation of these items can be found in Kinder and Sanders (1996). There is by now ample evidence that racial predispositions, measured in this way, are an important determinant of opinions on racial matters. The more resentment people feel, the more opposed they tend to be to policies and candidates attempting to advance racial equality, even after controlling for other factors such as nonracial ideology (Alvarez and Brehm 1997; Kinder et al. 1989; Kinder and Sanders 1996; Mendelberg 1997; Sears et al. 1997; Sears et al. 2000).[12]

ADVANTAGES AND DISADVANTAGES OF THE EXPERIMENTAL TESTS

My methodological approach in this book is eclectic, reflecting my belief that the best social science is one that uses multiple methods. Although I make use of survey data, I rely primarily on experiments.

Controlled experiments on opinion leadership, although disadvantaged by their own weaknesses, nevertheless have the advantage of strong causal inference (McGraw 1991). My analysis of the 1988 National Election Study affords several important advantages. I was able to rely on a random national sample of actual voters and gauge their response on a "real-time" basis, as the campaign unfolded. But estimating the impact of campaign messages with survey data poses problems as well. The uncertainty about which individuals received what

---

[12] Another important virtue of this measure from my point of view is that it hardly changes in response to question order (based on a split ballot experiment embedded in the 1988 NES; see 1996, 347 n. 27). This is excellent evidence that it is indeed measuring a predisposition and not a top-of-the-head, easily changeable response.

level of exposure remains. So does the inability of a general measure of campaign exposure to tease out the effects of a particular element of the campaign from concurrent campaign messages and events, and to ensure that recipients of the message are different from nonrecipients only in exposure. Finally, there is the vexing problem of estimating the impact of the message net of simultaneous mood-of-the-times factors that can also shape public opinion.

To avoid these methodological problems, I designed experiments that control the exact content and circumstances of exposure, thereby estimating the unique and unbiased effect of the message of interest. Experiments feature control over the content of the message, which can be constructed according to the demands of the research question at hand; control over which other messages, if any, are sent at the same time; greater control over attention to the message, maximizing the independence of message reception and message impact; control over the conditions of exposure, ensuring uniform exposure; and in general, stronger causal inference through random assignment of subjects to message conditions (Graber 1993; Iyengar and Kinder 1987; Kinder and Palfrey 1993).

Experiments introduce problems of their own, largely related to the artificial nature of the laboratory and its attendant procedures and stimuli (Graber 1993; Kinder and Palfrey 1993). There have been important advances in political science experimentation in this direction, including efforts to make the laboratory setting more homelike (Iyengar and Kinder 1987) and recruiting a demographically diverse sample in place of the more usual procedure in social science experimentation of recruiting primarily students (Sears 1986). There have also been efforts to introduce experimentation into the survey interview by treating survey questions as the stimulus and using random assignment to match questions with respondents (Nelson and Kinder 1996; Kinder and Sanders 1996; Marcus et al. 1995; Sniderman et al. 1991; Sniderman and Piazza 1993; Sniderman and Carmines 1997; Sullivan et al. 1978). Even so, the laboratory remains the near-universal setting for controlled experiments in political science, particularly in public opinion.

The design of the welfare experiment in Chapter 7 is well suited to address these problems. For that study I implemented a fully randomized experiment in the homes of a random sample of eligible voters in Washtenaw County, Michigan. This provides some assurance that the results generalize to the setting where people normally go about consuming media messages and expressing opinions. And because it was applied to a sample of citizens who were contacted at random (as was the norms experiment in Chapter 8), the design minimizes perhaps the most common experimental threat to external validity—the reliance on samples of convenience, particularly college students.

I took several steps to address what is widely taken to be the primary defect of experiments—that they are artificial. The most significant step was field experimentation. Moving from the lab to people's homes has several methodological implications. Subjects contend with one stranger, the experimenter, rather than with a group of other subjects who are strangers, as is common practice in lab experiments. Second, the simple fact of being in one's home means that subjects were in a familiar setting. Third, the experimental treatment entailed watching television (mostly their own), hardly an unfamiliar task, which meets an important criterion for external validity, though the subsequent self-administered questionnaire is one of the classroomlike tasks traditional to experiments and objected to by Sears (1986). Fourth, the experimenter loses some of the authority conferred by a lab setting, leaving subjects with more of it. I relied on a group of undergraduate students in their early twenties to run the bulk of the sessions; consequently, respondents were often considerably older than the experimenter. Anecdotal evidence from the initial phone conversation with the respondents revealed that many of them volunteered out of a sense of kinship or loyalty to the University of Michigan or a desire to help a student with a research project, and so approached the at-home session with an attitude of magnanimity or mild curiosity. This is perhaps understandable in light of the recruitment story, which stressed that one of our purposes was to improve the performance of University of Michigan journalism students. While the experimenter was setting up video equipment, subjects would often offer a drink, initiate casual conversation, deal with their children, or finish up a household chore. Subjects in this experiment seemed, relative to lab experiments, less meek and compliant, freer to question the study, and generally acted out a host's role, one much more comfortable, familiar, and less susceptible to demanding characteristics than that of lab subjects.

The use in this and in the norms experiment of seemingly real candidates in a fairly professional-looking television news segment was also intended to increase external validity. The campaign information typically distributed in media experiments tends to have many things that real-world campaign information does not: lots of facts; a clear summary of policy positions; a list of candidate characteristics; and printed rather than visual and auditory information (e.g. Lodge et al. 1989; McGraw 1991; Sigelman et al. 1992). These studies have much to offer, though often by necessity they are stronger on internal than external validity. I tried to minimize this trade-off, but also, where possible, to maximize generalizability. Of course, the best corrective is to use different methods to reach the same result (Sigelman and Rosenblatt 1996).

CHAPTER 5

Crafting, Conveying, and Challenging Implicit Racial Appeals: Campaign Strategy and News Coverage

> The use of a trick or stratagem permits the
> intended victim to make his own mistakes, which,
> combined in a single result, suddenly change the
> nature of the situation before his very eyes.
> —Clausewitz, On War

SINCE THE 1960s, the American party system has divided along racial lines. The Republican party relies on and seeks to mobilize white voters, who tend to be more racially conservative, while Democrats count on the support of African Americans, who are by far the most loyal Democratic constituency. Campaigns can thus take on a racial character at all levels of office, not just in the South, and not only when a black candidate is on the ballot. At the same time, however, the norm of racial equality clearly functions as a constraint on the nature of racial campaigns. Crafting an appeal to a constituency of whites requires great care and subtlety. The structure of electoral coalitions, and the strong norm of racial equality, provide Republican candidates with incentives to use implicitly racial appeals. These appeals allow Republican candidates to play the race card with deniability.

That is, in essence, the account I have developed in the preceding chapters. But to persuade, this account must answer three questions. First, does the Republican party intend to craft deniable racial appeals, or is the racial message a largely unintended by-product of conservative appeals on social issues? Some scholars argue that rather than emphasizing race, the Republican party emphasizes social issues and values that do not only appeal to racially resentful whites (Abramowitz 1994; Black 1998; Sundquist 1983). Are code words in fact part of a strategy of covert racial appeals, or not?

Second, how quickly and decisively does the media challenge implicit appeals, contingent on what factors, and how effectively? The news media can determine how the parties' campaign messages are communicated to the public (Graber 1988; Jamieson 1992; Just et al. 1996; West 1997). But studies of implicitly racial appeals have not fully explored the ways in which the media facilitates—or challenges—implicitly racial appeals.

Third, how does the Democratic party respond to an implicitly racial appeal? Today, Democrats often shy away from discussing race for fear of alienating white voters (Glaser 1996; Edsall and Edsall 1991; Kinder and Sanders 1996). But perhaps the party loses by remaining silent in the face of Republicans' implicitly racial appeals. Challenges to race-baiting are a longstanding practice in American politics, as Chapters 2 and 3 showed. Southern candidates affiliated with racial liberalism have engaged in this strategy on and off for over a hundred years. So have leaders in the black protest tradition. Perhaps this antiracist strategy is more effective than silence.

Here I attempt to answer these three questions with an analysis of the 1988 presidential campaign, including media coverage of that campaign. The 1988 election is widely remembered as the time the Democrats were taken to task for their liberal policies and lost the presidential election due to the Republicans' superior capability to go negative. Perhaps nothing better exemplifies this account of the election than the case of Willie Horton. Horton was a young black man convicted of a grisly first-degree murder and sentenced to life in prison without parole in Massachusetts, where Michael Dukakis, later to become the Democratic presidential nominee, was governor. While on a weekend pass Horton kidnapped and brutally assaulted a white couple in their home, raping the woman and stabbing the man. The Republican party made Horton a centerpiece of its campaign, charging that Dukakis was soft on criminals. George Bush launched the campaign's first use of the Horton story in June, with the Bush campaign (including supposedly independent political action committees and state Republican organizations) intensifying the effort in October. The more intensely the Bush campaign focused on Horton, the more frequently he was covered by the news media. From the beginning, news coverage of the message was highly visual, conveying the story with racially stereotypic imagery, such as Horton's glowering mug shot. However, no officials (Democratic or Republican) and almost no mainstream journalists made verbal references to race in connection with Horton—until October 21, when Jesse Jackson charged the Republican campaign with using Horton as a racial appeal. On that very day, the campaign was transformed from implicit to explicit. Other prominent Democratic officials, including Dukakis's running mate Lloyd Bentsen, echoed the charge, and journalists, for a few days, considered whether or not the Horton appeal was racial. Nearly all treated the charge with skepticism, but as we shall see in the next chapter, simply raising the question of race in an explicit way would make all the difference to white voters' response.

During the course of the campaign, the news media provided three different frames for the Horton story: criminal justice, negative campaigning, and race. A frame is an organizing theme composed of several elements, such as key words, phrases, and images. Together these elements create a coherent narrative that suggests how to interpret an issue and what to think about it (Gamson and Lasch 1983). As a discussion of criminal justice, the Horton case was a symbol of what some considered a liberal, overly lenient treatment of criminals—issuing weekend furloughs to convicted murderers. As a campaign appeal, the Horton case embodied the tough electioneering of the Republicans, and the ineffectual attempts of the Democrats to launch a countercharge. Finally, Willie Horton also fit neatly into the still-salient stereotype of black criminality (Gilliam et al. 1995; Hurwitz and Peffley 1997; Entman 1992; Kinder and Sanders 1996; Valentino 1999).

The fact that multiple frames existed for the Horton story is fortuitous for my purpose. It allows me to find out whether the frame of crime, perceived at the time as racially neutral, provided the means for conveying an implicitly racial message—purposefully for Republicans, inadvertently for the media. My analysis suggests that when news coverage of Willie Horton used the Republican-supplied frame of crime, no verbal cues to race were included, yet Horton's image was heavily used. When, much later in the campaign, and after Jackson's intervention, the media covered the Horton story with the Democratic-supplied frame of race, that coverage included verbal and visual cues to Horton's race, thus communicating racially stereotypic cues explicitly. When the media adopted the crime frame, it allowed the Republican party to communicate racial cues with deniability. The race frame, by contrast, made the Republicans' implicit racial message more difficult to communicate with deniability. The Republican party may thus be most successful in appealing to white voters when it communicates racial cues within a nonracial verbal frame, and when the media follows suit. The party is least successful in its racial appeal when the media uses a verbal race frame to convey that appeal.

IMPLICIT COMMUNICATION, THE NEWS MEDIA, AND PARTISAN COMPETITION

Existing studies of the Horton message suggest that during some portion of the campaign, the racial facts of the Horton story, and certainly its symbolic racial meaning, were not stated baldly. Viewers, argued Jamieson, projected their racial fears and stereotypes onto the Bush campaign's ads; the ads themselves did not communicate racial views. Only one ad, "Weekend Passes," made by an independent political group, actually showed Horton's image; yet Jamieson believes that this ad, because it was disseminated by the news media, was enough to cause white viewers to project their racial fears onto the chief Republican ad on crime, "Revolving Door," which did not show or discuss Horton at all (1992). Jamieson concludes that "visceral and visual readings that do not inhere explicitly can be read implicitly in texts about out-groups" (1992, 36). Kinder and Sanders and Edsall and Edsall similarly suggest that the Horton story was an instance of racial "code words," a way for Republicans to wink at the white audience without getting caught (Kinder and Sanders 1996; Edsall and Edsall 1991).

It is still unclear, however, whether Republicans had an implicit racial strategy. Did they intend to appeal to whites' racial sentiments but to deny doing so? It is also unclear to what extent and in what ways the media allowed them to do so. Did the media convey the Horton message implicitly, and if so, how and why? Did the media learn its lesson and change its way of covering racial campaign appeals? Finally, it is also unclear what effect, if any, the Democratic response had. What role, if any, did the Democratic countermessage about Horton play in the news coverage of Horton, and did partisan competition neutralize the play of the race card?

The news media is prone to inadvertently aiding in the communication of implicit racial messages because in general it tends to convey racial stereotypes implicitly. Robert Entman has shown that racial stereotypes are conveyed by local news coverage of crime largely through racial images and without racially stereotypical words (1992). Black criminals are portrayed in a visually threatening way, for example, restrained by handcuffs, while white criminals are shown as relatively more respectable and less violent (see also Gilliam et al. 1995). At the same time, television journalists avoid overt expressions of racial prejudice. Martin Gilens found that the print media's images of welfare recipients also tend to communicate racial stereotypes (1997). Thus, the news media tends to communicate racially stereotypical content in a subtle way, through visual images. Although many observers now believe that the news media learned its lesson after 1988 and began to cover negative campaign messages more critically, my analysis of ten years of Horton coverage suggests that this lesson was not learned where racial messages are concerned. An analysis of 1988—of party strategy and of media coverage then and afterward—can thus provide more general implications about the media's role in racial campaigns and the pitfalls of the media's coverage of other racially relevant events.

I examined the public record about the campaign and conducted a content analysis of news coverage of Willie Horton, in order to find out whether, and why, the Horton story was conveyed implicitly or explicitly by Republicans and by the media. Specifically, I asked the following questions: (1) Did Republicans intend to use the Horton story to mobilize white voters with deniability, or was race a nonexistent (or peripheral) part of the Republicans' Horton tactic? (2) Did Republicans communicate the racial aspect of the Horton story in an implicit way, or was this done explicitly? (3) Did the news media convey Horton's race implicitly or explicitly? (4) If the media at any point conveyed the Horton story in an explicitly racial way, what prompted it to do so, and did the explicit coverage of Horton affect the frame provided for the Horton story?

In this chapter I provide evidence that the Bush campaign meant to employ the race card but to deny that it was doing so. A content analysis shows that where media coverage is concerned, this strategy succeeded. Between June 13, when Bush launched the Horton strategy, and October 20, just over two weeks before Election Day, only a handful of newspaper stories, and no magazine or television news story, mentioned the word "black" in connection with the name Horton. As a result, only a handful of the hundreds of news stories that mentioned Horton suggested that the Bush campaign was engaged in a racial strategy, or that the Horton story had racial overtones. At the same time, Horton's race was repeatedly displayed in the many network news broadcasts covering Horton. Much has been made of the impact of the unofficial "Weekend Passes" ad, which showed Horton's image and was disavowed by the Bush campaign. But in fact the media widely broadcast Horton's image without the ad's prompting. News coverage of the Horton case thus inadvertently aided in communicating an implicitly racial campaign appeal.

Neither was the media the actor responsible for taking the Republicans to task for their use of a racial story. This function was performed by Jesse Jackson, speaking as a prominent Democrat but perhaps more as a representative of the black protest tradition. Jackson, quite late in the campaign, abruptly seized the agenda and introduced the charge that the Republicans' Horton appeal was racist. Just as abruptly, the news media executed an about-turn and began to cover that story through the lens of race. Journalists did not accept the possibility that the Horton appeal was a play of the race card; quite the contrary. But they did give the charge, and the Republican countercharge, an intense—if very late—airing (and printing). It took the media approximately three years to validate the claim that the story of Horton had been a play of the race card. Nevertheless, as the next chapter will show, this acceptance was not necessary to neutralize the impact of the implicitly racial message. Jackson's challenge was sufficient.

THE BUSH CAMPAIGN'S DENIAL OF RACIAL INTENT

The Bush campaign denied that the Horton story had any racial overtones, much less that it was racially motivated. George Bush, campaign chairman James Baker, campaign manager Lee Atwater, media czar Roger Ailes, pollster Robert Teeter, and other high-level officials each steadfastly maintained, when asked, that the Horton appeal was not at all racially motivated. Late in the campaign, when asked about the possibility that the Horton story was racist, Bush told the press: "There is not a racist bone in my body." At about the same time, Baker maintained that the leaflets and ads with Horton's picture were produced without his approval (Drew 1989, 342). When the charge of racism was raised, Baker, Atwater, Ailes, and others repeatedly pointed out that the Bush campaign had never used Horton's image and had never referred to Horton's name in any of its paid advertising. In the immediate aftermath of the election, the Bush campaign emerged largely untainted by the charge of racism.

Atwater was probably the most vocal in this regard.[1] Taking stock of the campaign shortly after the election, Atwater told a public forum that his July

---

[1] In fact, in press interviews during and after the campaign, and at a public forum on the campaign at Harvard University, Atwater claimed that at first he did not know Horton was black,

boast to Republican leaders that he would make Willie Horton a household name and that Horton may even end up as Dukakis's running mate was "a mistake" (Runkel 1989, 116). Asked about his decision to downplay Horton in official campaign ads, Atwater explained:

> I am a white southerner and anytime I said anything I was accused of being a racist . . . but Willie Horton—there was nothing racial about Willie Horton. We resent the fact that it was used racially in the campaign because we certainly didn't, and we were very conscious about it. . . . We are very sorry if anyone took it racially, because we had a concerted effort in our campaign to make sure that race was not used in any way, shape, or form. . . . I do not think that people thought that the use of the furlough program was an injection of racism in this campaign. I have yet to see any data anywhere, in any shape or form, to sustain that. (Runkel 1989, 116–117, 127)

Ailes agreed: "If Willie Horton were white, we would have used the furlough program" (Runkel 1989, 120). In press interviews after the campaign, Ailes repeated this theme: "If Horton had been white," he told journalist Roger Simon, "we would have done more [Horton ads]" (Simon 1990, 301). "As a guy who has been in southern politics for 20 years," Atwater told the post-election Harvard forum, "there's no question in my mind that Republicans, Democrats, blacks, and whites all reject racist politics. If there were any racist politics in this campaign, it would have backfired on us, in the party" (Runkel 1989, 120).[2] Clearly, then, Atwater and Ailes perceived an acute need to distance the campaign from the charge of racism.

Atwater went to great trouble to deny links between the Bush campaign and other groups that did use Horton's image. These groups were mainly state Re-

---

and that when he found out about Horton's race, he had insisted that Horton's image or name not be used in any campaign appeals. Atwater said that his intent was to appeal to values, not racism (Runkel 1989, 114–117). Describing an impromptu discussion about Horton among a mixed-race group, which he had overheard at a restaurant in Virginia, Atwater said, "It was the white guy [who was angry about Horton] but it was the black woman who first brought it up, which was significant to me" (Germond and Witcover 1989, 164). When in late October Jackson and Bentsen charged the Bush campaign with racism, Atwater firmly denied the charge: "Race has nothing to do with this issue" (Sidney Blumenthal, "Willie Horton and the Making of an Election Issue," *Washington Post*, October 28, 1988). After the election Atwater claimed that during the campaign he had decided to reshoot the "Revolving Door" ad, now considered the most notable of the campaign, because he had worried that it showed "too many blacks in the prison scene" (Runkel 1989, 120).

[2] Even Atwater's so-called death-bed confession that he was wrong in using Horton, often taken as an apology for a racist tactic, was not that at all; it did not include a confession that the appeal was racially motivated, racially targeted, or designed to net racially motivated voters. When he told the *New York Times* in April 1989 that "I'm sorry [Horton] was black. In retrospect we should have used a white guy," Atwater was not admitting responsibility for playing the race card, but rather lamenting that he and the Republicans had been labeled racist. (Lee Atwater, "Second Thoughts on First Reactions to Race," *New York Times*, April 26, 1989).

publican organizations, which circulated and mailed leaflets and brochures, and a group called the National Security Political Action Committee (NSPAC), also known as Americans for Bush. At the same time that Atwater claimed that he and Ailes, upon learning that Horton was black, had made "a conscious decision not to use him in any of our paid advertising, on television or in brochures," he also said that "we figured at the time that we would have to try to police other people. There were so many groups. . . . The second decision we made was that the day we found any kind of brochure or television ad from an independent committee, we would denounce it publicly right off the bat" (Runkel 1989, 116). When a journalist pressed Atwater on why, if avoiding the use of Horton's face was so important, Atwater had not made this clear to the state parties, Atwater replied, "We did repeatedly. . . . We did it very early . . . right after [we mentioned Horton's name]" (Runkel 1989, 125). Bush officials thus were highly motivated to prevent the perception that their Horton message was a racial appeal. An important part of the Republican strategy was the effort to prevent such a perception. The evidence, however, suggests that Republican officials knew of Horton's race early on and used it, though with deniability.

EVIDENCE OF RACIAL INTENT

The Link between Independent Communication about Horton and the Bush Campaign

However strenuously the Bush strategists denied any link with independent operators, it is clear that many links in fact existed. A *Reader's Digest* article that first introduced Willie Horton to the nation in print was written by a freelance writer at his own initiative, but Andrew Card, Bush's first director of opposition research, admitted in an interview that he had contact with the writer before the article was published.[3]

Journalist Elizabeth Drew reported about one supposedly independent ad: "Before it even ran, one Bush campaign official read me the text of the 'independent' group's ad featuring Clifford Barnes, one of Horton's victims" (1989, 332). The same group had created "Weekend Passes," the only campaign ad that actually showed Horton's image. The producer of that ad, Larry McCarthy, had recently been employed by Roger Ailes, Bush's media director.

The hundreds of thousands of fliers displaying Horton's picture that were mailed to New York voters in the fall were sponsored by an organization oper-

---

[3] Dick Kirschten, "How the 'Furlough' Issue Grew and Dominated the Campaign," *National Journal*, October 29, 1988 The Republican National Committee sent every delegate to the Republican convention a reprint of the *Reader's Digest* article on Horton, thus ensuring that Horton's name was salient, but while the furlough program was raised often during the convention, Horton's name was "barely mentioned" (Drew 1989, 253).

ated by both state and national Republican officials, belying the claim that the national campaign knew nothing about the uses of Horton's image.[4] In press interviews, James Baker, deputy press secretary Mark Goodin, and other Bush campaign officials emphatically disavowed all state Republican ads and leaflets with Horton's picture, claiming that the campaign had no control over them. But when asked directly by the press, Bush did not deny his responsibility for the Maryland letter featuring pictures of Horton and Dukakis (Drew 1989, 342). Speaking to reporters late in the campaign, Bush said that "he did not mind" the use of Horton's picture in "independent" television advertising.[5] The officials of NSPAC, which produced the "Weekend Passes" ad, made clear that they did not receive a direct personal request from the Bush campaign to withdraw the ad until the ad had run for twenty-five days. "If they were really interested in stopping this," asked Floyd Brown, a consultant to NSPAC and a former Ailes employee, "do you think they would have waited that long to send us a letter?" (Simon 1990, 222). NSPAC's founder, Elizabeth Fediay, explained: "Officially the campaign has to disavow themselves from me. Unofficially, I hear that they're thrilled about what we're doing" (Simon 1990, 222). CBS's report on Federal Election Commission and congressional investigations into NSPAC provided evidence linking NSPAC's Fediay with an opposition research specialist officially employed in 1988 by the Bush campaign.[6] These pieces of evidence jointly suggest that the so-called independent efforts, partly responsible for the wide circulation of Horton's face, were hardly independent.

The Bush Campaign's Intentional Use of Race

Contrary to Bush officials' statements, the way they discussed the Horton case suggests that they knew of Horton's race early and that this influenced their use of his story.

The original news reports about the Massachusetts furlough program covered several white criminals along with Horton. Yet the Bush campaign said nothing about the white convicts who committed heinous acts while on furlough (Simon 1990; Jamieson 1992).

---

[4] "Bush Flier Features Convict," *New York Times*, October 24, 1988.

[5] Maureen Dowd, "Bush Says Dukakis's Desperation Prompted Accusations of Racism," *New York Times*, October 25, 1988.

[6] The opposition researcher, Candice Strother, had gathered voluminous information about Horton for the Bush campaign, including extensive clippings from a Massachusetts newspaper. She apparently passed on the information to Fediay, who passed it on to Larry McCarthy, commissioned to produce the Horton ad for Fediay's NSPAC. McCarthy told the FEC that he assumed the newspaper clippings came from the Library of Congress, but CBS found that this Massachusetts newspaper was not available there. After the election Fediay paid Strother $19,500 for unspecified opposition research although it was a non-election year. Strother then took a government job

From his first mention of Horton, Atwater spoke of him in a racially revealing way. Willie Horton was Atwater's invented name for William Horton, the name Horton had always used (Jamieson 1992). Atwater's recasting of William into Willie makes sense in light of the fact that Atwater was a white man raised in the Deep South during the 1950s and 1960s who was accustomed to referring to black men with overstated familiarity (Black and Oliphant 1989, 226; Jamieson 1992).

Early in the campaign, Atwater revealed that he did in fact know of Horton's race. In July Atwater told Republicans in Atlanta about "a fellow named Willie Horton who for all I know may end up being Dukakis's running mate" (Black and Oliphant 1989, 225; Drew 1989, 333); Atwater explained that he had seen Jesse Jackson with Dukakis, "so anyway, maybe [Dukakis] will put this Willie Horton on the ticket after all is said and done" (Black and Oliphant 1989, 225).[7] In September, well before Horton's race was remarked upon by the news media but while his face was being shown on television, a campaign strategist told Elizabeth Drew, "Every woman in the country will know what Willie Horton looks like before this election is over" (1989, 266). Possibly hoping to prod reporters to pursue the Horton story, Mark Goodin hung Horton's menacing picture by his desk at campaign headquarters.[8] A Bush aide told journalist Elizabeth Drew "with some satisfaction" that the campaign was having a desirable racial impact: "Dukakis's negatives with white voters are so high as to be insuperable" (1989, 305). Whether or not the aide's claim was true, it suggests that Horton's race was quite salient in the Bush camp. A biography of Bush reports that his aides knew from the start that Horton was black and that this made the appeal "both more devastating and dangerous" (Parmet 1997, 336). More than likely, the Bush campaign used the racial facts of the case intentionally—though subtly—as part of the overall strategy to recruit white voters without drawing the "racist" label.[9]

---

paying $100,000, which until then had not existed, and failed to report the fees she had received from Fediay on a required disclosure form (CBS Evening News, October 14, 1992).

[7] Atwater also bragged to Republicans in Houston, "By the time this election is over, Willie Horton will be a household name" (Drew 1989, 332). Ailes, too, had his moment of carelessness when he told the press, "The only question is whether we depict Willie Horton with a knife in his hand or without it" (Bernard Weinraub, "Campaign Trail: A Beloved Mug Shot for the Bush Forces," New York Times, October 3, 1988).

[8] Bernard Weinraub, "Campaign Trail: A Beloved Mug Shot for the Bush Forces," New York Times, October 3, 1988. See also Simon 1990, 219.

[9] Dan Quayle, Bush's running mate, seems to have been influenced by Horton's race in a way he could not fully control. Quayle's knowledge of Horton's race and his response to it can be seen by his vacillation on two separate questions posed to him about abortion. When Quayle was asked by an eleven-year-old girl whether she should be denied an abortion if raped by her own father, Quayle adhered to his strict pro-life position and told her yes (Drew 1989, 346). But when asked whether a woman raped by Willie Horton should be denied an abortion, Quayle made an exception: the woman should immediately go to the emergency room and undergo a "D. and C. [the standard abortion procedure] . . . a perfectly normal procedure that I would not put into the category of abortion" (NBC Nightly News, October 11, 1988; see also Drew 1989, 346).

Not only did Bush officials use Horton's case as part of a racial strategy designed to win over white voters; they clearly perceived Horton to be the centerpiece of their overall strategy. Atwater concluded during the campaign that Horton's furlough was the "silver bullet" he had been searching for, the issue that would single-handedly win the election for Bush. "It's the single biggest negative Dukakis has got," Atwater told a reporter in late October.[10]

The Source of the Implicitly Racial Strategy

Lee Atwater's racial use of Horton can best be understood in the context of Atwater's professional history. He got his start in politics during the early 1970s as an aide to South Carolina senator Strom Thurmond, the former Dixiecrat and pioneer of implicit racial appeals who switched to the Republican party in 1964 (Edsall and Edsall 1991). Atwater managed Thurmond's reelection campaign in 1978 as well (Black and Oliphant 1989, 206). Thus Atwater came of age as a professional political operative in the South just after southern politicians had traded in explicit for implicit racial campaigns (see Chapter 3). His hero was Richard Nixon, who won the presidency in 1968 with implicit racial appeals. Harry Dent, a Nixon strategist, was Atwater's mentor, and Atwater considered Nixon's southern strategy—appealing to racially resentful whites in the South—"a blueprint for everything I've done in the South" (O'Reilly 1995, 380–381). Atwater was highly conscious of the imperative for Republicans running in the South to appeal to racially tinged issues. In a heavily Democratic region, sticking to economic issues alone was bound to be a losing strategy. "Race," Glaser notes, "is never far from the minds of southern campaign managers. It cannot be" (1996, 43).

Atwater noted that he had been planning the 1988 campaign "at a certain level" since the early 1970s (Simon 1990, 305). "The Horton case," Atwater told the press early in the 1988 campaign, "is one of those gut issues that are values issues, particularly in the South, and if we hammer at these over and over, we are going to win."[11] When Atwater learned of the favorable focus group response to the Willie Horton strategy, obtained in a northern New Jersey suburb, he quickly understood its significance—voters outside the South would resonate to the same "values" issues that would win over the South. Nixon had won the presidency with a southern strategy that, because it was implicit, migrated quite naturally to the North. Atwater would do the same for Bush.

---

[10] Sidney Blumenthal, "Willie Horton and the Making of an Election Issue," *Washington Post*, October 28, 1988. Well before October, Republican-run focus groups across the country convinced Atwater and his associates that the furlough issue, communicated through the Horton case, was the most powerful one at their disposal (Simon 1990, 216).

[11] Andrew Rosenthal, "Foes Accuse Bush Campaign of Inflaming Racial Tension," *New York Times*, October 24, 1988.

Atwater thus concluded, based on his experience in southern campaigns, that a Republican candidate for the presidency had to make appeals to race but mask them. Atwater did not arrive at this strategy from scratch, nor did he acquire it in 1988. It was already considered a tried-and-true method by the top echelons of the Republican party.[12]

Atwater's essential strategy, then, may well have been to "play dumb and keep moving," in the words of one journalist (Simon 1990, 308). Atwater seemed to think of his political skill as a form of martial prowess, and believed that subterfuge was a crucial part of his toolkit. He carried with him everywhere a translation of Sun Tzu's *Art of War* and other classic martial texts, in which passages about deception were conscientiously underlined, and liked to show them to reporters (Simon 1990, 308).[13] For a person with such a martial view of electoral campaigns, making appeals to racial resentment without getting caught at it is likely to seem vital and proper.[14]

Thus, not only was the Horton story crafted as an implicitly racial appeal; its success, believed those who had crafted it, rested on its ability to remain implicitly racial. The key to the success or failure of this strategy was the news media.

HOW THE MEDIA CONVEYED THE HORTON STORY AS AN IMPLICITLY RACIAL MESSAGE

How was the Horton story actually conveyed in a way that was racial but appeared not to be? Typical of modern presidential campaigns, the Bush campaign relied heavily on the news media. As much as Republicans constructed their own paid media in an implicitly racial fashion, the news media ultimately determined whether the Horton story would be lodged in most voters' minds as implicitly or explicitly racial. For citizens, the news is a crucial means of obtaining political information. In 1988, Times-Mirror polls estimated that 84 percent of the adult population of the United States used television or newspapers for information on national affairs (Slass 1990, 14).

The content analysis that follows considers which frames—racial or nonracial—were constructed for the Horton story by the news media, and what type

[12] One component of Atwater's early plan that clearly was implemented in 1988 was to target the Sun Belt with the issue of crime: California and Texas were the focal points of the most intensive coverage of the crime issue, including "saturation radio" ads, more television ads, more direct mailings, and the personal oversight by the chief campaign managers in these states (Drew 1989, 342). Black and Oliphant report that "Weekend Passes" was shown widely in the South during the summer, well before it was shown in other regions (1989, 226).

[13] The two other books Atwater said he read "over and over" were Machiavelli's *The Prince* and Clausewitz's *On War* (Simon 1990, 308). Bush's biographer indicates that Bush knew of Atwater's penchant for deception and realized the need for it (Parmet 1997, 394).

[14] Atwater is probably the most important figure in the racial strategy behind Horton's case. But James Baker was chiefly responsible for focusing the campaign from mid-August onward on the crime issue, of which Horton was a crucial piece (Drew 1989).

of actor constructed each frame. The analysis also asks whether an authority figure (such as the reporter or an independent source) endorsed the final frame in which the Horton appeal was cast as racial. More importantly, the analysis also shows how racial meaning was conveyed by the media. Racial meaning could have been conveyed through references to any of the following racial elements of the story: Horton's race, his victims' race, the Bush campaign's intent to appeal to white voters' racial sentiments, and the Democrats' charge that the Horton message was racist. Horton's and his victims' race were the racial elements that the Bush campaign intended to convey. The racial elements of the story that they hoped would not be conveyed were their own racial intent and the charge that the message was racist; this was exactly what the Democrats eventually tried to convey. My analysis distinguishes between verbal and visual references to Horton's race, a distinction that is crucial to the strategy of implicitly racial messages.

I conducted a quantitative and qualitative analysis of news coverage of Willie Horton. Included are all stories in newspapers defined by Nexis as "major," all stories appearing in Nexis's database of major news magazines, and all broadcasts by the three major networks in 1988. A story or broadcast segment was included if it mentioned Horton's name at any point.[15] The first Horton story broadcast on network news was in December 1987, when the furlough issue was a local news item in Massachusetts and thus relevant to Dukakis's run for the Democratic presidential nomination.[16]

THE IMPLICIT PHASE OF THE HORTON MESSAGE

No Verbal Reference to Race

Did the news media facilitate the implicitly racial strategy and convey the Horton story without explicit—that is, verbal—reference to race? I begin with the results of the major newspaper analysis.[17] Figure 5.1 divides the verbal references in these stories into several categories: a reference to Horton's race; a reference to the Bush campaign's racial intent or to the racial effect of the message (described with words such as "racial" and "racist"); a reference to another racial actor (primarily black voters or white voters). I also coded

[15] Tapes of the television news broadcasts were borrowed from the Vanderbilt Television News Archive. In Nexis, I used two independent search terms: "Horton" and "furlough." The latter was necessary since Nexis omitted some stories that mentioned Horton from the first results list. The broadcast analysis is based on unedited footage provided by Vanderbilt. In Nexis, the full text of the news stories was available. Stories about other individuals by the name of Horton were deleted from the set.

[16] The *Eagle-Tribune* of Lawrence, Massachusetts, pursued the story diligently, running over 200 stories on the furlough issue and contributing to the petition drive that ultimately led Dukakis to revoke the furlough program in April 1988 (Simon 1990, 212).

[17] Between June 1988 and May 1998, 1,167 major newspaper stories mentioned Willie Horton.

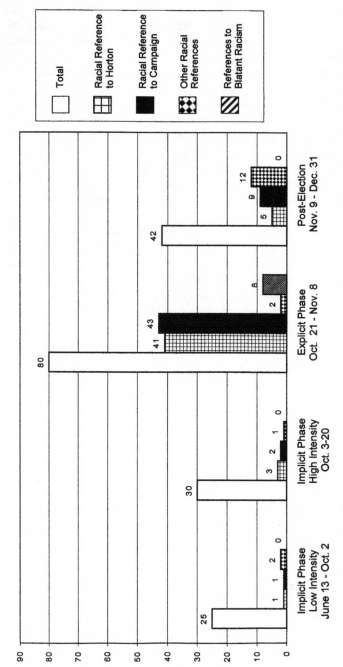

Figure 5.1. Verbal references to race in major newspaper stories about Willie Horton during the 1988 campaign. The figure excludes stories that contained the search words but with the wrong meaning, e.g., *race* as a synonym for *contest* rather than *ethnicity*, or references to others named Horton. Stories may be counted in more than one category. The categories are defined in the appendix. (Courtesy of Lexis-Nexis)

whether or not a reference to a racial campaign was accompanied by the adjective "blatant" (and its synonyms).

It is clear from the results that the Horton story had several distinct phases. During the implicit phase it was framed by the news media as a story about crime, not race. Figure 5.1 shows that there were fifty-five stories about Willie Horton in the early part of the 1988 campaign, beginning in June and extending through October 20. Only four of these mentioned Horton's race, and three referred to the campaign's racial overtones. The crime frame was so effective at concealing the racial overtones of the Horton story that even the *Washington Post*, which ran the first story with the racism frame, and which after the election was among the most consistent in using that frame, ran an editorial on July 8 condemning Dukakis for furloughing Horton.[18] Until the final three weeks of the campaign, race was nearly nonexistent in print coverage of Horton.

The analysis of television news confirms this pattern, and provides direct evidence about the news frame. Table 5.1 shows that just as the newspapers largely failed to mention race in the implicit phase, none of the television news stories about Horton included any verbal racial reference—not to Horton's race, not to his victim's race, and not to any racial strategy or racial impact his case might have.[19] Table 5.1 also displays the results of my coding of the frame provided by the anchor's introductory remarks and the reporter's conclusion. These remarks constructed one of three frames (or a combination of these): crime, general campaign strategy, and the general negative tone of the campaign. In no story during the implicit phase did anchors or reporters provide a racial frame. No one at this time either mentioned Horton's race or discussed partisan racial tactics or racial targets.

These results suggest that whatever the racial overtones of the story, they were communicated nonverbally, in a way that did not draw attention to them.

Widespread and Frequent Visual Cues to Race

The crucial racial element of the Horton story—the element sufficient to render the story racial—was Horton's race. In order for coverage to count as implicitly racial, it must have provided voters with information about Horton's race frequently and widely. Of course, to aid in the Republicans' implicitly racial strategy, the news coverage had to refer to Horton's race with subtlety. Visual references to race tend to be salient to white viewers but they are likely not to call attention to racial intent as readily as verbal references.

---

[18] Richard Cohen, "William Horton's Furlough," *Washington Post*, July 8, 1988.
[19] Nor did they include any other visual reference to race, except for the occasional African American appearing in the candidates' audiences.

TABLE 5.1
Framing of Willie Horton in Television News Broadcasts during the 1988 Campaign

Date	Network	Anchor's Frame	Reporter's Frame [a]	Democrats Charge Racism	Republicans Deny Racism	Independent Source Charges Racism	Reporter Neutral or Skeptical	Reporter Asserts Racism
Nonracial Phase: Horton Not Yet Introduced by Bush Campaign								
12/2/87	CBS	C	C					
1/21/88	NBC	C	C					
Implicit Phase (Low-Intensity): Bush Campaign Initiates Its Horton Message								
6/22/88	NBC	C/N	C					
6/26/88	CBS	C	S					
7/20/88	CBS	C/N	C/S					
9/22/88	ABC	C	C/S					
Implicit Phase (High-Intensity): Bush Campaign Intensifies Its Horton Message:								
10/7/88	ABC	C/S	C/S					
10/7/88	NBC	C/N/S	C/S					
10/11/88	NBC	I	I/S					
10/19/88	NBC	C/S	N/S					
10/19/88	ABC	C/S	C/N					
10/20/88	CBS	N/S	N/S					
Explicit Phase: Jesse Jackson Labels the Horton Message Racial								
10/21/88	CBS	N/S	N/R	*				*
10/23/88	ABC	N/R	N/S	*				*
10/24/88	NBC	N/R	N/R/S	*	*			*
10/24/88	CBS	R	S	*	*			*
10/24/88	ABC	N	R/S	*	*			*
10/25/88	ABC	N/R	N	*	*			*
10/26/88	CBS	N/R	I	*				*
10/27/88	CBS	N/R/S	I					*
10/28/88	NBC	S	S					
10/30/88	NBC	I/S	S					
10/30/88	ABC	I/S	I/S					
11/2/88	CBS	N/S	S					
11/4/88	ABC	N/S	I					

Source: Vanderbilt Television News Archive. *Note:* Multiple codes used where applicable. Includes all network evening news broadcasts in which Horton's name was mentioned. Intercoder reliability, calculated for two coders, is 100% for the anchor's frame, and 96% for each of the other columns.

Frame Codes:

Nonracial: S = Strategy or horse race; N = Negative campaigning; C = Crime or furlough issue; I = Other issue

Racial (in bold): **R** = Racial strategy or campaign.

[a] Code based on reporter's last sentence.

Was Horton's face circulated frequently and widely enough for a significant number of people to have seen it? Voters had the opportunity to see Horton in several different media: in a newspaper; in a magazine; in Republican campaign literature distributed by state party organizations; in "Weekend Passes," the NSPAC ad broadcast on cable channels; or through television news coverage (available on ABC, CBS, or NBC). The graphics in newspapers and magazines were scarce, and probably not a significant source of exposure to visuals of Horton.[20] One important source of the visual reference to Horton's race was the printed campaign propaganda distributed by the Republican party, but it is unclear how many people were actually exposed to it.[21] "Weekend Passes" ran for twenty-five days beginning in the second week of September (Jamieson 1992, 17).[22] It is unlikely, however, that a large number of viewers saw it. It was shown on cable television, for which the estimated market share in this

[20] The newspaper coverage of Horton was particularly devoid of visuals. This is true not only of the initial, implicit phase, but throughout the campaign, even in the explicitly racial phase. Only two Horton stories between June 13 and October 20 were accompanied by a photo or portrait of Horton, as found in a Nexis search. The scarcity of Horton images in the newspapers did not change considerably in the explicit period. There were only two stories with an image of Horton between October 21 and November 8, five stories between November 9 and the beginning of the 1992 presidential campaign, five stories during that campaign, and one story after it. The Nexis search was: "Horton" and "Graphic (Horton) or Graphic (murderer) or Graphic (convict)," deleting erroneous hits. Some of the stories did reach a large circulation, however, such as the *New York Times* story on "Weekend Passes," appearing on page one, which included Horton's image from the ad ("Bush, his disavowed backers and . . .").

The magazine coverage also did not show Horton's image frequently. During the implicit period, only three magazine stories on Horton included his photo. But the magazine coverage, although sparse, reached a much larger audience than the newspaper coverage. The photos appeared in three major magazines early enough during the campaign that they had the potential to racialize, implicitly, all subsequent discussion of Horton and the furlough issue. The oft-noted *Reader's Digest* article on the furlough program, "Getting Away with Murder," appeared on June 12, but did not contain Horton's picture or any racial references (Dick Kirschten, "How the 'Furlough' Issue Grew and Dominated the Campaign," *National Journal*, October 29, 1988). It was read by an estimated fifty million readers, according to Goldman and Mathews (1989, 306), though this number may be inflated, even accounting for the reprints commissioned by the RNC and distributed in many states (Black and Oliphant 1989, 226). The *Digest's* circulation then was twenty-eight million, including over sixteen million subscriptions (*National Journal*, October 29, 1988).

[21] In Maryland in mid-September, the state party distributed eight thousand letters with Horton's and Dukakis's pictures (and the not very subtle claim that "all the murderers and rapists and drug pushers and child molesters in Massachusetts vote for Michael Dukakis") (Germond and Witcover 1989, 422). In New York, during the week of October 17, 1988, the state party mailed a campaign flier to several hundred thousand New Yorkers that "prominently featured" Horton's photograph (Jamieson 1989, 417). In Illinois the state party distributed fliers with Horton's picture (Germond and Witcover 1989, 11). In Maine, the state Republican party distributed fliers warning that Jesse Jackson would be appointed secretary of state should Dukakis win.

[22] "Weekend Passes" appeared across the nation on cable channels CNN, CBN, Lifetime, and A&E (Kinder and Sanders 1996, 346 n. 9). The "Crime Quiz" ad produced by the official campaign only aired in Texas and California, beginning in late September, and it did not include Horton's name or picture (Simon 1990, 223).

period was under 1 percent. The official Republican ad produced by Ailes, "Revolving Door," began to air on October 5, but it did not show or mention Horton. In the third week of October, "victim ads," NSPAC commercials featuring Horton's victims, began to air (Jamieson 1992, 20), but Horton's image did not appear in these.

By far the most important source of Horton's image was thus television news. Television is more popular than print as a source of news. Most Americans not only consume news on television rather than in newspapers, but find the news they see to be more trustworthy than the news they read (Bartels 1992, 262; Campbell 1995, 6). Simon estimates that during the fall of 1988, the three network news shows reached over twenty-five million homes every night (1990). Research by Kiku Adatto estimates that a total of seventy million households watched coverage of the presidential campaign on weekday evening news programs (cited in Jamieson 1992, 276).[23] Television circulated Horton's image more effectively than any of the other media, and served as a boon to the Bush campaign because it was free (West 1997).

The results of the visual television news analysis are presented in Table 5.2. It is clear from the table that the networks provided Horton's picture often. His image was widely shown on television well in advance of the news coverage of "Weekend Passes," which is often believed to be the most significant source of exposure to Horton's image (Jamieson 1992). The news media widely circulated Horton's image without the so-called independent groups prompting them. All the Bush campaign had to do was mention Horton's name in connection with the furlough issue, and his image would be shown on all three network news that same night, often several times in the same story.

The first national evening news segment to mention Horton was broadcast on December 2, 1987, in response to the salience of the issue in Massachusetts. During the implicitly racial phase of the story, which lasted until Jackson charged the Bush campaign with using Horton as a racial appeal, there were twelve segments that mentioned Horton's name. All but two showed Horton's image, and six showed his image more than once. The images were all photos: his mug shot, in which he appears menacing and even crazed; a different close-up photo of him in which he appears almost as threatening as in the mug shot; and the "perpetrator walk," in which he is shown looming over police officers who are carrying him off to prison. Horton's white victims also appear more often than not, and almost never without Horton's face as a counterpoint. Of the eight segments showing the white victims, all but one showed both the victims and Horton.

While the "Weekend Passes" and "Revolving Door" ads were not necessary to the frequent broadcasts of Horton's image, the Bush campaign's increased

[23] This is a cumulative percent based on Nielsen data and referring to soundbites in non-interview segments of network evening news.

TABLE 5.2

Visuals in Television News Broadcasts Mentioning Willie Horton during the 1988 Campaign

Date	Network	Horton Mug	Horton Photo	Perp Walk	White Victim(s)	"Weekend Passes" Ad	"Revolving Door" Ad
Nonracial Phase: Horton Not Yet Introduced by Bush Campaign							
2/2/87	CBS[a]	*		*	*		
1/21/88	NBC[a]	*			*		
Implicit Phase (Low-Intensity): Bush Campaign Initiates Its Horton Message							
6/22/88	NBC	*			*		
6/26/88	CBS		*	*	*		
7/20/88	CBS	*	*	*	*		
9/22/88	ABC		*	*			
Implicit Phase (High-Intensity): Bush Campaign Intensifies Its Horton Message							
10/7/88	ABC		*	*	*		
10/7/88	NBC	*			*		
10/11/88	NBC						
10/19/88	NBC						
10/19/88	ABC		*	*			
10/20/88	CBS				*[b]		
Explicit Phase: Jesse Jackson Labels the Horton Message Racial							
10/21/88	CBS	*		*		*	*
10/23/88	ABC						
10/24/88	NBC	*		*		*	*
10/24/88	CBS						
10/24/88	ABC	*		*		*	
10/25/88	ABC						*
10/26/88	CBS	(Bentsen interview; no visuals)					
10/27/88	CBS	(Dukakis interview; no visuals)					
10/28/88	NBC				*[b]		
10/30/88	NBC		*[c]				
10/30/88	ABC		*[c]				
11/2/88	CBS		*				
11/4/88	ABC	(Dukakis interview; no visuals)					

Source: Vanderbilt Television News Archive.

Note: Includes all network evening news broadcasts in which Horton's name was mentioned.

[a] Horton's first name is given as "William," not "Willie."

[b] "Victim ads" also shown.

[c] Horton's photo shown in a state Republican leaflet.

focus on Horton, in Bush's speeches, in state party literature, and in paid ads, did intensify the media's broadcast of Horton's face. Between October 7, just after the Bush campaign launched its most intense Horton offensive, and the last day of the implicit period (October 20), the networks featured Horton in as many broadcasts as they had during the entire campaign to that date.

THE EXPLICIT PHASE: FROM THE CRIME FRAME TO THE RACE FRAME

As the campaign drew to a close, the meaning conveyed by the Horton story changed. The switch was initiated by Jesse Jackson, who accused the Republicans of using Horton's case to appeal to racial sentiments. The first television story on the accusation appeared on October 21 on CBS. Jackson's accusation was supported two days later by Dukakis's running mate Lloyd Bentsen (Simon 1990, 226).[24]

At this point, the Horton story took on a very different frame: racial strategy. Now, Horton's race and that of his victims was described verbally, in a way that drew explicit attention. These racial facts were always conveyed alongside the Democratic accusation that Republicans were engaged in a racial strategy, which was often accompanied by a Republican denial. The racial facts of the story were now widely discussed, but always as part of a frame about the Democratic charge of racist strategy.

The results of the newspaper content analysis, shown in Figure 5.1, demonstrate how abruptly the frames shifted. During the implicit phase, while the nonracial frames of crime and negative campaigning reigned, there were fifty-five Horton stories, and only five of these had a verbal racial reference to Horton or the campaign (9 percent). During this phase, 89 percent of the stories had no verbal references to race. By contrast, in the explicit phase, from October 21 to Election Day (November 8), there were eighty Horton stories, and only 41 percent had no verbal reference to race.[25] Coverage of Horton thus made a sudden and definitive switch from implicit to explicit. The majority of Horton stories now made a racial reference both to Horton and to the campaign.

Thus, the Horton story was conveyed, during most of the campaign, as a story purely about crime or, alternatively, electoral strategy or negative campaigning. Its racial overtones, because they were conveyed only visually, were so subtle that almost no news stories pointed them out. By contrast, in the second phase, Horton's race, and with it, the Republicans' racial strategy, became the dominant aspect of the Horton coverage.

---

[24] The first accusation actually came a few days earlier from Donna Brazile, an aide to Dukakis (and a black woman), but this received virtually no coverage. More recently Brazile served as Al Gore's 2000 presidential campaign manager.

[25] Search terms were: "race" or "racial" or "racism" or "racist" or "black!" or "African American!" or "white!," with erroneous references deleted.

The television coverage displays a similar pattern. Table 5.1 shows that the explicitly racial phase of the campaign yielded thirteen television news segments that mentioned Horton's name. In contrast to the implicit phase, in which there were no verbal references to race, now eight of the thirteen Horton stories included such a reference. These racial references were concentrated in the short span of seven days. Like the newspapers, television news framed the Horton case with the charge that the Bush campaign was using a racist tactic. In all these television stories except one, the media constructed the racist frame as an outgrowth of the frame of negative campaigning. It presented the Democrats' charge of racism as part of the attack and counterattack of a negative campaign.[26] At no point during the campaign did the news present the charge from a nonpartisan source. Neither did any television reporter appear to agree with the charge.[27]

In fact, as stridently as some journalists condemned Bush and his aides for their negative and even "sleazy" campaign, the news assessments of the election in its immediate aftermath largely ignored the racial element of Horton's case. The *New York Times*'s Tom Wicker, one of the most consistent and uncompromising critics of Bush during the campaign, minced no words in taking Bush to task. The "famous Willie Horton furlough," he wrote on Election Day, was "unfair," part of the "distortions and absurdities" of Bush's "low-road" campaign. But nowhere in Wicker's 740-word column was race mentioned in any way. Wicker directed his outrage at what he perceived to be the vilification of Dukakis, not the vilification of blacks.[28] Most other assessments of the election were no different in this regard.

The televised images of Horton continued despite the change in frame from crime to racism. They did, however, grow somewhat less frequent. As Table 5.2 shows, six of the thirteen segments in this phase included at least one photo of Horton, and three of these segments included multiple images of Horton (all of the three included his photos by showing parts of "Weekend Passes"). But while the visual element of the story continued more or less as it was, the verbal element was drastically different.

These figures and tables jointly show the sharp distinction between the implicit and explicit phases of the campaign. In the implicit phase, there was almost no talk of race. The racial element of the campaign was heavily visual.

[26] Dukakis never made any of these charges and in fact uttered not a single racial word. Perhaps because Jackson originated the charge, the media interpreted the charge of racism as a strategy aimed at mobilizing black voters. Bentsen did not echo the charge of his own initiative—he agreed with it only after he was pressed on it during a television interview.

[27] These two developments only occurred well after the election, as we shall see shortly. Slass finds that only about a quarter of the stories before the racism phase complained about the negative style of the campaign, while the vast majority of coverage during the racism phase did (1990).

[28] Tom Wicker, *New York Times*, "In the Nation: Sowing the Whirlwind," November 8, 1988.

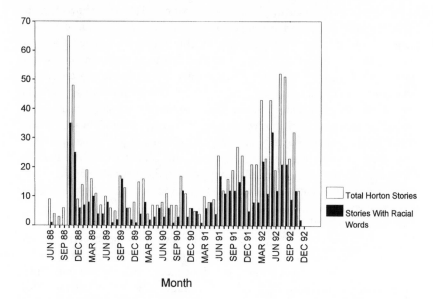

Figure 5.2. The number of Horton stories with racial words, 1988 to 1992. (Courtesy of Lexis-Nexis)

In the explicit phase, verbal discourse about race was widespread and frequent. The silence of the implicit phase was replaced by loud voices as officials and journalists, prompted by Jesse Jackson's protest rhetoric, suddenly began to speak about race and racism.

THE RACISM FRAME GAINS ACCEPTANCE—TEMPORARILY

After the election, a third phase of Horton coverage appeared. It was unlike the implicitly racial phase, which lacked verbal references to race while widely displaying images of Horton's face. It was also unlike the second phase, which framed the accusation of racism as partisan bickering. The third phase of coverage accepted the accusation of racism and discussed Horton as a clear example of the use of race. This frame, dominating coverage some three years after the election, suggested that the racial use of the Horton case had returned to haunt Bush and the Republicans.

Figures 5.2 and 5.3 display the results of an electronic search of the Lexis-Nexis database of major newspapers. While early in 1989 stories of Horton have a fairly highly proportion of verbal references to race (Fig. 5.2) or to

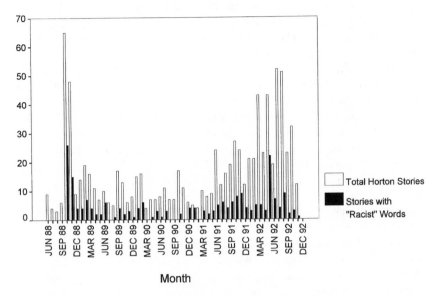

Figure 5.3. The number of Horton stories with "racist" words, 1988 to 1992. (Courtesy of Lexis-Nexis)

racism (Fig. 5.3), these stories are not as consistently frequent as the stories from the middle and late months of 1991. That period witnessed the height of the debate about Bush's veto of and opposition to the 1990 and 1991 civil rights bills, respectively. It was also the time when David Duke, the former Ku Klux Klansman, was running a nationally publicized campaign for governor of Louisiana.

Bush's opposition to the civil rights bill seems to be particularly influential in the media's acceptance of the racism frame. Beginning in March 1991, when Bush's aides began to signal their opposition to the 1991 civil rights bill, through November 1991, when Bush changed his mind and signed the bill, a monthly average of 5.1 Horton stories included a reference to racism. By contrast, the monthly average of Horton stories including a reference to racism during the period just after the 1988 election, from December 1988 to February 1991, was only 2.5. This trend is not limited to the word "racism" or its synonyms. Racial words as a whole show a similar increase, from a monthly average of 5.1 during the period after the 1988 election to 11.3 during the debate over the 1991 civil rights bill. The racial aspect of the Horton story thus greatly intensified between the end of the 1988 campaign and the controversy of Bush's veto.

It was Bush's veto of the 1990 bill and his threat to veto the 1991 version that seems to have been chiefly responsible for the media's acceptance of the race frame for Horton. The 1991 coverage of the bill included Horton's name much more often than did the 1990 coverage. From January to October 1990, the months when the 1990 bill was covered, only 10 of 959 stories about the bill also included Horton's name. By contrast, from November 1990 (the month after the veto) until December 1991 (when coverage began to wane), 59 of 1,290 stories mentioned Horton's name.[29] The media thus recalled Horton much more often after Bush vetoed a highly visible civil rights bill, when condemnation of Bush's stance on civil rights was at its peak. By far the most intense coverage of this type occurred in June 1991, just after Bush announced his intention to veto the 1991 version of the bill.[30] Thus, Bush's veto of the 1990 civil rights bill, coupled with his threatened veto of the 1991 version, was likely the chief cause of the media's decision to endorse the racism frame for the Horton case.

The 1992 election also serves as an instructive contrast period. The election as a whole vigorously resuscitated the Horton story—so much so that in 1992 there were nearly twice as many stories referring to Horton as in 1988 (212 versus 114). However, this increase is mostly due to the fact that Horton was much more prominent during the primaries in 1992 than he had been in 1988. During the 1992 primaries, the media was still preoccupied with its failure to challenge the Horton message as a dirty campaign tactic in 1988, putting itself and the public on guard against repeating that mistake. But by the general election, the media was no longer worried about the return of Willie Horton. A comparison of October 1988 and October 1992—typically the most intense period of a general election campaign—shows that indeed 1988 and not 1992 was the year of Willie Horton. October 1988 yielded many more Horton stories than October 1992, by a ratio of 3.3 to 1.

However, 1992, and not 1988, was the year of explicitly racial discourse about Willie Horton. In 1992, journalists commented more consistently on the racial overtones of the Horton story than they had in 1988. Figure 5.2 shows that during most of the 1992 campaign, a large minority of Horton stories included a racial reference of some kind. Still, the media did not bring up the use of Horton as an instance of use of racism, to judge by the use of "racism" words in Horton stories (see Fig. 5.3). The racism frame was only used to discuss the Horton story during the primaries, especially during coverage of the candidacy of Patrick Buchanan, and then, of the Los Angeles riot. The

[29] The Nexis search was "civil rights pre/2 bill or act," which finds stories that mentioned civil rights preceding the words bill or act.

[30] This occurred just as Bush went on a speaking tour to condemn what he called a "quota bill." The number of stories on the civil rights bill peaked in June 1991, at 273. From June through November 1991, a monthly average of 6.3 Horton stories included references to racism.

months of May, when the riot occurred, and June, when Bill Clinton and Sister Souljah sparred over the riot, clearly invigorated the racism frame. However, as strong as the press's preoccupation was with the three-way connection between Bush's prior use of Horton, his weak response to the problems that underlay the riot, and Clinton's response to the event, it was a short-lived preoccupation. Certainly it was too short-lived to affect the general election. During the general election campaign—the months of September, October, and early November—the number of stories with references to racism is tiny, particularly in contrast to the large number of stories that mention Horton. Overall, then, it appears that during the general election campaign of 1992, Horton reverted to a symbol of negative campaigning that, although it retained some connection to race, did not retain much of a connection to politicians' play of the race card.

The television analysis not only replicates this pattern, but also shows how the frame of racism gained acceptance after the 1988 election (see Table 5.3). The first news segments to clearly use the racism frame for Horton occurred more than three months after the 1988 election. NBC's coverage of David Duke's state legislative contest in Louisiana in February 1989 was the first to adopt this frame. While during the explicit phase of the 1988 presidential campaign the news media raised the possibility of racist meaning, it did so only by quoting Democrats making that charge. Now the media no longer framed the charge as a Democratic accusation, moving toward legitimizing it. It presented the racism charge against Bush from an independent, nonpartisan source. CBS's subsequent coverage of the Howard University student protest against Lee Atwater, who had been asked to join the university's board of trustees, also presented the charge of racism from an independent source, going further than the NBC story by avoiding a Democratic accusation altogether. This lessened the partisan frame and made the accusation seem still more credible.

Consonant with the results of my newspaper analysis, June 1991 was the last month in which the charge of racism was raised by a Democrat in any television news story. In fact, in the fall of 1991, as the Louisiana gubernatorial contest, pitting David Duke against former governor Edwin Edwards, heated up, it was a Republican official who charged Bush with racism in the Horton case.[31] Reporters' reliance on a nonpartisan source and especially on Republican sources for the charge of racism lent that accusation considerable credibility. Still, until September 1991 the reporter in these stories remained largely neutral. After that date, six of the thirteen Horton stories featured the reporter clearly suggesting, or even asserting as a matter of course, that racism underlay

---

[31] In March 1992, Buchanan echoed that charge while he campaigned against Bush in the Republican presidential primaries.

TABLE 5.3

Framing of Willie Horton in Television News Broadcasts after the 1988 Campaign

Date	Network	Anchor's Frame	Reporter's Frame[a]	Democrats Charge Racism	Republicans Deny Racism	Independent Source Charges Racism	Reporter Neutral or Skeptical	Reporter Suggests Racism
11/9/88	ABC	E	N/S					
11/9/88	NBC	N/S	R	*			*	
11/30/88	NBC	E	R	*	*		*	
12/31/88	CBS	N						
1/26/89	NBC	E	R	*				*
2/20/89	NBC	R	R	*		*	*	
2/20/88	NBC(2)	R	R		*			
3/7/89	CBS	R	RI			*	*	
3/7/89	NBC	R	RI			*	*	
3/8/89	NBC	E	RI			*	*	
10/25/89	NBC	E	E					
6/5/91	ABC	RI	R/RI	*	*		*	
6/5/91	ABC(2)	R	N/R	*	*		*	
9/4/91	NBC	E	S					
9/4/91	ABC	E	R		*			*
10/26/91	CBS	RI	E					*
11/2/91	CBS	R	R/S			*		*
12/4/91	CBS	R/S	S					*
2/8/92	CBS	E	S					
3/7/92	ABC	E/S	E/S			*		
3/30/92	CBS	N	N					
5/5/92	NBC	C	E		*			*
5/28/92	ABC	E	N	*	*	*		*
7/2/92	NBC	E/N	N					
8/18/92	ABC	E/N	E/S					
10/14/92	CBS	N	N/S		*			*
10/17/94	ABC	C/S	C/S					

Source: Vanderbilt Television News Archive.

Note: Multiple codes used where applicable. Includes all news broadcasts in which Horton's name was mentioned. Intercoder reliability, calculated for two coders, is 92% for the anchor's frame, and 100% for each of the other columns.

Frame Codes:

Racial (in bold): **R** = Racial strategy or campaign (includes David Duke); **RI** = Racial issue.

Nonracial: **S** = Strategy or horse race; **N** = Negative campaigning; **C** = Crime issue; **E** = Event or issue.

[a] Coding based on reporter's last sentence.

2 = Second story on some date.

the Horton case. In none of these stories did the reporter express skepticism or even try to indicate neutrality.[32]

Table 5.3 also shows that as the racism frame gained acceptance, it declined in use. The relationship between journalists' acceptance of the racism frame and their use of it seems to be negative. At least where racial strategy is concerned, journalists seemed to rely on a racism frame while that frame was still contested and the charge of racism was controversial. The more heavily they relied on a Democratic source to make the charge of racism, the more often they brought it up; the less they relied on a partisan source to make the charge, the less often they brought it up. Once the racism charge was no longer a source of controversy, it became much less useful to journalists as a frame for their stories.[33]

Visuals of Horton, as Table 5.4 shows, fit into this pattern. Visuals of Horton were scarce during the post-election coverage until June 1991. At that point the accusation of racism passed from Democratic to more credible sources, and interest in the "Weekend Passes" ad underwent a dramatic revival. Until then, only three of eleven Horton stories showed Horton's image. But for the next three years, thirteen of seventeen Horton stories did. "Weekend Passes" appeared in ten of these stories. "Revolving Door," even though it has been christened the classic ad of the 1988 campaign (Black and Oliphant 1989, 226), appeared in only two. The white victims completely disappeared from television news coverage. In the Horton visuals, it is Horton's mug shot that makes by far the most frequent appearance, overtaking the "perp walk" photo by about two to one. In ten of thirteen stories that showed the mug shot after June 1991, the mug shot is situated in the context of "Weekend Passes."

This evolution of visual coverage fits the pattern we saw in the verbal coverage. Of all the visuals available to reporters, it is the mug shot, and its close association with "Weekend Passes," that conveys most clearly the demagogic and racial nature of the Horton appeal. As the news media switched to an endorsement of the racism frame for the Horton campaign appeal, it also honed in on the visuals that best represented that frame. Horton's image at this point only had meaning to reporters in the context of what the Bush campaign had done with it, not in the context of crime policies. And in the view that some journalists now expressed, the Bush team had used Horton's image not only as a general dirty tactic, but specifically to play the race card. This judgment was clearly expressed a full three years after the election that the strategy had helped decide.

---

[32] Slass's qualitative analysis (1990) of stories appearing during 1989 in the *Washington Post* and *New York Times* found that only three of the twenty-three stories attributed responsibility for Horton to Bush.

[33] On journalists' reliance on controversy see Paletz and Entman (1981, 16–17).

TABLE 5.4

Visuals in Television News Broadcasts Mentioning Willie Horton after the 1988 Campaign

Date	Network	Horton Mug	Horton Photo	Perp Walk	White Victim(s)	"Weekend Passes" Ad	"Revolving Door" Ad
11/9/88	ABC						*
11/9/88	NBC						
11/30/88	NBC	*					
12/31/88	CBS		*				
1/26/89	NBC						*
2/20/89	NBC						
2/20/89	NBC(2)						
3/7/89	CBS	*		*		*	
3/7/89	NBC						
3/8/89	NBC						
10/25/89	NBC						
6/5/91	ABC						
6/5/91	ABC(2)	*		*		*	
9/4/91	NBC	*		*		*	
9/4/91	ABC	*				*	*
10/26/91	CBS	*					
11/2/91	CBS	*					
12/4/91	CBS	*		*		*	
2/8/92	CBS	*				*	*
3/7/92	ABC						
3/30/92	CBS	*				*	
5/5/92	NBC	*				*	
5/5/92	NBC(2)						
5/28/92	ABC	*				*	
7/2/92	NBC	*					
8/18/92	ABC						
10/14/92	CBS	*		*		*	
10/17/94	ABC	*		*		*	

Source: Vanderbilt Television News Archive.

Note: Includes all news broadcasts in which Horton's name was mentioned.

2 = Second story on same date.

In sum, the meaning of the Horton story continued to evolve well after the 1988 election. First, independent news sources, and even a sprinkling of Republican sources, gradually replaced Democratic sources in charging racism. Then, reporters ceased expressing skepticism or neutrality about the charge. They made this switch with a good deal of finality—the last expression of skepticism occurred in a news broadcast in early June 1991, and has not been repeated since. Finally, in the fall of 1991, during the course of reporting on Bush's opposition to the civil rights bill, reporters began, albeit sporadically, to express the view that the racism charge was largely merited. The media shied away from calling the Horton story racist until a consensus on its racism seemed to emerge. Once it was deemed legitimate, however, the racism frame dissipated.

Just as journalists had inadvertently allowed the Republicans to implement the Horton appeal in an implicit fashion, after Jackson's charge they disallowed, apparently just as inadvertently, the Republicans' implicitly racial strategy. Journalists now provided voters with explicitly racial coverage of the Horton story. That coverage consisted of verbal descriptions of Horton's race and that of his victims, most often coupled with the charge that the Horton appeal was intended to reach white voters or appeal to their racial sentiments. Visual images of Horton and the story of his exploits continued, but to these were added explicitly racial descriptions of the facts of the case and of the racial intent behind the appeal. The frame of race was added, composed of the race of the actors in the drama and the race and racial views of the target audience for the drama. The frame merged two different race frames into one—the racial facts of Horton the crime story, and the racial facts of Horton the campaign appeal.

During the 1988 campaign, many news reports handled the Democrats' charge of racism as if it were a dirty tactic equivalent to the Republicans' negative campaigning. The closest journalists came to condemning the Horton appeal was to label it a negative partisan tactic, not a negative racial tactic. Only after the campaign was over did the Horton appeal develop a reputation as an obvious play of the race card. My analysis shows that this did not happen until 1991, three years after the Horton appeal had done its work.

Only then did journalists accept the charge of racism—and the frame of which it was part—as valid. As the debate raged over the 1991 Civil Rights Act, journalists finally began to give credibility to the race frame employed by Jesse Jackson three years earlier, and to offer their own endorsement of it. They still described Horton's race and raised the issue of racial appeals, as they had late in 1988, but now, they also concluded that the Republican use of Horton in 1988 had been racist.[34]

Why Did Journalists Cooperate with the Implicitly Racial Strategy?

James Devitt's comprehensive analysis of network news coverage of crime sheds light on the reason journalists cooperated in the Republicans' implicit strategy. Devitt compared general television news coverage of crime in the months before and after the Horton appeal rose to prominence in June 1988. He found that visual depictions of black criminals were much more stereotypical after Horton coverage began. Black criminals were more often shown re-

---

[34] My analysis suggests that while the Horton case was recalled often during 1989, and was accompanied by racial references then, the frame of racism was not fully accepted until mid-1991.

strained by police (29 percent after vs. 6 percent before), more likely to be seen in jail (27 percent vs. 11 percent), and less likely to be shown wearing suits or other respectable clothing. No such change occurred in news coverage of white criminals; they were no more likely to be shown in threatening ways than before. Moreover, white criminals were more likely to be shown wearing suits and speaking at press conferences or in interviews, and hence seemed less threatening and alien. Devitt's analysis rules out the possibility that the coverage reflected an increase in the rate of violent crimes committed by African Americans (this rate did not increase). The most likely explanation, argues Devitt, is that reporters and producers were primed by the facts made available to them about the Horton case to seek out crime visuals that fell into line with that case. Clearly, Devitt's evidence also shows that Horton's case guided reporters toward more racially stereotypical portrayals of crime. In other words, Horton's story activated white journalists' racial stereotypes, leading them to cover crime in a more racially stereotypical way than before. This explanation seems even more likely when we consider the general tendency of the news media to portray African Americans in a stereotypical way and to portray whites in a way that enhances their prestige and authority vis-à-vis African Americans (Entman 1992; Gilens 1997; Gilliam et al. 1995; Reeves 1997; van Dijk 1991).

It is also possible that reporters simply did not see their job as that of a referee. According to Teun van Dijk, "the concept of 'racism' remains taboo in the press" (van Dijk 1991, 14). Perhaps many journalists did note the racial undertones of the Horton appeal, but felt it was not appropriate for them to mention it. According to this explanation, the more central the Horton appeal became to the campaign, the harder it was to maintain their silence on its racial overtones, but journalists still felt that they could not legitimately raise the charge of racism themselves. So while reporters said nothing of the message's racial overtones, they may have been fully aware of them and simply awaiting an opportunity to convey their impressions to the public. That opportunity had to come in the form of a partisan accusation from the other side. The Democrats did not oblige reporters until quite late in the campaign, and so they are ultimately to blame for the fact that the race card received such extensive and uncritical play.

This explanation is possible, but unlikely. Journalists did not hesitate to take the parties to task during the campaign. In fact, according to Table 5.1, the three networks broadcast six news segments on the Horton appeal that relied on the frame of negative campaigning (50 percent of all Horton segments) before a single broadcast raised the issue of race. And recall that the most strident critics of Bush's use of Horton, such as columnist Tom Wicker, took Bush to task in harsh terms, but made no mention of his racial strategy.

Perhaps journalists were reluctant to take the parties to task on matters of race. After all, race is a much touchier subject for news reporters than character assassination. This too does not seem likely. The *Washington Post*, perhaps the most likely newspaper to print a story or editorial about Republican racism, ran an editorial on October 31, at the peak of the explicitly racial phase, when Jackson's and Bentsen's charge had had plenty of time to be duly considered. Rather than agreeing that there had been racial overtones to the Horton appeal, the *Post* decried the Democrats' accusation and pleaded with both sides to engage in "reasoned discourse." The Democrats, said the editorial, only make such discourse more difficult when they take "every hesitation [on racial issues] to be racist." On social and racial issues, the president, whoever he is, should be a peacemaker. He ought to lead the country in a "period of R&R" on these matters and "turn down instead of magnify the volume of debate" on them.

In other words, the *Washington Post* considered it inappropriate to charge the Republican campaign with racism because journalists believed that the charge was not accurate. And even if the charge was true, journalists believed that making the charge would ultimately retard racial progress. The media was not reluctant to take the parties to task on matters of race. After all, the *Post* did just that to the Democrats when they charged racism. Journalists apparently believed that for anyone to accuse a major candidate or party with racism was counterproductive. Over the course of the next ten years, journalists changed their collective mind on this issue only briefly, during extraordinary times when highly unusual racial events occurred that seemed to make the charge of racist campaigning obviously accurate.

It is crucial to note that reporters who covered the presidential campaign seemed to know, during the implicit phase, that Horton was black, but simply did not think it a relevant fact to mention. Elizabeth Drew's reportorial book on the 1988 election is particularly useful to examine because, as she notes, it recounts "what I saw and how I saw it at the time," and thus "all judgments (or misjudgments) are left as they were" (1989). Drew first mentions race in connection with Horton in September, well after the Bush campaign launched its first Horton offensive in June. During the last week in September she notes that the Bush campaign is uncertain over "whether to use Horton's picture in an ad," but she remarks on Horton's race in literal parentheses: "(Horton, who is black, has a somewhat menacing visage)" (1989, 266). On October 12, well over a week after the Bush campaign launched its concerted fall offensive on Horton, Drew judged, for the first time, that the furlough issue "conveys a subliminal message about race" (1989, 305). By then, the Horton tactic had been played nearly to the hilt by the Bush campaign—all ads, official and otherwise, were in place and running repeatedly. Drew eventually concluded, "Never had the appeal to racism been so blatant and so raw." But she wrote this several weeks after the election (1989, 333). If the appeal to racism had been so blatant and raw, Drew would have noticed it earlier than mid-October. Yet she didn't remark on the racial strategy at all until then; and when she did, she called it "subliminal," not "blatant."

The most likely explanation for journalists' complicity with the implicitly racial strategy is that journalists were affected by this strategy in the same way as white voters. Devitt's analysis supports this, as does the lack of evidence for the alternative explanations. In the next chapter I analyze the responses of white voters to the two phases of Horton coverage, the implicit and the explicit. The evidence there suggests that the implicit phase activated white voters' racial resentment, which was then deactivated during the explicit phase. During the implicit phase, racial resentment had a large impact on vote choice and on opinions about race-targeted policies, such as affirmative action. But during the explicit phase, which had even more intense and widespread coverage of Horton, racial resentment had a significantly smaller impact. Journalists and editors, who are overwhelmingly white, tend to believe in the same racial stereotypes as white voters; and although they consciously reject blatant racial stereotypes, Gilens has suggested that they may rely on these stereotypes subconsciously, as a "seat-of-the pants" way to decide how to appeal to their (largely white) audience (Gilens 1999, 144–153). Journalists and editors are unlikely to be aware that the implicit racial messages they communicate are in fact powerfully racial. Without this awareness, there is also no attempt to make the implicit explicit.

Implications for the Mobilization of Race in an Egalitarian Age

Other analyses of the 1988 campaign that have taken the media to task for its coverage tend to focus on the "dirty" quality of the Horton appeal. Jamieson's excellent analysis develops a nuanced account of the many distortions introduced by the Bush campaign and by the media in its coverage of Horton (1992). But while a campaign's distortion of truth is a large obstacle to a healthy deliberative democracy, it is not the main roadblock to an egalitarian polity. From the perspective of racial politics, deceit by itself is not the problem. The problem with the coverage of Horton is not so much that it distorted the truth about crime, or that it allowed Bush to smear Dukakis. The heart of the problem is that it allowed Bush to smear African Americans and to get elected as a result. The Horton message was intended to perpetuate racial conflict in the service of electoral gain, and it did so to the disadvantage of a subordinate racial group and of all Americans' democratic aspirations.

From the point of view of reforming campaigns and media coverage, this distinction makes a considerable difference. Ad watches, in which journalists evaluate ads, may correct the problem of inaccuracy and relevance, and disallow the smearing of candidates. But they may not be as effective at countering implicitly racial appeals unless they point out the racial overtones of the ad and make race explicit. In addition, while several media scholars have worried that the news media may unwittingly reinforce the power of campaign ads (Jamieson 1992; Just et al. 1996, 134; West 1997), the ads are not the main problem where racial priming is concerned. The news coverage of Horton worked in concert with the Republicans' implicitly racial strategy even without the "Weekend Passes" ad. Only twelve percent of the news broadcasts about Horton showed Horton's image from the "Weekend Passes" ad, and only sixteen percent showed the "Revolving Door" ad. It was not journalists' blurring of the line between ads and news that caused the most damage. Rather, it was the widespread failure to realize the damage that implicitly racial communication can cause. That failure was both the media's and the Democrats'.

The Republicans in 1988 mobilized race despite the norm of racial equality. It is fitting that they were halted not by the institution best situated to regulate the free market of political discourse—the media—but rather, by the same black protest strategy that launched the age of equality. Jesse Jackson singlehandedly initiated the challenge to the implicit message, and apparently without the pre-approval of the Dukakis campaign. He did so as a black Democrat and as a political outsider. Lloyd Bentsen echoed Jackson's charge several days later, but only when directly asked for his view of the matter on a television news show. Jackson's accusation can best be understood as a part of the black protest tradition. As we saw in Chapter 3, the NAACP came of age as a civil rights organization when it denounced the Supreme Court nomination of Judge John Parker on the grounds that Parker had made racist campaign speeches. The NAACP continued to challenge the racist speech of prominent public figures, contributing to the erosion of the norm of racial inequality. When Jackson took issue with the Horton appeal he was engaging in this form of black protest, albeit within the framework of electoral politics. In a testament to the strength of the norm of racial equality, Jackson's protest appears to have worked; without it, it is likely that few journalists or officials would have accused the Republicans of playing the race card.

The news is a joint product of the orientations and perceptions of reporters and of the public actions of political actors (Terkildsen et al. 1998; Gamson and Wolfsfeld 1993). Political actors' rhetoric of protest can mitigate the tendency of the news media to reinforce racial stereotypes and to avoid the explicit discussion of sensitive racial topics. Jackson's rhetorical protest, his charge that Republicans were appealing to racial sentiment, was the force that impelled the Democrats and the media to speak to the issue of race. As we shall see in Chapter 6, although it failed to persuade the media, Jackson's protest was sufficient to deactivate the racial impact of the Horton appeal on white voters.

APPENDIX

1988 Presidential Election Timeline

March 15: Bush secures nomination
June 7: Dukakis wins last primaries
June 9: Bush launches June offensive, including Horton message
June 12: *Reader's Digest* story on Horton appears
June 13: First major newspaper story on Horton appears
June 18–24: Bush's summer offensive on crime peaks
June 27: First major news magazine story with Horton's picture appears
July 18–21: Democratic convention
August 15–18: Republican convention
September 7: "Weekend Passes" ad begins showing on cable television
September 25: First presidential debate
October 3: "Revolving Door" ad begins showing nationally; "Weekend Passes" is pulled
October 5: Vice presidential debate
October 13: Second presidential debate
October 21: Jesse Jackson charges Horton message is racist; journalists begin to cover the charge and to include verbal references to race in their stories
November 8: Election Day

Categories for Figure 5.1

Racial references to Horton = black, African American
Racial references to the campaign or the Horton message = race, racist, racial, racism, and any permutation of bigot (e.g., bigotry, bigoted, etc.)
Other racial references = black, blacks, African American, African Americans, white, whites, minority, minorities
Blatant racism references = blatant, extreme, apparent, blunt, direct, naked, patent, overt, explicit, flagrant, glaring, obtrusive, conspicuous, obvious, brazen, outrageous, shameless, egregious, prominent, audacious, evident, marked, noticeable, manifest, plan, distinct, striking, clear, indisputable, open, and their permutations

Racial References in Television News Broadcasts
Mentioning Horton, 1988 to 1992

October 21, 1988, CBS
Black leaders, black voters, inner city, Harlem, black criminals, black and brown faces

October 23, 1988, ABC
black leaders, black vote, black turnout, racist campaign, white woman, blatantly race conscious signals, fear in whites, alienation from blacks, racist appeal

October 24, 1988, NBC
Racial fears, racist overtones, blatant appeal to racism, charging racism, black inmates, elements of racism, denied racism, racism charge, black murderer, white couple, if [Horton] were not black, anti-black, blacks

October 24, 1988, CBS
Black murderer, blatant appeal to racism, racial tension

October 24, 1988, ABC
Racist appeal, black man, white woman, racist overtones, racism, black vote, black communities

October 25, 1988, ABC
Denied racial intent, black murderer, white woman, Horton's black color

October 26, 1988, CBS
Racism, racist fears, criminal happens to be black, not racist, Bush a racist, black photograph, black churches

October 27, 1988, CBS
Racism

November 9, 1988, ABC
Blacks

November 9, 1988, NBC
Racial division, black voters, white middle class, racist elements, blacks and the civil rights movement, white voters, black leaders

November 30, 1988, NBC
Black leader, race conscious signals, no racism was intended

January 26, 1989, NBC
Racial fears, not racial, blacks, middle-class blacks, black church, black leaders, black appointments, black community

February 20, 1989, NBC
Race, black legislator, minority set asides, subtle racism, Klan, racist overtone

March 7, 1989, CBS
Black men

March 7, 1989, NBC
Black agenda

March 8, 1989, NBC
Anti-black sentiment

June 5, 1991, ABC
Race, race relations, race against race, not racist, charges of racism, civil rights, minority, racial quota

September 4, 1991, ABC
Race of Horton, race, racial Horton ad

October 26, 1991, CBS
White voters, black voters, racial quota, minority, white, race, civil rights

November 2, 1991, CBS
Racism, race card, coded racial terms

December 4, 1991, CBS
Klansman, racial division, race, racially tinged issues

March 7, 1992, ABC
Racism, bigotry, race

May 5, 1992, NBC
Whites, blacks, Martin Luther King, civil rights bill, Bush insists he was not playing on racial fears, nothing to do with race

May 28, 1992, ABC
White middle class, black underclass, race, white resentment

October 14, 1992, CBS
Racially charged [and] divisive, black criminal's attack, white couple

CHAPTER 6

The Impact of Implicit Messages

He who knows the art of the direct and the indirect
approach will be victorious.
—Sun Tzu, The Art of War

THE REPUBLICAN STRATEGY to make implicit appeals to whites seems to have hit its mark in 1988. The Willie Horton message has come to epitomize the play of the race card in elections. While by now many observers have detected racial overtones in that message, the last chapter showed that during most of the campaign, it was conveyed by the Republican party and by the media as a message about crime rather than race. Yet to date no evidence exists that the Horton story was effective because it was implicit. Despite many scholars' recognition that candidates play the race card and that they do so in subtle ways, few studies have directly examined the impact of racial campaign communication on white voters, and even fewer have seriously attended to the distinction between implicit and explicit appeals.[1]

So far, I have provided no evidence that the Horton story affected voters, or that it did so because it was implicit. Did the story actually garner votes? And when the story changed from implicit to explicit, did it cease to work? If implicit appeals really are more powerful than explicit ones, now that the norm of equality is so strong, that is exactly what we should expect. As the media coverage of Willie Horton suddenly shifted from exclusively visual cues to joint visual and verbal references, the impact of racial resentment should have lessened as well. Is this in fact what happened? We also do not know yet whether the Horton message worked as a story about crime or one about race. Perhaps it primed worries about crime rather than racial resentment. Or perhaps it primed a general conservative approach to politics. Did the Horton story appeal to white voters' racial resentment or to concerns and ideas that owe little or nothing to race?

To find out, I turned to the national sample of adults surveyed by the National Election Study (NES) during the 1988 presidential campaign. I analyzed only white or Hispanic respondents who actually cast votes in 1988. The con-

[1] Jamieson (1992) provides examples of voter response to Horton, drawn from focus groups. West's study (1997) focused on the content of the Horton story rather than on its effect on the public. See Chapter 1 for a detailed discussion.

tent analysis in Chapter 5 revealed that the campaign divided, quite sharply, into an implicit phase and an explicit phase. Using the date on which this happened, I divided the NES sample into people interviewed during the implicit period and those interviewed during the explicit period. I use the successive dates of interview within each period as an index of increasingly greater exposure to the Horton message of that period. This technique allows me to match respondents to the type of Horton message in a way that does not contaminate one type of message with the other. Chapter 5 also showed that the implicit phase divided rather sharply in the intensity of the message. To find out whether intensity mattered, I further divided the implicit period into two categories, low exposure and high exposure. The dividing point is October 3, when the Bush campaign launched its Horton offensive in a concerted way.

Campaign appeals to race ultimately must prove themselves capable of mobilizing support for candidates who employ them; otherwise they would eventually fade from the electioneering repertoire. This chapter analyzes the response of voters as it occurred, that is, as the campaign unfolded, not after the election was decided.[2] Such a real-time analysis can disentangle the impact of the implicit and explicit phases of a campaign. It can show whether or not the Horton story's implicit phase was the powerful one, and whether the implicit phase primed voters' racial resentment more powerfully than did the explicit phase.

RACIAL RESENTMENT AND VOTE CHOICE IN 1988

Can we expect that racial resentment affected vote choice in 1988? Several scholars have argued that racial resentment played a significant role during the 1988 presidential election. Jamieson's nuanced analysis of the media portrayal of Willie Horton suggested that this portrayal resonated with whites' stereotyped notions about blacks (1992). Analysis reported by Kinder et al. (1989) has established this claim in a robust way (see Kinder and Sanders 1996). As these analyses demonstrate, the level of racial resentment itself did not change significantly, but its effect did. Racial resentment had a substantial, albeit indirect, effect on whites' vote decisions in 1988. In fact, the impact of racial resentment increased with exposure to the Horton message. The longer respondents were exposed to the campaign, the more powerful the impact of resentment on their choice of president. The effect of resentment increased as the Horton message intensified. Furthermore, the effect of Horton exposure did not extend to nonracial predispositions such as moral conservatism. The Horton message's racial cues got through to white voters and benefited George Bush.

---

[2] Using date of interview as a proxy also avoids the measurement error problems plaguing self-report measures of exposure (Bartels 1993).

But my argument here is more specific. It is the very implicitness of a racial appeal that allows it to work. As soon as the appeal becomes explicit, its power should wane. When white voters are made aware of a racial appeal's racial overtones, the appeal should have less sway. So far we have no way of knowing whether this is true. We know that the Horton appeal activated racial resentment. But we do not know whether, contrary to my argument, it was most powerful when it was explicit, toward the end of the campaign. Perhaps Abigail Thernstrom is correct in arguing that "subtlety in campaigns risks political ineffectiveness; only overt appeals are reliably heard" (1987, 202). Perhaps the Horton appeal was weakest when it was implicit. The Horton message would indeed be weak when implicit if any one of my assumptions is false: if norms against saying something that may sound racist are not so strong; or if most white voters do not change their opinions and evaluations when a candidate violates the norm; or if the appeal's racial cue is insufficiently strong when it is exclusively visual. Each of these possibilities would predict that the Horton appeal works more powerfully when it is explicit. This possibility was succinctly put by one observer of the election who did not see what all the fuss was about: "The average voter . . . just plain don't [sic] feel guilty for being scared of black criminals," he explained. "They [sic] didn't understand why it was racist to talk about reality" (quoted in O'Reilly 1995, 387).

Consider Jamieson's analysis of the 1988 election, which made a good case that the media's portrayal of Horton had racial meaning. Jamieson finds that the news coverage of Horton clearly communicated to voters the essential fact of Horton's race. Of Jamieson's ninety-three focus group participants, eighty-eight knew, by the last week of October, that Horton was black (1992). But this finding does not tell us about the specific power of implicit appeals. By the end of October the explicit phase of the campaign was well under way. Perhaps people learned of Horton's race primarily during the explicit phase, and picked up no racial undertones during the implicit phase.

Yet to be answered, too, is the question of whether the Horton message spoke to crime along with—or even in place of—race. The main alternative argument about the Horton message is that it was intended to speak to the crime issue at least as much as to racial concerns, if not more so, and that this was how the message in fact succeeded. As Abigail Thernstrom has argued about "subtle" appeals, the use of "code words" is "telling, yet not decisive"; voters may respond to a multifaceted message "on grounds unrelated to race" (1987, 203).

The implicit message's distinctive ability to prime racial predispositions, and its failure to prime nonracial predispositions, particularly those related to concern about crime, are the two primary hypotheses I test in this chapter. I take up each in turn, beginning with the matter of implicitness, and ending with the matter of crime.

CONSTRUCTING THE HORTON EXPOSURE CATEGORIES

To find out the distinct effect of each type of message, I used the date of pre-election interview as a proxy measure for the type and the intensity of the message to which respondents were exposed when they made political evaluations and preference decisions. While advantageous, this method also presents some problems. As I noted in Chapter 5, the implicit coverage of Horton varied in intensity over time. My content analysis revealed that there were far fewer newspaper stories and television news broadcasts about Horton in September than in October. No doubt this has much to do with the fact that, as I noted in Chapter 5, the Bush campaign launched a concerted effort to place the furlough issue, and Horton in particular, at the forefront of voters' thoughts during the crucial four weeks preceding the election.

Such a wide discrepancy in the volume of Horton stories means that the effect of exposure to the implicit coverage of Horton was likely to have been much weaker during September than October. Rather than posing a problem, though, this affords the opportunity to study the impact of the implicit message at two levels of intensity: low and high. The Bush campaign's October offensive began on October 3. I use this date to distinguish the low- and high-exposure phases.

The most important distinction to draw is between the implicit and explicit coverage. Conveniently, the content analysis in Chapter 5 revealed a sharp break between the two, centered on October 21. This is the date when Jesse Jackson's accusation of racism was first broadcast on network television. I use this as the dividing line between the implicit and explicit phases of the campaign. The explicit phase continued until the election on November 8.

The problem of intensity is a potential concern in this phase, too. I would not trust the contrast between implicit and explicit coverage if the intensity of exposure is highly uneven across the two. If the high-intensity phase of the implicit message is considerably more intense than the explicit phase, then finding a higher impact during the implicit phase could mean simply that people were exposed to more of Horton. I would have less confidence that the result is due to the switch from implicit to explicit.

Fortunately, such is not the case. In fact, Table 5.1 showed that the number of Horton stories nearly tripled in the explicit phase. In addition, the explicit phase, because it took place toward the end of the campaign, coincided with the peak of viewer attention to the campaign. From October 18 to November 4, a period which closely overlaps the explicit period, 68 percent of a national sample of eligible voters reported that they followed news coverage of the presidential campaign either very closely or somewhat closely (Buchanan

1995). If anything, this stacks the deck against finding a stronger impact during the implicit period.

The three Horton exposure categories, then, are as follows. Low exposure to the implicit message began on September 6, the first date of interview, and ended on October 2. High exposure to the implicit message began on October 3 and ended on October 20. Exposure to the explicit message began on October 21 and ended on November 7, the last date of interview before the election.[3]

MODELLING THE IMPACT OF RACIAL RESENTMENT GIVEN IMPLICIT VS. EXPLICIT MESSAGES

Did the racial impact of the Horton story depend on the story's implicitness? Did the Horton story activate racial resentment in perceptions of and feelings toward the candidates more strongly when it was implicit or when it was explicit? In other words, is there evidence of racial priming, and does it occur when the implicit message was most intense? To find out, I estimated Equation 6.1, described in the appendix to Chapter 6. I indexed exposure to the Horton message by counting the number of campaign days up to the date of the voter's pre-election interview. Each phase of the Horton message has its own count, so that the impact of a phase does not continue into the next phase. This yields a distinct interval-level exposure measure for each period—low-exposure implicit, high-exposure implicit, and explicit. A response provided just before the election is the sum of the total impact of each of the three distinct phases. I also included terms estimating the unique impact of racial resentment in each period (resentment is scaled on the 0–1 interval, 1 being the most resentful). Included, too, is a set of exogenous control variables.[4] All variables and models are summarized in the appendix.

This specification has two advantages, each bearing on the question of how to estimate the increasing impact of resentment with increasing exposure. For one, it allows the effect of a message to increase incrementally with successive days, but the rate of increase is allowed to vary from one period to the next. Second, the model is a reduced form equation. Previous work has found that racial resentment only had an indirect effect on vote choice, working through such variables as assessments of the candidates (Kinder and Sanders 1996). A reduced form equation is thus a preferred specification over a model that includes endogenous variables. In a later section I will conduct a parallel analysis that replaces resentment with predispositions regarding crime as a way to compensate for relying on a reduced form equation.

---

[3] Mitch Sanders points out that the NES's method of assigning respondents to date of interview avoids nonrandom effects of timing (1994, note 5).

[4] Control variables include partisanship and demographic measures. See appendix for details.

If a given message activates racial resentment, the total effect of resentment at the end of the relevant exposure period will be greater than zero (at the standard .05 level). I expect that the intense implicit message will activate resentment and the explicit message will not. The effect of resentment during the low-exposure period is possible, and if it exists certainly would buttress my argument, but it is neither necessary nor likely. We should see some effect of resentment in the low-exposure implicit period, a greater effect in the high-exposure implicit period, and a declining effect in the explicit period.

On the left-hand side of Equation 6.1 are arrayed a series of dependent variables measuring response to the campaign. Most important is the difference in feeling thermometer evaluations of Bush and Dukakis. Ideally, I would examine the actual choice voters made on Election Day. However, by Election Day every voter in the NES has been exposed to all phases of the campaign. I had to find a substitute to actual vote choice that was measured as the campaign unfolded. To that end I examined the difference between a voter's general feelings about Bush and Dukakis. This feeling thermometer difference score is a good measure of a global, affective response to the candidates, and it predicts vote choice extremely accurately (Abramson et al. 1994, 166). I also included a continuous variable that takes the difference between the perception of each candidate's opposition to government assistance to blacks. I constructed this from two identical closed-ended items, one about Bush and the other about Dukakis, asking the respondent to say whether the candidate believed that the government should help blacks or that blacks should help themselves. Finally, I included a measure derived from open-ended responses to a set of questions about what respondents liked or disliked about the two candidates. Responses were originally coded along many different dimensions. The dimension of interest here is whether the candidate supports or opposes law and order. Included, for example, is mentioning as a reason to vote for Bush his tough stance on criminals or his support for the death penalty, or mentioning that Dukakis would not support the death penalty as a reason to vote against him. From these responses I constructed a dichotomous measure of support for Bush or opposition to Dukakis on the law and order dimension.[5] These variables are summarized in the appendix.

---

[5] I tried to construct a more sophisticated measure, but respondents tended overwhelmingly to mention law and order only once, leaving me with no alternative to the dichotomous variable. Other questions of interest exist in the NES, of course, but they were asked only in the post-election questionnaire. My analysis requires dependent measures asked during the pre-election interview; by the post-election interview the distinct effects of each Horton message will have dissipated by the last message, or their effects will have blended together. Other relevant dimensions had very skewed distributions, such as 5 percent vs. 95 percent, so they were set aside. These were racial crime (candidate codes 970 and 976); racial policy stands (codes 991 through 993, 946–948, 1217–1218, 1229–1230); and nonracial crime policy stands (codes 982–984, 988–990).

TABLE 6.1

The Effect of Racial Resentment with Exposure to Three Types of Horton Messages

Candidate Assessment	Low-Exposure Implicit Message			High-Exposure Implicit Message			High-Exposure Explicit Message			N	Fit
	Total Effect	F	p	Total Effect	F	p	Total Effect	F	p		
Bush-Dukakis Global Evaluation[a]	0.28	4.43	0.04	0.45	11.28	0.00	0.08	0.10	0.75	902	0.42
Bush-Dukakis Perception on Race Policy[a]	−0.04	0.15	0.70	0.25	5.23	0.02	−0.22	1.30	0.25	903	0.07
Bush-Dukakis Evaluation on Law and Order[a]	0.14	1.40	0.24	0.24	2.24	0.13	0.30	1.14	0.29	903	0.05

Source: 1988 NES (white or Hispanic validated voters).

[a] Estimated with OLS. Fit column contains adjusted R^2. "Law and order" equation estimated with robust standard errors.

RACIAL PRIMING BY IMPLICIT MESSAGES

Table 6.1 displays the total effect of racial resentment in each of the three successive message periods—low-exposure implicit, high-exposure implicit, and explicit—along with the F ratio for the total effect and its significance level.[6] The first row in Table 6.1 shows the effects of resentment on a difference score of feeling thermometer ratings of Bush and Dukakis, a global assessment of the candidates that stands in for vote choice. Resentment had a statistically significant effect on this difference score during each of the two implicit periods, but not during the explicit period. The effect was especially strong during the high-exposure implicit period.

This model's predicted candidate evaluations are displayed in Figure 6.1, separately for Republicans, Independents, and Democrats.[7] Figure 6.1 converts Table 6.1's total effects to a scale ranging from 1, a complete preference for Bush over Dukakis, to 0, a complete preference for Dukakis over Bush, with .5 representing indifference between the two candidates. As the implicit appeal increases in intensity, it increases white voters' support for Bush and their opposition to Dukakis. This is only true for resentful people. The implicit coverage moves the resentful to support Bush and oppose Dukakis regardless

---

[6] The sample in all the analyses in this chapter consists of white or Hispanic respondents who were validated as 1988 voters.

[7] Holding all other variables in the equation at their means.

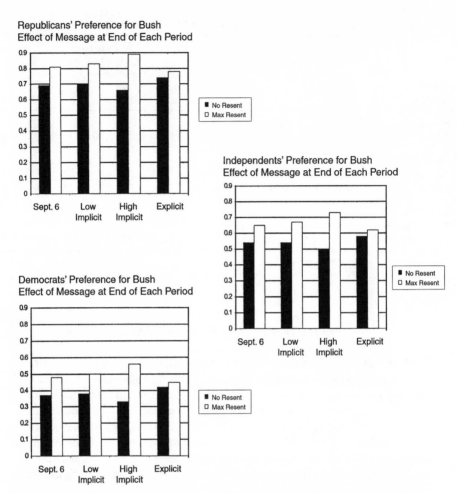

Figure 6.1. The electoral impact of implicit and explicit phases of the campaign, by voters' partisanship. The scale ranges from 1, a preference for Bush over Dukakis, to 0, a preference for Dukakis over Bush. (White or Hispanic Voters.)

of their party identification; in fact, the implicit appeal is sufficiently powerful to move Democrats over the .5 threshold, from pro-Dukakis to pro-Bush. When the coverage turns from implicit to explicit, support for Bush plummets sharply, again among the resentful and for all partisan groups.

To fully understand the meaning of the coverage effects during the implicit and explicit periods, imagine two individuals who consider themselves politically independent, and who are identical to each other except that one is highly resentful and the other highly sympathetic toward African Americans. As the media's implicitly racial coverage of Horton peaks on October 20, these two individuals are easily distinguishable. The resentful person moderately likes Bush and moderately dislikes Dukakis (approximately .7 probability of voting for Bush, as shown in Figure 6.1), while the sympathetic person feels fairly neutral about both Bush and Dukakis (approximately .5 probability of voting for Bush, as shown in Figure 6.1).[8] Then these individuals experience two and a half weeks of intense, explicitly racial coverage. Election Day arrives. Now the two individuals are virtually indistinguishable in their feelings toward the candidates. The resentful person is no more likely than the racially sympathetic person to lean toward Bush.

By contrast, consider the impact of the next-most powerful variable in the model. The effect of identifying as a Republican rather than an independent, across the entire campaign, is .32 on the Bush-Dukakis difference score (on a scale of 1 to -1; $t = 10.48$).[9] Thus, at the peak of the *implicit* coverage of Horton, resentment had a larger impact on candidate preference than did Republican identification (.45 versus .32). Yet only two and a half weeks of *explicitly* racial coverage of Horton made this powerful impact of resentment disappear.

The results for perceptions of the candidates' stands on government assistance to blacks reveal a similar pattern, as Table 6.1 shows. The high-exposure implicit period clearly activated racial resentment, while the other two periods did not. The effect here is smaller than it is on the global affective evaluation. But it is remarkable that an effect exists at all. The candidates never addressed the issue of assistance to blacks. Yet despite the total silence on this issue, resentful and unresentful voters made quite different inferences about what the candidates would do about assistance to blacks. Resentful people perceived a greater gap between Bush and Dukakis than did racially sympathetic people, with Bush seen as less prone than Dukakis to assist blacks.[10]

It is possible that racial priming extended to evaluations of the candidates on the issue of law and order. The results regarding law and order are less conclusive than for the other candidate evaluations. In contrast to the pattern for global evaluations of the candidates and for perceptions of the candidates' stands on racial issues, coverage of Horton had no statistically significant effects on evaluations of the candidates on law and order.[11] Still, the impact of resent-

---

[8] The difference between these two individuals is the effect of resentment, displayed in Table 6.1: .45 − 0 = .45.

[9] In the opposite direction, identifying as a Democrat rather than an independent only makes a difference of −.34 (t = 10.87).

[10] By contrast, the next largest coefficient in the equation for perceptions of the candidates on racial issues is for rural residence (b = .10, SE = .04). The effect of Republican identification is .06 (SE = .02).

[11] The law and order variable, alone of the three I have so far considered, is dichotomous. Hence, it requires a probit estimation. The probit model, however, lacked variance in some categories, and so could not be estimated. I therefore estimated the model with OLS and robust standard

ment during the intense, implicitly racial period approaches the significance threshold, while the coefficients in the other periods do not, suggesting that the high-exposure implicit period may have activated resentment, while neither of the other periods did so.[12]

Racial priming clearly occurred during the 1988 presidential campaign. The Horton message, designed to be an implicitly racial appeal, and conveyed in that fashion by the news media, worked as intended. Bush benefited from it while Dukakis lost ground. Keeping the message implicit was important to its ability to achieve the intended result of mobilizing whites' racial fears, stereotypes, and resentments. When the racial nature of the message was explicitly pointed out, it lost much of its racial power.

DID EXPOSURE TO HORTON PRIME CRIME PREDISPOSITIONS?

The Crime Alternative

Of course, just because exposure to an implicit message activates racial resentment does not mean that this message works more powerfully as a racial message. At its strongest, my argument states that implicit messages cause racial priming far more than any other kind. The final test of this argument should show what exposure did not do. Specifically, we need to know whether exposure to the implicit message failed to prime concern about crime. More than any other, this is the alternative explanation that requires consideration.

This crime alternative states that regardless of the racial content in the implicit message—all of it visual—the Horton story was nevertheless dominated by a message about crime and criminal justice. Those who denied the charge of racism during and after the 1988 campaign believed that the Bush campaign's discussion of crime in general, and the furlough issue and Horton's case in particular, were primarily about crime and had little to do with race. The journalist Robert MacNeil, in summarizing what he took to be Horton's impact, reported that voters' response was " 'I'm going to vote for George Bush because

---

errors. Although OLS with a dichotomous dependent variable tends to generate inefficient coefficients, they are consistent, and the inefficiency can be corrected by calculating robust standard errors (Hanushek and Jackson 1977, 195). The next-largest coefficient in the model is for jobless (−.10, SE = .05).

[12] I estimated a series of models to test for main effects of the Horton messages (that is, the overall effect of each type of coverage on the response, regardless of resentment or any other activated predisposition). These models include two dummy variables (coded 0 or 1), one for the high-intensity implicit period and one for the explicit period (with the low-intensity implicit period as the excluded third category). I found no effect of any Horton message on any of the variables here except on evaluations of the candidates on law and order (the impact of the high-intensity implicit period is .31 [SE = .12], of the explicit period .39 [SE = .13]).

I can't vote for a man who lets murderers out of jail.' "[13] While many commentators now view the Willie Horton case as a clear racial appeal, in 1988 it was widely perceived primarily as a message about crime and misguided liberalism, not race. Some observers and scholars continue to downplay its racial element. Farah and Klein's and Hershey's studies of the campaign (both 1989) characterized the Horton episode entirely as an issue of personal security or crime and punishment. A study of public response to "Willie Horton" crimes focused on brutal crime and criminal justice and ignored race altogether (Anderson 1995). According to Barone and Ujifusa's *Almanac of American Politics*, voters inferred from the Horton episode the obvious and not altogether inaccurate message that Dukakis might carry liberalism to unreasonable extremes. They argue that "such an inference was neither racist nor irrational" (1989, xxxvi). Hagen similarly argues against the "fascination in some quarters with the hidden meanings—especially the hidden racial meanings—of campaign rhetoric and political advertisements, to the exclusion of more obvious and pertinent considerations" (1995, 80). Thernstrom believes that in general, "subtle" appeals are more about nonracial issues than they are about race (1987).

This view deserves a serious hearing, even by those who may view the racial content of the Horton message as blatant and inescapable. While Horton's case was only one of several elements in Bush's discussion of crime, it was, as the most symbolic element, a rich composite of crime-related issues and concerns, especially misguided social reform policies. And after all, as Chapter 5 demonstrated, of the dozens of news stories about Horton during the implicit period, none mentioned the racial overtones that, three years later, many concluded had so obviously been there all along. If all the journalists and observers who wrote or broadcast the news believed that the message was about crime more than race, it is likely that voters watching them at home believed this too. And if they believed this, it is plausible that their opinions and evaluations of the candidates reflect that belief. A visual cue is powerful, adherents of the crime alternative might grant, but it is not the only game in town. The verbal content of campaign discourse counts for something too. When the verbal discourse is entirely about crime, it should provoke at least some response on issues of crime.

The Crime Model

To test this alternative, I examine a predisposition regarding crime that would have been activated by the campaign's discussion of crime. I made use of a set of questions that provided respondents the opportunity to discuss, in their own words, the most important problems facing the country. This is the closest

---

[13] Quoted in Jamieson (1992, 33). See also Barone and Ujifusa's summary (1989).

equivalent to racial resentment available in the domain of crime. The answers articulated by respondents were coded along a variety of dimensions. The one of interest here groups together mentions of the problems of crime, violence, or criminal justice. Examples include "crime," "violence," "too much crime," "streets aren't safe," "mugging, murder, shoplifting," and "drug-related crime." This category ranks eighth out of the eighty problems mentioned by respondents. The variable is summarized in the appendix.

I estimated a crime model that parallels as closely as possible the racial model in Equation 6.1. In place of the multiplicative terms for exposure and resentment, I included multiplicative terms for exposure and worry about crime (see Equation 6.2 in the appendix).

On the left-hand side are two familiar variables: feeling thermometer difference, assessing global affective evaluation of the candidates, and the law-and-order dimension in evaluating the candidates. In addition, I included a closed-ended question, fortunately found in the pre-election questionnaire, asking which candidate would better solve the nation's drug problem. Ideal would have been questions about the candidates' stands on furloughs or the death penalty, but unfortunately these were not available in the pre-election questionnaire.

The Impact of Concern about Crime

The first order of business is to find out whether worry about crime is separate from racial resentment. In fact, the two are almost entirely unassociated ($r = .01$; this fluctuates almost not at all with the Horton period). Apparently, during times when the worry about crime is widespread, that worry owes little to racial resentment. When crime, violence, and drugs are frequently portrayed in the media as a national epidemic, many people who are not racially resentful also believe these problems to be serious.

Table 6.2 presents the results from the crime model, in the same fashion as the race model in Table 6.1. Table 6.2 is dramatically different from Table 6.1. For one thing, it includes no significant effects in the expected direction. Whereas the implicit message clearly primed racial resentment, it clearly did not prime worry about crime. The only statistically significant effect in the table has the wrong sign, suggesting that those not worried about the problem of crime were most inclined to perceive Bush as the tougher crime fighter. If we relax the .05 threshold, then the low-intensity implicit message seems to have primed worry about crime on evaluations of the candidates' conduct of the war on drugs. People worried about the nation's crime problem were more inclined to trust Bush to fight drugs during the low-intensity implicit period. But nothing else in this table supports the crime alternative. The effect of the

TABLE 6.2
The Effect of Worry about Crime with Exposure to Three Types of Horton Messages

Candidate Assessment	Low-Exposure Implicit Message			High-Exposure Implicit Message			High-Exposure Explicit Message			N	Fit
	Total Effect	F	p	Total Effect	F	p	Total Effect	F	p		
Bush-Dukakis Global Evaluation[a]	0.03	0.08	0.77	−0.05	0.12	0.73	0.22	0.86	0.35	905	0.41
Bush-Dukakis Evaluation on Fighting Drugs[b]	0.56	2.68	0.10	0.24	0.27	0.60	0.80	0.99	0.32	898	−845.80
Bush-Dukakis Evaluation on Law and Order[a]	−0.09	1.22	0.27	0.10	0.38	0.54	−0.45	7.41	0.01	906	0.05

Source: 1988 NES (white or Hispanic validated voters).

[a] Estimated with OLS. Fit column contains adjusted R^2. "Law and order" equation estimated with robust standard errors.

[b] Estimated with ordered profit; F column contains Chi-square ratios, Fit column contains Log Likelihood ratios. Profit estimates for "law and order" were unobtainable due to lack of variance in some of the independent variable combinations.

Horton message on feelings toward and views of the candidates does not rest on the activation of a sense of urgency about crime.[14]

Did the Implicitly Racial Message Activate General Conservatism?

One last alternative possibility is that the implicit coverage of Horton activated a more general ideological orientation toward politics. True, the worry about crime does not seem to have been primed by the Horton coverage. But worry about crime is not the only predisposition to which the Bush campaign's crime message may have appealed. Getting tough on criminals is a stand that fits well within the general framework of political conservatism. Perhaps the nonracial predisposition toward conservatism, rather than the racial predisposition to resent African Americans, was primed by the implicit coverage.

[14] I replicated the results in Tables 6.1 and 6.2 using a trimmed model that omitted all control variables except Republican and Democrat. Also, a probit analysis of candidate evaluation on law and order failed to estimate the effects of two of the three crime worry interactions because they perfectly determined the dependent variable, so I had to rely on OLS with robust standard errors. There are also no main effects of Horton coverage on evaluations of the candidates on fighting drugs.

TABLE 6.3
The Effect of Conservatism with Exposure to Three Types of Horton Messages

Candidate Assessment	Low-Exposure Implicit Message			High-Exposure Implicit Message			High-Exposure Explicit Message			N	Fit
	Total Effect	F	p	Total Effect	F	p	Total Effect	F	p		
Bush-Dukakis Global Evaluation	0.21	11.23	0.001	0.26	13.82	0.0002	0.52	15.13	0.0001	894	0.46
Bush-Dukakis Perception on Race Policy	−0.05	0.88	0.35	0.08	1.71	0.19	−0.23	4.10	0.04	895	0.07
Bush-Dukakis Evaluation on Law and Order	0.12	3.95	0.05	0.08	0.93	0.34	−0.22	1.85	0.17	895	0.06

Source: 1988 NES (white or Hispanic validated voters). Effects are estimated with OLS (with robust standard errors for "law and order").

To find out, I modified the model used to obtain the results in Table 6.1. Equation 6.3 includes the terms from Equation 6.1 but adds a set of terms for conservatism that exactly parallel the set of terms for resentment. That allows me to estimate the activation of ideological conservatism net of the activation of racial resentment. The results show, first, that the effects of resentment change almost not at all relative to those in Table 6.1.[15] Controlling on the activation of conservatism does not make the activation of resentment go away. The implicit message activated resentment even when I account for the activation of conservatism. Moreover, as Table 6.3 shows, the pattern of effects attributable purely to conservatism is quite different from the pattern of effects we have seen for resentment. While resentment tends to peak with the implicitly racial coverage of Horton, conservatism tends to peak when the coverage turns explicitly racial. Apparently, the explicit message is not altogether without impact. It does succeed in activating an important predisposition. But that predisposition is not racial. Conservatism is not activated by implicit racial messages and deactivated by explicit ones; racial resentment is.

This pattern runs against our understanding of how communication works. Intuitively, we believe that an audience responds according to the surface content of the message. In their pioneering study of the impact of television news,

[15] The total effects of resentment, in the order of Table 6.1, are as follows (F ratios in parentheses). For feeling thermometer difference: 0.21 (3.02) for low implicit, 0.42 (10.04) for high implicit, −0.24 (0.90) for explicit. For perceptions of stands on race policy: −0.03 (0.11), 0.21 (3.68), −0.07 (0.10). For evaluation of the candidates on law and order: 0.12 (1.08), 0.20 (1.61), 0.49 (2.49). Table 6.3 displays N and fit statistics and the ideology effects.

Iyengar and Kinder found that a news story about a given issue affects the audience on that issue (1987). In the case of matters strongly regulated by norms, however, we cannot count on such a straightforward pattern. Instead, a message that deals with a socially sensitive matter in an explicit way may well evoke a predisposition that does not deal with the matter in a direct way. When the matter causes discomfort, the more explicit the message, the more oblique the response becomes. By the same token, an implicit message evokes a predisposition that does deal specifically with the sensitive matter. Implicit communication means that the audience responds in a direct fashion to a message that it does not consciously perceive, and fails to respond directly to a message that it does consciously perceive.

CONCLUSION

The surface content of campaign discourse would seem to be a good clue to what voters hear when they tune in to the campaign. But the Horton appeal shows that the surface meaning of the crime issue was entirely deceptive. While all the talk was about crime and criminal justice policies, nearly all the impact was on race. The implicit phase of the Horton message activated whites' racial resentment, not their worry about crime or their general conservatism. In this way it shaped evaluations of the candidates, including a global, affective evaluation as well as more specific perceptions and evaluations of which candidate would be more supportive of government assistance to blacks or would implement punitive criminal justice policies such as the death penalty. The Horton message—while it was implicit—helped George Bush win the election.

The results I reported here are based on survey data that stand in for campaign messages and media coverage. Such a method has its vulnerabilities, as does any method. It is possible that I have captured the impact not of racial messages but of some other event that unfolded simultaneously. The fact that conservatism was not primed during the implicit phase and was primed during the explicit phase suggests that the effects I attribute to implicit communication were not caused by some simultaneous nonracial campaign event. One might argue that resentful people increased their support for Bush in October but decreased it during the two weeks before the election because they are more susceptible to the general shift in favor of the likely winner during the heart of the campaign but in favor of the underdog at the end. However, a similar analysis of the 1992 campaign found no fluctuation in the impact of racial resentment over the course of that campaign (Kinder and Sanders 1996, 257–258). It is unlikely that the pattern of racial priming is due to some nonracial campaign dynamic. Still, some uncertainty remains about what exactly caused the pattern of voter response. Perhaps the statistical estimates are undermined by measurement error in the exposure variable. These problems are inherent to any study that does not measure actual exposure to a message.

For reassurance that the results are robust, I conducted an experiment that allowed me to verify and control the circumstances of exposure to the message (see Mendelberg 1997). I randomly assigned groups of white Americans to one of two conditions. One group was exposed to an implicit Horton news segment. The other group saw instead a control news segment about pollution in Boston Harbor (which for a time was a salient issue in the campaign). I measured participants' level of racial resentment in advance of the experiment, then exposed them to their randomly assigned message, and then asked them a series of questions about their political opinions and predispositions.

The results show that the implicit racial message primed racial resentment. Resentful people exposed to the implicit message expressed more racially conservative opinions than their counterparts in the control condition (their opinions on nonracial matters remained similar to those of the control group). Unresentful people showed no movement, except in a slightly more racially liberal direction. In a further replication of the results presented here, the implicit message did not prime worries about crime. Thus the same pattern—the power of implicit messages, specifically via racial priming—obtains regardless of the method.

The Horton appeal was rooted in longstanding practice within the Republican party, as we saw in Chapters 3 and 5. But 1988 was only the second time in American history that a racial appeal had helped a candidate win the presidency. The success of the implicit Horton strategy sparked a wave of similar tactics. Elizabeth Drew was correct in predicting that the negative style of the 1988 presidential campaign—in particular, its racial component—would be emulated by future campaigns. The racial campaign style of 1988 was echoed in such statewide campaigns as the 1991 gubernatorial election in Mississippi (in which little-known Republican Kirk Fordice upset incumbent Democrat Ray Mabus by opposing quotas, saying that welfare recipients should be forced to work, and attacking policies for coddling criminals), the 1991 Duke-Edwards gubernatorial contest in Louisiana, Buchanan's 1992, 1996, and 2000 presidential bids, the 1994 California gubernatorial and senatorial campaigns of Wilson and Huffington, respectively, Ridge's 1994 gubernatorial campaign in Pennsylvania, and others. In the 1996 Helms-Gantt senatorial contest in North Carolina, the North Carolina Republican party mailed half a million fliers pairing a photograph of black Democrat Harvey Gantt with black members of Congress and asking, "Eva [Clayton] is bad enough . . . do you want Harvey too?"[16]. The appeal resembled Helms's racial ad of 1990 but avoided racial words. All these campaigns included implicit references to race: charges that the welfare underclass takes advantage of hard-working tax payers,

---

[16] Kevin Sack, New York Times, November 3, 1996.

calls for punitive crime policies, or attacks on federal affirmative action "quota" bills. The implicit strategy will not go away any time soon. As long as candidates believe they will profit, they will continue to use it.

The evidence presented here shows that the racial impact of the Horton appeal was due to the implicitness of the message. Racial priming occurred only while all the candidates, party officials, and journalists dealt with the story as one of crime *and* while the Republicans and the media provided a visual racial cue. It was during this implicit phase of the Horton story that racial resentment was most powerful—in fact, far more powerful than concern about crime and more powerful than general ideological conservatism. When the Democrats charged Republicans with using Horton as a racial appeal, and the media coverage reflected that charge—that is, when the coverage turned explicit—the Horton story caused racial resentment to have almost no effect. Thus, paradoxically, when campaign discourse is clearly about race—when it is explicitly racial—it has the fewest racial consequences for white opinion; when it is on the surface not at all about race, but makes a subtle allusion to racial stereotypes, it has the biggest racial consequences.

The results also suggest that the intensity of a racial message matters a great deal. The impact of the implicit Horton message was much more muted in September, when it was conveyed much less frequently and widely. Political strategists recognize the influence of message intensity and they act accordingly. Their decisions about when and how often to buy air time for their ads is among their most important (West 1997). Strategists' concern with message intensity turns out to be well justified in my analysis.

Of course, intensity is not the only important factor. In the case of racial communication, whether a message is implicit seems to be more important than whether a message is frequent and widely disseminated. The explicit phase of the campaign yielded much smaller racial effects than the high-exposure implicit phase, despite the fact that the explicit phase had three times as many newspaper stories.[17]

The results shed light on the role of the news media in implicit political communication. Journalists did not accept the charge of racism and the race

---

[17] A final question about the Horton message concerns individuals' political knowledge. Zaller has made a particularly strong case for including political knowledge as a conditioning variable in analyses of media effects (1992). My view of racial appeals does not generate a priori expectations about knowledge in one direction or another. Nevertheless, I tested Zaller's notion with a series of equations predicting the dependent variables in Table 6.1. Each equation included the terms presented in Equation 6.1, along with a set of interaction terms between exposure and knowledge, and between exposure, knowledge, and resentment. Because of the difficulty of estimating fourth-order interactions, in estimating these equations I used a trimmed model that replaced the twenty-four control variables with two dummy variables for partisanship. The knowledge variable is a continuous scale of political information, constructed with the knowledge items that Zaller used. I did the same for the crime model. None of the analyses turned up a significant interactive effect

frame of which it was part until nearly three years after the election, as Chapter 5 showed. They finally did so during the national debate over the 1991 Civil Rights Act and particularly as Bush threatened once again to veto a significant civil rights bill. At that point journalists began to allow independent sources rather than Democratic ones to charge the 1988 Bush campaign with appealing to racial stereotypes, fears, and resentments, and to endorse the charge themselves. The results reported in this chapter, showing resentment's weak impact during the explicit phase, suggest that journalists' acceptance of the Democrats' charge of racism was not necessary. Despite the fact that during the explicit phase of the campaign reporters were largely skeptical or neutral about the charge of racism, and that they framed it as yet another example of partisan mud-slinging in a dirty campaign, the explicit coverage of Horton nevertheless was sufficient to neutralize Horton's racial impact. Getting white voters merely to consider the possibility that the Horton story was a racial appeal was sufficient to undermine the Republicans' racial strategy. The media's use of the frame of negative campaigning in covering the charge of racism did not seem to have interfered significantly with the effectiveness of that charge. Of course, it is likely that had the media covered the charge of racism with the racism frame during the election, rather than waiting three years to do so, the impact of the Horton story would have been neutralized more effectively.

The role of the media highlights the dynamic nature of implicit communication. The message that the Bush campaign sent never changed—it remained implicit throughout the campaign. What changed was the implicit nature of the media coverage of that message. Prodded by the Democrats' charge of racism, the news media began to cover the Republican message in explicitly racial terms. Instead of conveying a racially threatening image without racial words, the media conveyed the image together with racial adjectives such as "black criminal" and "white couple." Thus, if the media conveys a partisan message that begins implicitly but adds to it verbal references to race, the message ceases to be implicit. At that point, even if the party continues to send the message in its implicit form, voters receive the message through the media in its explicit form.

Several scholars have recommended that the media encourage what Kathleen Hall Jamieson calls candidate engagement (Buchanan 1995; Jamieson 1992). Jamieson would like journalists to press the candidates on the details of their programs and to elicit a meaningful dialogue between them. It is possible that had the media done so, someone in the Democratic camp may have charged racism sooner. But engagement by itself would not have assured that outcome. Engagement is supposed to bring out the truth about candidates' claims and get them to specify clearly what they would do in office (Jamieson

---

of knowledge with either resentment or concern about crime. Most likely, however, more analysis is needed to understand the mediating impact of sophistication and exposure.

1992, 254). But in the case of implicit appeals, what is more to the point is the need for the media to reframe—or to encourage the opposition to reframe—an implicit appeal as an explicit one. Jamieson does suggest that reframing is the most effective means of combating implicit communication, but this remedy is not included in her list of reforms, and there is little evidence that journalists have attempted it. Even if George Bush and James Baker had admitted to making misleading statements about Dukakis's furlough program, and even if the furlough issue had been widely recognized as irrelevant, the implicitly racial undertones in their appeals would have gone unchallenged.

More effective than engagement is a challenge to the racial undertones of the implicit message. The media were not well suited to doing so, and as Chapter 5 suggested, they are not likely to become better at it in the future. But the Democratic party is well-positioned to undertake that challenge, despite its vulnerability to the appearance of being too racially liberal.

The Democrats' big fear, during the 1988 presidential election, in southern congressional and gubernatorial elections, and in other elections as well, has been that if they speak explicitly about race they will lose crucial white votes. They are right to fear losing white voters. When more than a small percentage of Democratic support comes from blacks, Democrats lose elections (Abramson et al. 1998). Losing their already tenuous hold on white voters is fatal for Democrats. At the same time they must not alienate their core black constituency (Black 1998; Glaser 1996; Kinder and Sanders 1996), hence their overwhelming reluctance to abandon their strategy of public silence on race. The Democrats are correct in perceiving that their best interests lie in shifting the electoral agenda away from race and toward economic issues on which blacks and working-class whites can agree. The Democrats can still pursue racially liberal policies while in office, and in fact it is in their interest to do so. By eroding racial inequality they will aid in bridging the racial divide that renders them so electorally vulnerable. But as many African Americans recognize, highlighting these efforts to white voters is likely to erode Democratic support among whites (Glaser 1996).

Once an implicit racial appeal gains attention, however, silence on race is no longer a reasonable strategy for the Democratic party. As many observers of the 1988 election noted, Dukakis's major blunder was to fail to respond to the repeated attacks of the Republicans. Whether or not a candidate should respond with "negative advertising" when attacked is still an open question.[18] But a direct response does seem to be the smart strategy in the case of implicit racial appeals. The results of this chapter underscore just how dramatically the Democrats' fortunes changed once they brought the message's racial meaning to the surface. It was their switch from silence to an antiracist message that set

---

[18] See the exchange in the "Forum" section of the *American Political Science Review* (1999, 851–910).

in motion the significant change in news coverage of the Horton story. The consequent change in whites' response to the campaign is quite clear in my analysis. The Democrats received a net gain from abandoning silence in favor of antiracist discourse.

We do not yet know what it is about explicit messages that neutralizes racial predispositions. In order to draw conclusions about explicit messages, we must disentangle the various verbal references to race included in these messages. I will take up this task in the next chapter.

APPENDIX

Variables

Racial Resentment (RESENT): A continuous variable coded on the 0–1 interval, 1 = resentful (mean = .60, SD = .22). It is an unweighted average of four items, variables 961 to 964 (Cronbach's alpha = .74). See Chapter 4 appendix for wording.

E: A count of the number of days from September 6 to the interview date. It ranges from 1 to 63 (mean = 30, SD = 17).

E_2: A count of the number of days from October 3, the first day of the high-intensity period, to the interview date. This variable equals zero if the respondent was interviewed before October 3, 1 if the interview was on October 3, 2 if the interview was on October 4, and so on. It ranges from 0 to 45 (mean = 12, SD = 17; 597 cases received a value of 0).

E_3: A count of the number of days up to the interview date from October 21, the first day of the explicit period. This variable equals zero if the respondent was interviewed before October 21, 1 if the interview was on October 21, 2 if the interview was on October 22, and so on. It ranges from 0 to 18 (mean = 12, SD = 22; 711 cases received a value of 0).

Worry about Crime (CRIMEPR): A dichotomous variable measuring salience of crime as a national problem. It is coded 1 for any mention of crime problems on open-ended responses to four questions, 0 otherwise (mean = .07, SD = .26). Any mention in variables 813, 814, 815, or 817, code 340, was coded as 1. Those missing on all four variables were excluded from analysis. I tried a variation drawn from the "single most" important problem (817), and another variation with 813 alone, but there were too few cases to use these versions.

Z: A set of exogenous control variables, included as dummy variables: Republican, Democrat (independent is the excluded variable), family income above $75,000, refused to reveal income, disabled, unemployed, fundamentalist, Hispanic, South, West, resides in a large city, resides in a town, resides in a rural area, high school graduate, high school graduate and some college,

college graduate, advanced degree, interviewer race, Jewish, unskilled worker, service worker, gender, and union householder.

Conservatism (CONSERVATISM): A trichotomous variable measuring nonracial ideology. It is coded 0 for liberal, .5 for moderate, and 1 for conservative (mean = 68, SD = .43).

Dependent Variables

Bush-Dukakis Feeling Thermometer Difference (BDFT): A continuous variable taking the difference of feeling thermometer evaluations of Bush and Dukakis. It ranges from 1 (warm toward Bush and cold toward Dukakis) to -1 (cold toward Bush and warm toward Dukakis; mean = .08, SD = .47). Constructed from variables 154 and 155.

Bush-Dukakis Difference on Racial policy (BDDIFFR): A continuous variable taking the difference of perceptions of the candidates' opposition to government assistance to blacks. It ranges from 1, the perception that Bush opposes and Dukakis favors assisting blacks, to -1, the perception that Dukakis opposes and Bush favors assisting blacks. Constructed from 334 or 342, Bush's stand on government assistance to blacks, minus 333 or 341 for Dukakis.

Bush-Dukakis Evaluation on Law and Order (BDLAW2): A dummy variable assigning a value of 1 when law and order is mentioned as a reason to vote for Bush or to vote against Dukakis (n = 153), and 0 otherwise (mean = .17, SD = .37). It is constructed from variables 104 to 108 (codes 968, 975, 977, 978, 1042) for Bush and 122 to 126 against Dukakis (codes 968, 969, 972, 973, 104). Respondents missing on every variable were set aside.

Evaluation of Candidates' Effectiveness on the Drug Problem (CAND-DRUG): An ordered trichotomy measuring evaluations of the candidates' relative effectiveness in solving the drug problem in the United States. It is coded 1 for Bush, .5 for neither or both or don't know, and 0 for Dukakis (mean = .54, SD = .41). Based on variable 394.

Equation 6.1 (Resentment model)

$$\text{RESPONSE} = a + b_1 (E*RESENT) + b_2 (E_2*RESENT) + b_3 (E_3*RESENT) + b_4 (E) + b_5 (E_2) + b_6 (E_3) + b_7 (RESENT) + b_{8-32} (Z)$$

Equation 6.2 (Crime Worry model)

$$\text{RESPONSE} = a + b_1 (E*CRIMEPR) + b_2 (E_2*CRIMEPR) + b_3 (E_3*CRIMEPR) + b_4 (E) + b_5 (E_2) + b_6 (E_3) + b_7 (CRIMEPR) + b_{8-32} (Z)$$

Equation 6.3 (Resentment and Ideology model)

$$\text{RESPONSE} = a + b_1 (E*RESENT) + b_2 (E_2*RESENT) + b_3 (E_3*RESENT) + b_4 (E) + b_5 (E_2) + b_6 (E_3) + b_7 (RESENT) + b_8 (E*CONSERVATISM) + b_9$$

$(E_2*CONSERVATISM) + b_{10} (E_3*CONSERVATISM) + b_{11} (CONSERVATISM) + b_{12-36} (Z)$

Total Effects of Resentment

1. The Total Effect of Resentment with Exposure to the Low-Exposure Implicit Message:

$b_7 + (b_1 * E)$ [where E = 27, the last day in the first period]

2. The Total Effect of Resentment with Exposure to the High-Exposure Implicit Period:

$b_7 + (b_1 * E) + (b_2 * E_2)$ [where E = 45, the last day of the first two periods combined, and E_2 = 18, the last day in the second period]

3. The Total Effect of Resentment with Exposure to the High-Exposure Explicit Period:

$b_7 + (b_1 * E) + (b_2 * E_2) + (b_3 * E_3)$ [where E = 63, the last day in the three periods combined, E_2 = 36, the last day in the last two periods combined, and E_3 = 18, the last day in the third period]

Note: The hypothesis test sets a total effect to zero and uses the F distribution (or Chi-square if probit was used) to calculate significance. The total effects of worry about crime and of conservatism are calculated with the above equations, but replacing each resentment term with the parallel crime or conservatism term.

CHAPTER 7

Implicit, Explicit, and Counter-Stereotypical Messages: The Welfare Experiment

*Everyone sees what you seem to be, few experience
what you really are.*
—Machiavelli, *The Prince*

RACIAL POLITICS in the contemporary United States is characterized by a paradox. On the one hand, negative racial predispositions continue to influence whites' political preferences, especially their views about government efforts to ameliorate racial inequality. But on the other hand, blatant racism has been repudiated. Whites routinely endorse the principle of racial equality in national surveys. Direct appeals to whites' racial stereotypes and antagonisms seem few and, when they occur, are usually met with scathing denunciation. In the 1988 presidential election, the campaign of George Bush went to great lengths to deny any racial intent in using the story of Willie Horton. The perception exists that for a candidate there is no quicker route to political suicide than being identified as a racist.

With so little overt discussion of race, how does racial politics continue to operate? More specifically, how could white citizens be attracted to the Republican party on racial grounds when both the party and an overwhelming majority of white citizens repudiate racism? The answer is that a good deal of racial communication can take place without any direct verbal reference to race. I have begun to provide evidence on this point, but the argument remains tenuous without knowing more about how implicit appeals work so effectively. If racial appeals have the greatest power when they are deniable, it is possible that voters are not fully aware of the nature of the message. Implicit messages may allow whites to express resentment toward African Americans without realizing that the message is racial, and thus without awareness that their opinions are based on race. We need to find out whether whites in fact perceive the implicit message as nonracial.

A second important element of my argument also requires elaboration. In Chapters 5 and 6 I used the term "explicitly racial" both to describe an appeal that explicitly derogates blacks and the use of explicitly racial words to call attention to an implicit appeal's racism. In the 1988 presidential campaign, when Jesse Jackson accused the Republicans of playing to whites' racial sentiments with the Willie Horton appeal, the mass media not only conveyed this charge, but also reiterated the Republicans' original appeal along with verbal references to Horton's race. Journalists thus communicated the Republicans' message explicitly at the same time that they conveyed Jackson's challenge.

How do we distinguish between different kinds of explicitly racial references? Politically, it matters whether an explicit communication itself conveys a racist appeal or whether it only accuses another message of conveying a racist appeal. The former is an appeal that denigrates African Americans, while the latter is an attempt to defend or warn against that appeal. While in reality these two seem to go hand-in-hand, the core of my argument is about appeals that denigrate African Americans. I have been contrasting implicit and explicit messages because, despite having identical meaning, one is likely to work and the other to fail. One does not violate the norm of equality while the other does. To charge a political adversary with racism is a risky tactic for politicians. Public figures indeed seem reluctant to do it; it took Jackson nineteen weeks to work up to it, and he was not even a candidate; Dukakis never did agree with the accusation. But accusing a politician of racism does not constitute a violation of a deeply held norm in the way that uttering a derogatory statement about blacks does.

My study closely contrasts a clearly worded derogatory message about African Americans with one that conveys an identical message much more indirectly. Such a design enables us to discover whether an explicitly derogatory message in fact suppresses racial stereotypes, fears, and resentments, and takes us closer to understanding the process by which voters construct the racial meaning of implicit messages. The results suggest that the racial impact of an anti-black message is far weaker when the message is explicit. More importantly, whites give weight to their resentment only with a racial appeal that does not seem to them to be about race; they suppress their racial resentment after viewing a message that crosses the line of public acceptability. When a campaign message is explicitly anti-black, white citizens reject the message and, in the process, avoid relying on their negative racial predispositions in reaching decisions about politics.

There is one final wrinkle to the design of the study. The results in the previous chapter suggested that an implicitly racial message can activate racial sentiments, and that it does so more powerfully than a message that has nothing to do with race or with a message that contains a great deal of overt racial references. The design I employ in this chapter intends to settle more decisively whether a visual racial cue is necessary for this to occur. If the visual reference to African Americans is what makes the implicit appeal work, than replacing that visual reference with an image of white people engaged in the same behavior should neutralize the impact of this appeal. I call this kind of message counter-stereotypical.

In the spirit of extending the reach of my findings, I have turned from presidential to gubernatorial elections, and from the issue of crime to the issue of welfare dependency. Economic dependency has been racialized in quite explicit ways in American history, as we saw in Chapters 2 and 3. It continues to carry strong racial associations (Gilens 1995, 1997). Thus, it particularly lends itself to implicit racial messages.

To carry out the contrasts required by my argument, I relied on an experimental design. I went to great lengths to recruit a nonstudent sample and to even greater lengths to make sure that the people in my study were exposed to the message in the setting in which they always consume messages. I contacted households randomly from the phone directory of Washtenaw County, Michigan, and I conducted the experiment in my participants' own homes. (See the Chapter 4 appendix for a methodological discussion.)

In sum, the design of the experiment allows me to contrast the impact of an implicitly racial message featuring a gubernatorial candidate's anti-welfare appeal with the impact of messages that were identically constructed, but were either explicitly racial or counter-stereotypical. I can then conclude that whatever the implicit message does that the other messages do not must be the result of a reference to race that is at once covert and anti-black.[1]

IMPLICIT, EXPLICIT, AND COUNTER-STEREOTYPICAL MESSAGES

The central hypothesis of this chapter is that messages that make a negative but implicit reference to blacks are more likely to prime whites' racial resentment. Operationalized, this means that an implicitly racial appeal should activate racial resentment in whites' minds, leading them to express greater opposition to government efforts to ameliorate racial inequality. Unlike messages that are explicitly racial and messages that counter stereotypes, implicit messages are expected to increase the tendency of resentful whites to reject policies designed to redress the problems of African Americans.

This hypothesis in turn suggests three alternative hypotheses, one about whites' response to welfare, the second about whites' response to blacks, and the third about the nature of the predispositions in question. First, on the one hand, any allusion to a racially tinged issue like welfare may racialize a campaign, even if it alludes to white recipients. In that case, added racial symbolism may not be required for racial priming to occur. The Nixon White House

---

[1] The strongest test would examine a message without any racial images at all. However, I argue that racial images dominate the nonracial images and words they accompany. That is controversial enough to test, especially when candidates routinely deny it.

tapes show how strongly welfare dependency was associated with blacks in the minds of some of the nation's elites. Chief of staff H. R. Haldeman's diary included this entry from 1969: "President emphasized that you have to face that the whole [welfare] problem is really the blacks. The key is to devise a system that recognizes this, while not appearing to. . . . Pointed out that there has never in history been an adequate black nation, and they are the only race of which this is true" (quoted in Feagin and Vera 1995, 113). Perhaps, then, welfare has inescapable racial meaning. If saying the word "welfare" is enough to bring to mind derogatory views of African Americans, then even messages counter to stereotypes will succeed as well as implicitly racial messages in priming negative racial predispositions.

On the other hand, any allusion to blacks, even one that seems overtly racist, may prime negative racial predispositions. According to this alternative hypothesis, racial predispositions are not so ambivalent, and egalitarian norms are not so powerful. Negative racial sentiments may be sufficiently strong and prevalent that politicians who articulate them stand to gain more than they lose. On this view, calling a candidate's message racist helps to neutralize it, but for the same reason that any attack on a candidate's message works. Although we saw in Chapter 6 that Jesse Jackson's charge that the Horton message was racist made resentful people less likely to support Bush, this does not necessarily mean that an implicit derogatory reference to blacks works better than the explicit version. Remove the accusation of racism, leave the explicit derogatory reference to blacks, and find the same racial priming effect as with implicit messages. Explicit as well as implicit appeals may prime racial resentment.

There is yet a third alternative. Implicitly racial messages may seem to be priming racial predispositions. But perhaps they are really priming nonracial predispositions that may be related to racial predispositions, especially a general tendency to think conservatively about politics. In Chapter 6 we saw that controlling on conservatism does not lessen implicit appeals' ability to prime racial resentment. This time, I test the conservatism alternative in a different way, by seeing whether a message changes a person's decision to identify as a conservative. A racial message may work by activating a person's nonracial predisposition, but it may also work by changing it.

The experimental design I discuss below tests these alternatives against each other by pitting an implicitly racial message against (1) a message that counters racial stereotypes by showing white welfare recipients (the "counter-stereotypical" message) and (2) a message that makes an explicit negative reference to race (the "explicitly racial" message). By pitting an implicitly racial message against the other two styles, we can find out if it succeeds by offering a negative portrayal of blacks without mentioning race.

TABLE 7.1
Explicit, Implicit, and Counter-Stereotypical Messages

Message Style	Visual Reference	Verbal Reference
Explicitly racial	Blacks	Blacks
Implicitly racial	Blacks	None
Counter-stereotypical	Whites	None

AN EXPERIMENTAL TEST OF IMPLICIT VERSUS ALTERNATIVE MESSAGES

I relied on random assignment to generate equivalent groups of whites, and exposed each group to a different message about welfare. One group saw a message that was explicitly racial, another group a message that was implicitly racial, and a third group a message that was counter-stereotypical. All messages featured the identical conservative argument—that welfare recipients are an unfair burden for American society—and differed only in their racial style.

As Table 7.1 shows, the explicitly racial message implicated black welfare recipients both visually and verbally; the implicitly racial message implicated black welfare recipients visually, making no verbal identification; and the counter-stereotypical message implicated white welfare recipients visually, making no verbal identification. The contrast across three messages that are identical in every way except racial style can tell us whether negative racial predispositions are primed most powerfully by campaign messages that refer to racial stereotypes covertly and deniably.

For this purpose I manufactured three television news stories about gubernatorial candidates in Michigan. I invented every feature of these stories, including the candidates, but the script stuck to political realities (e.g., a gubernatorial contest was in fact about to begin). I went to great lengths to present realistic candidates and relied on trained television personnel to ensure that the script and its execution conformed to local news style. Scenes of African-American and white welfare recipients were matched on relevant dimensions, as were candidate scenes.[2]

The format of each treated news story was the same. A voice-over describing two potential candidates for Michigan's upcoming gubernatorial contest accompanied scenes of the candidates campaigning and of the subject matter of their issues. The Democrat and Republican were described in detail as essentially moderate candidates whose histories, concerns, and various issue positions were nearly identical. Their primary concern was reported to be the North

---

[2] Scenes chosen did not reveal candidates' true identities. The experiment was conducted in the first half of 1993.

American Free Trade Agreement. The experimental manipulation was introduced toward the end of the story: the voice-over detailed the Republican's critique of Michigan's welfare provision, either verbally targeting blacks (in the explicit condition) or making no mention of race (in the implicit and counter-stereotypical conditions), while scenes of either black (in the implicit and explicit conditions) or white (in the counter-stereotypical condition) welfare recipients appeared. (See appendix for script.)[3]

Participants were randomly selected from the Ann Arbor/Ypsilanti phone book and contacted by mail. They were informed that their household had been selected to participate in two unrelated studies conducted jointly by University of Michigan students for their degree requirements. One study was supposedly designed to improve the training of journalism students through evaluations of a television news story. The other was described as a study of opinions about current issues.

Follow-up contact was made by phone. Callers reiterated the purpose of the "two studies," secured consent, explained that we needed preliminary information, and asked about citizenship, age, race, partisanship, two open-ended questions on health care and government spending, a question about gender roles, and two questions that assessed racial resentment (see Chapter 4 for a discussion of this construct).[4]

Households were randomly assigned to message conditions. All eligible individuals in a household were included if possible (household N ranged from 1 to 4; total N per condition ranged from 68 to 78). The treated news stories were sandwiched between innocuous filler segments. After viewing the news stories participants answered a questionnaire on the news to maintain the ostensible purpose of the study and to create a time buffer for later opinion assessment. This was followed by several self-administered questionnaires: on political views, on news memory, and on suspicion of the study.[5] Except for education, the effort to create a diverse sample was, for an experiment, quite successful (the education distribution is representative of the highly educated local population).[6]

---

[3] Actually, there were six welfare messages: each style included one individualistic message that focused on the problems with welfare recipients and one systemic message that focused on rising demand for welfare. I report pooled results as this framing made little difference.

[4] The preliminary questions screened for vote eligibility and race, established rapport, and concealed the racial focus of the study. Viewing took place several days later.

[5] Debriefing items yielded several suspicion dimensions; those who guessed the purpose of the study were not included ($N = 27$), as is standard practice in deception experiments.

[6] Sample age ranged from 18 to 101 (mean = 43). Median household income was $45,000. Fifty-six percent were men. Work status was as follows: 58 percent full time, 10 percent part-time, 9 percent students, 1 percent disabled, 5 percent homemakers, 10 percent retired, 3 percent unemployed or laid off. Forty-seven percent were Protestant, 20 percent were Catholic, 9 percent were Jewish, 20 percent were not religious, and 5 percent had another religion. The sample was highly educated: 46 percent had some post-graduate education. Partisanship was as follows: 34 percent Democrats, 22 percent Republicans, 38 percent independents.

The two racial resentment questions and their distributions are presented in Table 7.2. I created a scale by averaging the two items, with the least resentful response set to 0 and the most resentful set to 1. The tendency away from resentment apparent in the individual item distributions is reflected in a low scale mean of .37 (SD = .23).[7] This is a much lower sample mean than is normally found in national probability samples, consistent with the abnormally high education level of the county population (Kinder and Sanders 1996; Sniderman and Piazza 1993). Nevertheless, the proportion of those who are extremely unresentful on both items is quite small (12 percent).

THE DISTINCTIVE IMPACT OF IMPLICIT MESSAGES

Message Classification

The first order of business is to verify that the messages are in fact perceived differently by viewers. For this purpose I asked respondents to choose from a list of statements those they considered accurate descriptions of the news story (see appendix).[8] If the messages in fact have different racial styles, then respondents exposed to an explicitly racial message will be more likely than the others to classify their message as a racial appeal. To find out, I regressed responses to a question asking whether the message was a racial appeal on resentment, a set of 0–1 dummy variables representing the message styles, and a religion variable that was not randomly distributed across conditions, included as a control (Pietist/fundamentalist religious affiliation). Because the responses were binary ("racial appeal" or not), I estimated the coefficients with a dichotomous probit model. The results suggest that of all the messages, only the explicitly racial style was considered racial: the model yields a single substantial effect, for explicit messages (b = 1.37, SE = .46).[9] Viewers of an implicitly racial

---

[7] Pre-testing ruled out trait measures of racial predispositions because they aroused suspicion about the study. One item was reflected in constructing the scale. Pearson r = .21. For the scale, pre- and post-exposure r = .72; difference of means is negligible (.02; paired t-test p = .05).

[8] The experimental groups differed on several demographic variables despite random assignment. Consequently, I reestimated all models with Protestant, Jewish, Pietist/fundamentalist, age, and education (and income, to control on racial resentment). A group that viewed a message about the environment had significantly different characteristics and thus could not be included.

[9] N = 237, 84 percent of cases predicted successfully. The set of 0–1 dummy variables representing the message styles consisted of explicit, implicit (b = .66, SE = .47), and counter-stereotypical (b = .52, SE = .48). The contrast group received a nonracial message about the environment. Unfortunately, rejection of the "racial appeal" description is confounded with missing data (the dependent variable is coded 1 = agreement, 0 does not), which underestimates agreement. Resentment had an impact of −.80, SE = .48, t = −1.69. Ranging from unresentful to resentful, 39 percent to 14 percent of explicit-message viewers indicated it was a racial appeal; in contrast, only 16 percent to 4 percent of implicit-message viewers said their message was racial and 13 percent to 3 percent of counter-stereotypical message viewers said their message was racial. Estimates hardly vary when I add ideological conservatism and the full set of demographic controls listed in note 6.

TABLE 7.2
Racial Resentment

Item 1: It's really a matter of some people not trying hard enough: if blacks would only try harder, they could be just as well off as whites. Do you agree strongly, agree somewhat, disagree somewhat, or disagree strongly?

Agree Strongly	4%
Agree Somewhat	26%
Disagree Somewhat	35%
Disagree Strongly	33%
Don't Know	1%
No answer	2%
Total	101%

Item 2: Generations of slavery and discrimination have created conditions that make it difficult for blacks to work their way out of the lower class. Do you agree strongly, agree somewhat, disagree somewhat, or disagree strongly?

Agree Strongly	23%
Agree Somewhat	42%
Disagree Somewhat	21%
Disagree Strongly	12%
Don't Know	1%
No answer	2%
Total	101%

Resentment: (unweighted average of items 1 and 2)

Low Resentment	0.00	12%
	0.17	19%
	0.33	27%
	0.50	26%
	0.67	12%
	0.83	2%
High Resentment	1.00	2%
Total		100%

Source: Ann Arbor-Ypsilanti area field experiment, 1993, $N = 251$.

message did not, for the most part, consider it to be a racial appeal, while many viewers of the explicit version did.

Impact of Racial Resentment on Policy Views

Does the implicitness and the stereotypical nature of a message matter to whites' reliance on racial resentment? To find out, I estimated Equation (7.1) with OLS, separately for each of five policy domains: race, welfare, poverty, social welfare spending, and defense spending (see appendix). Each policy domain is represented by a scale constructed on the 0–1 interval (1 = conservative) from unweighted averages of relevant items (see appendix for item wordings and scale reliabilities).[10]

Each message style is included as a dummy variable (coded 0 or 1), with those exposed to implicitly racial messages as the contrast group. Resentment is included as an unweighted average of the two items in Table 7.2, scaled on the 0–1 interval, and coded so that positive coefficients are expected (ideology and the remaining control variables are scaled this way too for comparability; see Table 7.4 in the appendix for details on these variables and their effects). Of interest are the effect of racial predispositions with exposure to implicitly racial appeals (b_1), and the change in that effect with exposure to explicit and counter-stereotypical appeals (b_4 and b_5). If b_1 is large and positive, and b_4 and b_5 are negative, then implicit racial appeals are particularly effective racial primes. (Table 7.4 in the appendix reports the remaining coefficients.)

And indeed they are. Table 7.3 shows that the implicitly racial message elicits a sizable effect from resentment on race policy views, and does so distinctively. With exposure to an implicitly racial message, a person sympathetic to blacks differs from a person who resents blacks by 57 points on a 100-point scale, a difference that places them at complete opposites on the issue of government intervention in racial matters. With counter-stereotypical and explicitly racial messages, however, resentment makes a much smaller difference to opinion on racial issues. With a counter-stereotypical or an explicitly racial message, the same pair of people, one resentful and one not, only differs by 27 or 33 points on a 100-point scale (these are total effects, i.e., $b_1 + b_5$ and $b_1 + b_4$). A message about welfare that is not implicitly racial reduces the power of racial predispositions by nearly 50 percent.[11]

[10] A missing data algorithm computed scale scores for cases with missing data from values on the remaining items (consequently, alpha estimates may be somewhat biased). Most unpopular is welfare, closely followed by government intervention in matters of race. Spending on the poor and spending in general, on the other hand, receive a good deal of support. For a similar pattern see Smith (1987).

[11] $b_4/b_1 = 42\%$; $b_5/b_1 = 53\%$. While diminished, the total effect of racial predispositions (.27 and .33) does not disappear.

TABLE 7.3

Baseline and Incremental Effects of Resentment on Policy Views, by Message Style

	Message Style					
Policy	Implicitly Racial (Baseline Effect) (b_1)	Explicitly Racial (Incremental Effect) (b_4)	Counter-Stereotypical (Incremental Effect) (b_5)	Adjusted-R^2	SE	N
Race	0.57[a]	−0.24[b]	−0.30[b]	0.34	0.19	194
	(0.10)	(0.14)	(0.15)			
Welfare	0.16[c]	0.08	0.10	0.24	0.20	197
	(0.11)	(0.15)	(0.16)			
Poverty	0.19[b]	0.07	0.19	0.37	0.19	196
	(0.10)	(0.14)	(0.15)			
Spending	0.21[b]	−0.04	−0.01	0.39	0.21	198
	(0.11)	(0.16)	(0.17)			
Defense	0.15[c]	0.00	0.12	0.26	0.19	195
	(0.10)	(0.14)	(0.15)			

Note: Entries are OLS unstandardized regression coefficients, representing baseline or incremental effects relative to the implicitly racial group (standard errors in parentheses). Models include Pietist/Fundamentalist and Jewish affiliations, age, education, and ideology. Racial predispositions and ideology are coded on the 0–1 interval, 1 = conservative (see appendix).

[a] $P \leq .001$ (one-tailed)

[b] $p \leq .05$

[c] $p \leq .10$

Racial predispositions do have some influence over opinion in policy domains other than race, but these effects are much smaller than in the case of race (15 to 21 versus 57 points). More important, these effects, unlike the effect on race policy, do not vary with the nature of the message. Explicitly racial and counter-stereotypical messages do not change the impact of racial predispositions on views in any domain other than race: not on opposition to welfare, not on resistance to aiding the poor, not on holding the line on government spending, not on increasing defense spending. The evidence so far suggests that when it comes to priming racial predispositions, implicitly racial messages are distinctively powerful, and then primarily in the domain of race.[12] A message that white voters do not recognize as racial but that cues racial stereotypes elicits the strongest racial response. Campaign appeals have their

[12] Analysis of variance indicates no main effects of message exposure. Implicitly racial messages do not affect policy views regardless of racial predispositions. Resentment also does not change in response to any of the messages: the overall difference of means is .02, p = .46, and a one-way ANOVA on post-message resentment yields an F of .49, p = .82.

greatest racial impact when they have a racial component but are perceived as nonracial.

Racial Predispositions Versus Conservatism

But perhaps racial priming in fact masks the priming of nonracial predispositions—ideological conservatism in particular. To find out, I reestimated Equation 7.1 with an extra pair of 0–1 dummy variables, representing the interaction of conservatism and each message style (again, the implicitly racial group in each set of dummy variables was excluded). If racial predispositions are primed most powerfully by implicitly racial messages even with a control on ideological priming, then the case for racial priming is more solid.

Figure 7.1 presents the total effect of racial predispositions and ideological conservatism on race policy views, separately for each message. The effect of racial predispositions on race policy views still varies with the racial style of the message, remaining virtually unchanged from the pattern in Table 7.3. The distinctive power of implicit appeals to prime racial predispositions is not undermined by taking ideology into account. The priming effect characteristic of implicitly racial appeals does not in any way stand in for activated nonracial predispositions. (See the bottom of Figure 7.1 for full details.)

Figure 7.1 also shows that each message style elicits a distinctive psychological process. The impact of racial predispositions dominates the impact of ideology only with exposure to implicitly racial messages; the impact of ideology in turn dominates the impact of racial predispositions only with exposure to explicitly racial messages; and counter-stereotypical messages are not particularly successful in priming either set of predispositions. Implicitly racial appeals seem to be the most effective racial primers because they contain a racial reference and they do not suggest the need for self-censorship: they are both racial and subtle.

The explicit message's ability to prime conservatism at the expense of resentment requires some explanation. Conservatism was measured after people were exposed to the message. Therefore, the explicit message may have influenced people's tendency to identify as conservative. Regressing ideological identification (a continuous measured scaled 1 for conservative) on the message styles, resentment, the interaction of each style with resentment, and the familiar set of demographic controls reveals only one coefficient that is even remotely statistically significant: on the resentment*explicit message interaction (b = .59, SE = .29, one-tailed p = .10).[13] It appears that the explicit message is distinctive in leading some resentful people to identify as conservative more than they would otherwise. Conservatism may dominate resentment when

---

[13] $N = 251$; SE for the equation = .25.

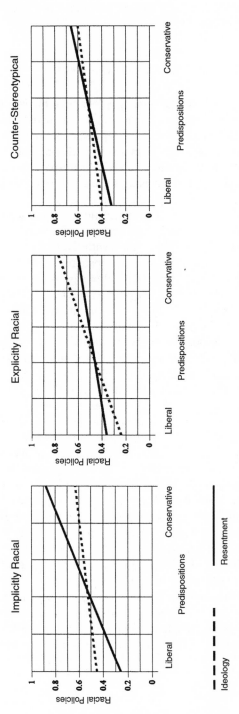

Figure 7.1. Effect of resentment and ideology on opposition to racial policies, by message. Based on unstandardized ordinary least squares (OLS) regression estimates from the following model (standard errors in parentheses): .31 (.06) + .62 (.10) Resent + .18 (.09) ID − .07 (.07) Explicit + .05 (.08) Counter − .38 (.14) Explicit* Resent − .28 (.15) Counter* Resent + .35 (.13) Explicit* ID + .02 (.13) Counter* ID − .002 (.001) Age. Line calculations rely on mean values for remaining variables. Resent = Resentment (0–1 interval); ID = ideology (0–1 interval); adjusted R-square = .39; SE = .21; N = 194. Explicit and Counter are 0–1 dummy variables, with implicitly racial exposure (and its multiplicative terms) the excluded categories. Pietist/Fundamentalist and Jewish affiliations and education had no significant effects, hence the trimmed model.

people are exposed to explicitly racial messages because the resentful are more likely to turn to conservative identification and to ground their opposition to egalitarian racial policies in a race-neutral, general ideology.

In sum, the largest and most consistent impact of implicitly racial messages about welfare is not to change opinions about welfare so much as to enhance the influence of racial resentment on opinions about race. Racial resentment is primed distinctly by implicitly racial messages, not by explicitly racial or by counter-stereotypical messages, and primarily on policies that directly deal with race. The implicit message is the only one that contains a racial cue yet is not recognized by most whites as racial. Clearly, there is something peculiarly and powerfully racial about implicitly racial messages. The combination of derogatory racial reference and implicitness is the only factor that can account for this.

CONCLUSION

The evidence presented here suggests that racial campaign appeals do indeed shape the considerations individuals bring to their policy decisions. But the style of a racial message makes all the difference. When politicians engage in explicitly racial appeals, or when they offer counter-stereotypical portrayals of welfare, racial predispositions exercise a smaller impact on opinions about policies dealing with race. By contrast, implicitly racial messages mobilize whites' racial predispositions with considerable force. These appeals are not considered racial by the vast majority of white viewers. Yet, paradoxically, it is their racial reference that dominates white citizens' political decisions.

There is room for optimism too, however. Conservative rhetoric about welfare does not have inevitable racial consequences. When the racial component of a message is neutralized with the simple move of showing white welfare recipients, the white public's racial "component" is much less influential. A candidate can be a staunch conservative and rely on dramatic appeals, and still easily minimize consequences that are detrimental to a democratic polity. Counter-stereotypical portrayals of welfare recipients, which underscore the reality that most people who receive welfare are white, is likely to lead white citizens to view government efforts to improve the lives of African Americans in a more positive light. Racial predispositions can be activated by implicit messages, but that does not mean that stereotyping is inevitable. Should the public debate over welfare cease to reinforce racial stereotypes, taking on a counter-stereotypical character, white citizens would rely on racial stereotypes much less—particularly when considering issues that deal expressly with race.

The magnitude of such a change in coverage can be inferred from Figure 7.1. That figure shows that with exposure to counter-stereotypical messages, the most resentful people lean closer to neutrality regarding policies such as affirmative action and spending to aid blacks than they do to strong opposition; with an implicitly racial message, the most resentful people are much closer to strong opposition than they are to neutrality (the least resentful people do not vary their position much).[14] If candidates campaign in a counter-stereotypical way, rather than with implicitly racial appeals, resentment would likely cease to have a large impact on the views of white voters, and the white majority would become considerably more receptive to government efforts to ameliorate racial inequality.

The other piece of good news is that when campaign rhetoric is so racially charged that it is patently racist, its white viewers are also less likely to rely on their racial predispositions in reaching policy decisions. But these explicitly racial messages elicit a psychological process that implicitly racial and counter-stereotypical messages do not: they lead resentful whites to reject their racial predispositions as grounds for deciding racial matters, and to turn instead to conservative ideology.

Why this is so is a matter for speculation. It is possible that because resentful whites are resolved to conform to egalitarian norms in matters of race, they search for principled grounds for maintaining resistance to government-engi-neered racial equality, especially when egalitarian norms of public discourse are violated by a candidate. Whites in this study and in national surveys are not at all reticent about expressing opposition to policies like affirmative action (the Michigan sample's mean conservatism on race policies is 57 on a 0 to 100 scale). That opposition only becomes problematic for resentful whites when they witness a candidate engaging in explicit racial rhetoric. At that point they appear to monitor the basis for their opposition and choose ideological justifi-cations for it, rejecting their racial predispositions. An egalitarian norm may not moderate whites' opposition to policies that aid African Americans, but it may moderate the racial determinants of that opposition, leaving room for nonracial determinants such as ideological conservatism. All this, of course, is speculative, but it does follow from the theoretical framework I have built to explain the impact of implicitly racial appeals, and it is testable.

How can we connect the experimental findings in this chapter with the conduct of real campaigns? In Chapter 6 we observed that the Republicans' racial message in the 1988 presidential campaign ceased to work when it was rendered explicit by the Democrats and the media. But what element of the explicit phase of the campaign was responsible for neutralizing racial resent-ment? Was it the use by journalists of the terms "black" and "white" to describe Horton and his victims? Or was it the Democrats' charge of racism? The results

---

[14] When resentment = 1 (the most resentful), the model used for Figure 7.1 predicts an opposi-tion of about .65 on the race policy scale, which is closer to the scale's neutrality point of .5 than it is to the scale's "strong opposition" point of 1. With the implicit message, opposition is at about .88, much closer to 1 than to .5.

of the welfare experiment suggest that the former may be sufficient. When journalists make clear that a candidate's implicit message is in fact about race, voters are likely to become aware that the message is racial. That awareness renders the implicit message explicit. But in the real world of politics, the media rarely supplies this type of explicit coverage on its own. By charging the opposition with stepping over the bounds of the norm, a party prods the media to cover the message in an explicit way. At a minimum, a party that highlights the violation of norms causes an important indirect effect.

Implicit appeals seem to be powerful because they are both racially derogatory and implicit. But the impact of implicit messages depends on awareness and on commitment to the norm. The next chapter takes up these mediating processes in greater detail.

APPENDIX

Script

(All tapes begin with scenes of the anchor, then the Democrat and Republican campaigning, then an auto factory; throughout, the anchor's voice-over describes the candidates.)

Tape 1: Counter-stereotypical (white recipients)
An important difference between the candidates concerns Michigan's welfare budget. In his last campaign, Hayes said people take advantage of welfare at the expense of hard-working taxpayers. He claimed welfare has become a way of life for many, and criticized Michigan's above-average rates of welfare cheating. He said able-bodied welfare recipients should have to work in return for benefits.

[Anchor shot.] It's early in the gubernatorial campaign, and observers caution that John Engler, until he says otherwise, is still a candidate for re-election. But it's never too early to start campaigning, as John Hayes and James Reed know. And at least for now, welfare reform may emerge as the main issue in this campaign pre-season.

Tape 2: Implicitly racial (black recipients)
(Same voice-over as tape 1.)

Tape 3: Explicitly racial (black recipients)
An important difference between the candidates concerns Michigan's welfare budget. In his last campaign, Hayes said some people, *especially blacks*, take advantage of welfare at the expense of hard-working taxpayers. He claimed welfare had become a way of life for many *black people*, and criticized Michigan's above-average rates of welfare cheating. He said able-bodied welfare recipients should have to work in return for benefits.

Tape 4: Counter-stereotypical (white recipients)

An important difference between the candidates concerns Michigan's welfare budget. In his last campaign, Hayes cited several recent studies suggesting that the welfare budget is growing. He said compared to 1989, there were more people on the welfare rolls and more welfare applications.

Tape 5: Implicitly racial (black recipients)

(Same voice-over as tape 4.)

Tape 6: Explicitly racial (black recipients)

An important difference between the candidates concerns Michigan's welfare budget. In his last campaign, Hayes cited several recent studies suggesting that the welfare budget is growing. He said compared to 1989, there were more people, *especially blacks*, on the welfare rolls, and more welfare applications, *especially from blacks*.

Variables

(Scales are on the 0–1 interval, 1 = conservative, based on an unweighted average.)

Race Policies (Cronbach's alpha = .81)

1. Some people feel that the government in Washington should make every effort to improve the social and economic position of blacks. Others feel that the government should not make any special effort to help blacks because they should help themselves. Where would you place yourself on this scale? (Seven-point)

2. If you had a say in making up the federal budget this year, for which of the following programs would you like to see spending increased and for which would you like to see spending decreased: Programs that assist blacks? (Increased/ Same/ Decreased/ Don't know)

3. Some people say that because of past discrimination, blacks should be given preference in hiring and promotion. Others say such preference in hiring and promotion is wrong because it discriminates against whites. (Five-point Likert and Don't know)

4. Because of past discrimination it is sometimes necessary for colleges and universities to reserve openings for black students. Others oppose quotas because they say quotas give blacks advantages they haven't earned. What about your opinion— do you favor or oppose quotas to admit black students? (Five-point Likert and Don't know)

5. What do you think the chances are these days that a white person won't get a job or a promotion while an equally or less qualified black person gets one instead? (Very likely/ Somewhat likely/ Not likely/ Don't know)

TABLE 7.4
Miscellaneous Effects on Policy Views

	Conservatism (0–1)	Fundamentalist (0–1 dummy)	Jewish (0–1 dummy)	Education (0–1)	Age (18–101)	Counter-Stereotypical (0–1 dummy)	Explicit (0–1 dummy)	Constant
Race	0.29	0.03	0.04	-0.06	-0.002	0.07	0.05	0.31
	(0.06)	(0.04)	(0.06)	(0.06)	(0.001)	(0.06)	(0.06)	(0.07)
Welfare	0.35	0.03	-0.02	-0.05	0.000	-0.06	-0.05	0.53
	(0.06)	(0.04)	(0.07)	(0.06)	(0.001)	(0.07)	(0.07)	(0.07)
Poverty	0.45	-0.03	-0.07	0.05	-0.001	-0.13	-0.01	0.25
	(0.06)	(0.04)	(0.06)	(0.06)	(0.001)	(0.06)	(0.06)	(0.07)
Spending	0.60	-0.05	-0.08	0.04	0.000	-0.05	0.03	0.00
	(0.07)	(0.04)	(0.07)	(0.06)	(0.001)	(0.07)	(0.07)	(0.08)
Defense	0.19	-0.02	-0.13	-0.25	0.000	-0.07	0.02	0.45
	(0.08)	(0.05)	(0.08)	(0.07)	(0.001)	(0.06)	(0.06)	(0.09)

N range = 194–198. See Equation 7.1 and the description in the appendix.

Welfare (Cronbach's alpha = .71)

1. Requiring that people must work in order to receive welfare. (Five-point Likert and Don't know)

2. Reducing welfare benefits to make working for a living more attractive. (Five-point Likert and Don't know)

3. Welfare spending? (Increased/ Same/ Decreased/ Don't know) (see spending series for stem)

Poverty

1. Government aid to the poor (see assist blacks; replaces "blacks" with "poor")

Spending (Cronbach's alpha = .73)

1. Some say the government should provide fewer services even in areas such as health and education in order to reduce spending. Other people feel it is important for the government to provide many more services even if it means an increase in spending. (Seven-point)

2. Child Care (Increased/ Same/ Decreased/ Don't know) (see spending series for stem)

3. Health Care (Increased/ Same/ Decreased/ Don't know) (see spending series for stem)

Defense

Some people believe that we should spend much less money for defense. Others feel that defense spending should be greatly increased. (Seven-point)

Ideology

Here is a seven-point scale on which the political views that people might hold are arranged from extremely liberal to extremely conservative. Where would you place yourself? (Seven-point and Don't know)

Message Classification

Circle *as many as you think are correct*: A candidate who tried to appeal to racial feelings.

Equation 7.1:

Opinion = a + b_1(Resentment) + b_2(Explicit) + b_3(Counter-stereotypical) + b_4(Explicit*Resentment) + b_5(Counter-stereotypical*Resentment) + b_6(Ideology) + $b_{(7-7+k)}$(Demographic Controls)

CHAPTER 8

Psychological Mechanisms: The Norms Experiment

It is itself a form of deceit, when it is completed; yet
not deceit in the ordinary sense of the word, since no
outright breach of faith is involved.
—Clausewitz, *On War*

RACIAL PROBLEMS are among the most difficult for Americans to resolve even
under the best of circumstances. What makes them particularly trying is that
discourse about them often takes place under cover of other issues. The previous chapters have documented the impact of implicitly racial campaign communication. I have shown why and how it is used by politicians, how it is
conveyed by the media, and what exactly makes it implicit. In Chapters 6 and
7 I provided several types of evidence that politicians' implicit appeals make a
great deal of difference to white citizens' opinions.

The question these findings pose is how, psychologically, a subtle reference
to race works. Why does it work more powerfully than an overt reference? After
all, common sense, supported by the literature on political communication,
suggests that the opposite is true. The more the message focuses on the issue
of crime the more it should influence opinion about crime and the less it should
affect opinion about racial matters. The same could be said of communication
about welfare. We expect that a message should influence opinion about whatever it is that viewers perceive to be the subject of the message (Iyengar and
Kinder 1987; Krosnick and Brannon 1993). When viewers perceive a message
to be about welfare (or crime) rather than race, as Chapter 7 showed that they
do, their predispositions about that issue domain should be activated, and
their opinion about that topic should change. Yet I find that it is their racial
predispositions that are evoked, and their opinion about race policy that
changes most.

Why does a message whose content is perceived to be about one issue operate on views about another issue? How is it that "what is said is not always
what is heard" (Jamieson 1992, 9)? By the same token, what is it about the
explicitness of a message that decreases its effectiveness? Put differently, what
psychological mechanisms help determine whether a message increases—or
decreases—whites' reliance on negative racial predispositions?

CONSCIOUS CONTROL VERSUS AUTOMATIC RACIAL PRIMING

In Chapter 4 I suggested an explanation based on the notion that people control their response to their environment to different degrees in different circumstances. Normally, a message that contains a subtle racial cue succeeds because it makes a person's racial predispositions more accessible—more ready for subsequent use—without the person being aware of this. Greater accessibility causes a person to form opinions more in line with the activated predisposition. This is what I have referred to as racial priming. However, people are not always sure they want to give more weight to their negative racial predispositions. Under some circumstances, this automatic, nonconscious process becomes conscious. At that point, people can decide how much weight to give to their resentment. They may choose not to give it any more weight than before. In fact, they may choose to give it less weight than they normally do.[1] All a message must do to achieve racial priming is to make racial predispositions more accessible—as long as it does this outside of awareness. As soon as a person is alerted to the need to pay conscious attention to her response, accessibility is no longer sufficient to make the person rely on racial predispositions. Becoming alert may even cause a person to ignore the accessible predispositions more than they normally do, resulting in the opposite of a priming effect—a contrast effect.

Control can be rooted not only in reason but in emotion too. Negative racial predispositions may contain attributions and beliefs, such as the attribution of racial inequality to the faults of African Americans, but also feelings and affect, such as fear. Racial resentment has cognitive content—for example, the perception that blacks engage in inappropriate behavior—but also includes a moralistic feeling of resentment. When a person gives weight to his resentment, he is allowing himself to express sentiments, beliefs, values, and more. Controlling the expression of negative racial predispositions thus entails, in part, control of an emotional response. Emotions are subject to what Frijda calls the "law of care for consequence," which dictates that "every emotional impulse elicits a secondary impulse that tends to modify it in view of its possible consequences" (1988, 355). Emotions encounter a control mechanism, itself part of the package of emotional response, which can override even powerful emotions and prohibit them from dictating behavior.

Just as with cognitive control, in which a belief determines the extent to which a predisposition will be given weight, the extent to which emotional control is exercised is determined by the demands of the situation. Control over an emotional response erodes, for example, when others seem to be letting

---

[1] Racial priming is also known in the psychological literature as an "assimilation effect," and the opposite is known as a "contrast effect" (Moskowitz 1993).

themselves go (1988, 355). Evidence for this proposition in the political domain is scarce, but it does exist. For example, emotions seem to mediate the impact of threatening information on people's decision to tolerate an extremist, disliked political group (Marcus et al. 1995).

The missing link in what I have said so far is the psychological function of norms. The reason many whites do not implement their racial predispositions in all situations is that they have learned to inhibit them in response to the presence of a norm of racial equality. Some have done so because they have internalized the norm. For these people, the norm is not merely descriptive or injunctive but personal. For others, the norm is not quite personal but it is injunctive, working through a person's wish to maintain her social approval. In Chapter 4 I presented the overwhelming evidence for the proposition that white Americans have become egalitarian on matters of principle in near-universal proportions, that the norm is descriptive, injunctive, and, for many, personal. A debate continues about the sources of this change and the number of people for whom the norm is genuinely personal. But that a sea change has occurred is beyond question.

What the dramatic trend toward endorsing the ideal of racial equality suggests, unequivocally, is first that the norm concerning racist expression in public has become markedly more egalitarian. The fact that over 90 percent of national white samples endorse the fundamental principle of racial equality as an abstract matter indicates few things for certain; one thing it does indicate for certain is that whoever publicly speaks words that strike the audience as racist is likely to face social censure. A politician who appears to violate the norm against racist public expression is likely to suffer adverse political consequences. White voters, even those sympathetic to racially resentful statements, may nevertheless reject the message, and the candidate, if it appears to violate the norm of nonracist public expression. This hinges on how the message is consciously classified.

The second implication of the sea change is that a person's control over their response to a message hinges in part on their sense of security about their own normative placement. People are often highly sensitive to their perception of what others think (Bennett and Klockner 1996; Herbst 1993; Mutz 1998; Noelle-Neumann 1974). It is the unease with the possibility of one's own violation of the norm that, in part, creates the need to monitor one's response. Placing a person in the mainstream of the norm of racial equality may reassure him that he need not worry about controlling his response. Placing him outside the mainstream and near the extreme of the norm, on the other hand, may sufficiently threaten him (even if he does not accept the truth of that placement) that he will be more likely to monitor his response. Of course, some individuals are likely to be chronic self-monitors. They may more readily control their response than others do. I will return to these possibilities shortly.

LEVEL OF RESENTMENT

Highly resentful people are those who face the direst problem when it comes to relying on their racial predispositions in reaching political decisions. Ambivalence about how much weight they should give to their predispositions should be especially strong for them. One possible reason is that they are ambivalent between conflicting considerations, torn between a heartfelt commitment to equality on the one hand and resentful predispositions on the other. The other possibility is that they are driven primarily by social considerations. Although they endorse the ideal of racial equality at a superficial level, they may not place it high on their personal priority list. What they are likely to want is to conform to the social norm of equality so as not to be considered extremist. In the privacy of their homes and when speaking to another white, resentful whites are often not reluctant to say that they resent black people, because they view their resentment not as a general, irrational prejudice but as a specific, contingent judgment that is justified by the facts (Lamont 1999). When provided with "safe" ways to express their resentment, they do not shy away from doing so (Kuklinski et al. 1997). They are much less likely to feel free to express their racial views when talking to a black than a white survey interviewer (Sanders 1996).[2] It is highly resentful people who are likely to face strong social censure if they speak their minds, since their views are the ones most often subject to the charge of racism. They are the ones to suffer the most severe reaction should they express their views fully. A person with high levels of racial resentment is thus especially likely to be susceptible to situational considerations and social desirability pressures in deciding whether to express racial resentment.

People with low levels of resentment may also be susceptible to situational cues. However, the cues of greatest influence to them are likely to be those that signal which value is most appropriate in a given situation. People with low resentment are much more concerned with adhering to their own internal code of behavior and much less susceptible to social pressures than are highly resentful individuals (Devine et al. 1991; Plant and Devine 1998; Zuwerink et al. 1996). This does not mean that they are impervious to the automatic activation of derogatory racial beliefs. Low-resentment individuals are no less susceptible than others to the automatic activation of derogatory racial stereotypes (Devine 1989; Fazio et al. 1995; on gender bias see Banaji and Greenwald 1995; Banaji and Hardin 1996). But when allowed conscious access to their reaction, they suppress their stereotypes with greater vigor (Devine et al. 1991). People who score high on a scale specifically developed to measure the motiva-

---

[2] African Americans also change their responses depending on the race of their interviewer, but for different reasons (Davis 1997).

tion to control prejudiced responses may not avoid the automatic activation of their stereotypes, but they control their response to that activation (Dunton and Fazio 1997). Unlike highly prejudiced individuals, who are less worried about the correctness of their true opinion than they are about the social acceptability of their expressed opinion, low-resentment people control their response out of internalized values. This is somewhat akin to Monroe's (1995) argument that the toughest moral decisions of ordinary people are informed less by a conscious calculation of social cost or gain than by an instinctual and general sense of self, by a sense of the kind of person one is.

Thus low-resentment individuals, who normally are impervious to the effects of racial priming, may suffer those effects when they let down their usual guard. However, it is the highly resentful who should be particularly susceptible to the nature of the racial message and to whether expressing resentment is socially safe (more on this later on). There may be a difference in the type of motivation for the two groups, with the low-resentment group driven more by internal standards and the high-resentment group driven more by social desirability.

PSYCHOLOGICAL MECHANISMS

It seems, then, that citizens may, under some circumstances, choose whether or not to give weight to their racial predispositions in making political choices. A message may result in more or less racial priming depending upon people's control over their response. But what psychological mechanisms lead people to control their response? And is it the actual opinion that is monitored, or simply the expression of opinion? Is psychological control primarily designed to form an opinion that the person can live with given her own internal standards, or to protect the individual from social censure? I will examine three mechanisms that may facilitate or inhibit the ability of a message to prime racial resentment: an emotional reaction to the possibility that one may violate the norm of racial equality; a general personality tendency to self-monitor for socially acceptable responses; and a conscious awareness of the racial nature of a message.

Let us consider the first mechanism first. A person who has a strong emotional reaction to violating the norm of racial equality is likely to be more conscious of her own thoughts regarding racial matters. She is likely to monitor the extent to which her opinion on matters of race policy violates the norm, and guard against giving much weight to negative racial predispositions. She may even monitor her response to a candidate who communicates a racial message.

The second mechanism is a personality tendency to self-monitor. This mechanism has more to do with opinion expression than opinion generation. It deals more with the decision whether or not to reveal a racially conservative opinion than with whether or not to form the opinion. There is some evidence that self-monitoring has a great deal of influence over political evaluations. Terkildsen (1993) found that self-monitoring overrules prejudiced people's inclination to discriminate against black candidates. In fact, people who were prejudiced but highly inclined to monitor their reaction overcompensated for their prejudice and demonstrated a contrast effect by supporting a fictitious dark-skinned black candidate more than his light-skinned or white replicas. On the other hand, people who were prejudiced but not inclined to monitor their response simply expressed their prejudice and opposed black candidates over an identical white candidate (opposition to the dark-skinned candidate was greatest). Without the tendency to attend to social norms about race, prejudiced whites rely on their prejudice in choosing candidates. Attention to the norm begets the neutralization of prejudice in political choice. Terkildsen's study does not say conclusively whether the outcome results from a desire to conform to others' opinion or a desire to conform to an egalitarian self-concept. Still, self-monitoring has been conceptualized as a social desirability mechanism, and this is the most plausible interpretation of its effect.

The third and final mechanism is message classification. This mechanism too is related to racial norms. As we saw in Chapter 7, white citizens do not perceive the subtle racial reference in implicit messages as a violation of racial norms. Conversely, they tend to perceive the explicitly racial message as violating these norms. When they decide that a message violates racial norms, they may in turn inhibit their own racial predispositions in making subsequent decisions. This would explain why people rely on their racial predispositions after exposure to implicitly racial messages even though they do not classify these messages as racial. Conversely, it explains why people rely less on their racial predispositions in response to explicit messages that they do classify as racial. As a result either of personal commitment to egalitarian ideals or of a desire to adhere to dominant social norms against racist expression, classifying a message as racial leads individuals to mitigate the influence of their negative racial views on their political judgments. An awareness of the racial nature of the appeal, then, is likely to mediate the racial impact of the message. It should regulate the extent to which a racial message results in racial priming.

EXPERIMENTAL DESIGN

Overview

To test these hypotheses, I designed the norms experiment. After assessing subjects' racial and nonracial predispositions, I randomly assigned white subjects to a mainstream or extreme condition. In the mainstream condition, subjects were informed that their racial predispositions are in the mainstream of the racial norm. In the extreme condition subjects were informed that their racial predispositions are on the extreme of the norm. Because the impact of violating the norm is likely to be mediated by a negative emotional response to that violation, I included an extensive assessment of emotional reactions immediately following the norm manipulation. Each subject was then randomly assigned to viewing a message that was either implicitly racial, explicitly racial, or nonracial. I expect that informing people that they may be violating the norm decreases the effect of implicitly racial messages. White citizens would then be less resistant to government intervention in racial discrimination and government assistance to blacks. They would also be less inclined to support a candidate who employs a racial appeal.

Emotional response to norm violation is one control mechanism that may regulate the response to a subsequent message. Two other factors may regulate a person's racial response: whether the message is perceived as a racial appeal, that is, as a violation of norms, and whether the perceiver has a general tendency to monitor her own behavior. Accordingly, I asked subjects, toward the end of the session, whether they thought the message was a racial appeal and whether it dealt with a racial issue. I also measured subjects' general tendency to monitor themselves (see appendix).

A random sample of central New Jersey residents received a recruitment letter for a study of citizens' views of the political process. They were contacted by phone for a fifteen-minute initial interview that prescreened for race and eligibility to vote, and allowed me to measure racial and nonracial predispositions without the contamination of the experimental manipulations. They were invited to attend a follow-up session on the Princeton University campus.[3]

Message Conditions

Small groups of participants were randomly assigned to view one of three manufactured television news reports: implicitly racial, explicitly racial, or nonra-

---

[3] The study relied on white telephone interviewers who underwent several hours of training. At no point did the interviewers disclose the purpose of the study. The average participant had the following demographic characteristics: male (63%), college-educated, forty-nine years old, full-time worker (68%) with a $50,000 to $84,000 annual household income. Catholics made up a plurality (33%), followed closely by Protestants (32%), and then the unaffiliated (20%) and Jews (16%). Republicans constituted 35%, Democrats 33%, and Independents 26% (of these, 46% were Democratic leaners, 22% Republican leaners). Ideological moderates made up the bulk of the sample (39%) with conservatives at 28% and liberals at 25%. Relative to the county and to national samples, this sample was wealthier, older, more male, and better educated, but its partisan and ideological distribution is similar. They were promised a modest reward of either ten dollars or a Princeton University mug.

TABLE 8.1
Message Conditions

Message Style	Visual Reference to Race	Verbal Reference to Race	Issue
Explicitly racial	Blacks	Blacks	Welfare
Implicitly racial	Blacks	None	Welfare
Nonracial	None	None	Environment

cial (see Table 8.1).[4] I produced the news reports with local news format and style in mind. They each featured two possible candidates for New Jersey governor. All except the nonracial segment dealt with the issue of welfare; the nonracial segment focused on the environment. The implicit story featured a Republican candidate criticizing the New Jersey welfare system. He argued that too many recipients take advantage of hard-working taxpayers. During this verbal message viewers were exposed to several seconds of scenes showing black welfare recipients, but at no point was race mentioned verbally. The explicit message was identical but the verbal message included the word "blacks." In both news segments the Democratic candidate replies briefly that the state's welfare problem is not serious and will be solved with increased employment. (See appendix for script.) All the manufactured news segments feature the same two candidates, and each segment was also embedded in two innocuous news stories.

Norm Manipulation

In order to manipulate people's sense of conformity to the egalitarian racial norm, I gave them information suggesting either that they conform to the norm or that they are close to violating it (see Fig. 8.1). Before they watched the news, participants saw a pair of scales, the first labeled either "Ethnic Relations" or "The Environment," and the second labeled "Defense and Foreign Relations." Participants were told that these displays show where the answers they gave during the phone interview are located relative to the answers of three groups in society: Democrats, Republicans, and the Ku Klux Klan. The Klan qualifies as an extremist group that is widely disliked. Marcus et al., for example, found that of a list of eleven extremist political groups, the Klan was by far the group most disliked (1995).[5] Locating participants in relation to the Klan should get them to think of whether they are too close to a group that epitomizes the violation of the norm of racial equality.

---

[4] A fourth, counter-stereotypical condition had insufficient cases for analysis and I set it aside.
[5] Many other recent studies confirm this (Chong 1996; Nelson et al. 1997).

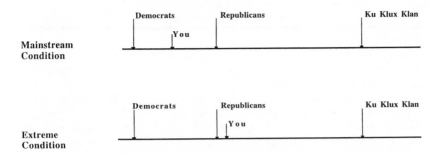

Figure 8.1. Norm conditions: display seen by subjects in the norm experiment.

Subjects were randomly assigned either to the mainstream condition—in the middle of the two parties—or the extreme condition—immediately to the right of the Republican party, with the Klan looming in the distance as the next possible reference group (to make the manipulation believable, the "extreme" condition placed the respondent just to the right of the Republican party and still rather far from the Klan). Each of the two scales that a participant saw ("Ethnic Relations" and "Defense," or "Environment" and "Defense") placed the participant in the same location. In all analyses that follow, I grouped together the "Ethnic Relations" with the "Environment" conditions since the dimension label made no difference.[6]

Measurement

I measured racial resentment with three items, displayed in Table 8.2.[7] As Table 8.2 shows, the three items correlate well with each other. They were averaged into a continuous variable ranging from 0 to 1, where 1 is most resentful. The mean of this resentment distribution is .5 with a standard deviation of .29. Because I was testing different hypotheses about high-resentment and low-resentment people, I divided the resentment distribution into three categories: low resentment (0 to .33), moderate resentment (.34 to .67), and high resentment (.68 to 1). The modal group is the moderate one, consistent with national samples.

[6] Apparently participants reacted so strongly to the Klan contrast group that the issue label of the dimension on which they were compared to the Klan did not matter to them.

[7] Participants' predispositions were assessed by phone in advance of the experiment. The racial questions were buried among nonracial items. The post-manipulation questions were self-administered by computer and are primarily questions about government policy and, to a lesser extent, about the candidates featured in the news report. (In both pre- and post-questionnaires the racial items came after the nonracial items.) The manipulations did not change the responses to any of the three items (paired t-tests on all three items are nonsignificant).

TABLE 8.2
Racial Resentment Items from Norms Experiment: Description and Correlations

Racial Resentment
(Response are in five-point Likert format ranging from strongly agree to strongly disagree, with counterbalancing to prevent acquiescence bias. Responses were recoded on the 0–1 interval, 1 = Resentful.)
Most people—blacks and whites alike—agree that the average white person in America is more likely to have a good income, get a good education, and to have a regular job than the average black person is. Here are some reasons that have been given as to why the average black American is not as well off as the average white American.

1. It's really a matter of some people not trying hard enough; if blacks would only try harder they could be just as well off as whites.

2. Generations of slavery and discrimination have created conditions that make it difficult for blacks to work their way out of the lower class.

3. Irish, Italian, Jewish, and many other minorities overcame prejudice and worked their way up. Blacks should do the same without any special favors.

Descriptive Statistics

	Cases	Mean	Std. Dev.
Blacks Try harder	228	0.38	0.36
Generations of Slavery	228	0.50	0.37
Irish Overcame	228	0.61	0.36

Pearson Correlation Coefficients

	Blacks Try Harder	Generations of Slavery	Irish Overcame
Blacks Try Harder	1.0000		
Generations of Slavery	0.3513	1.0000	
Irish Overcame	0.5766	0.3853	1.0000

The dependent variables are support for the candidates and opinion about racial policy. Candidate choice was measured with a question asked early in the post-manipulation questionnaire: "Which candidate would you vote for, if you had to choose?" Subjects could respond with either "James Reed, the Democrat," "John Hayes, the Republican," or "I wouldn't vote for either." A vote for the Republican was coded 1, a vote for the Democrat was coded 0, and a vote for neither was coded .5 (those who refused to answer were excluded from the candidate choice analysis). The overall mean hovers around a tie, at .47. Opinion on race policy was measured with five items averaged into a continuous index ranging from 1 (most racially conservative) to 0 (most racially liberal) (see appendix). Typical to most samples of white citizens, this sample is on the racially conservative side, with a mean of .61.

Procedure

Subjects were prescreened for citizenship and race, and their predispositions (racial and nonracial) assessed by phone. Several days later they arrived for the experimental phase of the study. They were seated in front of a computer screen that showed them a randomly assigned pair of scales displaying where they stood relative to others on two issues. They were then asked a series of questions about how the displays made them feel. Subjects were then shown a randomly selected, manipulated news segment. They answered questions about their political opinions and preferences on the candidates, the news they watched, various issues, and (at the end) various groups. The session ended with a full debriefing.[8]

THE EFFECT OF NORMS

Two main questions are at hand: is the greater impact of implicit appeals conditioned by their ability to appear to conform to social norms, and does the disadvantage of explicit appeals lie in their failure to do so? To begin to answer these questions, I contrasted the responses of four groups: people exposed to implicit appeals and told they are mainstream, people exposed to implicit appeals and told they are extreme, people exposed to explicit appeals and told they are mainstream, and people exposed to explicit appeals and told they are extreme. The responses of these groups are also contrasted to the responses of the two control groups (nonracial appeal with mainstream placement, and nonracial appeal with extreme placement). Each of these groups is further divided into three resentment levels. This model is estimated with a range of 172 to 188 cases (contingent on the dependent variable).

The three-way interaction between resentment (three levels), message (three types), and norm (mainstream and extreme) is statistically significant (F = 2.443, p = .05), as I expected.[9] However, the norm manipulation seems not to have worked quite in the way I expected. Those who were told they were extreme actually showed a greater tendency to vote for the candidate who made the conservative appeal (racial or, in the control condition, environmental) (F = 2.881, p = .09). Rather than decreasing whites' proclivity to endorse conservative candidates, extreme normative placement actually increases it. Nevertheless, the results reveal that the impact of resentment on candidate choice is negligible when the candidate does not engage in a racial appeal. Resentment

[8] No follow-up was possible because the controversial nature of the manipulations required on-site debriefing.

[9] The other effects are: For norm placement, F = 2.881, p = .09; for resentment, F = 2.393, p = .09; for the two-way interaction, F = 6.922, p = .001).

makes a good deal of difference to candidate choice, but only when candidates communicate racial messages.

The pattern of opinion on racial policy is largely similar to that of candidate choice. As in the case of candidate choice, there is a significant three-way interaction between message, norm, and resentment (F = 3.286, p = .01). The main difference is that, consistent with previous findings, racial resentment has a large main effect on opinions regarding what the government should do about racial inequality (F = 50.970, p ≤ .001).

Because the norm display was not interpreted in the same way by everyone, these results cannot provide a clear test of the impact of norm placement. But the results provide some support for the notion that norms matter.[10] The question is, *how* do norms matter—through what psychological mechanisms? To answer this question I examine the possibilities I laid out at the chapter's beginning: emotional reactions, self-monitoring, and message classification.[11]

EMOTIONAL REACTIONS TO NORM VIOLATION

The results of the norms experiment suggest that in looking for the impact of emotional reactions to norms, we should look particularly at people with low levels of resentment. When Patricia Devine and her colleagues studied the negative feelings people experience when they contemplate violating norms of

[10] Placing people in the mainstream of the norm enhances the impact of the implicit message, as I expected—but only among those low in resentment. Mainstream placement followed by an implicitly racial message elicits a much higher probability of voting Republican than any other pair of conditions (mean of .63 versus .36, F = 4.61, p = .05). In earlier chapters we saw that the low-resentment group was not influenced by implicitly racial appeals (or by explicitly racial appeals, for that matter). However, in this experiment, their probability of choosing a Republican candidate is indistinguishable from that of highly resentful individuals. They switch sides altogether, from solidly Democratic (in the extreme placement condition) to solidly Republican. Finding out that they are mainstream apparently gives people low on resentment a license to behave in a way that is for them unusually conservative. But they do not behave that way in response to any appeal. It is the combination of being placed in the mainstream and being exposed to an implicitly racial message that leads these voters to choose a candidate they would otherwise reject. By contrast, telling moderately resentful whites that their beliefs are mainstream makes them much more likely to reject the conservative candidate, if his message is racial (explicit or implicit). For the moderately resentful, the display is descriptive, not normative. When placed in the extreme, they simply accept that they are more conservative than most and proceed to support a conservative candidate. When placed in the mainstream they accept this and act more liberal than they otherwise would. Finally, the highly resentful are not swayed by any combination of message and norm.

[11] As in the previous chapters, I reestimated all the models that included racial resentment with a set of identical models that included, instead, ideological self-identification as a measure of a nonracial conservative predisposition. I was unable to estimate a model that included both ideology interactions and resentment interactions, which I was able to do in previous chapters. The results indicate that ideology has no interactive effects on policy and some but less consistent interactive effects on candidate choice than those provided by racial resentment.

conduct toward minority groups, they found that the level of resentment mattered a great deal. People low in prejudice, they concluded, experience stronger emotions when they consider violating the norm than do others (Devine et al. 1991).

To examine the possibility that such emotional reactions to the norm of equality mediate the impact of racial messages, I adapted the procedure used by Devine and her colleagues. I provided the subjects in my norms experiment with a list of feelings and asked them to indicate the degree to which the norm display made them feel each emotion. The emotional reactions were: "uncomfortable with the display," "depressed by the display," "embarrassed by the display," "annoyed with myself," "disappointed with myself," and "disgusted with myself." Subjects rated the applicability of each emotion on a 1-to-7 scale (see appendix). The six emotional responses were averaged in a continuous index scaled 0 for no response to 1 for strongest response.[12]

The two norm manipulations—mainstream and extreme—although they were not received in the same way by everyone, did in fact result in different emotional responses. The extreme placement more than doubled the level of emotional upset experienced by subjects in the mainstream condition (means of .21 versus .09, t = 17.67, p ≤ .0001). And as expected, low-resentment people were more upset than were others (mean = .20 versus .14 and .13 for the other resentment levels, one-way F = 2.68, p = .07). There was also a two-way interaction between norm placement and resentment, with the low-resentment people feeling most upset with the extreme placement (low-resentment means = .07 and .30 in the mainstream and extreme conditions, respectively, versus .10 and .16 for moderately resentful and .09 and .17 for highly resentful people). Low-resentment people are in fact more likely to interpret the extreme placement as a sign that their views on matters of race may violate the norm and to be upset by the possibility that they violate the norm.

The main question, however, is whether emotion conditions the impact of racial priming. Does a negative emotional reaction to one's own violation of the norm moderate the impact of an implicitly racial message on one's policy and candidate choices? To find out, I estimated the impact of emotional upset on candidate choice and race policy in interaction with the three messages. For this analysis, I created from the continuous emotional response variable a dichotomous variable indicating a strong or weak negative emotion.[13] Analysis

---

[12] Coefficient alpha for the six-item emotion scale is .84.

[13] The dichotomous emotion variable cuts the sample nearly in half, at 1/12 of the scale, in order to compensate for the downward skew of the distribution (strong emotion = 49 percent of the sample). I also estimated the model with a second version that cut the scale at .33 (strong emotion = 18 percent of the sample). Ideally I would include an interaction between the norm manipulation (mainstream vs. extreme), emotional response (present vs. absent), resentment level (high, moderate, low), and message style (implicit, explicit, nonracial). However, too many of the cells in this analysis are empty.

of variance shows that emotional response does in fact interact with the message and level of resentment, both on race policy (F = 2.37, p = .06) and on candidate choice (F = 2.25, p = .11).[14]

A series of one-way ANOVAs of the impact of emotional response, separately for each resentment level, can pinpoint the impact more precisely. Figure 8.2 displays the group means of candidate choice and race policy.[15] The size of the emotion effect is impressive, and in the anticipated direction. The implicit appeal clearly worked much more effectively when people were not upset about their normative placement. Those who felt upset were much less likely to prefer the candidate who engaged in the implicit appeal. Those low on resentment were also much less likely to resist egalitarian race policies (for the low-resentment group, p ≤ .01 on race policy, p ≤ .05 on candidate choice; for the high-resentment group, p ≤ .10 on candidate choice); the moderate group showed no significant effects.

While the moderately resentful are not affected by their emotional response (and as we saw earlier, they tend to be unmoved in the first place), both high-resentment and low-resentment people are influenced by their emotional reaction, at least on candidate choice. This supports my expectation that resentful voters inhibit their racial response to an implicit appeal when they fear they may violate racial norms, but it also suggests that low-resentment people can act in a resentful way under specific normative circumstances. These results are not decisive on the question of whether low-resentment people are driven less by social norms than by internal moral standards. Clearly, when they are not upset about violating the norm, they allow themselves to act in ways that are highly unusual for their resentment level. Perhaps, contrary to Devine's view, low-resentment people are as attuned to the violation of social norms as the highly resentful. The next two sections will provide further evidence on this question.

A further question remains: does this pattern repeat itself where the explicit message is concerned? One possibility is that the effect of the explicit message is just as sensitive as the effect of the implicit message to the violation of norms. Perhaps people inhibit their response to the explicit message only when they feel upset about violating norms, just as they did for the implicit message. The other possibility is that the impact of the implicit message is particularly vulnerable to the operation of racial norms. An implicit message should work very well when voters believe their own response to be acceptable. The implicit message should *not* work well when voters worry that their response may not be acceptable. Explicit messages, by contrast, are rejected by nearly everyone. In the case of explicit messages, equanimity in the face of the norm manipula-

---

[14] Setting aside the nonracial message.
[15] Figures 8.2 and 8.4 include the overall mean for each group when the significance level is larger than .10.

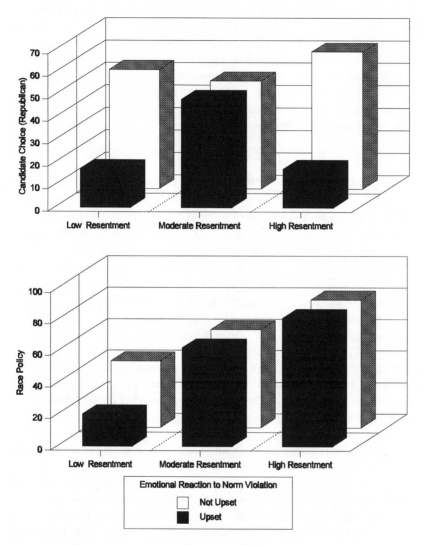

Figure 8.2. The impact of an implicit appeal, by emotion.

tion—either because it strikes a person as not believable, or because it is not perceived as a violation of the norm, or for some other reason—may not mediate the impact of the message because the message is likely to be classified as a racial appeal and rejected on that basis. I will take up the effect of message classification in a later section. For now, the question remains whether emotional upset has the same conditioning effect where the explicit message is concerned.

The answer is that it does not. A series of one-way ANOVAs, paralleling the tests done for the implicit appeal, yields no effect of emotional response among those exposed to the explicit message (at the .10 threshold). The explicit message does not lead to a higher likelihood of conservative racial choice among people unmoved by the norm manipulation. This holds within each resentment level, and for candidate choice as well as race policy preferences. Only the impact of the implicit message is susceptible to whites' worry that they may violate the racial norm.

THE ROLE OF SELF-MONITORING: DOING AS OTHERS DO

So far I have considered people's emotional response to the possibility that they are in violation of the norm. A second possible mechanism by which racial messages succeed or fail is a personality tendency toward self-monitoring. Self-monitors are sensitive to cues about social norms and alter their responses to fall in line with behavior that is socially desirable. Low self-monitors know their own beliefs and act on internal standards, not on situational cues. High self-monitors are sensitive to the standards of others and act according to the demands of the situation.

The logic of self-monitoring suggests that the explicit message fails because it triggers people's general proclivity for self-monitoring. Conversely, perhaps the implicit message succeeds because it does not trigger self-monitoring. If so, then we should find that the effect of self-monitoring on candidate evaluation and on opinion about racial policies is strongest when I place citizens in the normative extreme and expose them to an explicit message. This effect should be strongest among people with high resentment, in line with Terkildsen's findings (1993).

Self-monitoring is measured by an eight-item scale, using an agree-disagree format (see appendix). The items include "When uncertain I look to others," and "my behavior usually expresses my true beliefs" (reverse-coded).[16] The scale reliability is quite low (.30), much lower, for example, than in Terkildsen's sample (1993, 1051). This requires that the results be interpreted with caution.

Does self-monitoring enhance the impact of normative placement? In this study, the results suggest not. On race policy opinion and on candidate choice, self-monitoring has no impact, either by itself or in interaction with resent-

---

[16] I included the self-monitoring scale in the post-treatment questionnaire, to avoid suggesting to respondents that they self-monitor before the video. Don't know responses were coded in the middle to preserve cases; the results are similar when setting these responses aside.

ment, normative placement, or message.[17] Self-monitoring, then, does not mediate the impact of either implicit or explicit messages.

There is one more possibility. Perhaps self-monitoring does not so much
mediate the impact of emotional response as it causes it. Perhaps people who
self-monitor respond emotionally more strongly than others do. If so, then the
impact that emotional response has is partly due to self-monitoring. The results, however, turn out not to be so.[18]

In sum, self-monitoring does not seem to influence people's response to the
norm placement, to the message, or to the combination of the two. The ability
of emotional reactions to norm violation to moderate or enhance the impact
of implicit messages is likely not a product of social desirability but rather of
genuine, internalized values. When the norm of racial equality becomes personal, and not simply descriptive and injunctive, the emotions evoked by violating that norm can inhibit the impact of an implicit racial message. A caution-
ary note is in order, however. It may be that it is not self-monitoring that fails
here but rather the self-monitoring scale. The scale in this study may not measure the underlying construct very well. The reliability of the scale in this
sample is much lower than usual. This may be due to the fact that it was
administered toward the end of the session. The results presented here should
thus be taken as suggestive, not definitive.

THE IMPACT OF MESSAGE CLASSIFICATION

We have seen that a negative emotional response is one mechanism that regu-
lates white citizens' response to racial appeals. Self-control lies in passion, not
simply in reason. But what of reason? Does the perception of the message
inhibit and facilitate that ability of the message to prime racial stereotypes,
fears, and resentments? We saw in the previous chapter that explicit and implicit messages are perceived very differently by white citizens. An appeal is
much more likely to be classified as racial if it is explicit rather than implicit.
An implicit appeal is classified as racial by only a small proportion of whites.

---

[17] I tested all combinations of self-monitoring and the other variables (norm placement, resentment, and message) but none were significant and in the expected direction. As we saw earlier in
the chapter, however, the norm placement manipulation in itself is less meaningful than the emotional reaction to it. Perhaps self-monitoring conditions the effect of the emotional response to
norm placement. This hypothesis turns out to lack support as well. On race policy and candidate
choice, the three-way interaction of emotion, monitoring, and message is nonexistent ($F = .05$,
$p = .95$ on policy; $F = .58$, $p = .56$ on candidate choice).

[18] One-way ANOVA explaining emotional response (continuous) by self-monitoring yields
a null result ($F = 1.34$, $p = .25$). Two-way interaction between self-monitoring and the norm
manipulation, and three-way interaction between self-monitoring, norm, and resentment are not
significant.

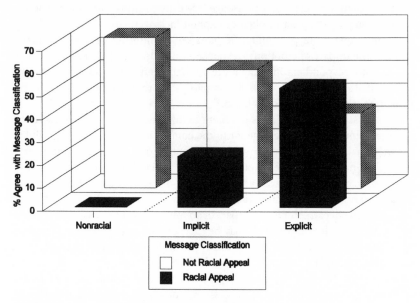

Figure 8.3. Classifying the message as "racial."

It is likely that the extent to which the message is classified as racial matters for its ability to prime negative racial predispositions. Not only emotion but cognition, in particular the nature of perception, probably matters to the impact of a racial message.

To measure whether the message was classified as racial, I asked respondents (toward the end of the session) to indicate whether or not each item in a list of descriptions fit the news story they had watched. Among the descriptions: "It dealt with a candidate who tried to appeal to racial feelings" (see appendix). As Figure 8.3 shows, there is a clear difference between the three messages. Fifty-two percent of those who watched the explicit message categorized it as a racial appeal and 33 percent categorized it as not racial. By contrast, only 22 percent of those watching the implicit message perceived it as a racial appeal and 52 percent denied that it was racial. Finally, no one exposed to the nonracial message believed that it was a racial appeal, and 66 percent said it was not racial. If we take the perception of the message as its measure, implicit messages resemble nonracial messages much more than they do explicit messages. Yet, as we saw in previous chapters, implicit messages prime negative racial predispositions much more effectively than do explicit messages. Perhaps that is because explicit messages are perceived as too racial. If explicit messages fail to prime racial predispositions because they are perceived as too racial, we should find that when white voters classify the message as "racial" it ceases to work.

Does classifying the message as a racial appeal matter to the message's impact? If message classification matters, it should do so by decreasing the impact of the message on candidate choice and on opinion about race policy. When a person does not consider the message to be a racial appeal, she is more likely to allow the message to influence her. Conversely, when a person classifies the message as a racial appeal, she is likely to reject it and control her own response as well.

To test for this possibility, I conducted a series of one-way ANOVAs, separately within each resentment/message combination. The results reveal that classification affects the impact of the explicit message but not the implicit message. In particular, highly resentful individuals change their response considerably, depending on whether they perceive the explicit message to be racial. Figure 8.4 displays the mean response to the explicit message, on candidate choice and race policy, for low-, moderate-, and high-resentment groups, contrasting those who perceived the message as racial against those who did not.[19] It is clear that perceiving the message to be a racial appeal decreases its impact on highly resentful people. People who are moderate or low in resentment are unaffected. On race policy, the highly resentful who classify the message as racial lower their opposition to race policy to nearly the same level as the moderately resentful. The impact is especially dramatic on candidate choice: while 75 percent of the highly resentful who do not perceive the message as racial chose the Republican candidate, only 39 percent of those who perceive the message as racial chose him. Put differently, perceiving the message as a racial appeal makes a difference of 36 points, shifting the choice from Republican to Democratic.

CONCLUSION

This chapter examined three psychological mechanisms that could hinder or facilitate the impact of implicit and explicit racial appeals: a negative emotional reaction to (false) feedback that one's racial views violate the norm of racial equality; a general self-monitoring personality trait; and the conscious classification of the appeal as a racial one. Each of these is a way by which the norm of racial equality might mitigate whites' response to a racial message. Each has the potential to override the priming of negative racial predispositions. I find evidence that the first and third mechanisms matter. The second mechanism—self-monitoring—does not seem to make a difference, though this result may be an artifact of unreliable measurement.

[19] As in previous figures, I provide the overall group mean when the one-way result is not significant.

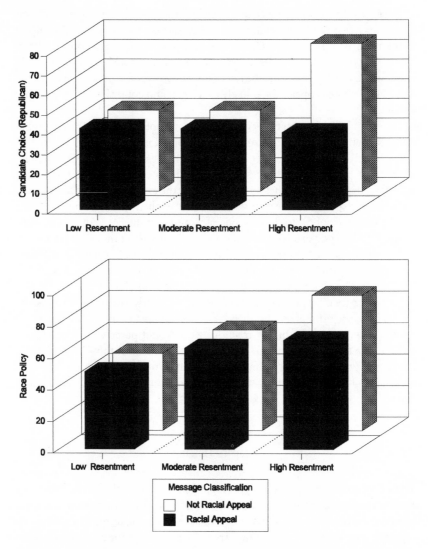

Figure 8.4. The impact of an explicit appeal by classification.

As I expected, people with low or high levels of racial resentment are those whose racial response depends on where they are placed relative to the racial norm. Classifying the message as an appeal to race also matters, particularly to people with a high level of resentment. Those with a moderate level of resentment do not change their racial response as a result of any of the three mechanisms. Whether or not white voters are susceptible to racial priming—whether or not a racial message causes them to give greater weight to negative racial stereotypes, fears, or resentments—depends, importantly, on whether or not they feel upset about the possibility of violating racial norms, and whether they perceive the message to be racial.

Low-resentment individuals in the previous chapters have largely been unmoved by racial appeals. In this study, however, they proved to be susceptible to racial priming under some circumstances. When I suggest to low-resentment individuals that their views are in the mainstream and quite far from the Klan, they become much more likely to choose conservative racial policies and candidates. If placed on the extreme, however, they are completely unresponsive to a racial appeal, just as they are under normal circumstances (when no one places them relative to others). Emotion, it turns out, is an important mediator of this effect. If white Americans low on resentment are unmoved by the possibility that they violate the racial norm, they allow themselves to respond to a racial appeal, moving to the right in their political choices. We can infer that responding to a racial appeal is an unusual response for them from the robust fact that low-resentment individuals in the previous chapters were uninfluenced by racial appeals. The findings here testify to the influence that even low levels of racial resentment can have under particular circumstances. And those circumstances have to do with people's sense of their normative standing.

Still, it is high-resentment individuals whose response to a racial message is most consistently dependent on psychological control mechanisms. They are influenced not only by their emotional response to being placed on the normative extreme, but also by whether the message strikes them as racial. Resentful people who are exposed to a racial message respond far less than they usually do if they are first provoked to feel upset about violating racial norms. They also inhibit their response to the message if they classify the message as a racial appeal.

These findings suggest that the people who find it most problematic to resonate to a racial appeal are the people with high levels of resentment. They differ from others primarily in the vulnerability of their racial response to feelings of norm violation and to the awareness that the message is racial. Put differently, racial consciousness matters most to the response of highly resentful whites. A racial message is capable of evoking their resentment even when the message is explicit, as long as they deny that it is racial. In refusing to recognize the racial nature of the message, they allow themselves to respond to it. By allowing the racial content of the message into full consciousness, they inhibit their racial response. What influences the racial response of resentful people, in other words, is whether or not they consciously recognize the message as racial. A message is at its most powerful when it contains racial content but is not consciously recognized as racial. A message backfires among the very constituency it targets when it contains racial content that triggers the realization that it is in fact a racial appeal. Consciousness of the racial nature of the appeal is an important mediator of the appeal's success or failure.

We can now shed more light on the previous chapters' analyses of the 1988 presidential campaign. In Chapter 5 we saw that Jesse Jackson's protest sparked a debate about whether the Horton message was used by the Bush campaign for racial effect. The accusation that Horton was being used to appeal to whites' racial stereotypes and fears shifted the nature of the discourse from an implicitly racial discussion, ostensibly about crime but really about race, to an explicitly racial discussion fully focused on race. In Chapter 6 we saw that this sudden and dramatic shift toward explicit discourse dampened the impact of white voters' racial predispositions. I can now say with greater confidence that this shift in discourse and the accompanying decrease in the impact of resentment likely was mediated by a consciousness of the racial nature of the appeal. As long as the appeal was implicit, resentful voters did not classify the Horton appeal as racial. Consequently the appeal was successful in priming racial resentment in an automatic fashion, outside of awareness. When Jackson and then Lloyd Bentsen challenged it and called it a racial appeal, even though the challenge was conveyed by the media without its endorsement, many resentful people began to doubt their classification of the message as nonracial. This in turn meant that no longer was racial priming taking place as an automatic, nonconscious process. Resentful individuals now shunted the process of giving weight to their racial predispositions from the nonconscious, automatic track to the conscious, controlled track.

A final word about how social norms regulate racial messages. Often what scholars have in mind when they speak of the impact of norms is that people whose private opinion conflicts with the majority's opinion will censor their expression when in public. This is not, however, what seems to have happened in the study I reported here. Norms did affect the racial response, but they did not do so via self-monitoring. The evidence here favors the genuine suppression of racial stereotypes, fears, and resentments, and goes against the possibility that people formulate an anti-black or racially conservative opinion but decide not to express it. People who feel upset about violating the norm of racial equality guard against giving their racially resentful views more weight, even in their private opinions.

This result makes sense particularly when we consider the study's response context. Scholars of the interview situation often find that responses can be highly susceptible to the need to report more socially desirable opinions (Finkel et al. 1991). Whites tend to moderate their endorsement of racial resentment in response to such situational cues as a black interviewer (Kinder and Sanders 1996). The greater the confidentiality and privacy of the response, the less it is socially desirable, on matters of race and other socially sensitive topics (Dovidio and Fazio 1992; Kuklinski et al. 1997; but see Krysan 1998 for a more complex set of results).

It may matter, then, that the response in the present study was provided under unusually private circumstances. Most often, survey respondents and experimental subjects engage in a face-to-face or telephone conversation with an interviewer, or, in a more private situation, they fill out a self-administered questionnaire that they know will be handled by a person. In this study, however, people reported their opinions and beliefs directly and anonymously to a computer screen. That is likely to make a great deal of difference to the social desirability effect. People asked about such sensitive behavior as drug use are more inclined to confess all when asked to provide opinions to a computer than to an interviewer or a paper questionnaire (Romer et al. 1997; Turner et al. 1998). Self-administered interviewing by computer elicits a greater willingness to disclose embarrassing behavior, particularly when self-presentation concerns are salient (Tourangeau and Smith 1996). Allowing people to express their racial opinion to a computer screen under conditions of full confidentiality is likely to have reduced social conformity pressures. In turn, that means that people's changing response had more to do with whether they gave greater or lesser weight to their racial predispositions, and less to do with whether they felt more or less safe in expressing an undesirable response.

The effect of self-monitoring, then, may be contingent on whether the situation assures privacy. Self-monitoring should have a greater impact in a situation that highlights the need to guard against other people's opinion of oneself. The influence of the other two mechanisms—emotional reaction to norm violation, and classification of the message as racial—suggests that even when people feel free to express their true opinions, they may still want to guard against a racial response. Why would a person want to uphold a norm when no threat of sanction exists? Perhaps because she has internalized the norm. It is not so much the desire to appear to others as a norm-conformist that drives the resentful to censor their response. Rather, it is the desire to maintain a self-concept as a person who fits within the norm. The norm effect is limited to people who felt upset about the possibility that they violate the norm; the possibility that one may violate a norm, if it shakes people up emotionally, can make the difference, even if one knows one will not get caught at it.

Issue discourse that seems on the surface to be about one issue may actually serve as the means of discourse about another, more charged issue. But while candidates may use this fact to their political advantage in a calculated way, among white citizens much of this subterranean discourse results from a less strategic psychological process. White citizens mostly do not mean to obfuscate, to replace one issue with another, to hide their true racist response under a benign cover. The obfuscation takes place at an aggregate level; but at the individual level, what drives the outcome is whether a message is processed within or outside of awareness. The consequence of that awareness—a weaker response to racial appeals—seems to be influenced by the goal to avoid being a racial extremist. It is not simply a matter of wanting not to sound like a racist.

APPENDIX

Display Instructions

We are going to show you how the opinions you expressed to us by phone compare to the opinions of other people who answered the same questions. We averaged your opinions together and represented them by the marker labeled "You." We also averaged the opinions of other people, and grouped them into Democrats, Republicans, and the Ku Klux Klan. We positioned your marker so it shows how close your opinions are to the opinions of others. The closer your opinions are to the opinions of a group, the closer your marker is to that group's marker. The farther away your opinions, the farther away is your marker. The displays are generated by a computer program that takes into account how many people in a group held the same opinion as you, and how many disagreed with you. It also takes into account how strong the disagreements were.

Emotional Responses to the Norm Placement Display

Each question that will appear below is a feeling. Please indicate whether this display of your opinions on racial and ethnic relations creates that feeling in you, where a response of "1" means that the feeling does not apply to you at all, and a response of "7" means that it applies very much to you.

Uncomfortable
Depressed
Embarrassed
Annoyed with myself
Disappointed with myself
Disgusted with myself

Self-Monitoring Scale (True or False; Don't know responses coded in the middle)

We're interested in learning a little about you as a person in social situations. Please indicate if each statement is true or false as it applies to you:

I can only argue for ideas which I already believe (reverse coded)
When I am uncertain how to act in social situations I look to the behavior of others
I laugh more when I watch a comedy with others than when alone
I would not change or modify my opinions in order to please someone else or win a favor (reverse coded)

I am not always the person I appear to be

My behavior is usually an expression of my true attitudes and beliefs (reverse coded)

I am not particularly good at making other people like me (reverse coded)

I can look anyone in the eye and tell a lie

Message Classification

Which of the following is a correct description of the news report?

0. Not Correct
1. Correct
8. Don't Know

It dealt with industry jobs

It dealt with the environment

It showed a candidate with glasses

It dealt with a candidate who tried to appeal to racial feelings

It showed scenes from a garbage dump

It showed scenes of black welfare recipients

It dealt with racial issues

It dealt with a candidate who said taxes should rise

It showed the families of the candidates

Racial Policy Items

1. Some people feel that the government in Washington should make every effort to improve the social and economic position of blacks. Others feel that the government should not make any special effort to help blacks because they should help themselves.

1------2------3------4------5------6------7

Help Blacks   Help Selves

2. Some people say that because of past discrimination blacks should be given preference in hiring and promotion. Others say that such preference in hiring is wrong, because it discriminates against whites.

1------2------3------4------5------6------7

Strongly Favor   Strongly Oppose
Preferences   Preferences

3. Some people say that because of past discrimination it is sometimes necessary for colleges and universities to reserve openings for black students. Others oppose quotas because they say quotas give blacks advantages they haven't earned.

1------2------3------4------5------6------7

| Strongly Favor | Strongly Oppose |
| Quotas for Blacks | Quotas for Blacks |

4. What do you think the chances are these days that a white person won't get a job or a promotion while an equally or less qualified black person gets one instead?

Very Likely
Somewhat Likely
Not Very Likely

5. If you had a say in making up the federal budget this year, for which of the following programs would you like to see spending increased and for which would you like to see spending decreased or kept the same?

Increased
Same level
Decreased
Don't Know

Video Scripts

(Open with a segment on caffeine use, show one of the following treated segments, and end with a segment on rare cattle breeds:)

VIDEO 1: COUNTER-STEREOTYPICAL

(BUST SHOT—ANCHOR). If you thought it was too early to campaign for '97, think again! It seems the preseason for the New Jersey governor's race has already started. The election is still months away, but already some candidates are mapping out their campaign strategies. Governor Whitman is reportedly interested in a place on the Republican presidential ticket next year. That would leave the field wide open for two new candidates.
(DISSOLVE TO INSERTS AS BELOW:)

(VOICE-OVER—REED CAMPAIGN)
(SCENES OF CANDIDATE REED) One likely candidate is Democrat James Reed, who served fifteen years as a high-ranking official in the New Jersey Department of Social Services. He now owns a computer software business. Reed has already put together a small campaign staff and is out on the campaign trail. His agenda includes: limiting special interest influence in state government, controlling health care costs, reducing tuition at state universities, and curbing high taxes. His campaign aides say he will focus on the issues he talked about as a state official, but will also put his business experience to use.

(VOICE-OVER—HAYES CAMPAIGN)
(SCENES OF CANDIDATE HAYES) Republican John Hayes is another man who has his eyes on the governor's seat. Hayes is a native of New Brunswick, where he runs a successful real estate business. After several years in city government, he lost a close race for the state senate two years ago. During that campaign, he stressed raising educational standards, reducing government spending, and ending government gridlock. Sources close to Hayes say he'll soon announce his intention to run and they expect his campaign to be very similar to the one he ran in 1993.

(VOICE-OVER—AUTO FACTORY SCENES) Hayes and Reed agree that the first priority in New Jersey should be jobs. They're both concerned about the employment situation and the status of the state's economy. Hayes thinks tax breaks for businesses that relocate to New Jersey are a good idea, but may not create enough jobs in New Jersey. Reed thinks that the North American Free Trade Agreement approved by Congress last year may hurt New Jersey's ability to keep and attract new industry jobs. He thinks the state should move quickly to protect laid-off workers.

(VOICE-OVER—WELFARE SCENES)
(FEATURING WHITE RECIPIENTS) The candidates are taking very different positions concerning New Jersey's welfare budget. Hayes says people take advantage of welfare at the expense of hard-working taxpayers. He claims welfare has become a way of life for many, and criticized New Jersey's above-average rates of welfare cheating. He says able-bodied welfare recipients should have to work in return for benefits.

(DISSOLVE TO:)
(BUST SHOT—ANCHOR ON SET) Reed, when asked about his position, said there are more important issues. He believes New Jersey's welfare problems are not as bad as those in other states. And he says that once taxpayers have secure jobs, paying for welfare won't be as much of a concern.
It's early in the gubernatorial campaign, and observers caution that Christine Todd Whitman, until she says otherwise, is still a candidate for reelection. But it's never too early to start campaigning, as John Hayes and James Reed know. And as the campaign gets under way, one issue that seems sure to come up is welfare.

VIDEO 2: IMPLICITLY RACIAL

(SAME VOICE-OVER)
(VOICE-OVER—WELFARE SCENES)
(FEATURING BLACK RECIPIENTS) The candidates are taking very different positions concerning New Jersey's welfare budget. Hayes says people take advantage of

welfare at the expense of hard-working taxpayers. He claims welfare has become a way of life for many, and criticized New Jersey's above-average rates of welfare cheating. He says able-bodied welfare recipients should have to work in return for benefits.

VIDEO 3: EXPLICITLY RACIAL

(RETAPE VOICE-OVER)
(VOICE-OVER—WELFARE SCENES)
(FEATURING BLACK RECIPIENTS) The candidates are taking very different positions concerning New Jersey's welfare budget. Hayes says that people, especially African Americans, take advantage of welfare at the expense of hard-working taxpayers. He claims welfare has become a way of life for many, especially for African Americans, and criticized New Jersey's above-average rates of welfare cheating. He says able-bodied welfare recipients should have to work in return for benefits.

VIDEO 4: NONRACIAL

(VOICE-OVER—ENVIRONMENT)
(GARBAGE CLEAN-UP SCENES) The candidates are taking very different positions concerning environmental cleanup. Hayes says that environmental clean-up is too costly and that New Jersey residents don't think environmental preservation is all that important to the state's economy. He says that anti-pollution regulations create too much red tape, causing businesses to lose profits. Hayes also says regulations hinder the efforts of state government to attract more businesses to New Jersey. He says that the state should not force businesses to clean up their dump sites.

(DISSOLVE TO:)
(BUST SHOT—ANCHOR ON SET) Reed, when asked about his position, said there are more important issues. He believes New Jersey's anti-pollution regulations are not as bad as those in other states. And he says that once taxpayers have secure jobs, anti-pollution measures won't be as much of a concern.

. . . And as the campaign gets under way, one issue that seems sure to come up is environmental pollution.

Part Three

IMPLICATIONS OF IMPLICIT RACIAL APPEALS

CHAPTER 9

Implicit Communication beyond Race: Gender, Sexual Orientation, and Ethnicity

COMMUNICATION IS NOT only implicit on matters of race. The story I have told about race has implications for implicit communication in other domains, and outside the borders of the United States. To understand implicit discourse in electoral campaigns one must examine three variables: norms, parties, and citizens' predispositions. These variables operate outside the case of race, and can thus shape campaign communication about other social cleavages. The value that each variable takes on, however, is not necessarily the same for all social cleavages. Each variable may change across cases. A norm may or may not be egalitarian; the party system may or may not align on a particular cleavage; and citizens' predispositions may or may not contain resentments, fears, and stereotypes about the subordinate group in question. Only when norms are egalitarian, when the parties divide on the cleavage in question, and when many citizens have negative predispositions toward the subordinate group in question should we expect implicit appeals about that group. When norms are not egalitarian, or citizens' predispositions do not include stereotypes, fears, and resentments, or parties decline to appeal to these predispositions, then implicit appeals should be scarce or nonexistent. To understand how the argument about race sheds light on the electoral dynamics of other social cleavages, let us examine the cases of gender, sexual orientation, and, outside the borders of the United States, ethnicity.

RACE VERSUS GENDER

Consider the similarities and contrasts between race and gender.[1] On their face these two cases appear quite similar. Women and African Americans have had to contend with widespread negative predispositions about their group characteristics. For much of American history, women were considered inherently inferior to men, just as African Americans were considered to be inherently

---

[1] I will be using the terms "African Americans," "women," and "gays and lesbians" as mutually exclusive, even though these groups intersect and even though there are crucial differences between, say, African-American women and white women. I do this as shorthand for differentiating between the dimensions of race, gender, and sexual orientation.

inferior to whites (Jackson 1998). Women mobilized to gain significant civil rights for themselves, just as African Americans have done (women mobilized in three historical waves). In the process of successful mobilization, norms changed dramatically for each group: it is no longer acceptable to be a sexist, just as it is unacceptable now to be a racist.

As in the case of race, the norm of gender equality can be seen clearly in public opinion. Among the longest time series on the question of women's equality comes from the NES question on women's role. Responses to this question reveal a slow and steady support for the notion that "women and men should have an equal role" as against the competing idea that "women's place is in the home." The percent choosing an equal role for men and women was 49 percent in 1972 and increased to between 50 percent and 60 percent in the 1970s, to between 60 percent and 70 percent in the 1980s, and to nearly 80 percent in the late 1990s. Already in the 1970s, majorities of both Republicans and Democrats favored the idea that women should have an equal role in society, with men at least as supportive as women.[2] Another indicator of normative change comes from the symbolic question of a woman president. In the 1930s, Gallup polls found that a large majority of the nation's adults would refuse to vote for a woman for president. But that percentage gradually dwindled. Already by the 1950s a majority indicated it would vote for a woman for president, and by the 1980s that majority reached well over 80 percent (Darcy et al. 1994, 176).[3] The norm of gender equality is thus both descriptive and injunctive, just as in the case of race.

Similarly, while whites reject the idea of African Americans' inherent inferiority, yet fear and resent African Americans' advancement, so in the case of gender equality norms coexist uneasily with lingering negative predispositions. There are important differences, however, between whites' negative predispositions toward African Americans and men's negative predispositions toward women. In the case of gender, the negative predispositions do not contain fear, resentment, and other negative emotions so much as role expectations. These predispositions are not about the distribution of political power and relations within the public sphere as much as the distribution of private power and relations within the private sphere. Negative predispositions about gender focus on the spheres of home, family, and sexuality, with spillover effects in the workplace and in political participation.

One aspect of negative predispositions about women is that women's work, whether in the workplace or the home, tends to be devalued, granted less social prestige than men's, and undercompensated (Burns et al. 1997; Koppelman

---

[2] Based on my analysis of the 1948–1998 NES cumulative dataset (vcf0834 = women's role, vcf0303 = party identification, and vcf0104 = sex). All analyses use weight variable vcf0009 and year variable vcf0004.

[3] "If your party nominated a woman for president, would you vote for her if she were qualified for the job?"

1996, 121). Women are still clearly disadvantaged relative to men in economic power, and not just because of a glass ceiling in the workplace. The notion that men are better suited to handle important decisions translates into inequalities in the home as well as the workplace. Another aspect of negative predispositions is the expectation (their own and others') that women take primary responsibility for children and for the home, which creates a set of structural disadvantages for women in the economic and social realms (Koppelman 1996, 122). Unlike men, women who choose not to fulfill that expectation and do not take primary responsibility for the care of their children or their home are perceived as deviant. While it is the primary responsibility of women, the work that women do in the home is valued less than the work that men do as part of their primary responsibility—earning income. Women often accept their own devaluation. Women have higher rates of clinical depression, they tend to undervalue their own work and even their own human worth, and they tend to attribute their failures to internal rather than external causes (Rhode 1989, 182). Finally, negative predispositions about women include the notion that women do not deserve the same degree of control over sexuality that men do. Women continue to have less control over their own sexuality and reproduction than men, which reinforces their unequal power and denies them equal justice (MacKinnon 1987; Rhode 1989).

Both egalitarian norms and lingering inegalitarian predispositions are evident in research on gender inequality in marriage. On the one hand, large majorities of both men and women disagree that "it is more important for a wife to help her husband's career than to have one herself" (Simon and Landis 1991, 273). This finding suggests the presence of a norm of equality between men and women. But consider what happens when respondents are presented with a scenario such as this: "Suppose both husband and wife work at good and interesting jobs and the husband is offered a very good job in another city. Assuming they have no children, which one of these solutions do you think they should seriously consider?" Large majorities of both men and women indicate that the "wife should quit and relocate with the husband." When the sexes in this scenario are reversed, majorities of both men and women indicate that the "wife should turn down the job" (Simon and Landis 1991, 272). Predispositions about gender are negative, not in the way that they are for race, but in a way that emphasizes women's primary responsibility for the home and children and which reinforces women's inequality relative to men.

In a similar vein, Burns et al. found that approximately 90 percent of both husbands and wives in their national survey disagree with the view that husbands should control family decisions, and agree that housework should be shared equally. Again, this finding indicates the presence of a norm of equality. But actual practice reflects lingering negative predispositions about women. When questioned about their own households, 72 percent of husbands reported being responsible for major household financial decisions, while only

26 percent of wives reported being responsible for these decisions. And approximately 75 percent of wives but only 11 percent or less of husbands report that they do "all" or "most" of the housecleaning or child care (Burns et al. 1997, 377, 378, 380; note that both husbands and wives seem to underestimate the wife's contribution, judging by Table 1). Studies of dual-income households confirm that even when married women work full-time outside the home, they still do the lion's share of the housework, and earn less than their husbands (Hochschild 1989). This inequality tends to give husbands greater control over family decisions and somewhat more free time, and husbands who enjoy these privileges are provided with an advantage in political participation over husbands whose home is more egalitarian (Burns et al. 1997).

Thus, women are no longer devalued simply for being women, as they once were, and men accord women full equality in principle (see also Jackson 1998). Yet some negative predispositions about women linger, and in practice, women still lead lives that provide fewer privileges, less personal freedom, narrower life choices, less prestige, less authority, less economic power, less political influence, and less justice relative to men.

Women and African Americans each have mobilized successfully, have achieved significant rights for themselves, and now benefit from a strong norm of equality. Each group faces lingering disadvantages. These similarities end, however, when it comes to the nature of the disadvantage. Cultural predispositions toward women differ from cultural predispositions toward African Americans.

Along with this difference in predispositions has come a difference in the nature of party coalitions. To put it simply, the two major parties have diverged from each other a great deal on race but not much on gender. True, the parties have taken different stands on some issues of gender. Family leave in the workplace, for example, has been advocated by Democrats, not Republicans. But for the most part, differences such as this have not been central to the activities or platforms of either party. From the late 1940s on, the Democratic platform, which might be expected to champion the rights and preferences of women, paid much more attention to racial minorities than it did to issues regarding women and matters of particular interest to women (Gerring 1998, 200, Figure 13).[4] The parties have not differed much on the question of whether women should have expanded opportunities and improved lives; in fact, although in 1980 the Republican platform removed its endorsement of the Equal Rights Amendment, in the 1970s and 1980s the Republican platform devoted more attention to women's rights than the Democratic platform (Costain et al. 1997, 219; Prasad 1999, 23).

---

[4] "Socio-cultural" issues were defined by Gerring as not including racial minorities. On the parties' lack of attention to women during the 1950s and 1960s, see Harvey 1998.

This may be due in part to the dramatic increase in the representation of women and their increasing influence within both parties.[5] Women office-holders of both parties, to a greater extent than men, tend to work on issues that benefit women or on which women and men have different preferences (Thomas 1990, 1994, 1998; Dodson and Carroll 1991; Welch 1984). Women are more liberal than men among both Republican and Democratic members of Congress (Clark 1998; Welch 1984). Similarly, women activists of both parties are more liberal than their male colleagues on women's issues and on foreign policy (Rapoport et al. 1999). During the 1970s and 1980s, women party activists had an impact on the nomination process and platforms of their parties, sometimes through an "anticipatory effect" by which party leaders an-ticipate women's demands (Jennings 1990, 235). In state legislatures where women make up more than a small proportion, women are not only more active on issues of concern to women but they also influence their male col-leagues in favor of their causes (Darcy et al. 1994, 184). Thus, at the same time that the parties began to attend to issues of gender, women became increasingly numerous and influential within both parties (as officeholders and delegates). Each party has increasingly tried to respond to women's distinctive prefer-ences, which may have muted the potential differences between the parties on matters of concern to women. Perhaps the most salient gender issue has been abortion, and the Democrats have indeed taken a much more pro-choice posi-tion than the Republicans; but women voters are deeply divided on the issue and are no more pro-choice than are men (Sears and Huddy 1990).[6] Thus both parties are driven in the same direction—toward greater rights and benefits to women or to the causes women hold dear.

Further evidence that the parties differ in their treatment of race and gender comes from the clear difference that emerges between race and gender when we examine public perceptions of the parties. By comparison with race rela-tions, the status of women, and government's role in advancing it, has re-mained peripheral to voters' perceptions of the parties (Jennings 1990). Con-sider the two NES time series on perceptions of distance between the two parties, one about women's equal role and the other about aid to minorities. These two time series reveal a clear difference between the issues of race and gender. Between 1972 and 1998, on average, 70 percent of voters perceived a

---

[5] In state legislatures (the level at which women have gained the most seats), 60 percent of the women in 1992 were Democrats and 40 percent Republicans (Dolan and Ford 1998, 86).

[6] Not so among members of Congress. During the 1990s women were more pro-choice than men within both parties. In fact, in support of the argument that gender differences mute the overall partisan difference on gender issues, the gender gap was much larger among Republicans than Democrats. The 1995 House vote on an abortion bill illustrates this quite clearly. The percent-ages of those voting for allowing abortions at defense facilities were as follows: Democratic men, 75 percent, Democratic women, 97 percent, Republican men, 15 percent, Republican women, 53 percent (Clark 1998, 125).

difference between the parties on the issue of aid to minorities, while 53 percent perceived a difference on the issue of women's equal role.[7]

On the matter of which party's position is closer to the voter's own, the differences between the issues of gender and race are again revealing. The NES asks each respondent to indicate his or her own position and the position the respondent thinks each party has taken on aid to minorities and on women's role. The proximity of the voter's own position to the position the voter thinks each party takes can then be calculated. Of interest here is whether the percentage of voters who are closer to either party exceeds the percentage of voters who are equally close to both parties. On aid to minorities, in five out of the eleven election years in which the relevant questions were asked, the percentage of voters who are closer to one party or the other exceeds the percentage of voters who are close to both parties equally (that is, the "parties are equally proximate" category is not the plurality category). But on women's role, in only two out of the seven years in which the relevant question was asked is this true. Put differently, the percentage of national elections in which voters perceived a difference between their own position and that of one party is 45 percent on racial matters but only 29 percent on women's role. Across all the available elections, voters are, on average, equally distributed between proximity to the Republican party, the Democratic party, and both parties on the matter of aid to minorities, but a plurality of voters are close to both parties equally on the matter of women's role.[8] The parties differ less on gender than on race.

Thus, candidates do not experience pressure to appeal to voters' sexist predispositions. No party seeks to appeal to sentiments that keep women at a disadvantage to men. In fact, the gender gap in vote choice, which materialized in the 1980s and shows signs of growing, has created incentives for both parties to compete not for men's votes but for women's (Trevor 1999, 62). This incentive is enhanced by the fact that women now make up 52 percent of eligible voters and have, in every national election since 1984, consistently turned out to vote at higher rates than men (during presidential election years the turnout gap hovers at around 2 percentage points) (McGlen and O'Connor 1998, 68–75). The parties' attempt to gain women's votes is complicated by the fact that

[7] The perceived difference between the parties for aid to minorities ranged from 60 percent (in 1978) to 86 percent (in 1980); for women's role it ranged from 40 percent (in 1972) to 69 percent (in 1980). On both issues the percentages are approximately twenty percentage points lower in the 1970s than in subsequent decades. These percentages are based on my analysis of the 1948–1998 cumulative NES dataset. The variables are the position of the Democratic party minus that of the Republican party, on the question of aid to minorities and on women's equal role, respectively: (vcf0537-vcf0518) and (vcf0537-vcf0538). The percentages are the cumulative percent across values 2, 3, 4, 5, 6, and 7 (anything other than a minimal difference).

[8] Based on my analysis of the 1948–1998 NES cumulative dataset. The variables on aid to minorities are vcf0830, vcf0517, and vcf0518, and on women's role they are vcf0834, vcf0537, vcf0538.

most women do not have a political identity as women and do not make political cal decisions based on their perception of what women need or deserve (Sears and Huddy 1990).[9] In general, women's political choices have much less to do with a desire to improve the position of women and much more to do with a preference for fighting against what they perceive as social vices (pornography, drugs, gun violence), for dovish foreign relations, and for a safety net for vulnerable elements of the population (Conover and Sapiro 1993; Cook and Wilcox 1991; Gilens 1988; Shapiro and Mahajan 1986; T. Smith 1984).

Still, women have developed into a group with a distinct set of political preferences and have increased their presence in the voting population to such an extent that they have become, collectively if not individually, a more powerful voting bloc than men. Bartels estimates that since 1980 women have had 56 percent of the total voting power in presidential elections (1998, 62). Thus, neither major party has an incentive to appeal to men who want to keep women in a subordinate position, and both parties have incentives to appeal to women. Anna Harvey has argued that historically, both parties attempted to recruit women voters when women became a powerful voting bloc, and, as long as women's interest groups had credible electoral leverage, both parties tried to show that they were responsive to women through public policy (Harvey 1998). In 1984, for example, when Ronald Reagan's advisers learned of the gender gap in pre-election polls, they drastically increased the proportion of female delegates to the party's national convention in order not to appear to lag behind the Democrats (Jennings 1990, 225). This proved to be a weak (and unnecessary) attempt to pacify women. But the point remains that the parties have been increasingly preoccupied with how to win women's votes, not with how to appeal to men's predispositions about women.

In sum, while we can expect electoral campaigns that appear nonracial on the surface but are racial underneath, by the same logic, we can expect the absence of implicit (or explicit) messages in the case of gender. The little evidence that exists on the matter tends to support this hypothesis. A series of experiments and a content analysis of media coverage conducted by Kim Kahn suggest that gender stereotypes can actually advantage women candidates, especially in gubernatorial elections: women candidates are "viewed as more compassionate and more honest than identical male candidates" (Kahn 1992; see also Kahn 1994a, 1994b). Iyengar et al. found, in a similar vein, that women candidates reap electoral benefits from gender stereotypes in the sense that they are advantaged when they place gender and "women's issues" on the agenda (Iyengar et al. 1997). To be sure, women candidates and officeholders are not entirely advantaged by gender. These and other studies conclude that gender stereotypes make it difficult for women candidates to appear credible

---

[9] Although women voters do support Democratic women more than Democratic men, this difference is rather small (McGlen and O'Connor 1998, 75).

on "men's" issues such as crime or foreign policy, and that the media disadvantages women candidates or leaders by omitting their contributions in matters other than "women's issues" (Carroll and Schreiber 1997). Perhaps the greatest damage to women's equality has come from the way in which the media has covered the feminist movement (Huddy 1997). Still, the nature of gender predispositions is such that women candidates tend to gain advantages when they frame their positions in gendered terms, and they reap electoral benefits when the media does the same. And women citizens, unlike African-American citizens, are not the target of implicit campaign messages that portray them as less able or deserving.

Race and gender thus share much in common in American electoral politics, but the differences between them are sufficiently significant that their electoral dynamics play out quite differently. Political communication in electoral campaigns is implicit in the case of race but not in the case of gender. The implicitness of communication can serve as a lens through which to view the politics of many different types of social cleavage.

RACE VERSUS SEXUAL ORIENTATION

Sexual orientation is close to the case of race where party coalitions are concerned, but until recently it has been far from the case of race on the question of norms. Gays and lesbians, more than African Americans or women, suffer from social stigma (Gross 1991; Koppelman 1996, 149). The norm concerning sexual orientation has, in the last several decades, been quite inegalitarian. Still, popular sentiment has changed, slowly, in a way reminiscent of the way that white sentiment about African Americans changed during the 1940s and 1950s. "It is clear that mass opinion change has occurred within the past two decades, often to a striking degree," concludes Alan Yang in his comprehensive overview of poll trends from the 1970s to the mid-1990s (Yang 1997). In the public discourse about gays and lesbians, it is possible in the last decade or two to glean a slow but steady erosion of the norm of inequality. To be sure, the transformation is still in its infancy, and it has not affected all aspects of social relations to the same degree. But the political mobilization of gays and lesbians and the more positive portrayal of gays and lesbians in the entertainment media have succeeded in eroding the anti-gay norm, particularly during the 1990s (Cohen 1999; Cook 1999; Sniderman et al. 1991, chapter 3).

As in the case of norms about race and gender, the most direct indicator of the change in norms comes from surveys that ask about general principles of equality for the group in question. Perhaps the most telling survey findings are the responses to broad questions about equality for gays and lesbians. Consider the following poll question, asked in the fall of 1998: "Do you think that as a matter of principle, the federal government should treat homosexuals and heterosexuals equally, or don't you think so?"[10] Eighty-two percent of the national sample responded "yes," and only 14 percent said "no," with 4 percent not sure. The responses hardly varied with the respondent's party affiliation. This opinion pattern on such a principled matter is perhaps the most basic criterion for a public norm of equality. Other questions that tap symbolic political equality reveal a similar pattern of opinion. When asked, "In general, do you think that openly gay men or women should or should not be appointed as U.S. ambassadors to other countries," 57 percent of a national sample of adults surveyed by the Gallup organization in 1999 said yes, and only 34 percent said no. During the 1990s, the number of openly gay or lesbian office-holders tripled (from 49 in 1991 to 156 in 1998) (Cook 1999, 679). If the trend of the last ten or fifteen years continues, we can expect a growing norm of equality on sexual preference.

At the same time, however, sentiment about gays and lesbians and about some efforts to safeguard their rights is likely to remain negative. While symbolic equality is accepted by a clear majority of Americans, the heterosexual foundation of the family unit is still viewed as a moral precept that should not change. Affect toward gays and lesbians is still more negative than for almost any other social group (Yang 1997, 479). The same poll that found a majority accepting openly gay American ambassadors revealed that 64 percent disapprove of "clergy members, including priests, ministers, pastors or rabbis, performing marriage ceremonies and blessing marriage unions between two people of the same sex."

The combination of a growing egalitarian norm and lingering negative sentiment is likely to generate implicit appeals on sexual preference, particularly if the parties intensify their competition with each other on the issue. As Haider-Markel and Meier (1996) argue, when sexual orientation is framed as an issue of sexual morality, and is made salient by political actors, it often generates party competition. Under such circumstances, politicians find it relatively easy to attract the many voters who have a strong opinion on the issue.

There are clear signs that the parties are indeed dividing on the issue of implementing rights for gays and lesbians. In the 1990s there have been only two openly gay Republicans in Congress (Steve Gunderson and Jim Kolbe) but several Democrats. The first openly gay person to win a first term in Congress was a Democrat (Tammy Baldwin, in 1998). Efforts on behalf of gay rights (most prominently, Bill Clinton's initiative on gays in the military) have tended to come primarily from Democratic officials, resistance primarily from Republicans. Consequently, electoral appeals to anti-gay sentiment surfaced during the 1992 Republican National Convention with its discourse of "family values." The "family values" appeal quite likely was received by voters in part as an appeal against gay rights; Haider-Markel and Meier found that the county-level

---

[10] CNN/Time poll conducted by Yankelovich Partners.

percentage of the 1992 vote for George Bush was the most powerful predictor of that year's ballot initiatives on gay rights in Colorado and Oregon (Haider-Markel and Meier 1996). Thus, while the parties, and even candidates on the ideological extreme, have been extremely reluctant to make even very implicit appeals against women's equality, this is not the case for the issue of sexual orientation. Even the most extreme candidates avoid criticism of women's equal role in society, even of the more implicit type. But mainstream politicians have often criticized measures that advance equality for gays and lesbians and have condemned their sexuality as a violation of the moral order.

While egalitarian norms about sexual orientation are still weak, there are signs that attempts to mobilize anti-gay sentiment are already somewhat coded. As the norm has begun to change, the nature of anti-gay communication is slowly changing. In the 1998 congressional elections, anti-gay campaign messages failed to garner Senate seats for Republicans (in South Carolina, Wisconsin, Nevada, and Washington). Wisconsin congressman Mark Neumann, who explicitly said he would not hire anyone gay, lost to Democratic senator Russell Feingold (although clearly there were also other reasons for his defeat). Some mainstream politicians already show signs of reticence about being identified as anti-gay. When House Majority Leader Dick Armey publicly referred to openly gay Democratic congressman Barney Frank as "Barney Fag," he was taken to task immediately and strongly, not only by Democrats and journalists but also by a former Republican member of Congress who is gay. When Armey spoke to reporters to apologize for his remark, he was so shaken that, according to journalists, his jaw trembled.[11]

The norm about sexual preference is slowly becoming more egalitarian. At the same time, many Americans remain uneasy about gays and lesbians and continue to condemn them. The parties are beginning to align on the issue, with Democrats for greater equality and Republicans against. The combination of these three key factors—norms, party alignments, and citizens' predispositions—is fertile ground for the rise of implicit communication. The following example from the 2000 presidential primaries illustrates this dynamic. Both Democratic candidates, Bill Bradley and Al Gore, appealed for the votes of gays and lesbians, with Gore first going the extra step of declaring that he would make support for gays in the military a litmus test for appointments, and then retracting the statement. Republicans not only made no appeals to gays and lesbians, but were quick to appeal to voters' negative predispositions about gays and lesbians by attacking the Democrats for their pro-gay position. On January 20, days after Gore's statement, the Republican National Committee

[11] Nancy Mathis, " 'Barney Fag' remark roundly condemned; Majority Leader Armey blames media for broadcasting his 'stumbled word,' " *Houston Chronicle*, January 28 1995. See also the op-ed piece by Bob Bauman, a former Republican congressman from Maryland, "The Man Who Talked Too Much," *New York Times*, February 4, 1995.

announced that it would air a television commercial criticizing Gore's statement. Thus, clearly there is a party split on the issue of sexual orientation. But given normative constraints, the Republicans cannot explicitly accuse the Democrats of siding with gays. The result is a somewhat more implicit appeal: Jim Nicholson, chairman of the Republican National Committee, summarized the Republican appeal by saying that Gore was "pandering to the far left while at the same time trying to hide from the general public the fact that he would compromise U.S. security to socially engineer the military."[12] Republicans are not using the words "homosexual," "sexual orientation," "gay," or "lesbian." Instead, they are using terms such as "far left" and "social engineering." As in the case of race, the concern over "social engineering of the military" is probably genuine, not merely a mask for the issue of sexual orientation. Nevertheless, the safer issue of the military can act as a rhetorical vehicle for the more normatively risky issue of sexual orientation.

Once again, elections provide the incentive, and campaigns the opportunity, for parties to forge implicit discourse in the strategic service of gaining elective office. By the same token, silence in the face of such appeals is likely to be a losing strategy for the party standing for greater equality. As the norm of equality regarding sexual orientation grows, that party will win by contesting the meaning of implicit appeals, that is, by showing that implicit anti-gay appeals are in fact anti-gay, and thus that they violate the norm of equality.

The three key factors above can be examined in the cases of other subordinate groups in American politics. The result, I hope, is a clearer understanding of the distinct position in American electoral politics occupied by each group. But while my argument specifies the uniqueness of each group's position, its logic is highly generalizable. Not only can the argument shed light on the dynamics of group politics within the United States, it can be applied to other countries as well.

ETHNICITY AND IMPLICIT COMMUNICATION IN EUROPE

We can expect implicit communication in any country with electoral procedures that has witnessed an egalitarian change in norms about a subordinate group but in which conflict over the group's status persists. Ethnicity provides a range of examples, each of which illustrates the interplay between a polity's egalitarian norms, the widespread presence of negative predispositions toward a subordinate group, and the rhetorical strategy of the parties. That interplay determines whether or not implicit political communication will arise. Vivid

---

[12] Katharine Q. Seelye, "Gore Meets with Gay Leaders Before Homestretch in Iowa," *New York Times*, January 21, 2000.

examples of this interplay can be found in postwar Europe, where one of the most dramatic normative transformations in this century has occurred.

Many European nations have had a centuries-long history of anti-Semitism.[13] Although anti-Jewish sentiment has taken different forms depending on the time and the place, the common thread seems to be the rejection of a group perceived to be inherently alien. Often, Jews were segregated or subjected to discrimination because of their religion. But even when they converted to Christianity and fully assimilated into the dominant culture, they were still set apart and persecuted. Christians developed a variety of justifications for anti-Semitism. They said they disliked Jews because of Jews' economic status (sometimes because of poverty, other times because of wealth), or their occupations (which sometimes brought them into competition with Christians, other times were perceived as exploiting Christians, and other times were irrelevant to Christians and thus deemed useless), or their reluctance to assimilate into the dominant culture (or their success in doing so, which made discrimination difficult), or, during the Spanish Inquisition and again in the Third Reich, because they were perceived to pose a threat to the dominant group's racial purity. While the nature of anti-Semitism has not been constant across time and place, its common thread—rejection of an ethnic group as inherently alien—has characterized much of Europe from the eighth or ninth century onward. Anti-Semitism was sufficiently widespread that it constituted a norm, one that grew in strength during the late nineteenth and early twentieth centuries (in part as a response to the emancipation of Jews and to changes in the status of some Jews, in part in response to large-scale Jewish immigration from the Russian Pale of Settlement, in part because of the rise of nationalism). "I have never met one German who liked Jews," remarked Nietzsche, who himself liked Jews very much even though—or perhaps because—he believed them to be a distinct, smarter race (in Poliakov 1985, 4).

On the eve of World War II, anti-Semitism in Germany, Austria, Poland, and other countries had become a very strong norm.[14] It is important to note that while anti-Jewish sentiment had taken on overt racial overtones and had become a political ideology, it was fundamentally part of a centuries-old fear

[13] My summary of anti-Semitism is based on the following: Bankier 1992; Bering 1998; Christie 1998, 137–143; Curtis 1986; Encyclopedia Judaica, s.v. "anti-Semitism"; Glock and Stark 1966; Mahler 1942; Poliakov 1985; Pulzer 1988; Steiman 1998; Weinryb 1942.

[14] This does not mean that during this period all Germans were stridently hostile to all Jews at all times (an argument made forcefully by Goldhagen 1996). As Bauer has pointed out recently, the fact that German society was characterized by latent cultural anti-Semitism does not negate the fact that Jews were accepted by many Germans in many social roles, that they had prospered economically, and that their active persecution was endorsed by many but not all major segments of society. Before 1940, the norm of anti-Semitism was more about the desire for less "Jewish influence" than about the wholesale abrogation of Jewish civil rights and liberties; by 1940, most historians agree, the norm had turned much more radical and more easily channeled toward genocide.

and resentment of ethnicity. Throughout the Nazi era, many Germans did not approve of the anti-Semitic violence used by the Nazis, but "the overwhelming majority approved social segregation and economic destruction of the Jews" (Bankier 1992, 83). After the defeat of the Nazi regime, public opinion surveys carried out by the Allies found that half the German public believed that national socialism was "a good idea badly carried out" and most of the remainder thought that "Nazism represented more good than evil"; the surveys also found that anti-Semitic feelings were widespread (Dalton 1993, 112). Thus, leading up to, during, and immediately after World War II, anti-Semitism was a reigning norm in east and central Europe, and was at bottom a norm of ethnic inequality.

Much as the North forced the South to change its ways on race after the Civil War, the Allied occupation forced the norm of ethnic inequality into retreat. The media and educational institutions took up the task of building new norms that discouraged ethnic intolerance as part of a program of "denazification" (Tent 1983). Inegalitarian political language came to be perceived as a symbol of continued German belligerence, and was thus branded illegitimate, part of the imposition of anti-Nazism "by institutional guarantee" (Grunenberg 1997, 87; Stern 1992). This took place in different ways in East and West Germany, and during the first two decades the norm was confined to a small segment of the population and was rather weak. But by the 1970s, the repudiation of Nazism became a strong injunctive and descriptive norm. In the 1990s, large majorities of Germans indicated that they would accept a Jewish president, and only about a quarter indicated that they would disapprove of Jews as neighbors (Kurthen 1997).

More general questions about the place of Jews in Germany and efforts against anti-Semitism reveal still more egalitarianism, with 81 percent rejecting statements such as "It is better not to have too much to do with Jews," and "It would be better for us Germans if all the Jews would go to Israel" (Bergmann and Erb 1997). Bergmann and Erb found in several national surveys that when Germans were presented with a list of twenty-three group labels and asked whether they liked or disliked each one, "Jew" was disliked by 20 percent, while 60 percent indicated they disliked "anti-Semite" (with "communism," "Third Reich" and "fanatic" the only labels to get more "dislike" response). On the principle of equality, perhaps the most direct indicator of the norm, 70 percent agree that "Jews and non-Jews should be treated the same, legally and generally" (Bergmann and Erb 1997). The norm has become a personal one for most Germans, 75 percent of whom agree that "I don't make any distinction between Jews and other people" (Bergmann and Erb 1997). German popular culture now has strong anti-Nazi elements. For example, popular television crime shows regularly feature Neo-Nazis as extreme deviants (Cornell 1997). Thus, ethnic tolerance became established as a new norm, not only in Germany but in many other countries in post-war Europe, although the strength of this norm varies from one country to another.[15]

As in the case of race in the United States, however, this strong norm of equality has not eliminated negative predispositions about subordinate ethnic groups, both Jews and others. Many Europeans have continued to regard Jews with suspicion or unease (Stern 1992). Survey findings from East and West Germany during the 1990s reveal that only a minority of West Germans disagree that "now, as in the past, Jews exert too much influence on world events"; a small minority of East and West Germans disagree that "Jews are exploiting the National Socialist Holocaust for their own purposes" (Bergmann 1997, Tables 2.3 and 2.4); and less than a third reject the notion that "many Jews try to profit from the history of the Third Reich at Germans' expense" (Bergmann and Erb 1997). Bergmann and Erb's 1987 survey of Germans found that 42 percent agreed that Jews were "crafty and shrewd" and 70 percent agreed that Jews "stick together," both elements of an old anti-Semitic stereotype (1997). East German samples tend to agree that there is a continuing need to "talk" about the Holocaust, but over two-thirds of West Germans think that Germans "should not talk so much" about it (Bergmann 1997, Table 2.5). In 1995, 36 percent of Germans answered in the affirmative when asked, "Was the expulsion of the Germans from the East just as great a crime against humanity as the Holocaust against the Jews?" (Olick and Levy 1997, 928). While Jews could no longer be discussed in a negative way in public, some politicians in Central and Eastern Europe have at times found more indirect ways to appeal to anti-Jewish sentiment.

Anti-Jewish sentiment has, to be sure, changed in important ways since 1945. Contemporary unease about Jews does not have an overt racialist character. Instead, it finds expression in resentment about the payment of material reparations and the demand that the nation continue to acknowledge responsibility for the Holocaust (a phenomenon that has appeared, at different times, in Germany, Austria, and now Switzerland [Kastner and Jedermann 1997; Mitten 1992]). So widespread has Germans' avoidance of responsibility for the Holocaust been that Olick and Levy went as far as to cast Germans as "an expertly equivocating and evasive population" on the subject of the Holocaust (1997, 928). This phenomenon has also been called "secondary anti-Semitism" and "secondary resentment," and it has been noted not only in Germany but in Austria, Switzerland, and other countries implicated in the Nazi regime (Kurthen 1997, 44; Umland 1999). Olick and Levy explained this resentment as flowing from many Germans' preoccupation "with their own victimhood" and their inability to "even imagine why anyone should think that collective guilt

[15] When a West German member of a right-wing party made anti-Semitic comments in 1951, the German government requested that the Constitutional High Court declare the party unconstitutional (Stern 1992, 371). By contrast, the reaction to elites' anti-Semitic rhetoric in Russia of the 1990s is completely benign.

was appropriate" (1997, 928; see Arendt 1950 for a much earlier statement on Germans' denial of responsibility). As in the case of race in the United States, a strong norm of equality regarding the subordinate group coexists with resentments, fears, and stereotypes about the group. These are negative predispositions that are not focused on inherent and fixed difference but rather on the proclivity of the group to threaten the dominant group or undermine its values and goals.

Negative predispositions about Jews are linked with negative predispositions about other ethnic groups. In Germany as in many other European countries, the failure to fully examine and repudiate anti-Semitism is closely linked with the fact that, as Olick and Levy note, Germans continue to regard " 'Germanness' " as "an ethnic rather than a civic category." Despite the real changes brought about in the aftermath of World War II, "ethnocultural national identification remained an untouchable cultural principle" (Olick and Levy 1997, 930). The refusal to examine and repudiate the fundamental notions of racialist nationality links the anti-Semitism of old with the anti-immigrant xenophobia of today. As Bergmann and Erb put it, "Because of its history, anti-Semitism is a singular phenomenon, but it is also part of a general xenophobic attitude, directed in today's Germany mainly against migrant workers and asylum seekers" (1997, 198).

The link I draw between anti-Semitism and anti-immigrant sentiment requires some comment in light of the debate among scholars of European politics about the appropriateness of drawing a parallel between Nazi Germany and contemporary polities, particularly post-unification Germany and post-Soviet Russia. Naimark (1996), for example, underscores the continuing anti-Semitism and authoritarianism in postwar Germany and draws parallels with anti-Semitism in post-Soviet Russia. Many scholars, however, disagree that any of these "isms" are strong in Germany. Prowe (1997), for example, argues that despite the similarities often noted between the Nazis of the 1930s and the current radical right, there are many important differences that ultimately render the contemporary radical right much less of a threat. The right's preoccupation with ethnicity, Prowe argues, is much less coherent, ideological, expansionist, and revolutionary (although Prowe is mistaken in claiming that unlike today's right-wing groups, the Nazis primarily directed their xenophobia at people living far away; in fact, the Nazis persecuted Jews both far and near). Others argue that parallels between contemporary Russia and Weimar Germany are also misguided (Williams 1996), or that the new Germany faces— and poses—a different set of democratic dangers than the old Germany (Markovits and Reich 1997).

Much of this scholarly controversy, however, seems to be devoted to the questions of whether the radical right will bring totalitarianism, undermine democratic procedures and institutions, and bring a resurgence of imperialistic expansion. My question is quite distinct from these: whether mainstream parties, or parties of the right who seek to become mainstream, can succeed in appealing to sentiments that harm subordinate groups—Jews or immigrants— by using indirect, implicit electoral appeals. When these scholars directly address this question, their answer tends to be similar to mine. For example, Williams also locates the chief harm to ethnic groups not in extremist parties but in the actions of the ruling mainstream coalition (1996, 12).[16] There are, of course, important differences in the norms regarding Jews and immigrants and in the nature of negative predispositions about each group. In Central Europe today, the norm regarding Jews is stronger than the norm regarding immigrants (and stronger than the norm against anti-Semitism was during the 1950s and 1960s), and negative predispositions about Jews tend to emphasize their illegitimate power while those about immigrants emphasize their illegitimate dependence and criminality. Nevertheless, the similarities between the cases of immigrants and Jews, and with the case of race in the United States, are instructive, as I will elaborate later on.

In sum, as in the cases of race, gender, and sexual orientation in the United States, the use of subtle appeals to anti-Semitism or to negative predispositions about other ethnic groups depends on the salience of anti-Semitism or ethnic sentiment among an electorally influential segment of the population. The greater the electoral benefit accruing from these appeals, the higher the likelihood of finding them.[17] Germany and Austria provide somewhat different but related versions of the interplay of anti-ethnic predispositions, party strategy, and the norm of equality. I now elaborate on each of these two cases in turn.

---

[16] One underplayed fact in this controversy is that the norm against anti-ethnic political expression is stronger in post-unification Germany than it is in post-Soviet Russia. Leaders who make overtly anti-Semitic or extreme anti-immigrant statements are forced to resign in Germany and to a lesser extent in Austria, but not in Russia. For example, Albert Makashov, a member of the Communist faction in the Russian parliament (then the largest faction), advocated that Jews be "sent to the grave," but only a few of his liberal opponents called for his condemnation, and their motion was defeated. Boris Yeltsin's justice minister opened a criminal investigation of Makashov's remarks, but because of his party's protection Makashov maintained his parliamentary immunity, which allowed him to make such subsequent remarks as the following, delivered to a convention of Cossacks: "[Jews] are so bold, so impudent, because we're sleeping. . . . It's because none of us has yet knocked on their doors or pissed on their windows. That's why they're such snakes and acting so bold" (Meier 1999). Makashov has been linked with a long-time anti-Semite, Alexander Prokhanov, deemed "the uncredited ideologue in [Communist leader] Gennady Zyuganov's shadow Cabinet" (Meier 1999). Just as the norm is not egalitarian among elites, so do citizens seem to lack it. Surveys of Russians estimate the lowest percentage of anti-Semites at 40 percent, with "hard-line" anti-Semites estimated at a lowest bound of 25 percent (Kenez 1996, 141).

[17] Subtle forms of ethnocentrism are pervasive in Germany's discourse about the Holocaust even when the issue of ethnicity is electorally dormant. There has been a widespread "grammar of exculpation" that includes "the perverse absence of actors—passive formulations ('the crimes committed in Germany's name'); vague terms describing the period ('the conditions at that time,' 'what happened during those years,' 'the Hitler-time'); elliptical references to the details ('what happened,' 'the crimes that were committed'); and pervasive qualification ('others suffered, but so did Germans')" (Olick and Levy 1997, 931).

IMPLICIT COMMUNICATION IN AUSTRIA

Post-war Austria has had such a strong norm against political speech about Jews that some Austrian journalists have called it a "taboo." Yet anti-Semitic sentiment remains quite strong. Austrians largely consider themselves to have been victims of the Nazis rather than perpetrators of anti-Semitic acts; thus many Austrians have avoided a close examination of the country's anti-Semitism. Writing about Austria in the late 1980s, Richard Mitten noted,

> There is no reason to suspect that anti-Jewish prejudice (as opposed to discrimination) has significantly dwindled, much less disappeared, from post–World War II Austria. The point being that there exists a kind of reservoir of more or less firm beliefs about Jews which, under certain circumstances, might be tapped for political ends short of discrimination. . . . Antisemitic prejudice does not appear as, and thus cannot easily be identified through, explicitly anti-Jewish utterances, much less discriminatory measures. This is so, I argue, precisely because of the negative sanction which in general attaches to such openly antisemitic statements and acts. (Mitten 1992, 7).

Some Austrian politicians have attempted to appeal to lingering anti-Semitism in indirect ways. When Socialist Bruno Kreisky, an agnostic descended from a Jewish family, campaigned to become Austria's chancellor in 1970, the incumbent chancellor, Josef Klaus, the chairman of the Conservative People's party, campaigned against him using a poster of himself with the caption "A genuine Austrian." Earlier, as foreign minister, Kreisky had made a name for himself as an ally of the Palestinian cause, but still, Arab newspapers were quoted in Austria to suggest that Kreisky may give in to "Zionist pressure."[18] Appeals to anti-Jewish sentiment would not make sense were it not for the presence at the time of over 300,000 former Nazis, who constituted what one Austrian politician termed "the bulk of the swing vote." Kreisky's opponents were constrained by the social norm from using the word "Jewish" outright, but found code words to achieve the same end. Subsequently, one newspaper, *Kronen-Zeitung*, declared that the norm against explicitly discussing Jews in political discourse had backfired and should be overturned. But in a close parallel to news coverage of the implicitly racial 1988 American presidential campaign, the newspaper did not challenge the anti-Semitic appeal until after

[18] This tactic resembles those used in biracial contests in the American Deep South. Keith Reeves points out that such slogans as "Webb Franklin stands for Mississippi tradition" are a subtle way for white Republicans to mobilize southern whites' racial prejudices in contests against black candidates (1997, 77). This claim is not without its critics. According to Abigail Thernstrom, claiming that such slogans as "Eddie Knox will serve all the people of Charlotte" and "Knox can unify this city" are racial appeals is "reaching too far" (1987, 204).

the election (and it was alone in its call for change). The implicit appeal was not challenged until after it had the opportunity to inflict electoral damage.[19]

Kurt Waldheim's presidential election campaign in 1986 provides a more recent example of the interplay of egalitarian norms against anti-Semitic speech, lingering anti-Semitic predispositions among the Austrian public, and implicit communication designed to conform to the former yet incite the latter for political gain. During that campaign, allegations surfaced about Waldheim's Nazi past. When these allegations were repeated and elaborated by the *New York Times* and by the World Jewish Congress (WJC), Waldheim's supporters in the center-right People's party implied that they were part of a Jewish conspiracy to derail Waldheim. Austrian newspapers that toed this line were "neither wholly explicit nor even fully elaborated," but they implied that there was a Jewish conspiracy to attack Waldheim and, through him, Austria (Mitten 1992, 199). Mitten's summary of the campaign makes clear how the interplay of egalitarian norms and anti-ethnic sentiments generates implicit political communication:

> To claim publicly that 'the Jews' were behind the Waldheim affair, or that there was an 'international Jewish conspiracy' which controlled the international press, would ordinarily meet with official public censure, while the expression of too openly derisory attitudes towards Jews sometimes even has temporary political consequences in Austria. Many who aided in the construction of the negative stereotypes which emerged in 1986 would protest vehemently their innocence of antisemitic prejudice, and in some cases not obviously insincerely. The point is not to ascribe conscious antisemitic hostility to the politicians and journalists involved, much less to imply that their actions or words reflected antisemitic prejudice in any unmediated sense. It is nevertheless possible to suggest that some journalists and politicians actively participated in, while several others exhibited a studied indifference towards, the construction of this new antisemitic *Feindbild* in Austrian political discourse. (Mitten 1992, 200)

Thus implicit electoral appeals to anti-Semitism emerged in Austria when the three conditions I have outlined for the United States were present there: an egalitarian norm that forbids outright expressions of hostility toward the subordinate group; widespread lingering stereotypes, fears, and resentments toward the subordinate group; and attempts by at least one political party to appeal to these sentiments while adhering to the norm.

In the case of both Kreisky and Waldheim, the party that appealed to anti-Semitism was in the mainstream, but extreme parties also engage in implicit appeals. They tend to do so when they attempt to become more mainstream,

---

[19] Paul Hofmann, " 'Taboo' on Kreisky's Ancestry Scored," *New York Times*, March 9, 1970. Three years later a prominent member of the right-wing Freedom party was forced to resign after declaring he could not work with Kreisky because he was a Jew ("Party Wards Off Austrian Dispute," *New York Times*, August 5, 1973).

either in order to increase their percentage of the vote or to increase their attractiveness to mainstream parties seeking to build parliamentary coalitions. This can be seen in Austria of the late 1990s, not with anti-Semitism but with a related set of stereotypes, fears, and resentments directed at immigrants and their children.

The leader of Austria's right-wing Freedom party, Jörg Haider, who was removed from his post as a regional governor in the early 1990s for making pro-Nazi comments, regained that post in 1999 and has built the party into a formidable electoral force by proclaiming his rejection of Nazi acts. In 1999 Haider campaigned against immigration, focusing on Nigerian immigrants arrested for dealing drugs and the threat of massive immigration from Eastern Europe. In the 1999 election Haider's party won the second-largest percentage of the vote (27 percent) and was positioned to enter Austria's governing coalition.[20] In a recent interview, Haider explained his past political failure: "They took some sentences of speech . . . and tried to criminalize it [sic]. My fault was not to be careful enough, not to see the danger sometimes."[21] Haider has adjusted his rhetoric to fall closer to the bounds of the egalitarian norm, but continues to appeal to anti-ethnic and anti-foreign sentiment. An extremist party can avoid the social and political proscription against direct anti-ethnic actions, and still mobilize the unease that many citizens experience toward people marked as foreign. That double-faced strategy has helped Haider to revive his own political career and has propelled his party toward growing electoral gains.

IMPLICIT COMMUNICATION IN GERMANY

Even more than in Austria, in Germany the imperative to reject Nazism has been extremely strong in recent decades, and Germans, perhaps more than Austrians, have made the norm of ethnic equality not merely injunctive and descriptive but internalized and personal (Blaschke 1998, 55–58; Olick and Levy 1997).[22] In Germany, pro-Nazi, racist, and anti-Semitic speech is a crime, reparations for the Holocaust are written into law, the Office for the Protection of the Constitution monitors far-right organizations, and far-right parties have been unable to cross the 5 percent threshold necessary to obtain seats in the national parliament (Blaschke 1998). Opposition to Nazism is "a central feature" of Germany's political culture (Olick and Levy 1997, 925). But racial

[20] Donald G. McNeil, Jr., "Europeans Move Against Austrians on Nativist Party," *New York Times*, February 1, 2000.

[21] Thomas W. Haines, "Right-wing Austrian Gaining Momentum; Freedom Party's Tireless Push," *Boston Globe*, June 9, 1999.

[22] William Drozdiak, "Kohl's Party Moves to the Right: Germany's Christian Democrats Hope to Make Up Lost Ground in Bitter Campaign," *Washington Post*, July 4, 1998.

notions about ethnicity are, nevertheless, still strong. As we saw in the case of the United States, where racial appeals rise in response to a shock to the political system, in Germany the steep rise in immigration, coupled with a high unemployment rate, seems to have sparked implicit ethnic appeals.

Despite several incremental reforms (as of this writing, the latest occurred during 1999), the country's citizenship laws still rest on "blood lineage" rules established in 1913 during a period of widespread racist notions about nationality (Kurthen 1995, 14; Pulzer 1988).[23] Germany has made citizenship quite easy to obtain for immigrants whose ancestors were German, even if those ancestors left Germany centuries ago. But the law has made citizenship relatively difficult to obtain for people whose ancestors are not German. Even after several reforms, German citizenship is a right to those with German "bloodlines" and not a right to those without. "Foreigners under age eighteen who were born in Germany or who became integrated over many years do not have a right to naturalization," notes one scholar, but "a twenty-year-old ethnic German from Kazakhstan, who speaks no or only broken German and who has never visited Germany receives preferential treatment in comparison to the offspring of a Turkish labor migrant born in Germany" (Kurthen 1995, 13). Approximately 7.2 million noncitizens resided in Germany in 1996, and only about 10,000 a year were naturalized in the early and mid-1990s. By contrast, despite the restrictive quotas enacted in 1993, immigrants of German ancestry have arrived at a rate of about 200,000 a year from the former Soviet Union and Eastern Europe; they constitute the largest proportion of new citizens.[24]

This legacy of racialism coexists uneasily with an egalitarian imperative first imposed after World War II by the Allies and adopted gradually by a large majority of Germans. Hate crimes against immigrants and their German-born children rose on the heels of large waves of immigration, but these crimes elicited a loud public outcry (well organized and coordinated by elites) and a strong police response (Blaschke 1998). Far right parties that complain about "foreign bandits" and want "German jobs for Germans" have managed to gain as much as 13 percent in some state elections but have failed to rise beyond low single digits in national opinion polls.[25]

An openness to foreigners was written into Germany's Basic Law after the war, yet immigrants have been treated as temporary migrants, as a source of needed labor or as political refugees, rather than as potential citizens—unless they were of German ancestry. Many Germans have negative predispositions

[23] "German government defends plans to revise citizenship law," San Diego Union-Tribune, January 6, 1999.

[24] As of 1995 the rate of naturalization among immigrants remained low (Kuechler 1996, 240). See also "What Makes a 'German'? Immigration Is Pivotal Issue in the Election," Minneapolis Star Tribune, July 20, 1998; Rick Atkinson, "Ethnic Germans get cold shoulder in homeland," Fort Worth Star-Telegram, April 7, 1996.

[25] Andrew Nagorski with Stefan Theil, "The German Melting Pot," Newsweek, April 21, 1997.

toward ethnic immigrants, believing that immigrants have caused Germany's record-high unemployment, that they tend to commit crimes, and that they like to live off the state's welfare benefits. Many Germans apparently neglect the reality of German immigration—that immigrants have been prevented by law from working during the first several years of their residency, the vast majority who are allowed to work do so and pay taxes, and statistically they are no more likely to commit crimes.[26] Unemployment has been caused primarily by economic factors other than immigration, and the vast majority of immigrants take jobs that native Germans do not want (Kurthen 1995; Prowe 1997).[27] Even in the early 1990s, as Germany was receiving more immigrants and refugees per year than the United States, Canada, and Australia combined, many scholars deemed immigration a net gain to Germany's economy because of Germany's low birth rate, its aging population, its unfilled menial jobs, and immigrants' occupational and trade niches (Kurthen 1995).[28] The fear and resentment of immigrants owe much more to an ethnically exclusive notion of German national identity than it does to real threats to Germans' material well being. The fear of crime and the resentment of welfare dependency are intense even in regions where there is no objective reason for them. The exaggerated nature of such sentiments owes much to many Germans' ethnic ideas about Germany and Germans.

As the issue of immigration has risen in salience, so has talk of the need to get tough on crime, to wean people off welfare, to protect jobs for native workers, and to limit immigration. In 1993 the country's asylum law was changed to restrict the number of immigrants allowed into the country. Of course, many countries restrict immigration for simple logistical reasons, so in itself Germany's attempt to do so does not necessarily derive from a racialist view of German nationality. And proposals to restrict immigration in recent years have been joined with attempts to ease the process by which foreign-born residents become citizens. Still, proposals that restrict immigration or focus on immigrants' criminal activity are offered in a climate of ethnically based unease, fear, and resentment of people who are perceived as foreign. The media has contributed to this climate by covering immigration topics in a way that suggests (often implicitly) that immigrants cause social problems and conflicts (van Dijk 1988, chapter 3). As a consequence, mainstream parties have recently found ways to

[26] Paul Geitner, "Party Criticizes German Campaign," *Associated Press*, AP Online, July 9, 1998.

[27] Even in the height of immigration in the early 1990s, approximately 80% of working-age immigrants who were allowed to work were able to find jobs, and most of those were unwanted by Germans. Francine S. Kiefer, "Germans Want Restrictions in Asylum Laws; Stream of East European Refugees Fills Shelters, Spurs Attacks by Worried Germans,"*Christian Science Monitor*, August 15, 1991.

[28] Nagorski and Theil, "German Melting Pot." See also Kiefer, "Germans Want Restrictions in Asylum Laws."

appeal to these ethnic and anti-immigrant sentiments while remaining within the constraints of the norm against overtly anti-ethnic speech.

During his long tenure as Germany's chancellor, Helmut Kohl liked to proclaim, "We are not a country of immigration." Kohl and his center-right Christian Democratic Union (CDU) party were associated throughout most of the 1980s and 1990s with the traditional notion of Germany as a nation-state of German ancestry, although in 1991 Germany eased its difficult naturalization requirements for minors.[29] But in the early and mid-1990s, after unemployment reached its highest level since World War II, and as discontent with immigrants rose, the main opposition party, the center-left Social Democratic party (SPD), began to seize the center from the CDU (Linke 1999). In 1992 the SPD changed its long-standing liberal policy on immigration and agreed to restrict immigration by asylum seekers. Germany's open-door policy for asylum seekers was written into the constitution to "atone for the Nazis' persecution of foreigners"; thus SPD leaders saw the party's change as a painful but necessary move forced on them by the climate of opinion about immigration (Kurthen 1995).[30] SPD leader Oskar Lafontaine and the party's rising star, Gerhard Schroeder, moved the party to the center on several key issues. Among these was immigration.

In the 1996 state elections, Schroeder, then Lower Saxony's minister president, made highly visible appeals on the issue of immigration. Lafontaine did as well, pointing to anti-immigrant violence—not to condemn it but rather to argue that Germany should restrict immigration.[31] Interestingly, Lafontaine focused on ethnic German immigrants. This presented him with the opportunity to offer a less ancestral view of citizenship, but he did not do so. Instead, he condemned ethnic German immigrants as "people who are as foreign as any other immigrant."[32] Many on the left wing of the SPD publicly opposed Lafontaine's and Schroeder's appeals on immigration, arguing that the party's humiliating defeat that year proved the futility of these appeals, as many of the anti-immigrant voters targeted by the SPD voted instead for the extreme-right Republican party.[33] But Schroeder seemed unharmed by this defeat, and already in early 1997 he emerged as a favorite in trial-heat polls for the 1998 national election (Baun 1997, 14). Schroeder quickly gained power in his party and, with the approval of Lafontaine, continued to make electoral appeals on

[29] Nagorski and Theil, "German Melting Pot."

[30] Terrence Petty, "Germany Shuts Out Refugees—Tough Asylum Law Goes Into Effect as Policy Changes," *Seattle Times*, July 1, 1993; Stephen Kinzer, "Germany Moves to Tighten Laws on Asylum," *Raleigh News and Observer*, December 8, 1992.

[31] Ian Traynor, "Domestic woe blunts German blood claim," *Guardian*, March 7, 1996.

[32] Atkinson, "Ethnic Germans get cold shoulder in homeland."

[33] Denis Staunton, "Kohl's Poll Victory Routs Euro Skeptics: Dr. Helmut Kohl Won Crushing Electoral Successes," *Irish Times*, March 26, 1996.

the immigration issue. In 1997 he proposed to expel immediately immigrants who commit crimes in Germany. During the 1998 parliamentary elections, the SPD adopted a law-and-order plank highlighting its proposals to fight crime and to limit immigration, which journalists noted "bore the stamp of Schroeder."[34] A close ally of Schroeder, Hamburg mayor Henning Voscherau, said it was "scandalous that criminal foreigners could not be expelled to date."

Taken in isolation, the expulsion of noncitizens who commit crimes is not necessarily ethnocentric. But given the context of long-standing ethnically exclusive notions of national identity, it is difficult to make a salient issue out of the deportation of ethnic criminals without conveying an anti-ethnic, xenophobic message. It is unlikely that Schroeder and his allies in the SPD meant to be anti-ethnic in any overt way. But they did mean to appeal to voters who believe in the concept of German bloodlines and are uneasy about immigrants, and in doing so, they crafted electoral appeals that relied, intentionally or not, on exclusive ethnic notions of nationality and derogatory beliefs about ethnic immigrants.

Kohl's center-right government did likewise. In the 1996 campaign for state elections, CDU-affiliated government officials argued that ethnic Germans who resettle in Germany should continue to receive their constitutionally protected right to citizenship.[35] During the 1998 parliamentary elections the CDU-led government warned African countries that if they refused to take back their citizens when they commit crimes in Germany, the German government would retaliate with economic measures. The focus of this rhetoric seems to have been Africans of unknown nationality living in Germany, of which there were only about 5,500 at the time.[36] As the Social Democrats gained ground in pre-election polls, and as an extreme-right party gained protest votes in that year's state election in Saxony-Anhalt, Kohl approved a rightward rhetorical turn for his campaign. His party's Bavarian sister party, the Christian Social Union (CSU), called for a "security initiative" that would expel all immigrants who commit serious crimes, step up searches for illegal immigrants, and better equip the police force—all expounded with great fanfare in Bavaria, a state with one of Germany's largest foreigner populations but one of its lowest crime rates. Thus Bavaria might seem to have little to fear from criminals, ethnic or otherwise, and yet the far right had recently made gains there in part through anti-immigrant appeals (Karapin 1998; Kuechler 1996, 238).[37] The CSU's Michael Glos declared, "We can no longer tolerate millions of our citizens being

---

[34] Tony Czuczka, "German Opposition Says It's Ready to Take Over," *Associated Press*, March 9, 1998.

[35] Atkinson, "Ethnic Germans get cold shoulder in homeland."

[36] "Updates with general debate on immigrant delinquency," *Agence France-Presse*, September 5, 1997.

[37] Drozdiak, "Kohl's Party Moves to the Right."

unemployed while over a million new work permits are issued to foreigners in Germany."[38] A CSU campaign proposal even suggested that "foreign children who commit crimes should be deported." "Foreign children" was, even in 1998, a broad category that conceivably included children born in Germany to non-German parents, who are not granted citizenship automatically because they have no German "bloodlines."[39]

But while Kohl approved a package titled "Effective Stemming of Undesired Immigration," he was careful to stay within the limits of the norm; he prevented the leaders of the somewhat more conservative CSU from including the line "Germany is not an immigration country" in its platform. In the past Kohl had not been shy about using that slogan himself, but by the 1998 campaign, with the rising visibility of anti-immigrant extremist parties, the slogan had taken on more extreme connotations. In fact, it seems that the CDU/CSU's crucial crime-fighting proposal was held up for three months during the campaign while Kohl fought with the CSU to omit this slogan (and similar examples of what he feared would be extreme anti-immigration language). Kohl's worry about violating the norm may have been enhanced by the Green party's circulation of an anti-CSU poster that read, "Beckstein [a CSU Bavarian state minister] would also expel Jesus." When the CSU criticized the poster, Green party leaders replied that Jesus and his parents were refugees and would have been deported if they had arrived in Bavaria.[40]

Comparing Race in the United States with Ethnicity in Germany

So far I have argued that the cases of Jews and of ethnic immigrants demonstrate important similarities, and that each is similar to the case of race in the United States. However, there are important differences as well. Let us take a closer look at the cases of Jews and ethnic immigrants in Germany. In Germany, there is a strong general norm against xenophobia and racism, but that norm is stronger for action directed against Jews than for action directed against immigrants. Jews, much more than immigrants without German ancestry, are accepted as true Germans. Negative predispositions are stronger regarding ethnic immigrants (such as Turks) than Jews (Bergmann and Erb 1997; Kurthen 1997). The issue of immigration, and not the status of Jews, is salient, and it has caused a shock to social, economic, and political arrangements.

---

[38] Nagorski and Theil, "German Melting Pot."

[39] Children born in Germany to non-Germans have a right to citizenship if they are between the ages of 16 and 23, have resided in Germany for at least eight years, have spent at least six years in German schools, and give up their former citizenship (Kurthen 1995, 13; Kuechler 1996, 252).

[40] Geitner, "Party Criticizes German Campaign."

Consequently, the parties are pursuing appeals that target immigrants, not Jews. Consequently too, discourse about immigrants is more often explicit than discourse about Jews. The term "Jew" is rarely paired with criticism, unlike the term "foreigner," although the more mainstream the party or its aspirations, the more cautiously this term has been used. Anti-Jewish statements are less often made—because the issue is not salient and the parties are not aligned on it—and when made, are much more subtle and indirect than anti-immigrant statements—because the norm is more powerful regarding Jews.

Nevertheless, the norm of ethnic equality does extend beyond Jews to cover other ethnic groups. Anti-immigrant discourse faces a degree of normative constraint that it would not have faced before the establishment of the norm after World War II. The trend over the 1990s shows that the norm is increasingly applied to immigrants. Kohl's comments on immigration became increasingly muted during the 1990s, as mentioned earlier. And in 2000, when Austria's right-wing Freedom party won enough votes to enter the Austrian government, Germany led the other members of the European Union in threatening to isolate Austria. This move was driven by a desire to enhance the reach of the norm of ethnic equality: "We had to send a very clear signal that behavior of a racist or xenophobic character will not be tolerated within the European Union," explained the Portuguese prime minister, speaking on behalf of the members of the European Union.[41] The party's leader, Jörg Haider, was the target of social censure and political pressure because he had a record of past anti-Semitic and pro-Nazi statements and because he advocated strict anti-immigrant positions. Austria's president swore in Haider only after requiring him to sign a pledge to maintain an Austria in which "xenophobia, anti-Semitism and racism have no place" and to oppose "every way of thinking which seeks to denigrate human beings."[42] The norm of ethnic equality is brought to bear on the issue of immigration when that issue comes to resemble the issues of xenophobia and racism.

While European anti-Semitism and immigration show instructive differences as well as significant similarities, immigration in Europe also provides an instructive contrast and similarity to the case of race in the United States. Unlike contemporary racial appeals in the United States, in Germany both the center-right and center-left parties have been crafting rhetorical strategies that implicitly appeal to anti-ethnic sentiment. The SPD has coupled anti-immigrant appeals during elections with pro-immigrant measures in its policymaking.[43] When the SPD came to power after the 1998 elections, it proposed to

---

[41] McNeil, "Europeans Move Against Austrians on Nativist Party."

[42] Roland Prinz, "Austrian Leader Swears in New Government," *Associated Press*, February 4, 2000.

[43] This resembles the Reconstruction elections, as Chapter 2 showed.

make it easier for immigrants who had long resided in Germany to become German citizens. However, the CDU's rhetorical response promises to push the SPD to keep making anti-immigrant appeals during electoral campaigns. The chairman of the CDU spoke on German television against the SPD's proposal and argued that integrating these ethnic residents would pose a great threat to national security. While the CDU coalition lost the 1998 German parliamentary elections, in the most recent European parliamentary elections in June 1999 the right-of-center parties won a majority for the first time in twenty years, at the expense of the socialist parties which had unseated them in individual-country elections as recently as 1998. The SPD may thus face strong electoral incentives to use anti-ethnic appeals in the next election.

By contrast, in the United States the center-left Democrats have mostly refrained from making racial appeals. The exceptions are instructive. When Bill Clinton ran for President in 1992, he used the Los Angeles riots of that spring, and its endorsement by a militant black singer, Sister Souljah, to reassure resentful or fearful whites that he was on their side. Clinton's rhetoric fit within his overall strategy of combating the longstanding Republican strategy of making implicit racial appeals against Democrats.[44] Other Democrats who seek to counter the Republicans' implicitly racial strategy may be tempted to do the same, although the evidence I have gathered suggests that rendering these appeals explicit, and finding an issue to trump race, may be effective enough that mimicking implicit appeals becomes unnecessary. Exceptions to the common partisan pattern also arise in elections in which Democratic candidates face stiff competition from fellow Democrats. In areas of the United States with weak party competition, such as New York City in the 1970s and 1980s, or much of the South in the 1960s and 1970s, Democrats tended to split into more and less conservative factions, with the more conservative faction sometimes engaging in implicit racial appeals.[45]

The hope for more egalitarian politics in both Germany (and Austria) and the United States lies in the actions of political elites. In Germany the SPD's rhetorical strategy is crucial in this regard. We saw in the case of the United States that the most effective way to counter implicit communication is to make it explicit—to show that it violates the norm of equality. The case of the United States showed, further, that the institution best able to do so is not the media, which is hobbled by its internal constraints, but the partisan opposition. Unfortunately, in Germany the opposition to implicit appeals has come from groups

---

[44] In Democratic presidential primaries, however, implicitly racial appeals are few and weak. Contrary to Bill Bradley's accusation in 2000, Al Gore did not use Willie Horton's name or image in 1988—he referred to several criminals and the furlough program, and did so only during a debate in New York (Simon 1990, 201).

[45] On New York see Rogers 2000; on the South see Chapter 3 and Black 1976.

without a great deal of influence. The Greens challenged the anti-immigrant appeals of the CSU in 1998, but they have less political influence than the SPD and thus can only sway public opinion so far.[46] When the leader of the CDU called immigration a threat to national security, Germany's Jewish community, which had been labeled a threat to national security during the Third Reich, was the most vocal group to condemn this rhetoric as racist.[47]

Despite the fact that the egalitarian norm is weaker when applied to immigrants rather than Jews, the counterstrategy of rendering the appeal more explicit should work in both cases, as I have argued it does in the case of race in the United States. However, in Germany that counterstrategy must consist of applying the norm developed for Jews to discourse about ethnic immigrants. When in 2000 Haider's Freedom party won six seats in the Austrian cabinet, Austrian president Thomas Klestil rejected two of the party's more extreme nominees, one of whom had authorized campaign posters against "over-foreignization," a term apparently encompassing immigrants ("foreigners") but also used in the past to incite anti-Semitism.[48] Thus it is the pairing of anti-Semitic and anti-immigrant appeals, rather than anti-immigrant appeals alone, that seems to violate the norm most strongly and thus will provoke the strongest censure from influential elites. Should the SPD decide to challenge implicit appeals on the grounds that they violate the norm of ethnic equality, it will move the terms of debate about citizenship and ethnicity in a more egalitarian direction. The power of such a rhetorical move can be greatly enhanced if the most influential elites, such as officials elected by a large majority, or respected business leaders, support it. The key to success is to underscore the link between Germany's racialist past, which targeted Jews, and Germany's continuing racialist definition of itself, which now targets, albeit in a more democratic fashion, other ethnic groups. Similarly, in the United States the key to success is to underscore the link between the racist past and the nation's continuing, albeit democratic, resistance to racial equality.

All this does not mean that Germany is once again headed toward totalitarianism, right-wing extremism, or expansionism. But it does suggest that German politics still revolves in part around anti-ethnic sentiment. Germany's citizenship laws, despite the reforms of the 1990s—including the reform proposed in 1999—have not eradicated the notion of bloodlines.[49] Immigration

---

[46] The center-right, although only mildly anti-Semitic at the time, was crucial to the rise of the Third Reich and its anti-Semitic program (Baranowski 1996).

[47] "German government defends plans to revise citizenship law."

[48] Prinz, "Austrian Leader Swears in New Government."

[49] Imre Karacs, "Kohl Scrabbles for Votes on Immigration and Workfare," *Independent*, August 13, 1998; "German Immigration Reform Signed into Law," *Deutsche Presse-Agentur*, July 20, 1999. Germany is the only major immigrant-receiving European country that does not formally allow dual citizenship. The 1999 reform undermines the notion of bloodlines, but, due to a "mighty

coupled with other developments has created political stresses and opportunities—a shock to the political system—and has sparked appeals based on the
notion of an ethnic state. The parallels with the Weimar Republic, however,
while striking, are easily misinterpreted. While the extreme right-wing parties
have made gains in German state elections, they have failed to make headway
nationally. The economic problems and the rise of these parties are nothing
compared to the crises plaguing Weimar Germany. Germans reject extremism
and trust Democratic institutions, Germany has procedures that safeguard
against extremist parties, and the mainstream parties show no signs of weaken-
ing or of turning to authoritarian practices—all of which brought the Nazis to
power (Berman 1998; Dalton 1993). But the health of democratic politics in
Germany does not mean that anti-ethnic politics lacks force (Baranowski 1996;
Minkenberg 1998). Anti-ethnic politics can thrive in a democracy with constitutional guarantees of minority rights, a healthy electoral competition, a strong
norm of equality, and no plans to conquer its neighbors. In these ways post-
unification Germany resembles Weimar less than it does the United States.[50]

In Europe as in the United States, and on cleavages including race, ethnicity,
and sexuality, political communication turns implicit when egalitarian norms
coexist with widespread hostility to a subordinate group. Mainstream parties
often decide to capitalize on popular sentiment against a subordinate group
when an important voting bloc holds this sentiment. Often this situation originates with a significant event, such as sharp increases in immigration, the exi-
gencies of war, large-scale protests that challenge racial hierarchy, or a health
crisis that mobilizes gays and lesbians. These events pose a shock to the political system and often spark a reaction, which if sufficiently widespread provides
one party with a new electoral opportunity. Sometimes the other major party
follows suit; other times it takes up the cause of the subordinate group. When
a party decides to mobilize that reaction for electoral purposes, it is significantly

---

societal groundswell against double citizenship," did not eliminate this notion: German-born children of foreigners are granted automatic citizenship but must still give up a second citizenship at
the age of twenty-three (Joppke 1999, 638, 640).

[50] These observations apply to many other European countries. When right-of-center parties
in fourteen of the fifteen members of the European Union suffered defeats in recent national
elections, many right-wing parties decided to highlight their anti-immigrant stance. Some extreme parties have tried to repackage their message in more acceptable terms. The National Front,
France's third-largest party, has split on the question of rhetorical pragmatism, with some leaders
defecting to form a more rhetorically mainstream party for the express purpose of forming an
alliance with mainstream politicians. A German example is Steffen Hupka, a regional leader of the
National Democratic party, who said that he stands "for German values, German culture, and
against the guilt complex imposed on us by powerful groups, especially in the United States" (a
veiled reference to Jews). See Harry Sterling, "French Fascists Are Softening Their Edge," *Toronto
Star*, February 9, 1999.

constrained by the existence of an egalitarian norm. Explicit criticism of subordinate groups under the protection of the norm can still be found, but only among parties and figures of the political extreme.[51] Any party with mainstream aspirations takes pains to conform to the egalitarian norm, and to deny having violated it if so accused. By the same token, the effective counterstrategy appeals to the norm by rendering the implicit discourse explicit.

[51] In France, the explicitly anti-Semitic and anti-immigrant National Front has gained seats in parliament with 10 to 15 percent of the vote in recent elections. Unlike the United States, in parliamentary systems a mainstream party may form a coalition with an extreme party, for example in the Austrian election of 1975 ("Party Wards Off Austrian Dispute," *New York Times*, August 5, 1973; Fay Willey with Milan J. Kubic, "Austria: Digging Up the Past," *Newsweek*, December 1, 1975).

CHAPTER 10

Political Communication and Equality

Reflecting on the matters set forth above and
considering within myself whether the times were
propitious in Italy at present to honor a new
prince and whether there is at hand the matter
suitable for a prudent and virtuous leader to mold
in a new form, giving honor to himself and
benefit to the citizens of the country, I have arrived
at the opinion that all circumstances now favor
such a prince, and I cannot think of a time more
propitious for him than the present.
—Machiavelli, *The Prince*

THE CAMPAIGN MESSAGES I have examined in this book point to a crucial but poorly understood aspect of American politics today: racial stereotypes, fears, and resentments shape our decisions most when they are least discussed. Racial communication is common, but it is often presented as if it were not about race at all. It is this strong but implicit reference to race that is most effective in priming racial predispositions and racializing the political choices of white citizens. The explicit reference to racial stereotypes, fears, and resentments often backfires. Thus, the most effective way to counter a racial message is to render it explicit, to show that it is in fact racial.

When influential elites read racism into a message, they can mobilize enough people against the message and increase the likelihood that the candidate who uses it is will be defeated. Transforming an implicit appeal into an explicit one is among the surest ways to neutralize it. The counterstrategy of remaining silent on race in the face of an implicit racial appeal is a losing strategy. More effective is the counterstrategy of bringing race to the surface, of showing the racial meaning of the message and thus preventing the opposition from using race in a deniable way. The votes of African Americans are undoubtedly important to the success of this explicit counterstrategy. But at least as important in majority-white elections is the response of white voters. In fact, calling attention to the racial nature of implicit appeals turns off the very same racially resentful voters who respond to these appeals.

The same variable can explain the success of implicit messages and the way to defeat them. That variable is the implicitness of the message. And implicit meaning rests, fundamentally, on awareness. An implicit message hostile to African Americans can convey a racial meaning without the full awareness of the white audience. The more consciously white voters hear "welfare" or "values" or "crime" and the less consciously they hear "race," the more effective the message is at priming voters' racial predispositions. By the same token, the more consciously white voters hear "race," the less effective the message becomes at conveying derogatory racial meaning. Awareness matters because of the norm of racial equality. That norm not only describes a massive commitment of whites to the idea that blacks and whites are equal, but also labels anything to the contrary as illegitimate and immoral. The norm of racial equality thus constrains not only what candidates feel free to say, but also the response of white voters.

NORMS, EQUALITY, AND CAMPAIGNS

The norm of racial equality emerged in the United States at a gradual pace, as the older norm of racial inequality eroded. Crucial to its growth were the actions of white and African-American elites and of the civil rights movement. By targeting symbolic expressions of inequality, movements are engaged in an important exercise of normative change. Perhaps more effective than a movement's attempts to challenge inegalitarian expression directly, however, is the movement's attempts to prompt the passage of important egalitarian laws. In general, laws can have a large impact on social norms (Sunstein 1996). Sunstein has gone so far as to describe Martin Luther King as a "norm entrepreneur" (1996, 929). There is no better way to establish a norm of equality than the passage of landmark civil rights legislation. Such legislation not only has instrumental, material consequences; it also has significant symbolic results, including the establishment of strong egalitarian norms. A norm, however, is not merely a symbol. It has consequences for the way that politics is conducted. A norm constrains the discourse of elites and leaves their appeals vulnerable to challenge. This discourse and the challenges to it in turn affect the votes that citizens cast and the types of government policies that they are willing to support.

Even when a norm of equality is firmly established, political conflict over the subordinate group's status often continues. The tension between equality and racism is dynamic, not static. Electoral competition brings this dynamic into sharp relief. The electoral arena provides politicians with incentives to appeal to white voters' resentments and fears about racial change. Over the course of two centuries, American parties made racial appeals in response to every significant threat to hierarchical racial arrangements. When the arrangements that privileged the dominant racial group were challenged, one party seized on the challenge as an opportunity to advance the cause of equality, while the other party perceived an opportunity to mobilize those uncomfortable with the challenge. In this fashion, a shock to racial arrangements causes the party system to align on the issue of race. In this fashion do racial appeals arise. Racial appeals would not exist without the party system.

By the same token, it is in the electoral arena that racial appeals can be neutralized. When a norm of equality reigns, campaigns provide the site where the meaning of implicit communication can be contested effectively. The news media is not as well suited to officiate over the contest of meaning as its self-defined mission would suggest. Journalists have set for themselves the task of providing accurate, relevant information in an objective and balanced manner (McQuail 1992). Included in that mission is the attempt to avoid coverage that reinforces social inequalities (Norris 1997). We have seen here, however, that the incentives and norms of the news business are not conducive to a timely and effective coverage of implicit campaign appeals. Journalists may not be much better than white voters at perceiving racial meaning in implicit messages, as Chapter 5 showed. This is perhaps not surprising for those who have long worried about the dearth of African-American reporters and editors. Certain reforms, such as ad watches, if executed properly, may improve the quality of campaign coverage, as Jamieson has argued (1992). However, ad watches and similar reforms cannot counter implicit communication unless they tackle implicit meaning. Ad watches are well suited to fact checks, but they are unlikely to be used by journalists to charge one candidate or party with making an implicit appeal to race. Journalists are extremely uncomfortable with such a role. Their profession is not well positioned to highlight for the public the harmful racial meaning of implicit messages. As a result, the news media too often serves as the conduit of implicit racial communication.[1]

Partisan competition, however, can work well enough. Candidates, unlike journalists, do have clear incentives to engage other candidates in a debate about the harm that an implicit appeal might do to a subordinate group. Partisan competition works when the party targeted for implicit appeals realizes that its best course of action lies in a vigorous contest over derogatory meaning. In the United States, African-American leaders have been far more willing than their white counterparts to engage in such a rhetorical contest. The 1988 election demonstrates just how powerful the black protest tradition can be in the context of elections, even in contests featuring white candidates and a white voting majority. But African-American leaders cannot succeed in influencing white voters without the cooperation of influential white leaders. Just as racial equality in the policy domain depends on multiracial coalitions, so does racial equality in the electoral domain depend on cooperation between African-American and white leaders in the public definition of racial messages.

---

[1] This does not excuse the media from doing all it can.

What, then, of the debate about racism in the United States? Does the evidence in this book suggest that racism is a thing of the past or that it continues unabated? The answer is neither, because it is more complex than these extreme positions allow. The historical trajectory I have laid out suggests that racism has declined in crucial ways. Among the most important changes of the twentieth century was the emergence of the norm of racial equality. But the norm, while powerful, can be gotten around. Some politicians try to get around it because they sense, accurately, that many white Americans have negative racial predispositions. A large segment of the white voting public believes that African Americans do not practice the important virtues that whites (and others, such as Asians) do. On the whole, many white voters believe, African Americans could be—but are not yet—equal to whites, because they are not as committed as they should be to hard work, self-reliance, a peaceful and law-abiding existence, and moral sexual behavior. What is new and what is old about these views? What is new is the firm belief that blacks can in fact be the equal of whites, and that many blacks have already become equal. What is old is the condemnation of many blacks on the familiar dimensions of work, violence, and sexuality. As in the past, these views about blacks, and the feelings they engender among whites, are not always prominent in the minds of white voters. But they can be primed all too effectively by politicians. Today as in the past, when politicians prime whites' racial stereotypes, fears, and resentments, they undermine the public will to remedy racial inequality, and they help to place in office people who are hostile or indifferent to the problem of racial inequality. Racial appeals, today as in the past, come at the expense of black progress. And without the full measure of equal opportunity for the descendants of its slaves, the United States will never come close to achieving its democratic aspirations.

Continuity, however, does not mean the absence of significant change. Politicians have engaged in racial appeals more implicitly since the norm of equality was established. The implicit character of racial appeals makes them more difficult to detect, but once detected, they are highly vulnerable. Implicitness can circumvent the norm of equality, but because of the norm, implicitness also provides a point of vulnerability. Before the civil rights revolution, the norm was inegalitarian, and racial messages were explicit and difficult to neutralize. One could not neutralize a racial appeal simply by showing that it was racial. During historical periods when the norm was inegalitarian, countering explicit messages required a dramatic reordering of the public agenda. Electoral communication had to shift the focus away from race and toward another, more pressing issue, often that of patriotism. In the age of equality, racial conflict continues, and so, therefore, do racial messages; but because they must be implicit in order to work, racial messages today are more vulnerable than their explicit counterparts were in the age of inequality. At its core, an electoral campaign is a contest over meaning. Because of this, a campaign can be either a site of racial subordination or a place where racial equality advances. Candidates and parties can counter racial appeals by showing that they are racial, thus pointing out that the elites who use them have stepped outside the boundaries of the norm of equality.

THE DEBATE OVER RACISM

My argument thus speaks to the long-standing and heated debate over the nature of American racial attitudes, yet moves beyond it. Some scholars argue that since the 1960s, public opinion on matters of race is shaped primarily, though not entirely, by nonracial concerns. According to this view, matters of ideology, education, and values such as the work ethic, all of which are not essentially about race, determine the political choices that whites make regarding race, just as these factors determine any other type of political choice. Nevertheless, argue Sniderman and his colleagues, racial considerations, while less important than nonracial considerations, are not completely impotent (Sniderman and Piazza 1993; Sniderman and Carmines 1997; Sniderman et al. 2000). But these considerations can be clearly separated from notions of hard work and morality, and in the final analysis we can easily recognize them as a simple loathing of blacks. Other scholars argue instead that public opinion on matters of race is shaped mostly by racial considerations, and that these considerations are more sophisticated than pure racial bigotry. Whites' racial predispositions cannot be reduced to a simple dislike of anything black (Kinder and Sanders 1996; Sears et al. 2000; Sidanius et al. 2000). White Americans' racial concerns are more selective and nuanced than that. A few whites do have a pure dislike of African Americans, but that type of racial prejudice has little to do with the racial politics of today. Opposition to preferential hiring, for example, is not grounded in sheer bigotry but rather in whites' tendency to apply the work ethic with particular negative force to the situation of African Americans (Kinder and Mendelberg 1995; Kinder and Sanders 1996; Sears et al. 1997). On its own, the need to work hard has little influence on whites' opinions on racial matters, but when applied to the situation of blacks it becomes quite powerful (Kinder and Mendelberg 2000).

I have come down clearly in support of the latter argument. However, both arguments, although opposed in significant ways, share my conclusion that elites can influence the extent to which white voters choose on the basis of their racial considerations. I have fleshed out the conditions under which the social cleavage of race matters in politics, particularly in elections, and the circumstances under which that cleavage subsides in significance. Whites' racial predispositions can be quite powerful, and indeed often are. But the extent to which they are powerful, and the degree to which people are aware of this power, is a matter of politics. Politics operates in two ways: within individual citizens, and in the discourse of elites. Both sides in the debate about racism have neglected the internal dynamics of racial attitudes, the ways in which the political psychology of white individuals matters for the potency of racism. Both sides have just begun to explore the impact of elite discourse on the racism of white citizens. I have tried to show how both aspects of politics matter, and moreover, how the two are linked.

In the last page of her book on the powerful ideology of the American Dream, Jennifer Hochschild concludes with two hopes that she takes to be quite different from each other: "Ideally, all Americans will fight their own worst instincts by mobilizing their best. . . . Alternatively, some Americans will use the dream's best features to contest other Americans taking advantage of its worst" (1995, 260). The present book has shown in detail both how Americans can "fight their own worst instincts by mobilizing their best" *and* how some "use the dream's best features to contest other Americans taking advantage of its worst." To advance our understanding of race and other cleavages, we must investigate how Hochschild's paths to progress depend on each other. Rather than forming two distinct alternatives, the two paths are in symbiosis. To move beyond the scholarly debate over the nature of racism, we must study simultaneously what political systems do and what political psychology does. When norms and party strategies mobilize our "best feature," our norm of equality, they encourage individual citizens to overcome their "own worst instincts" of racial stereotypes, fears, and resentments by "mobilizing their best"—their personal ideal of equality.

BEYOND THE RHETORIC OF REACTION

In the United States and Europe, emancipation, civil rights, and egalitarian reforms often bring reaction in their wake. Reaction can be communicated in different forms, and some are more effective than others. In his study of two centuries of reaction against equality, Albert Hirschman remarked, "Curiously, the reaction that was least *consciously* intent on reversing the ongoing trends or reforms became the one to have—or to be later accused of having had—the most destructive impact" (Hirschman 1991, 6; emphasis added). The egalitarian revolution that succeeds is the revolution that institutes a strong norm against inegalitarian speech. Consequently, the reaction that fails to conform to the new norm stands little chance of success. Reaction is most effective when it conforms to the new norm but pursues a policy that hinders the advancement of the group protected by egalitarian reforms.

The remedy to reaction, then, arises from the intersection of two variables I have studied here: norms and party strategy. That remedy is for the mainstream egalitarian party to challenge the use of implicit communication on the grounds that it violates an egalitarian norm. What makes this remedy effective is that it rests on actions that an influential and well-organized political group is well positioned to take. Challenging implicit communication serves that group's self-interest—winning elections—and is not incompatible with the group's ideology—championing the needs of those who are less well off.

Of course, all remedies have limits. As with any other campaign practice, a challenge to implicit appeals that is overdone will lose its effectiveness. Negative advertising has received a great deal of attention during the 1990s, from scholars, observers, and political practitioners. Messages that attempt to counter implicit appeals risk the perception that they are simply more mud in a mudslinging campaign. My analysis of exactly such a case, in Chapters 5 and 6, is reassuring because it finds that even when that perception is widespread, the counterstrategy I recommend can nevertheless neutralize the implicit message. Still, as many grow increasingly weary of campaigns that seem to them too dirty, the question of how much of the antidote is too much remains an open one.

The strategy I recommend faces an additional problem. Candidates who are challenged have increasingly been responding with an accusation in kind. Some candidates, when pressed on their use of racial appeals, argue in turn that it is not they but the challenger who is injecting race into the campaign. This is a believable and easy message to convey when the original appeal is subtle and highly deniable. How often, how legitimately, and how effectively this message is used remains to be seen.

Along with countering implicit appeals, there is another, more difficult remedy that follows from the logic of my argument. While it is less practical, this remedy can serve as an ideal for which democratic politics may strive. That remedy is to modify the norm so that it is more far-reaching, so that it fully confronts the third variable in my story: individual predispositions that lead people to stereotype, fear, or resent the subordinate group. Encouraging in this regard is the finding, reported in Chapter 7, that not all campaign messages on a racially loaded issue prime racial resentment. Candidates seeking to appeal to unease over abuses of welfare policies or to anxieties and anger about violent crime can do so without priming white voters' racial predispositions if they make clear that African Americans are not their target. Simply showing images of white welfare recipients or whites arrested for violent crimes is sufficient to attract voters with conservative leanings. Candidates who do so may not win as many votes as they can with implicit racial appeals. Messages about welfare or crime, unfortunately, pack their greatest punch when they implicitly allude to racial stereotypes, fears, and resentments. However, candidates who wish to appeal to nonracial forms of conservatism can do so. Elites can implement their commitment to "compassionate conservatism" (as voiced by George W. Bush) or a "kinder and gentler nation" (in the words of his father), in a way that is truly innocent of race. The choice between implicit racial appeals and counter-stereotypical appeals is a clear one, and it is the candidates' to make.

While the first efforts to practice a true politics of nonracial conservatism may prove electorally costly, the more leaders who engage in these appeals, the less costly they are likely to become. And should the media take up the practice of counter-stereotypical news reporting, it will likely make counter-stereotypical campaign appeals considerably easier for politicians to make.

EQUALITY AND CHANGE

Egalitarian change is often partial. In Germany and other European countries partial change has meant the failure to fully grapple with the racial roots of anti-Semitism and of negative sentiments toward other ethnic groups. This in turn informs the failure to fully accept the idea that nationhood resides not in ancestral bloodlines but in subjective identity. The norm of equality in Germany, Austria, and other European countries must be stretched to include not only the repudiation of anti-Semitic speech, but a proactive struggle with the ethnically exclusive nature of national identity.[2]

In the United States egalitarian change has also been partial. The solution here as elsewhere ultimately requires that the norm of racial equality be expanded. Doing so will require proactive efforts to end the informal yet institutionalized color line in neighborhoods, schools, workplaces, and social relations.

Perhaps no greater change has taken place in U.S. electoral politics than the extension of civil rights to African Americans, ephemerally in the nineteenth century and more permanently in the twentieth. Revolutions, however, must coexist with the remains of the old regime. Even as greater equality is accepted, it is resisted. The acceptance of equality represents real progress, but it does not close the door to resistance. The most significant episodes of change spark resistance while constraining its expression. Politicians and voters alike express resistance in more subtle form than before. Subtle resistance is nevertheless susceptible to a counterstrategy that harnesses norms on behalf of equality.

Understanding why, when, and how the language of group politics is implicit or explicit, and understanding what implicit and explicit discourse does under egalitarian and inegalitarian norms, is a way to understand large-scale political change and continuity. Thus, examining the origins, dynamics, and impact of implicit discourse is a way to understand how the central social cleavages of a society evolve over time.

[2] There is no necessary link between aggressive nationalism and ethnic exclusivity. In the American case, racism was often thwarted rather than reinforced by American military conflicts (Klinker and Smith 1999). As we saw in Chapter 2, a party that favors greater rights for the subordinate group can advance its program by highlighting the threat from a common outside enemy. Olick and Levy (1997) argue that the norm against anti-Semitic speech now stands in the way of Germans' full reexamination of their anti-Semitic past. If the norm leads to "atonement" in lieu of "introspection," then the current norm must be fundamentally changed, not simply stretched.

References

Abramowitz, Alan I. 1994. "Issue Evolution Reconsidered: Racial Attitudes and Partisanship in the U.S. Electorate." *American Journal of Political Science* 38: 1–24.

Abramson, Paul, John Aldrich, and David Rhode. 1989. *Change and Continuity in the 1988 Elections.* Rev. ed. Washington, D.C.: Congressional Quarterly Press.

———. 1994. *Change and Continuity in the 1992 Elections.* Washington, D.C.: Congressional Quarterly Press.

———. 1998. *Change and Continuity in the 1996 Elections.* Washington, D.C.: Congressional Quarterly Press.

Allport, Gordon W. 1954. *The Nature of Prejudice.* Cambridge: Addison-Wesley.

Alvarez, R. Michael, and John Brehm. 1997. "Are Americans Ambivalent Toward Racial Policies?" *American Journal of Political Science* 41 (2): 345–374.

Anderson, David. 1995. "Expressive Justice Is All the Rage." *New York Times Magazine*, January 15, 36–37.

Apostle, Richard., Charles Glock, Thomas Piazza, and Marijean Suelzle. 1983. *The Anatomy of Racial Attitudes.* Berkeley: University of California Press.

Arendt, Hannah. 1950. "The Aftermath of Nazi Rule: Report from Germany." *Commentary* (October): 342–353.

Ashmore, Richard D., and Frances K. Del Boca. 1981. "Conceptual Approaches to Stereotypes and Stereotyping." In David L. Hamilton, ed., *Cognitive Processes in Stereotyping and Inter-Group Behavior.* Hillsdale, N.J.: Lawrence Erlbaum.

Axelrod, Robert. 1972. "Where the Votes Come From: An Analysis of Electoral Coalitions, 1952–1968." *American Political Science Review* 66: 11–20.

———. 1986. "Presidential Election Coalitions in 1984." *American Political Science Review* 80: 281–284.

Ayers, Edward L. 1992. *The Promise of the New South: Life after Reconstruction.* Oxford: Oxford University Press.

Banaji, Mahzarin R., and Anthony G. Greenwald. 1995. "Implicit Gender Stereotyping in Judgments of Fame." *Journal of Personality and Social Psychology* 68 (2): 181–198.

Banaji, Mahzarin R., and Curtis Hardin. 1996. "Automatic Stereotyping." *Psychological Science* 7 (3): 136–141.

Banaji, Mahzarin R., Curtis Hardin, and Alexander J. Rothman. 1993. "Implicit Stereotyping in Person Judgment." *Journal of Personality and Social Psychology* 65 (2): 272–281.

Bankier, David. 1992. *The Germans and the Final Solution: Public Opinion under Nazism.* Oxford: Basil Blackwell.

Baranowski, Shelley. 1996. "Conservative Elite Anti-Semitism from the Weimar Republic to the Third Reich." *German Studies Review* 19 (3): 525–537.

Bargh, John A., and Paula Pietromonaco. 1982. "Automatic Information Processing and Social Perception: The Influence of Trait Information Presented Outside of Conscious Awareness on Impression Formation." *Journal of Personality and Social Psychology* 43: 437–449.

Barone, Michael, and Grant Ujifusa. 1989. *The Almanac of American Politics, 1990.* Washington, D.C.: National Journal.

Bartels, Larry M. 1992. "Electioneering in the United States." In David Butler and Austin Ranney, eds., *Electioneering: A Comparative Study of Continuity and Change*, 244–277. Oxford: Clarendon.

——. 1993. "Messages Received." *American Political Science Review* 87 (2): 267–286.

——. 1996. "Uninformed Votes: Information Effects in Presidential Elections." *American Journal of Political Science* 40: 194–230.

——. 1998. "Where the Ducks Are: Voting Power in a Party System." In John Geer, ed., *Politicians and Party Politics.* Baltimore: Johns Hopkins University Press.

Barkan, Elazar. 1992. *The Retreat of Scientific Racism: Changing Concepts of Race in Britain and the United States between the World Wars.* Cambridge: Cambridge University Press.

Baumgartner, Frank R., and Bryan D. Jones. 1993. *Agendas and Instability in American Politics.* Chicago: University of Chicago Press.

Baun, Michael J. 1997. "The SPD and EMU: An End to Germany's All-Party Consensus on European Integration?" *German Politics and Society* 15 (3): 1–23.

Bennett, W. Lance, and John D. Klockner. 1996. "The Psychology of Mass-Mediated Publics." In Ann Crigler, ed., *The Psychology of Political Communication.* Ann Arbor: University of Michigan Press.

Berelson, Bernard R., Paul F. Lazarsfeld, and William N. McPhee. 1954. *Voting.* Chicago: University of Chicago Press.

Bergman, Werner, and Rainer Erb. 1997. *Anti-Semitism in Germany: The Post-Nazi Epoch Since 1945.* Trans. Belinda Cooper and Allison Brown. New Brunswick, N.J.: Transaction Books.

Bering, Dietz. 1998. "Jews and the German Language: The Concept of Kulturnation and Anti-Semitic Propaganda." In Norbert Finzsch and Dietmar Schirmer, eds., *Identity and Intolerance: Nationalism, Racism, and Xenophobia in Germany and the United States.* Cambridge: Cambridge University Press.

Berman, Sheri. 1998. "Path Dependency and Political Action: Reexamining Responses to the Depression." *Comparative Politics* 30: 379–400.

Biocca, Frank. 1991. *Television and Political Advertising.* Vol. 1. Hillsdale, N.J.: Lawrence Erlbaum.

Black, Christine, and Thomas Oliphant. 1989. *All by Myself.* Chester, Conn.: Globe Pequot Press.

Black, Earl. 1976. *Southern Governors and Civil Rights.* Cambridge: Harvard University Press.

——. 1998. "The Newest Southern Politics." *Journal of Politics* 60 (3): 591–612.

Black, Earl, and Merle Black. 1987. *Politics and Society in the South.* Cambridge: Harvard University Press.

Blair, Irene V., and Mahzarin R. Banaji. 1996. "Automatic and Controlled Processes in Stereotype Priming." *Journal of Personality and Social Psychology* 70 (6): 1142–1163.

Blaschke, Jochen. 1998. "New Racism in Germany." In Daniele Joly, ed., *Scapegoats and Social Actors: The Exclusion and Integration of Minorities in Western and Eastern Europe.* New York: Saint Martin's Press.

Bobo, Lawrence. 1988. "Group Conflict, Prejudice, and the Paradox of Contemporary Racial Attitudes." In Phyllis A. Katz and Dalmas A. Taylor, eds., *Eliminating Racism*. New York: Plenum.

Bobo, Lawrence, and James R. Kluegel. 1991. "Modern American Prejudice: Stereotypes, Social Distance, and Perceptions of Discrimination Toward Blacks, Hispanics, and Asians." Paper presented at the annual meeting of the American Sociological Association, Cincinnati.

———. 1993. "Opposition to Race-Targeting: Self-Interest, Stratification Ideology, or Racial Attitudes?" *American Sociological Review* 58: 443–464.

Bobo, Lawrence, James R. Kluegel, and Ryan A. Smith. 1997. "Laissez-Faire Racism: The Crystallization of a Kinder, Gentler, Antiblack Ideology." In Steven A. Tuch and Jack K. Martin, eds., *Racial Attitudes in the 1990s: Continuity and Change*. Westport, Conn.: Praeger.

Braden, Waldo W. 1980. "The Rhetoric of a Closed Society." *Southern Speech Communication Journal* 45: 333–351.

Brady, Henry E., and Paul Sniderman. 1985. "Attitude Attribution: A Group Basis for Political Reasoning." *American Political Science Review* 79: 1061–78.

Branch, Taylor. 1988. *Parting the Waters: America in the King Years, 1954–1963*. New York: Simon and Schuster.

Brewer, Marilyn. 1988. "A Dual Process Model of Impression Formation." In R. Wyer and T. Srull, eds., *Advances in Social Cognition*, vol. 1. Hillsdale, N.J.: Lawrence Erlbaum.

Brundage, William Fitzhugh. 1993. *Lynching in the New South: Georgia and Virginia*. Urbana: University of Illinois Press.

Buchanan, Bruce. 1995. "A Tale of Two Campaigns, or Why '92's Voters Forced a Presidential Campaign Better than '88's and How It Could Happen Again." *Political Psychology* 16 (2): 297–320.

Burns, James MacGregor. 1985. *The Workshop of Democracy*. New York: Alfred A. Knopf.

Burns, Nancy, Kay Lehman Schlozman, and Sidney Verba. 1997. "The Public Consequences of Private Inequality: Family Life and Citizen Participation." *American Political Science Review* 91: 373–389.

Button, James W. 1978. *Black Violence: Political Impact of the 1960s Riots*. Princeton: Princeton University Press.

Campbell, Christopher P. 1995. *Race, Myth, and the News*. Thousand Oaks, Calif.: Sage Publications.

Carmines, Edward G., and R. Huckfeldt. 1992. "Party Politics and the Voting Rights Act." In B. Grofman and C. Davidson, eds., *Controversies in Minority Voting : The Voting Rights Act in Perspective*. Washington, D.C.: Brookings Institution.

Carmines, Edward, and James Stimson. 1989. *Issue Evolution*. Princeton: Princeton University Press.

Carroll, Susan J., and Ronnee Schreiber. 1997. "Media Coverage of Women in the 103rd Congress." In Pippa Norris, ed., *Women, Media and Politics*. New York: Oxford University Press.

Carter, Dan T. 1996. *From George Wallace to Newt Gingrich: Race in the Conservative Counterrevolution, 1963–1994*. Baton Rouge: Louisiana State University Press.

Casdorph, Paul D. 1981. *Republicans, Negroes, and Progressives in the South, 1912–1916.* Tuscaloosa: University of Alabama Press.

Channing, Stephen A. 1970. *Crisis of Fear: Secession in South Carolina.* New York: Simon and Schuster.

Chong, Dennis. 1996. "Creating Common Frames of Reference on Political Issues." In Diana Mutz, Paul Sniderman, and Richard Brody, eds., *Political Persuasion and Attitude Change.* Ann Arbor: University of Michigan Press.

Christie, Clive. 1998. *Race and Nation: A Reader.* London: I. B. Tauris.

Cialdini, Robert B., and Melanie R. Trost. 1998. "Social Influence: Social Norms, Conformity, And Compliance." In Daniel T. Gilbert, Susan T. Fiske, and Gardner Lindzey, eds., *Handbook of Social Psychology*, 4th ed. Boston: McGraw-Hill.

Clark, Janet. 1998. "Women at the National Level: An Update on Roll Call Voting Behavior." In Sue Thomas and Clyde Wilcox, eds., *Women and Elective Office: Past, Present, and Future.* New York: Oxford University Press.

Cohen, Cathy J. 1999. *The Boundaries of Blackness: AIDS and the Breakdown of Black Politics.* Chicago: University of Chicago Press.

Condit, Celeste M., and John L. Lucaites. 1993. *Crafting Equality: America's Anglo-African Word.* Chicago: University of Chicago Press.

Conover, Pamela Johnston. 1984. "The Influence of Group Identifications on Political Perception and Evaluation." *Journal of Politics* 46: 760–785.

———. 1985. "The Impact of Group Economic Interests on Political Evaluations." *American Politics Quarterly* 13: 139–166.

———. 1988. "The Role of Social Groups in Political Thinking." *British Journal of Political Science* 18: 51–76.

Conover, Pamela Johnston, and Stanley Feldman. 1989. "Candidate Perception in an Ambiguous World: Campaigns, Cues, and Inference Processes." *American Journal of Political Science* 33: 912–940.

Conover, Pamela Johnston, and Virginia Sapiro. 1993. "Gender, Feminist Consciousness, and War." *American Journal of Political Science* 37: 1079–1099.

Converse, Philip. 1964. "The Nature of Belief Systems in Mass Publics." In *Ideology and Discontent*, ed. David E. Apter. New York: Free Press.

Converse, Philip, Aage Clausen, and Warren E. Miller. 1965. "Electoral Myth and Reality: The 1964 Election." *American Political Science Review* 59: 321–336.

Cook, Elizabeth Adell, and Clyde Wilcox. 1991. "Feminism and the Gender Gap—A Second Look." *Journal of Politics* 53: 1111–1122.

Cook, Timothy E. 1999. "The Empirical Study of Lesbian, Gay, and Bisexual Politics: Assessing the First Wave of Research." *American Political Science Review* 93 (3): 679–692.

Cornell, Alan. 1997. "The Depiction of Neo-Nazism in Police Shows on German Television." *German Politics and Society* 15 (1): 22–45.

Costain, Anne N., Richard Braunstein, and Heidi Berggren. 1997. "Framing the Women's Movement." In Pippa Norris, ed., *Women, Media, and Politics.* New York: Oxford University Press.

Crigler, Ann, ed. 1996. *The Psychology of Political Communication.* Ann Arbor: University of Michigan Press.

Crosby, Faye, S. Bromley, and Leonard Saxe. 1980. "Recent Unobtrusive Studies of Black and White Discrimination and Prejudice: A Literature Review. *Psychological Bulletin* 87: 546–563.

Curtis, Michael. 1986. "Introduction: Antisemitism—The Baffling Obsession." In Michael Curtis, ed., *Antisemitism in the Contemporary World*. Boulder: Westview Press.

Dalton, Russell J. 1993. *Politics in Germany*. 2nd ed. New York: HarperCollins.

Darcy, R., Susan Welch, and Janet Clark. 1994. *Women, Elections, and Representation*. 2nd ed. Lincoln: University of Nebraska Press.

Darley, John M., and P. H. Gross. 1983. "A Hypothesis-Confirming Bias in Labeling Effects." *Journal of Personality and Social Psychology* 44: 20–33.

Davis, Darren W. 1997. "The Direction of Race of Interviewer Effects among African-Americans: Donning the Black Mask. *American Journal of Political Science*(1): 309–322.

Davis, David Brion. 1988 [1967]. *The Problem of Slavery in Western Culture*. New York: Oxford University Press.

Dawson, Michael C. 1994. *Behind the Mule*. Princeton: Princeton University Press.

Degler, Carl. 1982. *The Other South: Southern Dissenters in the Nineteenth Century*. Boston: Northeastern University.

DeRidder, Richard, Sandra G. L. Schruijer, and Rama C. Tripathi. 1992. "Norm violation as a precipitating factor of negative intergroup relations." In Richard DeRidder and Rama C. Tripathi, eds., *Norm Violation and Intergroup Relations*. Oxford: Oxford University Press.

Devine, Patricia. 1989. "Stereotypes and Prejudice: Their Automatic and Controlled Components. *Journal of Personality and Social Psychology* 56: 5–18.

Devine, Patricia, Margo J. Monteith, Julia R. Zuwerink, and A. Elliot. 1991. "Prejudice with and Without Compunction. *Journal of Personality and Social Psychology* 60: 817–830.

Devitt, James. 1998. "Priming Reporters: A Study on How the Willie Horton Case Altered the Portrayal of Criminals." Ph.D. dissertation, Annenberg School, University of Pennsylvania.

Dittmer, John. 1994. *Local People: The Struggle for Civil Rights in Mississippi*. Urbana: University of Illinois Press.

Dodson, Debra L., and Susan J. Carroll. 1991. *Reshaping the Agenda: Women in State Legislatures*. New Brunswick, N.J.: Center for the American Woman and Politics, Rutgers University.

Dolan, Kathleen, and Lynne E. Ford. 1998. "Are All Women State Legislators Alike?" In Sue Thomas and Clyde Wilcox, eds., *Women and Elective Office: Past, Present, and Future*. New York: Oxford University Press.

Dovidio, John F., and Russell Fazio. 1992. "New Technologies for the Direct and Indirect Assessment of Attitudes." In Judith Tanur, ed., *Questions about Questions: Inquiries into the Cognitive Bases of Surveys*. New York: Russell Sage Foundation.

Dovidio, John F., and Samuel L. Gaertner. 1986. "Prejudice, Discrimination, and Racism: Historical Trends and Contemporary Approaches." In John F. Dovidio and Samuel L. Gaertner, eds., *Prejudice, Discrimination, and Racism*. San Diego: Academic Press.

Drew, Elizabeth. 1989. *Election Journal: Political Events of 1987–1988*. New York: Morrow.

Dunton, Bridget C., and Russell H. Fazio. 1997. "An Individual Difference Measure of Motivation to Control Prejudiced Reactions." *Personality and Social Psychology Bulletin* 23 (3): 316–326.

Edsall, Thomas B., and Mary D. Edsall. 1991. *Chain Reaction: The Impact of Race, Rights, and Taxes on American Politics.* New York: W. W. Norton.

Egerton, John. 1994. *Speak Now against the Day: The Generation before the Civil Rights Movement in the South.* New York: Alfred A. Knopf.

Entman, Robert. 1989. *Democracy without Citizens: Media and the Decay of American Politics.* New York: Oxford University Press.

———. 1992. "Blacks in the News: Television, Modern Racism and Cultural Change." *Journalism Quarterly* 69 (2): 341–361.

Erickson, Paul D. 1985. *Reagan Speaks: The Making of an American Myth.* New York: New York University Press.

Farah, Barbara, and Ethel Klein. 1989. "Public Opinion Trends." In Gerald Pomper, ed., *The Election of 1988: Reports and Interpretations.* Chatham, N.J.: Chatham House.

Farley, Reynolds, and Walter R. Allen. 1987. *The Color Line and the Quality of Life in America.* New York: Russell Sage Foundation.

Fazio, Russell H. 1986. "How Do Attitudes Guide Behavior?" In R. M. Sorrentino and E. T. Higgins, eds., *The Handbook of Motivation and Cognition: Foundation of Social Behavior.* New York: Guilford Press.

———. 1989. "On the Power and Functionality of Attitudes: The Role of Attitude Accessibility." In A. R. Pratkanis, S. J. Breckler, and A. G. Greenwald, eds., *Attitude Structure and Function.* Hillsdale, N.J.: Lawrence Erlbaum.

Fazio, Russell H., and Bridget C. Dunton. 1997. "Categorization by Race: The Impact of Automatic and Controlled Components of Racial Prejudice." *Journal of Experimental and Social Psychology* 33 (5): 451–470.

Fazio, Russell H., Joni R. Jackson, Bridget C. Dunton, and Carol J. Williams. 1995. "Variability in Automatic Activation as an Unobtrusive Measure of Racial Attitudes: A Bona Fide Pipeline?" *Journal of Personality and Social Psychology* 69 (6): 1013–1027.

Fazio Russell H., D. M. Sanbonmatsu, M. C. Powell, and F. R. Kardes. 1986. "On the Automatic Activation of Attitudes." *Journal of Personality and Social Psychology* 50: 229–238.

Fazio, Russell H., and Carol J. Williams. 1986. "Attitude Accessibility as a Moderator of the Attitude-Perception and Attitude-Behavior Relations: An Investigation of the 1984 Presidential Election." *Journal of Personality and Social Psychology* 51: 505–514.

Feagin, Joe R., and Hernan Vera. 1995. *White Racism: The Basics.* New York: Routledge.

Fein, S., A. L. McCloskey, and T. M. Tomlinson. 1997. "Can the Jury Disregard That Information? The Use of Suspicion To Reduce the Prejudicial Effects of Pretrial Publicity and Inadmissible Testimony." *Personality and Social Psychology Bulletin* 23: 1215–1226.

Feldman, Glenn. 1995. *From Demagogue to Dixiecrat: Horace Wilkinson and the Politics of Race.* Lanham, Md.: University Press of America.

Feldman, Stanley, and John Zaller. 1992. "The Political Culture of Ambivalence." *American Journal of Political Science* 36: 268–307.

Finkel, Steven E., Thomas M. Guterbock, and Martin J. Borg. 1991. "Race-of-Interviewer Effects in a Presidential Poll: Virginia 1989." *Public Opinion Quarterly* 55: 313–330.

Fiske, Susan T. 1989. "Examining the Role of Intent, Toward Understanding Its Role in Stereotyping and Prejudice." In James S. Uleman and John A. Bargh, eds., *Unintended Thought: The Limits of Awareness, Intention, and Control.* New York: Guilford.

———. 1993. "Social Cognition and Perception." *Annual Review of Psychology* 44: 155–194.

Fiske, Susan T., and S. E. Taylor. 1991. *Social Cognition.* 2nd ed. New York: McGraw-Hill.

Foner, Eric. 1970. *Free Soil, Free Labor, Free Men: The Ideology of the Republican Party before the Civil War.* New York: Oxford University Press.

———. 1988. *Reconstruction: America's Unfinished Revolution, 1863–1877.* New York: Harper and Row.

———. 1990. *A Short History of Reconstruction, 1863–1877.* New York: Harper and Row.

Franklin, Charles. 1991. "Eschewing Obfuscation? Campaigns and the Perception of U.S. Senate Incumbents." *American Political Science Review* 85: 1193–1214.

Franklin, John Hope. 1971. "Election of 1868." In Arthur M. Schlesinger, ed., *History of American Presidential Elections*, vol. 2. New York: Chelsea House.

———. 1989. *Race and History: Selected Essays 1938–1988.* Baton Rouge: Louisiana State University.

———. 1993 [1976]. *Racial Equality in America.* Columbia: University of Missouri Press.

Franklin, John Hope, and Alfred Moss, Jr. 1988. *From Slavery to Freedom: A History of Negro Americans.* 6th ed. New York: Alfred A. Knopf.

Fredrickson, George. 1971. *The Black Image in the White Mind: The Debate on Afro-American Character and Destiny, 1817–1914.* New York: Harper and Row.

Freehling, William W. 1992. *Prelude to Civil War: The Nullification Controversy in South Carolina, 1816–1836.* 1966. Reprint, New York: Oxford University Press.

Frey, K., and Alice Eagly. 1993. "Vividness Can Undermine the Persuasiveness of Messages." *Journal of Personality and Social Psychology* 65: 32–44.

Frijda, N. H. 1988. "The Laws of Emotion." *American Psychologist* 43: 349–358.

Gaertner, Samuel, and John F. Dovidio. 1986. "The Aversive Form of Racism." In John Dovidio and Samuel Gaertner, eds., *Prejudice, Discrimination, and Racism.* New York: Academic Press.

Gamson, William A., and Kathleen E. Lasch. 1983. "The Political Culture of Social Welfare Policy." In Shimon E. Spiro and Ephraim Yuchtman-Yaar, eds., *Evaluating the Welfare State: Social and Political Perspectives*, 397–415. New York: Harcourt, Brace, Jovanovich.

Gamson, William A., and Andre Modigliani. 1987. "The Changing Culture of Affirmative Action." In Richard Braungart, ed., *Research in Political Sociology*, vol. 3. Greenwich, Conn.: JAI Press.

Gamson, William A., and Gadi Wolfsfeld. 1993. "Movements and Media as Interacting Systems." *Annals of the American Academy of Political and Social Science* 528: 114–125.

Gardner, R. C. 1994. "Stereotypes as Consensual Beliefs." In Mark Zanna and James Olson, eds., *The Psychology of Prejudice.* Hillsdale, N.J.: Lawrence Erlbaum.

Germond, Jack W., and Jules Witcover. 1989. *Whose Broad Stripes and Bright Stars?* New York: Warner Books.

Gerring, John. 1998. *Party Ideologies in America, 1828–1996*. New York: Cambridge University Press.

Giddings, Paula. 1984. *When and Where I Enter*. New York: Bantam Books.

Gilens, Martin. 1988. "Gender and Support for Reagan: A Comprehensive Model of Presidential Approval." *American Journal of Political Science* 32: 19–49.

———. 1995. "Racial Attitudes and Opposition to Welfare." *Journal of Politics* 57: 994–1014.

———. 1996. " 'Race Coding' and White Opposition to Welfare." *American Political Science Review* 90: 593–604.

———. 1997. "Race and Poverty in America: Public Misperceptions and the American News Media." *Public Opinion Quarterly* 60 (4): 515–541.

———. 1999. *Why Americans Hate Welfare*. Chicago: University of Chicago Press.

Giles, Martin, and Kaenan Hertz. 1994. "Racial Threat and Partisan Identification." *American Political Science Review* 88: 317–326.

Gillette, William. 1965. *The Right to Vote: Politics and the Passage of the Fifteenth Amendment*. Baltimore: Johns Hopkins University Press.

———. 1979. *Retreat From Reconstruction, 1869–1879*. Baton Rouge: Louisiana State University Press.

Gilliam, Frank et al. 1995. "Race, Crime and Broadcast News: An Experimental Approach." Paper presented at the Annual Meeting of the Midwest Political Science Association, Chicago.

Glaser, James M. 1996. *Race, Campaign Politics, and the Realignment in the South*. New Haven: Yale University Press.

Glock, Charles Y., and Rodney Stark. 1966. *Christian Beliefs and Anti-Semitism*. New York: Harper and Row.

Goings, Kenneth W. 1990. *The NAACP Comes of Age: The Defeat of Judge John J. Parker*. Bloomington: Indiana University Press.

Goldhagen, Daniel Jonah. 1996. *Hitler's Willing Executioners: Ordinary Germans and the Holocaust*. New York: Knopf.

Goldman, Peter, and Tom Mathews. 1989. *The Quest for the Presidency: The 1988 Campaign*. New York: Simon and Schuster.

Goodwyn, Lawrence. 1978. *The Populist Moment*. New York: Oxford University Press.

Gould, Stephen J. 1981. *The Mismeasure of Man*. New York: W. W. Norton.

Graber, Doris. 1984. *Mass Media and American Politics*, 2nd ed. Washington, D.C.: Congressional Quarterly Press.

———. 1988. *Processing the News: How People Tame the Information Tide*. 2nd ed. New York: Longman.

———. 1993. "Political Communication: Scope, Progress, Promise." In A. Finifter, ed., *Political Science: The State of the Discipline II*. Washington, D.C.: American Political Science Association.

Gray, Jeffrey A. 1982. *The Neuropsychology of Anxiety: Inquire into the Septo-Hippocampal System*. Oxford: Clarendon Press.

Greeley, Andrew M., and Paul B. Sheatsley. 1971. "Attitudes toward Racial Integration." *Scientific American* 225: 13–19.

Greenwald, Anthony G., and Mahzarin R. Banaji. 1995. "Implicit Social Cognition: Attitudes, Self-Esteem, and Stereotypes. *Psychological Review* 102 (1): 4–27.

Grofman, Bernard. 1992. "Expert Witness Testimony and the Evolution of Voting Rights Case Law." In B. Grofman and C. Davidson, eds., *Controversies in Minority Voting : The Voting Rights Act in Perspective*. Washington, D.C.: Brookings Institution.

Grofman, Bernard, and Lisa Handley. 1998a. "Voting Rights in the 1990s: An Overview." In Bernard Grofman, ed., *Race and Redistricting in the 1990s*. New York: Agathon Press.

———. 1998b. "Estimating the Impact of Voting-Rights-Related Districting on Democratic Strength in the U.S. House of Representatives." In Bernard Grofman, ed., *Race and Redistricting in the 1990s*. New York: Agathon Press.

Gross, Larry. 1991. "Gays, Lesbians, and Popular Culture." *Journal of Homosexuality* 21: 19–46.

Grossman, Lawrence. 1992. "Democrats and Blacks in the Gilded Age." In Peter B. Kovler, ed., *Democrats and the American Idea*, 127–145. Washington, D.C.: Center for National Policy Press.

Grunenberg, Antonia. 1997. "Antitotalitarianism Versus Antifascism—Two Legacies of the Past in Germany." *German Politics and Society* 15 (2): 76–90.

Haider-Markel, Donald P., and Kenneth J. Meier. 1996. "The Politics of Gay and Lesbian Rights: Expanding the Scope of the Conflict." *Journal of Politics* 58 (2): 332–349.

Hagen, Michael. 1995. "References to Racial Issues." *Political Behavior* 17: 49–88.

Hamilton, David L., and T. K. Torlier. 1986. "Stereotypes and Stereotyping: An Overview of the Cognitive Approach." In J. Dovidio and S. Gaertner, eds., *Prejudice, Discrimination and Racism*. San Diego: Academic Press.

Hanushek, Eric A., and John E. Jackson. 1977. *Statistical Methods for Social Scientists*. Orlando: Academic Press.

Harlan, Louis R. 1958. *Separate and Unequal: Public School Campaigns and Racism in the Southern Seaboard States*. Chapel Hill: University of North Carolina Press.

Harvey, Anna L. 1998. *Votes without Leverage*. Cambridge: Cambridge University Press.

Heard, Alexander. 1952. *A Two-Party South?* Chapel Hill: University of North Carolina Press.

Herbst, Susan. 1993. *Numbered Voices: How Opinion Polling Has Shaped American Politics*. Chicago: University of Chicago Press.

Hershey, Marjorie. 1989. "The Campaign and the Media." In Gerald Pomper, ed., *The Election of 1988: Reports and Interpretations*. Chatham, N.J.: Chatham House.

Higgins, E. T., John A. Bargh, and W. Lombardi. 1985. "The Nature of Priming Effects on Categorization: Learning, Memory, and Cognition." *Journal of Experimental Psychology* 11: 59–69.

Higgins, E. T., and G. King. 1981. "Accessibility of Social Constructs." In N. Cantor and J. Kihlstrom, eds., *Personality, Cognition and Social Interaction*. Hillsdale, N.J.: Lawrence Erlbaum.

Higgins, E. T., W. S. Rholes, and C. R. Jones. 1977. "Category accessibility and impression formation." *Journal of Experimental Social Psychology* 13: 131–154.

Hill, Kevin A. 1995. "Does the Creation of Majority Black Districts Aid Republicans? An Analysis of the 1992 Congressional Elections in Eight Southern States." *Journal of Politics* 57 (2): 384–401.

Himelstein, Jerry. 1983. "Rhetorical Continuities in the Politics of Race: The Closed Society Revisited." *Southern Speech Communication Journal* 48: 153–166.

Hirschfeld, Lawrence. 1993. "The Child's Representation of Human Groups." In D. Media, ed., *The Psychology of Learning and Motivation: Advances in Research and Theory*, vol. 3. San Diego: Academic Press.

Hirschman, Albert O. 1991. *The Rhetoric of Reaction: Perversity, Futility, Jeopardy*. Cambridge: Harvard University Press.

Hochschild, Arlie Russell. 1989. *The Second Shift : Working Parents and the Revolution at Home*. New York: Viking.

Hochschild, Jennifer. 1984. *The New American Dilemma*. New Haven: Yale University Press.

———. 1995. *Facing Up to the American Dream: Race, Class, and the Soul of the Nation*. Princeton: Princeton University Press.

———. 1999. "Affirmative Action as Culture War." In Michele Lamont, ed., *The Cultural Territories of Race: Black and white Boundaries*. Chicago: University of Chicago Press.

Hofstadter, Richard. 1973. *The American Political Tradition*. New York: Vintage.

Holly, Werner. 1989. "Credibility and Political Language." In Ruth Wodak, ed., *Language, Power and Ideology: Studies in Political Discourse*. Amsterdam: John Benjamins Publishing Company.

Holt, Thomas. 1979. *Black over White: Negro Political Leadership in South Carolina during Reconstruction*. Urbana: University of Illinois Press.

Holzer, Harold, ed.. 1993. *The Lincoln-Douglas Debates*. New York: Harper-Collins.

Huckfeldt, Robert, and Carol Kohfeld. 1989. *Race and the Decline of Class in American Politics*. Urbana: University of Illinois Press.

Huddy, Leonie. 1997. "Feminists and Feminism in the News." In Pippa Norris, ed., *Women, Media, and Politics*. New York: Oxford University Press.

Hurwitz, Jon, and Mark Peffley. 1997. "Public Perceptions of Race and Crime: The Role of Racial Stereotypes." *American Journal of Political Science* 41 (2): 375–401.

Iyengar, Shanto, and Donald Kinder. 1987. *News That Matters*. Chicago: University of Chicago Press.

Iyengar, Shanto, Nicholas A. Valentino, Stephone Ansolabehere, and Adam F. Simon. 1997. "Running As a Woman: Gender Stereotyping in Women's Campaigns." In Pippa Norris, ed., *Women, Media, and Politics*. New York: Oxford University Press.

Jackman, Mary. 1994. *The Velvet Glove: Paternalism and Conflict in Gender, Class and Race Relations*. Berkeley: University of California Press.

Jackman, Mary, and M. J. Muha. 1984. "Education and Inter-Group Attitudes: Moral Enlightenment, Superficial Democratic Commitment, or Ideological Refinement." *American Sociological Review* 49: 751–769.

Jackson, Robert Max. 1998. *Destined for Equality: The Inevitable Rise of Women's Status*. Cambridge: Harvard University Press.

Jamieson, Kathleen Hall. 1989. "Context and Meaning in Campaign Advertising." *American Behavioral Scientist* 32 (4): 415–424.

———. 1992. *Dirty Politics*. Oxford: Oxford University Press.

Jennings, M. Kent. 1990. "Women in Party Politics." In Louise A. Tilly and Patricia Gurin, eds., *Women, Politics, and Change*. New York: Russell Sage Foundation.

Jones, Jacqueline. 1985. *Labor of Love, Labor of Sorrow*. New York: Basic Books.

Joppke, Christian. 1999. "How Immigration Is Changing Citizenship: A Comparative View." *Ethnic and Racial Studies* 22 (4): 629–652.

Jordan, Winthrop D. 1968. *White over Black: American Attitudes toward the Negro, 1550–1812.* Chapel Hill: University of North Carolina Press.

———. 1974. *White Man's Burden: Historical Origins of Racism in the United States.* New York: Oxford University Press.

Just, Marion R., Ann N. Crigler, Dean E. Alger, Timothy E. Cook, Montague Kern, and Darrell M. West. 1996. *Crosstalk: Citizens, Candidates, and the Media in a Presidential Campaign.* Chicago: University of Chicago Press.

Kahn, Kim Fridkin. 1992. "Does Being Male Help? An Investigation of the Effects of Candidate Gender and Campaign Coverage on Evaluations of U.S. Senate Candidates." *Journal of Politics* 54 (2): 497–517.

———. 1994a. "The Distorted Mirror: Press Coverage of Women Candidates for Statewide Office." *Journal of Politics* 56 (1): 154–173.

———. 1994b. "Does Gender Make a Difference? An Experimental Examination of Sex Stereotypes and Press Patterns in Statewide Campaigns." *American Journal of Political Science* 38 (1): 162–195.

Karapin, Roger. 1998. "Explaining Far-Right Electoral Successes in Germany: The Politicization of Immigration-Related Issues." *German Politics and society* 16 (3): 24–61.

Kastner, Elizabeth, and Laurent Jedermann. 1997. "Hitler's Willing Bankers." *German Politics and Society* 15 (2): 96–112.

Katz, Daniel, and Kenneth W. Braly. 1933. "Racial Stereotypes of 100 College Students." *Journal of Abnormal and Social Psychology* 28: 280–290.

Katz, Irwin, and R. Glen Hass. 1988. "Racial Ambivalence and American Value Conflict: Correlational and Priming Studies of Dual Cognitive Structures." *Journal of Personality and Social Psychology* 55: 893–905.

Katz, Irwin, Joyce Wackenhut, and R. Glen Hass. 1986. "Racial Ambivalence, Value Duality, and Behavior." In J. Dovidio and S. Gaertner, *Prejudice, Discrimination and Racism.* San Diego: Academic Press.

Kelley, Stanley. 1983. *Interpreting Elections.* Princeton: Princeton University Press.

Kenez, Peter. 1996. "Russian Anti-Semitic Thought Today." *German Politics and Society* 14 (1): 140–151.

Kern, Montague, and Marion Just. 1995. "The Focus Group Method, Political Advertising, Campaign News, and the Construction of Candidate Images." *Political Communication* 12: 127–145.

Kessel, John H. 1968. *The Goldwater Coalition: Republican Strategies in 1964.* Indianapolis: Bobbs-Merrill.

Key, V. O. 1949. *Southern Politics in State and Nation.* Knoxville: University of Tennessee Press.

Kinder, Donald R. 1998. "Communication and Opinion." *Annual Review of Political Science* 1: 167–197.

Kinder, Donald R., and Tali Mendelberg. 1995. "Cracks in American Apartheid." *Journal of Politic* 57: 402–424.

Kinder, Donald R., and Tali Mendelberg. 2000. "Individualism Reconsidered: Principles and Prejudice in Contemporary American Public Opinion." In David O. Sears, Jim Sidanius and Lawrence Bobo, eds., *Racialized Politics: The Debate about Racism in America.* Chicago: University of Chicago Press.

Kinder, Donald R., Tali Mendelberg, Michael Dawson, Lynn Sanders, Steven Rosenstone, Jocelyn Sargent, and Cathy Cohen. 1989. "Benign Neglect and Racial Codewords in the 1988 Presidential Campaign." Paper presented at the annual meeting of the American Political Science Association, Atlanta.

Kinder, Donald R., and Thomas R. Palfrey. 1993. *On Behalf of an Experimental Political Science.* Ann Arbor: University of Michigan Press.

Kinder, Donald R. and Lynn Sanders. 1996. *Divided by Color.* Chicago: University of Chicago Press.

Kinder, Donald R., and David O. Sears. 1981. "Prejudice and Politics: Symbolic Racism versus Racial Threats to the Good Life." *Journal of Personality and Social Psychology* 40: 414–431.

Kleppner, Paul. 1985. *Chicago Divided: The Making of a Black Mayor.* DeKalb: Northern Illinois University Press.

Klinker, Philip A., with Rogers Smith. 1999. *The Unsteady March: The Rise and Decline of Racial Equality in America.* Chicago: University of Chicago Press.

Kluegel, James R., and Eliot R. Smith. 1986. *Beliefs about Inequality.* New York: A. de Gruyter.

Kolchin, Peter. 1993. *American Slavery: 1619–1877.* New York: Hill and Wang.

Koppelman, Andrew. 1996. *Antidiscrimination Law and Social Equality.* New Haven: Yale University Press.

Kousser, J. Morgan. 1991. "How to Determine Intent: Lessons from L.A." *Journal of Law and Politics* 7: 591–732.

———. 1992. "The Voting Rights Act and the Two Reconstructions." In B. Grofman and C. Davidson, eds., *Controversies in Minority Voting: The Voting Rights Act in Perspective.* Washington, D.C.: Brookings Institution.

Krosnick, Jon A., and Laura Brannon. 1993. "The Impact of the Gulf War on the Ingredients of Presidential Evaluations: Multidimensional Effects of Political Involvement." *American Political Science Review* 87: 963–978.

Krosnick, Jon A., and Donald R. Kinder. 1990. "Altering the Foundations of Support for the President through Priming." *American Political Science Review* 84: 497–512.

Krugman, H. 1986. "Low Recall and High Recognition of Advertising." *Journal of Advertising Research* (Feb./March): 79–86.

Krysan, Maria. 1998. "Privacy and the Expression of White Racial Attitudes." *Public Opinion Quarterly* 62: 506–544.

Kuechler, Manfred. 1996. "Deutschland den Deutschen: Migration and Naturalization in the 1994 Campaign and Beyond." In Russell J. Dalton, ed., *Germans Divided: The 1994 Bundestag Elections and the Evolution of the German Party System.* Oxford: Berg.

Kuklinski, James H., Michael D. Cobb, and Martin Gilens. 1997. "Racial Attitudes and the 'New South.'" *Journal of Politics* 59 (2): 323–349.

Kuklinski, James H., Robert C. Luskin, and John Bolland. 1991. "Where Is the Schema? Going beyond the S Word in Political Psychology." *American Political Science Review* 85: 1341–1356.

Kuklinski, James H., Ellen Riggle, Victor Ottati, Norbert Schwarz, and Robert S. Wyer, Jr. 1991. "The Cognitive and Affective Bases of Political Tolerance Judgments." *American Journal of Political Science* 35: 1–27.

Kurthen, Hermann. 1995. "Germany at the Crossroads: National Identity and the Challenges of Immigration." *International Migration Review,* Dec. 22, p. 914. New York: Center for Migration Studies of New York.

———. 1997. "Antisemitism and Xenophobia in United Germany: How the Burden of the Past Affects the Present." In Hermann Kurthen, Werner Bergmann, and Rainer Erb, eds., *Antisemitism and Xenophobia in Germany after Unification*. New York: Oxford University Press.

Kurthen, Hermann, Werner Bergmann, and Rainer Erb. 1997. "Introduction: Postunification Challenges to German Democracy." In Hermann Kurthen, Werner Bergmann, and Rainer Erb, eds., *Antisemitism and Xenophobia in Germany after Unification*. New York: Oxford University Press.

Lamont, Michele. 2000. *The Dignity of Working Men: Morality and the Boundaries of Race, Class, and Immigration*. Cambridge: Harvard University Press. New York: Russell Sage Foundation.

Lanzetta, J., D. Sullivan, R. Masters, and G. McHugo. 1985. "Emotional and Cognitive Responses to Televised Images of Political Leaders." In S. Kraus and R. Perloff, eds., *Mass Media and Political Thought*. Beverly Hills: Sage.

Lau, Richard. 1989. "Political Schemata, Candidate Evaluations, and Voting Behavior." In Richard R. Lau and David O. Sears, eds., *Political Cognition: The Nineteenth Annual Carnegie Symposium on Cognition*. Hillsdale, N.J.: Lawrence Erlbaum.

Lavine, Howard, John L. Sullivan, Eugene Borgida, and Cynthia J. Thomsen. 1996. "The Relationship of National and Personal Issue Salience to Attitutde Accessibility on Foreign and Domestic Policy Issues." *Political Psychology* 17 (2): 293–316.

Lewis, David Levering. 1993. *W. E. B. Du Bois: Biography of a Race*. New York: Henry Holt.

Litwak, Leon F. 1961. *North of Slavery*. Chicago: University of Chicago Press.

Lodge, Milton, Kathleen McGraw, and Patrick Stroh. 1989. "An Impression-Driven Model of Candidate Evaluation." *American Political Science Review* 82: 399–420.

Lublin, David. 1995. "Race, Representation, and Redistricting." In Paul Peterson, ed., *Classifying by Race*. Princeton: Princeton University Press.

Luebke, Paul. 1990. *Tar Heel Politics: Myths and Realities*. Chapel Hill: University of North Carolina Press.

Lynn, M., S. Shavitt, and Thomas Ostrom. 1985. "Effects of Pictures on the Organization and Recall of Social Information." *Journal of Personality and Social Psychology* 49: 1160–1168.

MacDougall, Malcolm D. 1977. *We Almost Made It*. New York: Crown.

MacKinnon, Catharine A. 1987. *Feminism Unmodified: Discourses on Life and Law*. Cambridge: Harvard University Press.

Macrae, C. Neil, A. B. Milne, and Galen V. Bodenhausen. 1994. "Stereotypes as Energy-Saving Devices: A Peek Inside the Cognitive Toolbox." *Journal of Personality and Social Psychology* 66: 37–47.

Mahler, Raphael. 1942. "Antisemitism in Poland." In Koppel S. Pinson, ed., *Essays on Antisemitism*. New York: Conference on Jewish Relations.

Malone, Christopher. 1999. "Between Freedom and Bondage: Racial Voting Restrictions in the Antebellum North, 1787–1865." Paper presented at the annual meeting of the American Political Science Association, Atlanta.

Mantell, Martin E. 1973. *Johnson, Grant, and the Politics of Reconstruction*. New York: Columbia University Press.

Marcus, George E., John L. Sullivan, Elizabeth Theiss-Morse, and Sandra L. Wood. 1995. *With Malice Toward Some: How People Make Civil Liberties Judgments*. Cambridge: Cambridge University Press.

Markovits, Andrei S., and Simon Reich. 1997. *The German Predicament: Memory and Power in the New Europe*. Ithaca: Cornell University Press.

Massey, Douglas, and Nancy A. Denton. 1993. *American Apartheid: Segregation and the Making of the Underclass*. Cambridge: Harvard University Press.

McAdam, Doug. 1982. *Political Process and the Development of Black Insurgency, 1930–1970*. Chicago: University of Chicago Press.

McCauley, C., C. Stitt, and M. Segal. 1980. "Stereotyping: From Prejudice to Prediction." *Psychological Bulletin* 87: 195–208.

McClosky, Herbert. 1964. "Consensus and Ideology in American Politics." *American Political Science Review* 58: 361–382.

McConahay, John B., Betty B. Hardee, and Valerie Batts. 1981. "Has Racism Declined? It Depends upon Who's Asking and What Is Asked." *Journal of Conflict Resolution* 25: 563–569.

McConahay, John B. 1986. "Modern Racism, Ambivalence, and the Modern Racism Scale." In J. Dovidio and S. Gaertner, eds. *Prejudice, Discrimination and Racism*. New York: Academic Press.

McCormick, J., and C. Jones. 1993. "The Conceptualization of Deracialization: Thinking Through the Dilemma." In G. Persons, ed., *Dilemmas of Black Politics*. New York: HarperCollins.

McGinniss, Joe. 1969. *The Selling of the President, 1968*. New York: Simon and Schuster.

McGlen, Nancy E. and Karen O'Connor. 1998. *Women, Politics, and American Society*. Englewood Cliffs, N.J.: Prentice-Hall.

McGraw, Kathleen. 1991. "Managing blame: An Experimental Test of the Effects of Political Accounts." *American Political Science Review* 85: 1133–1158.

McMillen, Neil R. 1994. *The Citizens' Council: Organized Resistance to the Second Reconstruction, 1954–1964*. Urbana: University of Illinois Press.

McQuail, Denis. 1992. *Mass Communication Theory: An Introduction*. Beverly Hills: Sage.

McPherson, James. 1988. *Battle Cry of Freedom: The Civil War Era*. New York: Oxford University Press.

———. 1992 [1964]. *The Struggle for Equality*. Princeton: Princeton University Press.

Meier, Andrew. 1999. "Moscow Dispatch: Hateful." *New Republic* 220 (13): 15.

Meier, August, and Elliott Rudwick. 1994. *From Plantation to Ghetto*. 3rd ed. New York: Hill and Wang.

Mendelberg, Tali. 1994. "The Politics of Racial Ambiguity: Origin and Consequences of Implicitly Racial Appeals." Ph.D. diss., University of Michigan.

———. 1997. "Executing Hortons: Racial Crime in the 1988 Presidential Campaign." *Public Opinion Quarterly* 61 (Spring): 134–157.

Metz, David, and Katherine Tate. 1995. "The Color of Urban Campaigns." In P. Peterson, ed., *Classifying by Race*. Princeton: Princeton University Press.

Minkenberg, Michael. 1998. "The Impact of the New Radical Right on the Political Process in France and Germany." *German Politics and Society* 16 (3): 1–23.

Mitten, Richard. 1992. *The Politics of Antisemitic Prejudice: The Waldheim Phenomenon in Austria*. Boulder: Westview Press.

Monroe, Kristen R. 1995. "Psychology and Rational Actor Theory. *Political Psychology* 16 (1): 1–23.

Monteith, Margo J. 1993. "Self-Regulation of Prejudiced Responses: Implications for Progress in Prejudice-Reduction Efforts." *Journal of Personality and Social Psychology* 65: 469–485.

Monteith, Margo J., Patricia G. Devine, and Julia R. Zuwerink. 1993. "Self-Directed versus Other-Directed Affect as a Consequence of Prejudice-Related Discrepancies." *Journal of Personality and Social Psychology* 64: 198–210.

Morris, Aldon. 1984. *Origins of the Civil Rights Movement.* New York: Free Press.

Moskowitz, Gordon B. 1993. "Person Organization with a Memory Set: Are Spontaneous Trait Inferences Personality Characterizations or Behavior Labels?" *European Journal of Personality* 7 (3): 195–208.

Moskowitz, Gordon B., and Robert J. Roman. 1992. "Spontaneous Trait Inferences as Self-Generated Primes: Implications for Conscious Social Judgment." *Journal of Personality and Social Psychology* 62 (5): 728–738.

Mutz, Diana C. 1998. *Impersonal Influence: How Perceptions of Mass Collectives Affect Political Attitudes.* New York: Cambridge University Press.

Myrdal, Gunnar. 1962 [1944]. *An American Dilemma: The Negro Problem and Modern Democracy,* vol. 1. New York: Random House.

Naimark, Norman M. 1996. "Post-Nazi Germany and Post-Soviet Russia." *German Politics and Society* 14 (1): 129–139.

Nelson, Thomas E. 1992. "Political Harmonics: Issue Framing and Attitude Expression." Unpublished manuscript, University of Michigan.

Nelson, Thomas E., and Donald R. Kinder. 1996. "Issue Frames and Group Centrism in American Public Opinion." *Journal of Politics* 58 (4): 1055–1078.

Nelson, Thomas, Rosalee A. Clawson, and Zoe M. Oxley. 1997. "Media Framing of a Civil Liberties Conflict and Its Effect on Tolerance." *American Political Science Review* 91 (3): 567–584.

Neuman, W. Russell, Marion Just, and Ann N. Crigler. 1992. *Common Knowledge: News and the Construction of Political Meaning.* Chicago: University of Chicago Press.

Nieman, Donald G. 1991. *Promises to Keep: African-Americans and the Constitutional Order, 1776 to the Present.* Oxford: Oxford University Press.

Nisbett, Richard, and Lee Ross. 1981. *Human Inference: Strategies and Shortcomings of Social Judgments.* Englewood Cliffs, N.J.: Prentice-Hall.

Noelle-Neumann, Elisabeth. 1974. "The Spiral of Silence: A Theory of Public Opinion." *Journal of Communication* 24: 43–51.

Norris, Pippa. 1997. "Introduction: Women, Media, and Politics." In Pippa Norris, ed., *Women, Media, and Politics.* New York: Oxford University Press.

Olick, Jeffrey K., and Daniel Levy. 1997. "Collective Memory and Cultural Constraint: Holocaust Myth and Rationality in German Politics." *American Sociological Review* 62 (6): 921–936.

O'Reilly, Kenneth. 1995. *Nixon's Piano: Presidents and Racial Politics from Washington to Clinton.* New York: Free Press.

Ortony, Andrew, Gerald L. Clore, and Allan Collins. 1988. *The Cognitive Structure of Emotion.* Cambridge: Cambridge University Press.

Page, Benjamin. 1978. *Choices and Echoes in Presidential Elections: Rational Man and Electoral Democracy.* Chicago: University of Chicago Press.

Page, Benjamin, and Richard Brody. 1972. "Policy Voting and the Electoral Process: The Vietnam War Issue." *American Political Science Review* 66: 389–400.

Page, Benjamin, and C. C. Jones. 1979. "Reciprocal Effects of Policy Preferences, Party Loyalties, and the Vote." *American Political Science Review* 73: 1071–1089.

Page, Benjamin, and Robert Shapiro. 1992. *The Rational Public.* Chicago: University of Chicago Press.

Paivio, A. 1991. "Dual Coding Theory: Retrospect and Current Status." *Canadian Journal of Psychology* 45: 225.

Paletz, David L., and Robert M. Entman. 1981. *Media Power Politics.* New York: Free Press.

Parmet, Herbert S. 1997. *George Bush: The Life of a Lone Star Yankee.* New York: Scribner.

Peffley, Mark, Jon Hurwitz, and Paul M. Sniderman. 1997. "Racial Stereotypes and Whites' Political Views of Blacks in the Context of Welfare and Crime." *American Journal of Political Science* 41 (1): 30–60.

Peffley, Mark, Todd Shields, and Bruce Williams. 1996. "The Intersection of Race and Crime in Television News Stories: An Experimental Study." *Political Communication* 13: 309–327.

Perry, H. L. 1991. "Deracialization as an Analytical Construct in American Urban Politics." *Urban Affairs Quarterly* 27: 181–191.

Persons, Georgia, ed. 1993. *Dilemmas of Black Politics.* New York: HarperCollins.

Petrocik, John R. 1981. *Party Coalitions: Realignment and the Decline of the New Deal Party System.* Chicago: University of Chicago Press.

Petrocik, John R., and Scott W. Desposato. 1998. "The Partisan Consequences of Majority-Minority Redistricting in the South, 1992 and 1994." *Journal of Politics* 60 (3): 613–633.

Pettigrew, T. F. 1981. "Extending the Stereotype Concept." In D. L. Hamilton, ed., *Cognitive Processes in Stereotyping and Inter-Group Behavior.* Hillsdale, N.J.: Lawrence Erlbaum.

Pettigrew, Thomas F., and Denise Allston. 1988. *Tom Bradley's Campaigns for Governor: The Dilemma of Race and Political Strategies.* Washington, D.C.: Joint Center for Political Studies.

Petty, Richard E., and John T. Cacioppo. 1981. *Attitudes and Persuasion: Classic and Contemporary Approaches.* Dubuque: William Brown Company.

———. 1986. *Communication and Persuasion.* New York: Springer-Verlag.

Pinderhughes, Diane. 1987. *Race and Ethnicity in Chicago Politics.* Urbana: University of Illinois Press.

Plant, E. Ashby, and Patricia G. Devine. 1998. "Internal and External Motivation to Respond without Prejudice." *Journal of Personality and Social Psychology* 75 (3): 811–832.

Poliakov, Leon. 1985. *Suicidal Europe, 1870–1933.* Vol. 4, *The History of Anti-Semitism.* Trans. George Klin. Oxford: Oxford University Press.

Popkin, Samuel. 1991. *The Reasoning Voter.* Chicago: University of Chicago Press.

Powell, Lawrence N. 1980. *New Masters: Northern Planters during the Civil War and Reconstruction.* New Haven: Yale University Press.

Prasad, Monica. 1999. "Ideological Inconsistency and Logical Bridges: The Role of Race in the Evolution of the American Party System." Paper presented at the annual meeting of the American Political Science Association, Atlanta.

Prothro, James W., and Charles M. Grigg. 1960. "Fundamental Principles of Democracy: Bases of Agreement and Disagreement." *Journal of Politics* 22: 276–294.

Prowe, Diethelm. 1997. "National Identity and Racial Nationalism in the New Germany: Nazism Versus the Contemporary Radical Right." *German Politics and Society* 15 (1): 1–21.

Pulzer, Peter. 1988. *The Rise of Political Anti-Semitism in Germany and Austria.* Rev. ed. London: Peter Halban.

Rable, George C. 1984. *But There Was No Peace: The Role of Violence in the Politics of Reconstruction.* Athens: University of Georgia Press.

Rapoport, Ronald B., Walter J. Stone, and Alan I. Abramowitz. 1990. "Sex and the Caucus Participant: The Gender Gap and Presidential Nominations." *American Journal of Political Science* 34 (3): 725–740.

Reeves, Keith. 1997. *Voting Hopes or Fears?* New York: Oxford University Press.

Rhode, Deborah L. 1989. *Justice and Gender: Sex Discrimination and the Law.* Cambridge: Harvard University Press.

Riddleberger, Patrick W. 1960. "The Radicals' Abandonment of the Negro during Reconstruction." *Journal of Negro History* 45: 88–102.

Riggle, Ellen D., Victor C. Ottati, Robert S. Wyer, James H. Kuklinski, and Norbert Schwarz. 1992. "Bases of Political Judgments: The Role of Stereotypic and Nonstereotypic Information." *Political Behavior* 14: 67–87.

Rogers, Reuel R. 2000. "Between Race and Ethnicity: Afro-Caribbean Immigrants, African-Americans, and the Politics of Incorporation." Ph.D. dissertation, Princeton University.

Romer, Daniel, Robert Hornik, Bonita Stanton, Maureen Black, Xiaoming Li, Izabel Ricardo, and Susan Feigelman. 1997. " 'Talking' Computers: A Reliable and Private Method to Conduct Interviews on Sensitive Topics with Children." *Journal of Sex Research* 34 (1): 3–9.

Romer, Daniel, Kathleen H. Jamieson, and Nicole J. de Coteau. 1998. "The Treatment of Persons of Color in Local Television News: Ethnic Blame Discourse or Realistic Group Conflict?" *Communication Research* 25 (3): 286–305.

Rosenberg, Gerald N. 1991. *The Hollow Hope: Can Courts Bring About Social Change?* Chicago: University of Chicago Press.

Rosenberg, S., S. Kahn, and T. Tran. 1991. "Creating a Political Image: Shaping Appearance and Manipulating the Vote." *Political Behavior* 13: 345–367.

Rosenstone, Steven J., Roy L. Behr, and Edward H. Lazarus. 1984. *Third Parties in America: Citizen Response to Major Party Failure.* Princeton: Princeton University Press.

Ruchames, Louis 1969. *Racial Thought in America: From the Puritans to Abraham Lincoln.* Amherst: University of Massachusetts Press.

Runkel, David R., ed. 1989. *Campaign for President: The Managers Look at '88.* Dover, Mass.: Auburn House.

Sanders, Lynn. 1996. "Integrated Interviews, Alternative Models: How Differently Whites Think When the Discuss Politics with Blacks." Paper presented at the American Politics Workshop, Princeton University, November.

Sanders, Mitch. 1994. "Beneath Stormy Waters: The Evolution of Individual Decision Making in the 1984 and 1988 Presidential Election." Paper prepared for the Conference on the Impact of the Presidential Campaign, Philadelphia, November.

Schuman, Howard, Charlotte Steeh, and Lawrence Bobo. 1985. *Racial Attitudes in America: Trends and Interpretations.* Cambridge: Harvard University Press.

Schuman, Howard, Charlotte Steeh, Lawrence Bobo, and Maria Krysan. 1997. *Racial Attitudes in America: Trends and Interpretation.* Rev. ed. Cambridge: Harvard University Press.

Sears, David O. 1986. "College Sophomores in the Laboratory: Influence of a Narrow Data Base on Social Psychology's View of Human Natures." *Journal of Personality and Social Psychology* 51: 515–530.

———. 1987. "Political Psychology." *Annual Review of Psychology* 38: 229–255.

———. 1988. "Symbolic Racism." In Phyllis Katz and Dalmas Taylor, eds., *Eliminating Racism.* New York: Plenum.

Sears, David O., P. J. Henry, and Rick Kosterman. 2000. "Egalitarian Values and Contemporary Racial Politics." In David O. Sears, Jim Sidanius, and Lawrence Bobo, eds., *Racialized Politics: The Debate about Racism in America.* Chicago: University of Chicago Press.

Sears, David O., and Leonie Huddy. 1990. "On the Origins of Political Disunity Among Women." In Louise A. Tilly and Patricia Gurin, eds., *Women, Politics, and Change.* New York: Russell Sage Foundation.

Sears, David O., Colette Van Laar, Mary Carrillo, and Rick Kosterman. 1997. "Is It Really Racism?" *Public Opinion Quarterly* 61 (1): 16–53.

Shapiro, Robert Y., and Harpreet Mahajan. 1986. "Gender Differences in Policy Preferences: A Summary of Trends from the 1960s to the 1980s." *Public Opinion Quarterly* 50: 42–61.

Shepsle, Kenneth A. 1972. "The Strategy of Ambiguity: Uncertainty and Electoral Competition." *American Political Science Review* 66: 555–568.

Sidanius, Jim, E. Devereux, and F. Pratto. 1992. "A Comparison of Symbolic Racism Theory and Social Dominance Theory as Explanations for Racial Policy Attitudes." *Journal of Social Psychology* 132: 377–395.

Sidanius, Jim, Pam Singh, John J. Hetts, and Chris Federico. 2000. "It's Not Affirmative Action, It's the Blacks." In David O. Sears, Jim Sidanius, and Lawrence Bobo, eds., *Racialized Politics: The Debate about Racism in America.* Chicago: University of Chicago Press.

Sigall, H., and R. Page. 1971. "Current Stereotypes: A Little Fading, A Little Faking." *Journal of Personality and Social Psychology* 18: 247–255.

Sigelman, Lee, and Alan Rosenblatt. 1996. "Methodological Considerations in the Analysis of Presidential Persuasion." In Diana Mutz, Paul Sniderman, and Richard Brody, eds., *Political Persuasion and Attitude Change.* Ann Arbor: University of Michigan Press.

Sigelman, Lee, Carol Sigelman, and Barbara Walkosz. 1992. "The Public and the Paradox of Leadership: An Experimental Analysis." *American Journal of Political Science* 36: 366–385.

Sigelman, Lee, and Susan Welch. 1991. *Black Americans' Views of Racial Inequality: The Dream Deferred.* Cambridge: Cambridge University Press.

Simon, Herbert. 1985. "Human Nature in Politics: The Dialogue of Psychology with Political Science." *American Political Science Review* 79 :293–304.

Simon, Rita J., and Jean Landis. 1991. *The Crimes Women Commit, The Punishment They Receive*. Lexington, Mass.: Lexington Books.

Simon, Roger. 1990. *Road Show*. New York: Farrar, Straus and Giroux.

Sitkoff, Harvard. 1971. "Harry Truman and the Election of 1948: The Coming of Age of Civil Rights in American Politics." *Journal of Southern History* 37: 597–616.

———. 1978. *A New Deal for Blacks: The Emergence of Civil Rights as a National Issue*. New York: Oxford University Press.

———. 1993. *The Struggle for Black Equality, 1954–1992*. New York: Hill and Wang.

Slass, Lorrie Beth. 1990. "A Changing Symbol: Willie Horton and the 1988 Presidential Campaign." M.A. thesis, University of Pennsylvania.

Smith, E. R. 1990. "Content and Process Specificity in the Effects of Prior Experiences." In R. Wyer and T. Srull, eds., *Advances in Social Cognition*, vol. 2. Hillsdale, N.J.: Lawrence Erlbaum.

Smith, Rogers. 1997. *Civic Ideals: Conflicting visions of Citizenship in U.S. History*. New Haven: Yale University Press.

Smith, Tom W. 1984. "The Polls: Gender and Attitudes toward Violence." *Public Opinion Quarterly* 48: 384–396.

———. 1990. "Ethnic Images." University of Chicago: National Opinion Research Center.

Smith, Tom W., and G. N. Dempsey. 1983. "The Polls: Ethnic Social Distance and Prejudice." *Public Opinion Quarterly* 47: 584–600.

Sniderman, Paul M., Richard Brody, and Phillip Tetlock. 1991. *Reasoning and Choice: Explorations in Political Psychology*. Cambridge: Cambridge University Press.

Sniderman, Paul M., and Edward Carmines. 1997. *Reaching Beyond Race*. Cambridge: Harvard University Press.

Sniderman, Paul M., Gretchen C. Crosby, and William G. Howell. 2000. "The Politics of Race." In David O. Sears, Jim Sidanius, and Lawrence Bobo, eds., *Racialized Politics: The Debate about Racism in America*. Chicago: University of Chicago Press.

Sniderman, Paul M., and Thomas Piazza. 1993. *The Scar of Race*. Cambridge: Harvard University Press.

Steiman, Lionel B. 1998. *Paths to Genocide*. London: Macmillan.

Stern, Frank. 1992. *The Whitewashing of the Yellow Badge: Antisemitism and Philosemitism in Postwar Germany*. Trans. William Templer. Oxford: Pergamon Press.

Stevenson, Adlai. 1953. *Major Campaign Speeches, 1952*. New York: Random House.

Stoker, Laura. 1996. "Understanding Differences in Whites' Opinions across Racial Policies." *Social Science Quarterly* 77 (4): 768–777.

Stouffer, S. 1955. *Communism, Conformity and Civil Liberties*. Garden City, N.Y.: Doubleday.

Strack, Fritz, Norbert Schwarz, Herbert Bless, Almut Kuebler, and M. Wanke. 1993. "Awareness of the Influence as a Determinant of Assimilation versus Contrast." *European Journal of Social Psychology* 23 (1): 53–62.

Sullivan, D. G., and R. D. Masters. 1988. "Happy Warriors: Leaders' Facial Displays, Viewers' Emotions and Political Support." *American Journal of Political Science* 32: 345–368.

Sullivan, John L., James Pierson, and George E. Marcus. 1978. "Ideological Constraint in the Mass Public: A Methodological Critique and Some New Findings." *American Journal of Political Science* 22: 233–249.

Sullivan, John L. 1982. *Political Tolerance and American Democracy*. Chicago: University of Chicago Press.

Sun Tzu. 1963. *The Art of War*. Trans. and with an introduction by Samuel B. Griffith. New York: Oxford University Press.

Sundquist, James L. 1973. *Dynamics of the Party System: Alignment and Realignment of Political Parties in the United States*. Washington, D.C.: Brookings Institution.

———. 1983. *Dynamics of the Party System*. Rev. ed. Washington, D.C.: Brookings Institution.

Sunstein, Cass. 1996. "Social Norms and Social Roles." *Columbia Law Review* 96: 903–968.

Swain, Carol M. 1993. *Black Faces, Black Interests*. Cambridge: Harvard University Press.

Takaki, Ronald. 1990. *Iron Cages: Race and Culture in Nineteenth-Century America*. New York: Oxford University Press.

Tate, Katherine. 1993. *From Protest to Politics: The New Black Voters in American Elections*. Cambridge: Harvard University Press.

Taylor, D. Garth, Andrew M. Greeley, and Paul B. Sheatsley. 1978. "Attitudes toward Racial Integration." *Scientific American* 238: 42–51.

Taylor, Shelley E., Susan T. Fiske, Nancy L. Etcoff, and Audrey J. Ruderman. 1978. "Categorical Bases of Person Memory and Stereotyping." *Journal of Personality and Social Psychology* 36: 778–793.

Tent, James. 1983. *Mission on the Rhine: Reeducation and Denazification in American-Occupied Germany*. Princeton: Princeton University Press.

Tindall, George Brown. 1967. *The Emergence of the New South, 1913–1945*. Baton Rouge: Louisiana State University Press.

Tocqueville, Alexis de. 1988. *Democracy in America*. Ed. J. P. Mayer. Trans. George Lawrence. New York: Harper Perennial.

Terkildsen, Nayda. 1993. "When White Voters Evaluate Black Candidates: The Processing Implications of Candidate Skin Color, Prejudice, and Self-Monitoring." *American Journal of Political Science* 37: 1032–1053.

Terkildsen, Nayda, Frauke I. Schnell, and Cristina Ling. 1998. "Formation: An Analysis of Message Structure, Rhetoric, and Source Cues." *Political Communication* 15: 45–61.

Thernstrom, Abigail. 1987. *Whose Votes Count? Affirmative Action and Minority Voting Rights*. Cambridge: Harvard University Press.

Thomas, Sue. 1990. "Voting Patterns in the California Assembly: The Role of Gender." *Women and Politics* 9: 43–56.

———. 1994. *How Women Legislate*. New York: Oxford University Press.

———. 1998. "Introduction: Women and Elective Office: Past, Present, and Future." In Sue Thomas and Clyde Wilcox, eds., *Women and Elective Office: Past, Present, and Future*. New York: Oxford University Press.

Timpone, Richard J. 1995. "Mass Mobilization or Government Intervention? The Growth of Black Registration in the South." *Journal of Politics* 57: 425–442.

Tourangeau, Roger, and Tom Smith. 1996. "Asking Sensitive Question: The Impact of Data Collection Mode, Question Format, and Question Context." *Public Opinion Quarterly* 60 (2): 275–304.

Trevor, Margaret C. 1999. "Political Socialization, Party Identification, and the Gender Gap." *Public Opinion Quarterly* 63: 62–89.

Trommler, Frank. 1998. "The Historical Invention and Modern Reinvention of Two National Identities." In Norbert Finzsch and Dietmar Schirmer, eds., *Identity and Intolerance: Nationalism, Racism, and Xenophobia in Germany and the United States.* Cambridge: Cambridge University Press.

Turner, C. F., L. Ku, S. M. Rogers, L. D. Lindberg, and J. H. Pleck. 1998. "Adolescent Sexual Behavior, Drug Use, and Violence: Increased Reporting with Computer Survey Technology." *Science* 80 (5365): 867–873.

Tursky, B., M. Lodge, M. A. Foley, R. Reeder, and H. Foley. 1976. "Evaluation of the Cognitive Component of Political Issues by Use of Classical Conditioning." *Journal of Personality and Social Psychology* 34: 865–873.

Uleman, James S., Alex Hon, Robert J. Roman, and Gordon B. Moskowitz. 1996. "On-Line Evidence for Spontaneous Trait Inferences at Encoding." *Personality and Social Psychology Bulletin* 22 (4): 377–394.

Uleman, James S., and Gordon B. Moskowitz. 1994. "Unintended Effects of Goals on Unintended Inferences." *Journal of Personality and Social Psychology* 66 (3): 490–501.

Umland, Andreas. 1999. "Antigypsism and Antisemitism." *Patterns of Prejudice* 33 (2): 87–89.

Valentino, Nicholas A. 1999. "Priming of Racial Attitudes." *Public Opinion Quarterly* 63: 293–320.

van Dijk, Teun A. 1988a. *News as Discourse.* Hillsdale, N.J.: Lawrence Erlbaum.

———. 1988b. *News Analysis: Case Studies of International and National News in the Press.* Hillsdale, N.J.: Lawrence Erlbaum.

———. 1991. *Racism and the Press.* London: Routledge.

Vertanen, Simo V., and Leonie Huddy. 1998. "Old-Fashioned Racism and New Forms of Racial Prejudice. *Journal of Politics* 60 (2): 311–332.

Wade, Richard C. 1967. *Slavery in the Cities: The South, 1820–1860.* Oxford: Oxford University Press.

Walton, Hanes Jr. 1992. "Democrats and African Americans: The American Idea." In Peter B. Kovler, ed., *Democrats and the American Idea.* Washington, D.C.: Center for National Policy Press.

Weinryb, B. 1942. "The Economic and Social Background of Modern Antisemitism." In Koppel S. Pinson, ed., *Essays on Antisemitism.* New York: Conference on Jewish Relations.

Welch, Susan. 1984. "Are Women More Liberal than Men in the U.S. Congress?" *Legislative Studies Quarterly* 10: 125–134.

West, Darrell M. 1997. *Air War: Television Advertising In Election Campaigns, 1952–1996.* Washington, D.C.: Congressional Quarterly Press.

White, Theodore H. 1965. *The Making of the President 1964.* New York: Atheneum.

Williams, Robert C. 1996. "Virtuous Republics and Eternal Empires: Goose Steppes, Weimar on the Volga, and Other Specious Analogies." *German Politics and Society* 14 (1): 1–16.

Williamson, Joel. 1984. *The Crucible of Race: Black-White Relations in the American South since Emancipation.* New York: Oxford University Press.

———. 1990 [1965]. *After Slavery.* Hanover, N.H.: University Press of New England.

Wills, Garry. 1969. *Nixon Agonistes: The Crisis of the Self-Made Man.* Boston: Houghton Mifflin.

Wilson, William Julius. 1987. *The Truly Disadvantaged*. Chicago: University of Chicago Press.

———. 1996. *When Work Disappears: The World of the New Urban Poor*. New York: Alfred A. Knopf.

Wood, Forrest G. 1968. *Black Scare: The Racist Response to Emancipation and Reconstruction*. Berkeley: University of California Press.

Woodward, C. Vann. 1966. *The Strange Career of Jim Crow*. New York: Oxford University Press.

———. 1971. *Origins of the New South, 1877–1913*. Baton Rouge: Louisiana State University Press.

———. 1991 [1951]. *Reunion and Reaction: The Compromise of 1877 and the End of Reconstruction*. Oxford: Oxford University Press.

Wyer, Robert, and T. Srull. 1980. "Category Accessibility and Social Perception." *Journal of Personality and Social Psychology* 38: 841–856.

———. 1981. "Category Accessibility: Some Theoretical and Empirical Issues Concerning the Processing of Social Stimulus Information." In E. T. Higgins, C. P. Herman, and M. P. Zanna, eds., *Social Cognition: The Ontario Symposium*, vol. 1. Hillsdale, N.J.: Lawrence Erlbaum.

Yang, Alan S. 1997. "Trends: Attitudes toward Homosexuality." *Public Opinion Quarterly* 61 (3): 477–507.

Yzerbyt, V. Y., G. Schadron, J. Leyens, and S. Rocher. 1994. "Social Judgeability: The Impact of Meta-Informational Cues on the Use of Stereotypes." *Journal of Personality and Social Psychology* 66: 48–55.

Zaller, John. 1992. *The Nature and Origins of Mass Opinion*. Cambridge: Cambridge University Press.

Zarate, M. A., and E. R. Smith. 1990. "Person Categorization and Stereotyping." *Social Cognition* 8: 161–185.

Zarefsky, David. 1990. *Lincoln, Douglas and Slavery: In the Crucible of Public Debate*. Chicago: University of Chicago Press.

Zillman, D. 1984. *Connections Between Sex and Aggression*. Hillsdale, N.J.: Lawrence Erlbaum.

Zuwerink, Julia R., Patricia G. Devine, Margo J. Monteith, and Deborah A. Cook. 1996. "Prejudice toward Blacks: With and without Compunction?" *Basic and Applied Social Psychology* 18 (2): 131–150.